MAASTRICHT AND BEYOND
Building the European Union

Maastricht and Beyond describes the negotiations that led up to the signing of the Treaty and its controversial ratification, and places these events in their historical context. It analyses clearly the main provisions of the Treaty, including the three-pillared structure – the European Community (including economic and monetary union), common foreign and security policy, justice and home affairs – and discusses their implications for the future of the European Union. Finally it draws conclusions from the Maastricht process and suggests how the next revision of the Treaty, scheduled for 1996, should build on what has been achieved so far, as well as rectifying some of the weaknesses in the structure and procedures of European integration. The book considers the possibility of a constitutional settlement that would strengthen the federal character of the Union.

All the contributors to the book have a deep practical and theoretical knowledge of the European Community. They take a generally positive, though far from uncritical, view of the Treaty of Maastricht, and wish to see the new Union succeed in its objectives.

The book is designed to deepen understanding of the European Union. It offers many new insights about the state of European unification and will be invaluable for students taking courses on European and EC politics, especially at graduate level, for politicians, diplomats, academics, journalists, lawyers, business people, national and EC officials. No other book in the English language gives such a comprehensive and up-to-date appraisal of the significance of the new European Union, or goes so far to redress widespread misconceptions about it.

The Editors: **Andrew Duff, John Pinder** and **Roy Pryce** are, respectively, Director, Chairman and Senior Research Fellow of The Federal Trust, the UK member of the Trans-European Policy Studies Association. The Trust was established in 1945 to study the theory and practice of federalism. The principal focus of its work has been the European Community and the place of the United Kingdom within it.

THE FEDERAL TRUST

The Federal Trust was founded in 1945 to be the research arm of Federal Union. The aim of the Trust is to study the theory and practice of federalism. The principal focus of its work has been the European Community and the United Kingdom's place within it.

The Trust conducts enquiries, organises seminars and conferences and publishes on a wide range of contemporary issues. Its 1993 publications included the following:

- Dick Taverne (rapporteur), *Towards an Integrated European Capital Market*
- Andrew Duff (ed.), *Subsidiarity within the European Community*
- Harry Cowie and John Pinder (eds), *A Recovery Strategy for Europe*

Its current work programme includes major enquiries into the role of national parliaments, Europe's information infrastructure and the financing and liberalisation of pension funds within the European Union.

The Federal Trust sustains an active programme of European education for sixth forms, universities and young leaders. It is also engaged in a study of the European dimension in British education and in the design and production of teaching materials about the European Union.

The Federal Trust for Education and Research, which is an independent registered charity, is the UK member of the Trans-European Policy Studies Association. The Federal Trust may be contacted at 158 Buckingham Palace Road, London SW1W 9TR.

MAASTRICHT AND BEYOND

Building the European Union

Edited by *Andrew Duff, John Pinder* and *Roy Pryce*

London and New York

First published 1994
by Routledge
11 New Fetter Lane, London EC4P 4EE

Simultaneously published in the USA and Canada
by Routledge
29 West 35th Street, New York, NY 10001

Reprinted 1995

© 1994 The Federal Trust

Typeset in Baskerville by
Florencetype Ltd, Kewstoke, Avon
Printed and bound in Great Britain by
T. J. Press (Padstow) Ltd, Padstow, Cornwall

British Library Cataloguing in Publication Data
A catalogue record for this book is available from the British
Library

Library of Congress Cataloguing in Publication Data
A catalogue record for this book is available from the Library of Congress

ISBN 0-415-10818-7

CONTENTS

CONTRIBUTORS

Malcolm Anderson is Professor of Politics at the University of Edinburgh and President of the European Communities Studies Association, Brussels. He was formerly Dean of the Faculty of Social Science at Edinburgh University.

Dieter Biehl is Professor of Public Economics at the Johann Wolfgang Goethe Universität, Frankfurt/Main. Previously he was Professor of Public Economics at the Technological University, Berlin.

Kieran Bradley is a member of the Legal Service of the European Parliament, and formerly served on the secretariat of its Legal Affairs Committee. He is a Visiting Professor at the Autonomous University of Barcelona.

Alan Butt Philip is Reader in European Integration and Director of the Centre for International Business Research, School of Management, University of Bath. He was Financial Controller of the 3i Group from 1970–75.

David Coombes is Professor of European Studies at the University of Limerick. He was Senior Research Fellow at the Policy Studies Institute and Professor of European Studies at Loughborough University.

Richard Corbett is Policy Adviser on constitutional questions and enlargement for the Socialist Group in the European Parliament. He was previously clerk to a number of its parliamentary committees.

Monica den Boer is Research Fellow at the Netherlands Institute for the Study of Criminality and Law Enforcement at Leiden. She was previously Research Fellow at the Department of Politics, University of Edinburgh.

Andrew Duff is Director of the Federal Trust.

vii

Geoffrey Edwards is Deputy Director of the Centre for International Studies, University of Cambridge, and Fellow of Pembroke College. He has previously worked in the Foreign and Commonwealth Office and at the Federal Trust.

John Fitzmaurice has worked in the Secretariat General of the European Commission since 1973. He is now Head of Unit in the Directorate for Relations with the European Parliament, Economic and Social Committee and the Committee of the Regions.

Christopher Johnson is UK Adviser to the Association for the Monetary Union of Europe. He is a former Chief Economic Adviser to Lloyds Bank.

Gary Miller is now working at the European Social Observatory in Brussels. He was Director of the Federal Trust from 1990–92.

Sir William Nicoll was Director General in the Council of the EC from 1982–91. Previously he was Deputy UK Permanent Representative to the EC on secondment to the Foreign and Commonwealth Office from the Department of Trade and Industry.

Simon Nuttall is Director (Far East) in the Directorate General for External Economic Relations in the European Commission. He was previously Head of the EPC Division in the Secretariat General at the Commission.

John Pinder is Chairman of the Federal Trust, visiting Professor at the College of Europe, Bruges, and Honorary President of the Union of European Federalists. He was Director of the Policy Studies Institute from 1964–85.

Roy Pryce is a Senior Research Fellow and former Director (1983–90) at the Federal Trust. He was previously a Director in the Directorate General for Information at the Commission and Professor and founding Director, Centre for Contemporary European Studies at the University of Sussex.

Alastair Sutton is a Partner of Forrester Norall and Sutton in Brussels, and Visiting Fellow at the Centre for European Legal Studies, University of Cambridge. He worked in Lord Cockfield's office at the Commission from 1985–88.

FOREWORD

The authors of this study share a common conviction about the crucial significance of the European Union for the future security and welfare of our part of the world. Few things affect the British, as other European peoples, more profoundly than the way in which we deal with our common problems in the fields of the economy, security, the environment and the polity. The Maastricht Treaty, which ushered in the Union, is a significant step forward to enable us to deal with these issues more effectively. Yet we are not uncritical admirers of the Treaty which, with its massive complex of amendments to the existing Community Treaties, is comprehensible only to specialists. Nor did we much enjoy the debates about ratification in the United Kingdom and some other member states which only added to the confusion. Clarification of the Treaty's content and possible implications is sorely needed. This Federal Trust book endeavours to respond to that need. But our central purpose is to analyse critically the content of the Treaty and to suggest ways to remedy its weaknesses.

The contributors have a wide range of practical and theoretical experience of the European Community. The Introduction recalls the context in which the decision to negotiate a treaty was taken. Part I outlines the course of the negotiations, the content of the Treaty and process of ratification. Part II deals with the powers of the Union and some implications for policy, Part III with the institutions. The final chapter draws some conclusions for future policies, for reforms which should be considered at the next Intergovernmental Conference to be convened in 1996, and for the further development of a Union constitution.

The chapters in Parts II and III are by authors who are specialists in the respective subjects and were thus able to bring their considerable expertise rapidly to bear on elucidation of the different aspects of the Treaty. The editors were responsible for Part I and for the Introduction and Conclusion as well as for seeking to achieve a coherent whole. While there are inevitably some differences of emphasis among the several authors, there is a large measure of agreement about the fundamental elements of the Treaty; and we are all convinced of the importance of public understanding of these fundamentals, on which the future development of the Union, and of Britain's place within it, must be based.

AD, JP, RP February 1994

ACKNOWLEDGEMENTS

The Federal Trust is most grateful to the authors who, in addition to submitting their own contributions on time, met together on a number of occasions to discuss the shape and content of the book. The editors also received helpful advice from Harry Cowie, Stanley Henig and Anthony Teasdale. Judy Keep and Tim Knowles helped with the production of the book.

ABBREVIATIONS

CAP	Common Agricultural Policy
CBI	Confederation of British Industry
CDU	Christian Democratic Union
CEAC	Conference of European Affairs Committees
CFSP	Common Foreign and Security Policy
CIS	Commonwealth of Independent States
Coreper	Committee of Permanent Representatives
COSAC	Conférence des organes specialisées dans les affaires communautaires
CSCE	Conference on Security and Cooperation in Europe
EC	European Community
ECB	European Central Bank
ECHR	European Convention for the Protection of Human Rights and Fundamental Freedoms
Ecofin	Council of Economic and Finance Ministers
Ecosoc	Economic and Social Committee
ECSC	European Coal and Steel Community
Ecu	European Currency Unit
EEA	European Economic Area
EEC	European Economic Community
Efta	European Free Trade Area
The Eleven	The Twelve minus the UK
EMI	European Monetary Institute
EMS	European Monetary System
Emu	Economic and Monetary Union
EPC	European Political Cooperation
ERM	Exchange Rate Mechanism
ETUC	European Trade Union Congress
EU	European Union
Euratom	European Atomic Energy Community
FBI	Federal Bureau of Investigation
Gatt	General Agreements on Tariffs and Trade

ABBREVIATIONS

GDP	Gross Domestic Product
GNP	Gross National Product
IGC	Intergovernmental Conference
IMF	International Monetary Fund
Nato	North Atlantic Treaty Organisation
OECD	Organisation for Economic Cooperation and Development
OJ	Official Journal
PFU	Public Finance Union
R&D	Research and development
R&TD	Research and technological development
The Six	Belgium, France, Germany, Italy, Luxembourg, The Netherlands
TUC	Trades Union Congress
The Twelve	Belgium, Denmark, France, Germany, Greece, Ireland, Italy, Luxembourg, The Netherlands, Portugal, Spain, UK
UN	United Nations
UNICE	Union of Industrial Employers' Confederations of Europe
WEU	Western European Union

INTRODUCTION

1

THE MAASTRICHT TREATY AND THE NEW EUROPE

Roy Pryce

The Treaty on European Union signed at Maastricht on 7 February 1992 was negotiated in the immediate wake of the most dramatic and profound changes in Europe since the end of the Second World War. Conceived in a continent still divided into rival political and economic systems, and launched on a wave of great optimism about the European Community (EC), it is now being applied in very different circumstances. The old tensions of the Cold War have gone; but so has the euphoria which briefly accompanied their demise. Europe is now beset by other problems, including a bloody conflict in the Balkans, recession and high unemployment, and growing concern about the region's longer-term economic prospects. The Treaty which was designed to take Europe further along the road to 'an ever closer union' has itself proved to be a source of controversy, especially in three countries, Denmark, France and the United Kingdom, where it was only ratified after prolonged and acrimonious debate.

Many questions have been raised about the contents of the Treaty. Among the most important are how effective a response it provides to the needs of the new Europe; whether its aims can be reconciled with a much wider membership; and the desirability and feasibility of its central aim of Economic and Monetary Union. The commitments to a common foreign and security policy and an eventual common defence policy are also controversial. So too is the structure of the new European Union, with two intergovernmental 'pillars' alongside the original Community. Some, like the British government, fought for these as a way of heading off a federal Europe; others accepted them only with reluctance. The Treaty incorporates an uneasy truce between the two sides: battle is likely to be rejoined at the review conference due to be convened in 1996.

In the light of both the controversy surrounding the Treaty and the other difficulties which the Community has encountered since it was signed, sceptics question whether or to what extent it will in fact be applied. They make no secret of their hope that Maastricht will prove to be 'a Treaty too far' and its provisions a dead letter. Others, on the contrary, argue that a strengthened Union is crucial for the future peace and welfare of Europe and its contribution to a better-ordered world.

These issues provide the central themes of this study. But before addressing them, it is first necessary to put them in a wider context. One of the alarming features of the debate about the ratification of the Treaty was how narrow and parochial a set of considerations was advanced by its opponents who focused almost exclusively on issues of national sovereignty. These are not negligible issues, but they should be put into proper perspective. That requires in the first place some reflections about the nature of the world in which we now find ourselves, the role of the European Community in it, and the challenges now facing the new Union.

THE GLOBAL SCENE

In the brief period of euphoria which followed in the immediate aftermath of the dissolution of the Soviet Union, George Bush spoke hopefully of the prospect of establishing 'a new world order'. But what we see appears to be continuing, if not greater, disorder. The relative stability of detente has been followed by disintegration, a revival of nationalism, and near anarchy in many parts of the failed empire and its appendages.

One major source of tension and potential conflict in the world has indeed been removed with the collapse of the Soviet Union and its empire. With it has also gone the arms race between the superpowers and the constant threat of a nuclear holocaust. But huge stocks of nuclear weapons remain in the former Soviet Union, under much less certain and firm control than before. Tensions within and between its successor states have created new threats to peace. The collapse of the old bipolar world has also led to uncertainty and instability in other regions. At the same time, the international community as a whole is now having to grapple with more and more problems which require a concerted response. These arise from the ever-increasing degree of interdependence of the peoples and countries of the world, brought about by modern communications technology. This is now rapidly revolutionising our institutions, ways of life and the intensity of our relations with other societies.

The degree of interdependence already achieved means that rules have had to be created to regulate some areas of international activity, most notably trade and communications. But in many others, including international currency dealings, anarchy continues to reign. The lack of solidarity between the countries and peoples of the world in the face of urgent common problems is also manifest in the persistence of huge disparities of wealth between rich and poor regions and countries. And now the threats to the environment not only of particular regions, but also to the world as a whole, are a dramatic example of a type of challenge with which the international community is now increasingly confronted, but with which at present it is ill-equipped to deal.

The fragility of the means currently available to the world community to meet such problems is daily apparent. The dissolution of the Soviet Union and the ending of its rivalry with the United States have done little to increase the world's collective capacity to tackle these major global issues. A special responsibility clearly rests with the USA which now enjoys a unique and unrivalled superpower status. But, paradoxically, the end of the conflict in which it emerged as the apparent victor has shown how little it can achieve on its own. An overwhelming preponderance of military power is not by itself sufficient. As successive US administrations have discovered, at the time of the Gulf War against Iraq, and more recently in Somalia and Bosnia, the use of such power needs the support of the United Nations to give it legitimacy. Moreover, the mood of the country, confronted by huge debts and recession, is also clearly against shouldering too many of the problems of the world. Hence the new emphasis on multilateralism.

This is a recognition that the only hope of finding solutions to most of the world's problems is by a collective effort. That is not a new discovery: the present century has seen a huge proliferation of both governmental and non-governmental organisations designed to promote this in many different spheres. But while the imperatives of interdependence have continued to grow, so too has the number of independent states. Today there are over 170 of them in the world compared with only 70 in the 1930s. These greatly increased numbers have complicated the problem of creating effective international institutions, especially at the world level. Fortunately, the United Nations and its associated bodies are no longer subject to the frustrations imposed by superpower rivalry. But the increasing recourse now being made to the UN has highlighted the weaknesses of the organisation, most of which arise from the limitations placed on it by its member states. There is clearly an urgent need to strengthen it in order to give it a greater capacity to take action – and at the same time to increase respect for it as the legitimate instrument of the world community.

But it is also apparent that a strategy for a better-ordered world requires not only action at the world level. There are many problems which can and should be tackled at a regional level. Otherwise the present overload of the UN and its related bodies will grow ever more serious. The development of such regional mechanisms, which was a part of the original strategy envisaged for the United Nations, now needs greater attention and urgency. A new world order does not only imply more effective world-level institutions: it means the development

ment of a capacity at a regional level to perform a range of important functions. Efforts to establish a new world order need to be underpinned in this way to increase their chances of success.

The recognition of this need has given rise in recent times to an increasing number of regional-level organisations in many parts of the world, including Central and Latin America, Africa, the Middle East and South-East Asia. Several have taken a lead from the European Community and have developed predominantly economic functions. But some have also taken on more explicitly political tasks, including mediatory or peace-keeping roles in their region, and all have found themselves seeking to aggregate the interests of their members in order to express and defend them in international negotiations and on the world stage.

These developments are welcome for a number of reasons, including the welfare gains they offer to their citizens, and the prospect they hold out of more peaceful and harmonious relations between the states taking part in them. Conflicts within a region can trigger much wider conflicts: in the case of Europe they led to two world wars. Effective regional groupings are a necessary part of the architecture of a better-ordered world. This was one of the motives behind the original creation of the European Community itself. The opening words of the Schuman Plan of 1950 which gave birth to it made this clear:

> World peace cannot be safeguarded without constructive efforts proportionate to the dangers which threaten it.
>
> The contribution which an organised and living Europe can bring to civilisation is indispensable to the maintenance of peaceful relations.

The preamble to the Maastricht Treaty echoes and repeats this objective, arguing that the purpose of a common foreign and security policy is to reinforce 'European identity and independence in order to promote peace, security and progress in Europe and in the world'. So it is in this wide context, both regional and global, that the provisions and the impact of the Treaty should be assessed.

THE EUROPEAN COMMUNITY ON THE EVE OF UNION

Over the past forty years, the members of the EC have succeeded, in spite of many setbacks, in advancing a long way towards their declared objective of an ever closer union. Not surprisingly, in view of the primacy given to the process of economic integration, the most striking achievements lie in that area. The most important is the creation of a vast internal market of over 340 million people providing free movement within it, with only limited exceptions, for goods, capital and services and the citizens of the member states. Since 1 January 1994 this market has been extended even further by the creation of the European Economic Area, consisting of the EC and five members of the European Free Trade Association (Efta): Austria, Finland, Norway, Sweden and Iceland. It is the world's largest free trade zone, comprising 372 million people. This is a huge achievement in the face of the dense jungle of restrictions which each of those states had erected to protect domestic suppliers. It is also of vital importance for the future of the European economy to enable its producers to achieve economies of scale which will allow them to compete successfully on world markets and so underpin the living standards of the citizens of the Union.

As a result of the common market, the Community is now the world's largest trading group and as most aspects of external economic policy are now handled by it as matters of common concern, it has become one of the three most important players on the world economic scene alongside the USA and Japan. The main thrust of its policies within Gatt has been for greater liberalisation, though there are important exceptions with regard to agriculture (where a high price is still being paid for its inclusion in the common market), and some imports from developing countries, Central and Eastern Europe, and Japan.

The Community, alongside its member countries, is also an important source of help to the developing countries. Much of this effort is focused on the sixty-nine signatories of the Lomé Convention in Africa, the Caribbean and the Pacific. Since British accession this has developed from a limited preferential trade and aid agreement with a group of former colonies of the original six member states into a broader set of arrangements which now include a stabilisation fund for some of their basic products and technical and financial assistance.

So the EC already occupies an important role on the world economic stage. It has 'clout' and the means to exercise it. What is clear is the importance for all the members of the Community of having achieved a set of common policies on trade and other areas of external economic relations, and the continuing need for the Community to be able to speak and act on behalf of its members in these policy areas.

In political terms, the achievements of the EC are also very considerable. It has in the first place made a crucial contribution to the profound changes that have occurred in the relations between its members, and in particular between France and Germany. The strategy of the gradual construction of a *de facto* solidarity to which the Schuman Plan looked forward has in fact worked, and the day-to-day working relations which have been established in the framework of the Community, as well as the high-level bilateral contacts which have complemented them, have transformed former enemies into partners. In the process, Western Europe has been transformed from being a cockpit of conflict into one of the most securely peaceful areas of the world.

An important role in this transformation has been played by the institutions set up by the member states to govern the Communities. A novel system of government has been created in which significant federal-type elements, represented by the Commission, the European Parliament and the Court of Justice, co-exist alongside the European Council and the Council of ministers which represent the member governments in which ultimate power is still firmly vested. Collectively these institutions, together with associated consultative bodies, provide a series of arenas where the concerted collective effort required in the building of the EC is carried on. The process now reaches out far beyond governmental and business circles and engages many hundreds of thousands of people in almost every walk of life.

But while the Community in its internal organisation has progressed far along the path towards a political union, this has not yet been fully reflected in the non-economic aspects of its relations with the rest of the world. So far the EC has rarely been able to take effective initiatives in the field of general foreign policy, and has more often found itself reacting to events. It has also lacked effective means of action in those areas where it has not been able to bring its economic muscle to bear. The limitations of this type of pressure have been clearly demonstrated in the case of the former Yugoslavia. There the inability of the member states of the Community to prevent its break-up and the slide into brutal war has been a dramatic illustration of the difficulties they face in trying to achieve effective common action even on their own doorstep.

Part of the reason for the reluctance of EC members to develop a common foreign and security policy can undoubtedly be ascribed to their dependence for so many years on the USA. Confronted in the post-war years by the menacing power of the Soviet Union and its satellites, the countries of Western Europe were glad to shelter behind the military protection offered by the US. For most of them the maintenance of that commitment through their loyalty to the Atlantic Alliance was a cardinal principle of foreign and defence policy. As the Cold War confrontation slowly changed into detente, and the two superpowers began to negotiate and even cooperate together, there was increasing pressure for a specifically European stance within the Alliance. But even the Six took only very cautious steps along that road, and although after entry Britain supported and encouraged the tentative cooperation on foreign policy issues that had begun to develop, it was always with two important reservations. One was that it should be kept strictly on an intergovernmental basis; the other that it should not rock the boat in the Atlantic Alliance.

The United States, for its part, which began by strongly encouraging the formation of the EC and shielded it in its early years from British hostility, has subsequently adopted a more hard-nosed policy. Conflicts of economic interest (especially, though not exclusively, over agricultural protection) now set the tone of day-to-day relations. This has been accompanied, somewhat paradoxically, by the view that Europe should grow up, learn to stand on its own feet, and take a greater share of responsibility for its own defence. This was already being strongly urged by Washington before the collapse of the USSR. What has happened subsequently, in particular the sharp reduction in US force levels in Europe, has reinforced and hastened an evolution that was already under way.

Some members of the Community, led by the UK, argue that now even greater care has to be taken not to rock the Atlantic boat for fear that its remaining American crew members may push off back home. Others believe that there are good reasons of self-interest for the USA's continuing commitment to the security of Europe and to the Atlantic Alliance, which has now acquired a new role as a guarantor of the independence of the emerging democracies of Central and Eastern Europe. But by now even most of those who were sceptical have been convinced by the uncertainties in Europe itself that the Union needs to continue – and now more rapidly – along the path that leads to a common foreign and defence policy. That is one of the commitments built into the Maastricht Treaty.

It remains to be seen how far and how soon that commitment will be honoured, for experience, and not least recent experience with the former Yugoslavia, has shown how difficult it is to achieve agreement in these policy areas. Underlying these difficulties are continuing and sharp divisions of policy with regard to the nature and future of the Union now formally created at Maastricht. These reach far back into the history of the Community.

The founding members of the European Community were notable for having pioneered a new approach to regional unity: integration rather than cooperation. Even today, for many other states intergovernmental cooperation remains the only acceptable mode of working together with others at both the regional and world level. The attractions of this are easy to understand. It is based on a recognition of the sovereign independence of each of those taking part, and preserves the appearance of that independence. The reality, however, is rather different, and there is always a price to pay. In the first place, any agreement to act together implies the acceptance of constraints on the future freedom of action of everyone taking part. So, over time, the areas for autonomous national decision-making are steadily whittled away. The costs of the use of a veto in the face of majority views also rise. But at the same time the formal need for consensus usually means prolonged discussion and decisions based on the lowest common denominator of agreement. Much effort and time are required to produce quite modest results.

In creating the EC its original six members set out on a more ambitious course, the eventual aim of which was described in the 1950 Schuman Plan as a federation. They chose this path for mainly political reasons, in revulsion against the excesses of nationalism and as a way of embracing Germany and preventing renewed Franco-German hostility. It meant aiming at not only an economic but an eventual political union, with a much more intensive set of mutual commitments and constraints than was required by intergovernmental cooperation. It also implied an institutional system in which the collective interest, as well as that of individual member states, was to be represented and in which majority voting was eventually to be adopted as the norm.

This was, however, an approach that was contested by a minority within the Six, most notably the Gaullists in France, and in the preamble to the 1957 Rome Treaties the less emotive expression of 'an ever closer union' was adopted. Economic integration through a common market and customs union then headed the agenda, but even that was to be achieved by stages. And when the Six began in 1970 to work together more closely in foreign policy areas, they did so very gingerly outside the framework of the Community; without any new Treaty commitments; and in a very pragmatic fashion, using the classic techniques of intergovernmental cooperation.

So in spite of the rhetoric of integration, even the six founder members of the Community moved cautiously towards union. They also subsequently showed great forbearance in accommodating the concerns of new members, and especially those of Britain and Denmark. It is a complete myth, sedulously fostered by successive British governments, that its continental partners are hell-bent on the construction of a centralised European super-state. As the negotiations leading up to the Maastricht Treaty showed, a majority of them wish to see a federal-type union but one in which the role of the Community is limited to those policy areas where common action is absolutely necessary. This is the antithesis of centralisation, for federalist principles require that power should be dispersed and exercised as close to the citizen as possible.[1]

The conflict between those who wished to see a further development of the federal elements in the Union and those who were determined to prevent this was a major feature of the negotiations leading up to the Maastricht Treaty. The result was an uneasy compromise between the two in the shape of a three-pillar structure with two intergovernmental pillars (one for foreign, security and defence policy, the other for justice and home affairs) alongside the EC.

This is a curious hybrid, which is even more *sui generis* than the

Community itself. It is certainly not a structure that will enable the Union effectively to pursue the tasks its members have assigned to it. But we should not be surprised that the growing needs and demands of interdependence should have produced such a strange new animal. The members of the European Union are in the vanguard of a search for ways in which a group of states can more effectively work together to meet the challenges of the contemporary world. That search implies a mutual willingness to accept constraints on the exercise of national sovereignty in exchange for the benefits of collective action. The more you put in, the more you can expect to get out. But there also has to be a sufficient area of consensus to produce decisions and sustain common action. So far the EC has succeeded in continuing on the path towards union in spite of disagreements about both its ultimate objective and the means to achieve it. But the negotiators of the Maastricht Treaty had to work hard to achieve a series of compromises to bridge the continuing differences on these issues.

The debates in a number of member countries which accompanied the ratification of Maastricht also sounded a number of warning bells about the future of the integration process. In the first place it was apparent that old divisions of opinion about the nature and role of the Community still persist, not only in notoriously sceptical countries like Denmark and Britain, but in France. This was in spite of the emphasis on the doctrine of subsidiarity in the Treaty. Secondly, they suggested that in a number of countries the general public is becoming more hesitant about, and in some cases resistant to, further measures which will visibly constrict a national government's remaining areas of autonomous action.

Subsequently, survey data gathered in the spring of 1993 showed that the decline in generalised support for closer unity that had occurred during 1991–92 had been arrested, and that an average of 73 per cent of the population of the member countries was still either favourable, or very favourable. On the other hand, there was a continuing decline in the numbers considering that membership of the Community was 'a good thing' for their own country: an average of 47 per cent compared with a peak of 59 per cent in 1991. Support for the Maastricht Treaty itself was at a low level of 41 per cent, against a background of widespread ignorance about it. So a few months before its final ratification, there were rather mixed signals from those about to become citizens of the new European Union.[2]

THE NEW CONTEXT IN EUROPE

It is against this uncertain background that the member states have now embarked on the implementation of the Maastricht Treaty. That in itself

11

was always going to prove a major undertaking, certainly as far as the achievement of its central objective of Economic and Monetary Union (Emu) by the end of the century was concerned. It has now been made more difficult by the onset of economic recession and the repercussions of the exchange rate crisis of the summer of 1993. But this is only one of a series of challenges confronting the member states. Another is the large number of applications, actual or potential, from countries wishing to join the Union. By mid-1993 eight had formally applied to join: three from the Mediterranean, Turkey (1987), Cyprus (1990) and Malta (1990); and a group of Efta countries – Austria (1989), Sweden (1991), Finland, Switzerland and Norway (all 1992). Many others had announced their intention of applying in the future or were discussing the possibility of doing so. These included the so-called 'Visegrad' countries, Poland, Hungary and the Czech and Slovak Republics; the two remaining Efta countries, Iceland and Liechtenstein; the Baltic states of Estonia, Latvia and Lithuania; and Slovenia, Bulgaria, Romania and Albania.[3]

The list is powerful evidence of the importance the European Union has already assumed in Europe. The possibility now exists for it to become the organising framework for virtually the whole of the continent. This is a fine opportunity to realise the dream of a united Europe, and one which could bring great benefits to the region as a whole. But it is a prospect which has also divided the existing members of the Union, some of whom see it as likely at best to make it more difficult to advance any further along the path to closer union, and at worst to threaten the degree of unity already achieved. This is why they, unlike the United Kingdom for instance, have given top priority to strengthening the Union as a precondition for further enlargement.

Much of the discussion about the future of the Union has understandably focused on these issues of strengthening and/or widening. But in the meantime, a great deal of diplomatic effort has had to be devoted by the member states to trying to deal with the more immediate problem of the bloody conflict in the former Yugoslavia. This arises directly out of the collapse of the communist regime and is a sharp reminder of the strength of the ethnic conflicts that it has released. Many of the hopes nurtured about the new Europe have foundered among the corpses and material destruction it has brought in its train. It has been a deeply shocking experience for the countries and people of Western Europe who had thought that such scenes had been banished from their continent. It has also administered a sharp blow to the prestige of the Community.

The inability of its member states to act decisively or effectively in the former Yugoslavia has seriously undermined their credibility not only in Europe itself but world-wide, and not least in the United States. It is now no longer sufficient for the Community to offer an example to the world of how to create a common market: the limitations of what that means have been cruelly exposed. This is likely to mean that the member states will now have to devote far more attention to other aspects of their Union, and in particular to efforts to create a security and defence policy, as well as the material means needed to give such policies teeth. It may well be that public expectations about the benefits to be derived from the new Union will also change, with more emphasis being given to its ability to provide security and peace than in the past.

The capacity of the member states to respond to both this and the other challenges the Union now faces will be severely tested in the coming years. How well they are able to do so will depend to a large extent on how they react to the most important of all the changes that the disappearance of the old division of the continent has brought in its train: the unification of Germany. The impact of this has many aspects: structural, political and economic. In structural terms unification has made Germany much larger than the other member states, with a population of 78 million compared with the 56–57 million each of Britain, France and Italy. Even in these crude terms it is now much larger than these countries whereas before it was roughly on a par with them, and was given the same weight as them in the Community's institutional arrangements. This has now begun to change: the number of German members of the European Parliament has been increased from 81 to 99, making them the largest single national contingent in the parliament. (Britain, France and Italy have just six additional members, making their total 87 each.)

One important question which arises from this structural change at the political heart of the Union is how this will affect the Franco-German relationship which has so far provided its central motor. That relationship has already had to adjust to change in the past: initially France was much the senior partner, both economically and politically. Over the years it came to terms with a Federal Republic which became at least its equal in economic terms: now it faces a further test of adaptation to take account of a partner which is not only larger, but occupies a dominant position in monetary matters, is economically more powerful, and is politically more assertive. The new Germany also now occupies a central role in the new Europe, both geographically and otherwise, and for the first time since the Second World War there is serious discussion among German policy makers of their national interests. As one of those invited in August 1993 to take part in a meeting in the Chancellor's office to discuss this remarked: 'We have never asked ourselves that question before.'[4]

Already the new Germany has had an important impact within the EC. Initially this was entirely positive: in response to fears about the

13

implications of unification Chancellor Kohl took the initiative with President Mitterrand to add political union issues to the agenda for the Maastricht negotiations. But the financial burden assumed at the time of unification to help the new Länder has had serious consequences not only for Germany but the Community as a whole. The weight of public debt that this has brought in its train, together with the relatively high interest rates which the Bundesbank maintained in order to try and contain the resulting inflationary pressures, has contributed to recession in the European economy at large. At the same time the policy of the Bundesbank, which understandably gave priority to its national role, triggered off intolerable speculative pressure against several other currencies within the European Monetary System and provoked monetary crises in September 1992 and July 1993. Sterling and the Italian lira had to leave the Exchange Rate Mechanism (ERM), and much wider exchange rate fluctuations were allowed within it. This development was widely interpreted by Eurosceptics as spelling the death-knell of Emu: it also created considerable tension in the Franco-German relationship.

The crucial nature of that relationship is underlined by the fact that there is no other combination able to provide the core motive force for the Union in the forseeable future. The UK government, though ostensibly seeking to be 'at the heart of Europe', fought hard against key elements in the Maastricht Treaty, and has to contend with a powerful group of Eurosceptics in the Conservative party which is more than ever divided over European issues. Only when the Tory party unites behind a more firmly pro-European strategy, as Labour and the Liberal Democrats have done, will the UK be able to play a more positive role within the Union. Italy, for its part, is struggling with serious domestic political problems: virtually a whole generation of its politicians having been discredited in the wake of the ending of the division of Europe. Few positive initiatives are likely at present from this country which has always been one of the EC's most ardent supporters.

There are some who argue that Italy is only the most acute case of a more general malaise which now threatens to undermine democratic structures and practices throughout Western Europe. Of this there is little evidence: indeed, it is reassuring to see that elsewhere too political change has been and is taking place peacefully and within accepted democratic structures. In several countries this has included significant devolution of power from national to regional authorities: in the case of Belgium it has meant the wholesale recasting of national institutions and the creation in their place of a federal state. But even this radical change has been accomplished peacefully and by constitutional means. And the new state, like all of its neighbours and partners in the Community, firmly sees its future as part of the new European Union.

One of the Union's early tests will be the way it handles the many demands for membership. As a first step through the maze, the EC established some basic priorities with regard to timing. It decided to deal first with four of the Efta countries: Austria, Finland, Norway and Sweden.[5] Negotiations with them were concluded early in 1994, with the aim of entry by January 1995. These Efta countries are due to be followed by the four Visegrad countries who hope that negotiations can begin as soon as possible after the next Intergovernmental Conference of 1996, leading to membership before the end of the century. Beyond that the picture becomes much less clear, and no formal commitments to the timing of negotiations with other candidate countries have been given. All of them pose problems, though in varying degrees. The eligibility of other countries in Eastern Europe, such as Romania and Bulgaria, is conditioned by their ability to adapt their economies to a free market regime, and to demonstrate that they have become acceptably democratic. Malta and Cyprus both present a special problem because of their size, with the added complication in the case of Cyprus of the continuing partition of the country due to the Turkish occupation of its northern part. As far as Turkey itself is concerned, its long-standing application for membership remains on the back-burner for both economic and political reasons.

It is still too early to predict how the process of enlargement will go. But it will certainly be protracted, and is unlikely to be smooth. Much uncertainty surrounds the prospects of several of the applicants. It may be that the initial concerns that accompanied the expectation of a vast enlargement of the number of members of the Union will prove to be unfounded. At all events, the uncertainty itself as well as the practical problems involved in successive enlargements are likely to weigh heavily on the agenda of the Union for many years to come.

Another aspect of this is the uncertainty of how far the new members who do join will be willing or able in practice to accept all the obligations of the existing members. This has become all the more problematic in the light of the various concessions made during the negotiations of the Maastricht Treaty to the UK and Denmark on a range of important issues including the commitments relating to Emu, citizenship and a common defence policy. The original idea of everyone marching together in step towards an ever closer union has already been undermined by these concessions, and there is now a very real prospect not only of a multi-speed but also a multi-tiered Union which could be very difficult to manage, and might ultimately prove to be seriously divisive.

This is the background against which the Maastricht Treaty is now being implemented. It has reassuring features as well as uncertainties: great opportunities as well as dangers. What is clear is that, in the midst of so much disorder and uncertainty in the world, the countries of the European Union – and potentially the rest of Europe – have the great

15

advantage of a well-developed regional instrument at their disposal, built up over many years of determined effort. It would be the height of folly to squander this, and a catastrophe if the new Union were for any reason to fail. That would mean in practice German domination of the heartland of Europe, which could very easily trigger a powerful nationalist response both within that country and, in reaction, amongst its neighbours both in the East and the West. Europe would then be plunged back into a cycle of fear, hostility and the threat of conflict from which it has only painfully learned to free itself over the past forty years.

It is British blindness to this danger that is one of the most alarming features of the current scene: the narrow concerns with the myths of national independence threaten to undermine what has been achieved by the Community, and to imperil the new Union. This is what is really at stake now. For all its imperfections, the Treaty of Maastricht is a necessary instrument for the continuation of that work, and the best hope for the creation of a secure, peaceful and prosperous Europe.

Part I

THE TREATY
OF MAASTRICHT

2

THE MAIN REFORMS

Andrew Duff

The Maastricht Treaty created a new European Union, based on the European Community, which 'marks a new stage' in the process of creating an ever closer union among the peoples of Europe.[1] Much of the Treaty followed well-tried precedent, building on past EC treaties and on the corpus of law and policy made by the common institutions over forty years. Other provisions of Maastricht are intended to respond to new external challenges of the Community, including enlargement. Some of the Maastricht Treaty was truly innovatory – not least with regard to its own structure.

Against the wishes of the Commission and the Dutch presidency of the Council, the Maastricht Treaty divides into three 'pillars'. The first (Titles II, III and IV) amends the EEC, ECSC and Euratom Treaties (as revised most recently by the Single Act), formally naming them the European Community. The second pillar (Title V) concerns foreign and security policy and is built upon the existing intergovernmental procedures of European Political Cooperation. The third (Title VI) covers justice and home affairs. The first and last sections of the Treaty (Titles I and VII) comprise a Preamble and Final Provisions and seek to bind the three pillars together into the European Union.[2]

THE NATURE OF THE UNION

The 'European Union' of Maastricht embraces the three pillars and manages relations between them. But the true nature of the relationship between the Community method and intergovernmental practices will be defined as much in practice as in theory. The three-pillar structure is indubitably complicated, and would be difficult to explain to anyone coming fresh to a study of European unification – with such explanation made more tricky by the competing interpretations subsequently put upon the Treaty by many of the leading players. The UK government has made much of the separateness of the three pillars; others have accentuated their interconnectedness. The British Prime Minister is not

19

only proud of his achievement at Maastricht in stopping the establishment of a single federal structure, he sees it as a blueprint for the future development of the Community. He told the Commons:

> At Maastricht we developed a new way, and one much more amenable to the institutions of this country – cooperation by agreement between governments, but not under the Treaty of Rome. It covers interior and justice matters, foreign affairs and security, and the option is available for it to cover wider matters in the future.[3]

Another Byzantine dispute left unresolved by Maastricht is the use and definition of the term 'federal'. The British fought successfully to have it left out – the 'ever closer union' of the Treaty of Rome survives instead. But that John Major accepted many federalist elements of the Treaty (such as subsidiarity), and even argued for the inclusion of others (such as the power of the European Court of Justice to fine member governments in breach of EC law) makes his struggle against 'federal' an historical curiosity.

The precise nature of the Union, therefore, remains unclear. The ambitious language of the Treaty, at times almost rhetorical, suggests aspirations on a grand scale. The objectives are large, and the competences of the Union wide. The Treaty is long, and when consolidated with the existing EC Treaties, runs to hundreds of pages. But Maastricht obviously does not represent the definitive version of European unity. The British government's interpretation of Maastricht as vindication of the intergovernmental approach appears to be sincerely held. But it is not a view that seems to be shared elsewhere in the Community. Beyond Maastricht, at least, the battle lines are clearly drawn.

ECONOMIC AND MONETARY UNION

The Treaty's main achievement was to lay down the objective of Economic and Monetary Union along with a timetable and schedule for its achievement.[4] According to Article 2, the purpose of Emu is to 'promote throughout the Community a harmonious and balanced development of economic activities, sustainable and non-inflationary growth respecting the environment, a high degree of convergence of economic performance, a high level of employment and social protection, the raising of the standard of living and quality of life, and economic and social cohesion and solidarity among Member States'. In setting these objectives, of course, the European Community was mostly revisiting familiar territory. But the goal of currency union had never before been established precisely in treaty form. Nor had the EC been capable previously of prescribing in detail the ways and means of reaching that goal. What was agreed and why?

The Treaty gives the Community exclusive authority over money. It pools the monetary sovereignty of the member states, and supersedes any independent activity by them in that field. It ascribes the management of the Emu to a new supranational institution, the European Central Bank to be set up in either 1997 or 1999 at the latest. It established a precursor of that institution, the European Monetary Institute, when the transition from the first to the second stage took place on 1 January 1994. In Stage One of Emu, which formally began on 1 July 1990, limited monetary functions and the technical preparations for the Monetary Institute were carried out by the (refurbished) Committee of Central Bank Governors that has existed since 1964.

The Treaty prescribes a single currency for the whole of the EC: the Ecu (or as German sensibilities insisted, the non-French Ecu, 'European Currency Unit'). The European Central Bank sits at the pinnacle of and has duties to coordinate a European System of Central Banks, comprising the central banks of the member states. In the Intergovernmental Conference (IGC) leading up to Maastricht, the UK had won no support for its proposal that a coordinated central bank system would be sufficient to manage a European Monetary Fund that would issue a 'hard' Ecu, that is, a parallel, common or twelfth EC currency.[5]

The Treaty establishes that progress towards Emu is to be orderly: the question at once arises of how determined it is also intended to be. The existing arrangements of the Exchange Rate Mechanism within the European Monetary System are left in place throughout Stages One and Two of Emu. This crucial decision means that independent currencies, although technically and politically tied to each other, are still competitive and markets will continue to speculate in EC currencies throughout the transitional phases. The delay in setting up the European Central Bank until Stage Three, made at German insistence with the tacit support of the UK against the wishes of France and Italy, meant that the ERM would become increasingly exposed as the moment of truth, the irrevocable fixing of currencies, drew closer. At the time of writing the authority of the European Monetary Institute has still to be determined, and its credibility tested. But uncertainty over the ratification of the Treaty had already, before the beginning of Stage Two, caused great instability and there must be doubt that the earlier date of 1997 remains a realistic target for decisions about currency union – at least according to the conditions of the Maastricht accord.

To make matters worse, there is continuing disagreement about the criteria by which to judge when the transition is to take place and who is to be involved. In the Treaty, the Germans won their battle for seemingly tough criteria. The provisions lay down that currencies participating in Stage Three must have enjoyed a stable relationship within the ERM for two years. Long-term interest rates must not be above 2 per cent of the average of the three member states with lowest inflation, and inflation rates shall not be more than 1.5 per cent above their average. Member states' budget deficits should not exceed 3 per cent of GDP, and their public debt ratio should not exceed 60 per cent of GDP – unless excesses are exceptional, temporary and diminishing.

In one sense, the resolution of the argument over the 'convergence criteria' has been put off by the decision to make the European Council, voting by qualified majority, responsible for choosing which countries shall participate in the currency union. Those that do not will be dubbed 'Member States with a derogation', and will be granted subsequent opportunities every two years to come on board. The process of discrimination has been eased, possibly, by the UK which exacted a protocol to the Treaty allowing the Westminster Parliament to exercise its own discretion about sterling's participation in Stage Three. In practice, no doubt, this dispensation makes little difference to the political context in which Britain and the EC will eventually decide to go forward to monetary union: no UK government could defy the House of Commons on such a matter, and some member states, including Denmark, will even hold a referendum on the issue. But the UK Protocol served further to reduce the credibility of the carefully contrived Emu clauses of Maastricht. Worse, it set an unfortunate precedent. In the course of ratification, the Bundestag decided to adopt unilaterally a similar provision. And the Danes, following their referendum debacle of June 1992, extracted from the European Council at Edinburgh a declaration that Denmark would not participate in the currency union.[6]

Furthermore, the ERM under pressure relies upon the active support of the stronger for the weaker currencies. When in the course of 1992 the full cost of German unification became apparent, the commitment of the Bundesbank to European monetary integration fell under suspicion. German participation in the currency union has taken on Augustinian qualities of virtue postponed. In August 1993 the narrow band of 2.25 per cent was widened to 15 per cent, compromising one of the important Maastricht convergence criteria that requires observance of the 'normal' fluctuation margins of the ERM without devaluation for at least two years. Moreover, the fiscal criteria have looked increasingly controversial as economic recession has deepened.

Nevertheless, despite the lack of urgency implicit in the phased time-table, the decision of the IGC to go irreversibly for a single currency and Central Bank was certainly historic.[7] The maintenance of future price stability has been made a keystone of integration. The Treaty determines that neither the EC itself nor its member governments will be able to finance their public deficits by printing money. The ECB cannot extend credit to government at any level – supranational, national or subnational. The constitutional protection of the European Central

Bank from political interference is asserted forcefully in the Treaty. The Bank can make regulations about EC monetary policy, hold the reserves of member states, and make recommendations to the Council of Economic and Finance Ministers (Ecofin) about the Ecu's international rate. The directors of the Central Bank will be appointed by Ecofin after consulting the Parliament, and will serve for eight years. The President of the Bank will report regularly to the other institutions. The arrangements for the management of the single currency are in a way the best formed of all the parts of this Treaty. And whatever the fate of the Emu project of Maastricht, it is difficult to foresee circumstances in which the Community could continue to develop without a reaffirmation of the need for a single currency run according to these or similar arrangements by a central bank.

Given EC control of the customs union, common trade policy, single market and single currency, it is an important element of Emu that the political management of the economy – in other words, fiscal policy – will be shared but well coordinated between the EC institutions and member governments. Emu means the 'adoption of an economic policy which is based on the close coordination of Member States' economic policies' within the Council;[8] 'Member States shall regard their economic policies as a matter of common concern';[9] member states and the Community shall comply with the guiding principles of stable prices, sound public finances and sustainable balance of payments. The Commission is charged with the duty to monitor the budgetary position of each member state. This surveillance can lead to strictures being made by the Commission and Council about the economic policies and performance of a member government, leading in extreme circumstances to the imposition of a fine. In Stage Three a new Economic and Financial Committee, replacing the Monetary Committee, will be set up and composed of representatives of the European Central Bank, Commission and member governments to oversee and report to Ecofin on capital movements. Clearly Ecofin will become very much more busy and important. The new Central Bank has a vital technocratic role. But the success of the Emu enterprise may rest ultimately on the ability of the Council to arrive at macroeconomic policies that are cogent and convergent.

COMMON FOREIGN AND SECURITY POLICY

The Maastricht Treaty seeks to respect the *acquis communautaire* in its design of a common policy in the fields of internal and external security. But it proposes that the Union's foreign affairs be formulated and managed in a qualitatively different way from its domestic ones, not least in that they are purported to be beyond the jurisdiction of the Court of

Justice. As we have noted, this tripod arrangement of pillars, presided over graciously by the European Council, is hailed by UK ministers as a triumph of Anglo-Saxon pragmatism over federalist militancy. Nevertheless, an element of scepticism is in order.

The Common Foreign and Security Policy (CFSP) provisions of the Maastricht Treaty build on the years of experience of the European Political Cooperation (EPC) procedure.[10] Although ministerial decisions will now be taken by the Council, CFSP remains intergovernmental in character and the jurisdiction of the Court of Justice does not extend to it. Nevertheless, under Article M of the Treaty neither CFSP nor its intergovernmental twin pillar of Justice and Home Affairs (Title VI) can impede the operation of the Community, and the Court of Justice is empowered to rule on any infringement of that Article. The Council and the Commission are instructed to ensure consistency between CFSP and the external political and economic relations of the Community, which remain both intact and the responsibility of the EC institutions.

The CFSP pursues its objectives through 'common positions' and 'joint actions'. Common positions correspond to the current practice of EPC. Joint actions are worked out according to a complicated procedure. On the basis of guidelines from the European Council, the Council decides by unanimity that a matter should be the subject of joint action. The Council also decides those items which can be covered by qualified majority. The majority required is the same as that provided by the EEC Treaty for qualified majorities when there is no proposal from the Commission: that is to say, a majority of at least fifty-four votes (out of a possible seventy-six) in favour cast by at least eight countries. The Council is served by a political committee.

CFSP shall include 'all questions related to the security of the Union, including the eventual framing of a common defence policy, which might in time lead to a common defence'.[11] Joint actions, however, are not foreseen at this stage in the defence field. In an important departure, Western European Union (WEU) is charged with the elaboration and implementation of decisions and actions having defence implications. This is the case even though Denmark and Ireland are only observer members of WEU. The WEU arrangement is to be reviewed in 1996.

The presidency of the Council will represent the Union on CFSP matters and in international organisations and conferences. This is something of a setback for the Commission, which had hoped to extend its previously dominant representation of the EC on external economic matters. It also impends danger: the Greek government's representation of the Union in the UN peace conference on the Balkans has not been to everyone's taste. However, the Commission wins the important power to make proposals to the Council on CFSP matters alongside member states. EU members of the UN Security Council are to concert and keep fully informed other member states. As permanent members of the Security Council, France and the UK undertake to ensure the defence of the positions and interests of the Union.

JUSTICE AND HOME AFFAIRS

Over the years, the Twelve have invented many examples of *ad hoc* machinery covering a wide range of interior affairs such as police and customs cooperation, asylum, extradition, deportation, visa policy and, most controversially of all, immigration. The establishment of the single market, with its requirements for freedom of movement of persons, has enlarged the interface of this intergovernmental activity with that of the EC itself, and the Commission has gradually become more involved in the process. The signature of the Schengen Agreement between the core member states of the Community is intended to create a virtual frontier-free zone: an ambition set for the whole EC by Article 8a of the Single Act, but as yet impeded by certain member governments which insist on keeping national barriers for political and technical reasons concerning crime control.

The Maastricht Treaty attempts to impose some order on this patchwork of diplomacy, and associates it more closely with the EC itself. The relevant articles of the Treaty, Title VI, comprise the third 'pillar' of the European Union.[12] The procedural arrangements are comparable to those for CFSP, and, similarly, administrative costs fall to the EC budget. The Council of ministers is to run things. A new body, the 'K4 Committee', is set up to coordinate the different intergovernmental activities. The Commission's position in these matters is enhanced, however, and it is to enjoy on this committee a limited and non-exclusive right of policy initiation. The European Parliament has only a marginal role. And (for the anti-federalists just as important) the Court of Justice continues to be largely excluded. Some limited use of majority voting is prescribed, but, as with foreign and security policy, according to the stricter qualification. The possibility is admitted that some aspects of member states' interior policy can in the future be transferred under the auspices of the EC, but only on a case-by-case basis according to a strictly unanimous Decision of the Council ratified by all member states.

Again, the importance of this innovation of Maastricht really lies in the future. A rapid maturing of EC citizenship would have obvious implications for the lack of parliamentary scrutiny in these sensitive areas. Moreover, the relationship of both intergovernmental 'pillars' with the EC will be tested severely, possibly to destruction, by continuing instability in Central and Eastern Europe. The EC's response to its own insecurity might be both easier to arrive at and more incisive were the conventional Community method, including some element of qualified majority voting, to be applied. It is likely that the EC governments will review the whole pillared structure of the Union at the next IGC in 1996.

THE MAIN INSTITUTIONAL REFORMS

Despite the tripartite structure of the Treaty, the European Union is served by a 'single institutional framework' presided over by the European Council which is made up of heads of state or government and the President of the EC Commission.[13] In the opinion of the British Foreign Secretary, the European Council is now seen as the 'apex, the architrave of the three pillars'; it will be the 'chief gainer' from Maastricht.[14]

Nevertheless, all the institutions benefit from Maastricht as a consequence of the Union's increased competences. Emu, CFSP and interior affairs aside, the Maastricht Treaty expands the scope of Community activity in a number of other policy sectors. The Council is enjoined to vote less by unanimity and more by majority vote. In several cases, where the Single Act required merely consultation of the Parliament, Maastricht provides for cooperation with it: in other words, for two readings of draft law. The scope of the assent procedure is also widened. All these relatively modest changes make the EC more democratic and efficient, and are to be welcomed.

The Treaty of Maastricht, however, remains more of a reflection of the current state of European integration than a boldly innovatory document. Indeed, a former judge of the European Court, Lord Mackenzie-Stuart, has called Maastricht a 'driving-mirror Treaty', writing down *de jure* what has been achieved by the Twelve and their EC institutions *de facto*. This is not to belittle the exercise. It is essential that, from time to time, what has been integrated functionally within the EC and what the member governments have chosen to cooperate on together are given a more solid legal basis than Article 235 and that the institutions are vested with full and specific authority. Apart from the creation of the monetary institutions, however, five other innovations were made that are likely to have profound institutional repercussions for European unification. These are:

1 the incorporation of the principle of subsidiarity;
2 the establishment of the concept of European citizenship;
3 the introduction of a co-decision procedure between Parliament and Council;

4 the involvement of Parliament with the Council in the appointment of
   the Commission;
5 the setting up of the Committee of the Regions.

There is also one innovation that may have strong negative implications
for European integration – the clutch of opt-outs from important Treaty
provisions, notably the Social Protocol.

SUBSIDIARITY

Subsidiarity is a traditional federalist concept. It seeks to guard on the
one hand against an excessive centralisation of government and, on the
other, against its exaggerated dispersal. It is also a principle to be found
in Catholic doctrine with the aim of enhancing the role of the lower or
smaller orders in the Church and of individuals in society. It first
appeared in Community parlance in the Tindemans Report on
European Union of 1975. It was deployed again explicitly in the
European Parliament's 1984 Draft Treaty, drawn up by Altiero Spinelli,
and implicitly in the Single European Act.[15] With the encouragement of
the Commission and at the insistence mainly of the Germans, subsidiarity was written into the Treaty of Maastricht in the form of a basic
guideline for future activity. The flood of single market legislation since
1985 had awakened suspicions that the EC was beginning to interfere
too much in the minutiae of daily life. The German government, in
particular, had to protect the constitutional position of the Länder. The
British saw subsidiarity as a chance to claw back to London powers
passed previously to Brussels in a (presumably) irresponsible moment.
In the event, the problematic ratification process suggested that the IGC
had been prudent to seek to constrain in some systematic way the
incremental growth of the activities of the Community.

 Subsidiarity, therefore, was incorporated up-front as a common principle of the Treaty.[16] Unsurprisingly, it is defined ambivalently. On the
one hand, subsidiarity is taken to mean that decisions should be taken as
closely as possible to the people they most affect. On the other, in the key
Article 3b, the EC should take action in those areas where it does not
have exclusive competence 'only if and in so far as the objectives of the
proposed action cannot be sufficiently achieved by the Member States
and can therefore, by reason of the scale or effects of the proposed
action be better achieved by the Community'. No action by the
Community should go beyond what is required to fulfil the Treaty.
Subsidiarity does not attribute competences to the EC or Union, which is
really the job of the Treaties, but merely suggests how their competences
should be exercised.

 It is relevant to recall that the Maastricht Treaty did not amend Article

235 of the EC Treaty, which allows the Council acting unanimously to add to the EC's existing armoury of powers in order to carry out Treaty objectives. Furthermore, a new Article F says that the Union 'shall provide itself with the means necessary to attain its objectives and carry through its policies'.

The debate within Community circles about how to apply the principle of subsidiarity was electrified during the course of 1992 by the Danish referendum defeat and then the *petit oui* in France. The Danish foreign minister Uffe Elleman-Jensen insisted that the Community needed to get closer to the citizens and practise open government if the situation were to be retrieved. Three European Councils, at Lisbon, Birmingham and Edinburgh, were devoted to reaching an agreed and workable definition of subsidiarity. In the end, the Commission succeeded in getting its version accepted. The Edinburgh Annex of December 1992 lays down three criteria to be fulfilled when the possibility of EC action is considered.[17] First, is the action proposed proportional to the scale of the problem at hand? Second, is there a transnational element? Third, can the EC act efficiently? The UK failed to persuade its partners that a new mechanism was required to allow the Council to turf out Commission proposals on the grounds of alleged breaches of subsidiarity. Subsidiarity will be considered along with the content of the proposal; the European Parliament and the Commission will perform according to existing procedures; and any challenge brought before the Court of Justice will be left until after the legislative process has run its course.

Those who wanted a maximalist interpretation of subsidiarity, however, lost two battles. First, it was accepted that the EC should not define subsidiarity to implicate the subnational disposition of member states. Their internal organisation in terms of regional and local government is thoroughly insulated, at least formally, from any interference by government at the supranational level. As we shall see below, however, the controversy over subsidiarity served at least to expose the extent to which some member states are very much more decentralised than others, the two extreme cases being Germany and Britain.

Second, the Commission's proposal (strongly supported by the Italians) for a 'hierarchy of norms' was defeated. This would have simplified and rationalised the EC's law-making by creating a powerful form of framework law in which both the principles and objectives of the legislation and the ways and means of its implementation would be tightly and clearly drawn. Unlike the existing jumble of EC acts, regulations, directives, decisions, opinions and recommendations, all EC law under a hierarchical regime would be binding in its entirety and directly applicable irrespective of whether it was specified to be implemented by member governments or the Commission. Unsurprisingly, the

Commission's assertions that the hierarchy of norms would strengthen the clarity and transparency of the EC law-making process backfired. Few member governments at the IGC had the stomach to campaign for an increase in the executive power of the Commission, implying as it did a diminution of the reserve executive power of the Council.[18] Accordingly, the controversial issue of 'comitology' – that is, the choice between regulatory, advisory or management committee for the execution of EC policy – was effectively suppressed at Maastricht. Despite subsidiarity, therefore, executive power in the EC is still blurred or, more accurately, shared confusingly between Commission and Council. But the Commission did manage to extract a significant declaration attached to the Treaty that commits governments to return to the issue of creating a clear legislative hierarchy at the next IGC in 1996.

The writing-in of subsidiarity to the Treaty is likely to be one of its lasting and most valuable achievements. Already, the Commission is being more circumspect in proposing and in accepting the proposals of others for yet more EC law. Some minor and superfluous legislation (actual and draft) will be dismantled. But there will be no wholesale rolling back of the powers of the Community. In fact, subsidiarity is clearly a two-edged sword which will strengthen the argument for EC action in appropriate cases. It is not a mathematical formula, but a logical one. By using its discretion about states' rights, the Court of Justice will be acting more and more in the role of a federal supreme court.

THE CITIZEN-ELECTOR

The Maastricht Treaty gives birth to the concept of a common citizenship for the European Union.[19] This act may be interpreted as being of deep symbolic importance, as it postulates the existence of a common popular sovereignty to complement – or rival – the common sovereignty of the states. In so far as a political citizenship may be beyond the control of government, its assertion in the European Community has the potential to be a contentious or even a subversive force. But the Maastricht Treaty takes no risks. Citizenship of the Union is limited to citizens of the member states and confined to an extension of electoral rights, to vote and to stand, in local and European elections for citizens residing in an EC country other than their own, a confirmation of the existing right to petition the European Parliament, the establishment of an ombudsman to investigate charges of maladministration by the EC institutions and a sharing of consular services outside the EC.

This extension of civil rights adds up to a modest step in the history of European integration – and a significant step forward from the previously wholly superficial harmonisation of passports. Nevertheless, although the Treaty declares its respect for the European Convention of Human Rights, it neither ratifies it on behalf of the Union (or Community), nor does it attempt (with the exception of those above) to define more modern civil rights and duties.[20] An EC citizen is defined as a national of a member state. No mention is made of civil protection for people from third countries legally resident within the Community. The right of freedom of movement of EC citizens throughout the territory of the Union is reaffirmed, but there is no stipulation about the rights that they may carry with them.

The European Parliament, which lays claim to be the repository of the pooled popular sovereignty of the European citizen, stands to gain most from these innovations of the Treaty of Maastricht. The Treaty also confirms the obligation to adopt a uniform electoral procedure. The existence of trans-European political parties is recognised in treaty form for the first time. They are expected to contribute to 'forming a European awareness and to expressing the political will of the citizens of the Union'.[21] More uniformity in the method of electing the Parliament will ensure that the British government is forced eventually to adopt a system of proportional representation so that seats won broadly match votes cast. It also opens up the possibility of a supranational list for the election of a limited number of MEPs. The recognition of the role of political parties draws attention to the need to fund and build coherent partisan forces dedicated, according to the spirit of subsidiarity, to working within the European dimension. This innovation, again, has important implications for the domestic politics of the member states. Lastly, the Parliament is given the right it has exercised for some years to request the Commission to propose legislation. This did not match the Parliament's request of the IGC that it be granted the right of direct legislative initiative, but it is comparable to the existing rights of the Council, and has significance.

So the European citizen of Maastricht is a skeletal creature. How he and she are fleshed out in the future in terms of civil, cultural and social rights will have serious consequences for the engagement of public opinion in EC affairs. The citizen's new dual identity will reinforce civil rights.

'CO-DECISION'

The Treaty leaves the institutions with at least six different ways of taking main decisions: the budgetary procedure (unchanged), assent (introduced by the Single Act), information (new in Maastricht), consultation (Treaty of Rome), cooperation (Single Act) and co-decision (Maastricht). The Council also retains the right in some instances to act unilaterally without informing the Parliament until after it has acted, notably concerning excessive public debts. The biggest change introduced by Maastricht is indeed the 'co-decision' procedure, which concedes to the European Parliament the right of legislative partnership with the Council.[22] This reform was sought by the MEPs since their first direct election by universal suffrage in 1979. The concession is far from being comprehensive across all policy sectors. The Parliament is still not exactly a co-equal partner of the Council, as its new power is to obstruct a determined Council rather than to press its own amendments to a conclusion. (Significantly, the minimalist UK government uses the term 'negative assent procedure' rather than 'co-decision'.) The shuttling of draft acts between the institutions and the conciliation procedures are complex and protracted. Nevertheless, Maastricht marks the point in the Community's development at which the Parliament became the first chamber of a real legislature. And the Council is obliged to act from time to time like a second legislative chamber rather than a ministerial directorate.

The European Parliament has for some years been a proper partner of the Council in the making of the EC annual budget. The co-decision of Maastricht means that it has now come of age as a law-making body. It would be perverse were co-decision not to be extended (and improved) eventually so that nothing becomes EC law unless passed by a majority of both Houses.

The co-decision procedure is laid down in Article 189b. It is pre-scribed in the Treaty for a number of sectors, including the internal market, free movement of workers, self-employed workers, trans-European networks and environment policy. In all but two curious cases, R&D and culture policy, the Council acts by qualified majority vote. The possibility of its scope being widened at the 1996 IGC is made explicit. Co-decision sits alongside a revised version of the 'cooperation pro-cedure', introduced by the Single Act, in which the Council retains the last word (Article 189c). Under both arrangements the Commission plays an important role as conciliator and possible arbiter between Parliament and Council (but less so under the co-decision procedure, where it may be frozen out). In other areas of the Treaty, such as citizenship, the structural funds and international agreements, the Parliament is granted the blocking power of a simple vote of assent. In future, therefore, where ministers are divided, MEPs can play a decisive role in determining the content of EC law. Under co-decision, there is no doubt that a determined Parliament can frustrate the will of member governments. Moreover, in many cases it is possible for the Parliament with the Commission to paralyse the Community indefinitely, thereby provoking a constitutional crisis. How these two collaborate, therefore, is now of fundamental importance.

THE APPOINTMENT OF THE COMMISSION

The last main institutional reform achieved by Maastricht is to involve the Parliament in the selection of the Commission President and to require its approval of the appointment of the college as a whole.[23] The Parliament has always had the power to sack the Commission as a whole, although it has never dared to use it. The truth was that there had been for years a reluctance to admit the too close accountability of the Commission to the Parliament, both by the Commission (for obvious reasons) and by member governments, who wished to resist simultaneously a great enhancement of the democratic credentials of the Commission as well as the concession of further power to the Parliament. The Treaty of Maastricht, however, allows the Parliament, acting by a simple majority, to block the nominations of the member states' governments to the Commission. If the Parliament were ever to achieve the necessary coherence to settle on an alternative Commission, say to include MEPs, it could shatter the member states' monopoly power to appoint the executive authority.

The change to the appointment procedure of the Commission is supplemented by making the mandate of the Commission co-terminous with that of the Parliament. One of the first tasks of MEPs elected in June 1994 is to approve the appointment of the new Commission (to take office in January 1995). These reforms were advocated strongly by the President of the Commission, Jacques Delors, as a means of strengthening further the Commission's accountability. Together they will enliven the Parliamentary election campaigns and inject a fresh element of partisanship into European federal democracy. For the new Parliament the appointment of the Commission and the success with which it exploits co-decision will be big tests of its political maturity.

THE REGIONAL DIMENSION

The Treaty establishes a new Committee of the Regions and allows for the first time ministers from autonomous subnational governments to represent member states in the Council.[24] This, too, amounts to a significant reform, especially in the light of the controversial debate over the interpretation of subsidiarity, the enlargement of the size of the Regional Development Fund and the creation, by Maastricht, of a new Cohesion Fund for the poorer member states.[25] The Committee has limited consultative powers, akin to those of the existing Economic and Social Committee (Ecosoc). Indeed, the regional body is to share its administration and facilities with Ecosoc. It must be consulted on specifically regional matters and may be consulted by either the Commission or the Council on anything. It can issue opinions on its own initiative.

The reaction of regional and local authorities to this innovation has been curiously ambiguous. There is, for one thing, a difficulty in the very divergent forms of subnational government within the EC, not least in the matter of the degree of autonomy. But there can be little doubt that the German Länder and the Spanish regional governments such as Catalonia will soon assert themselves inside the new body and seek to create a whole new regional dimension to the EC's representative system. Ecosoc, which has languished, may be quickly surpassed. The Committee of the Regions adds to the checks and balances of the Community method. Although it is far from fully integrated with the legislative process, its success will help to enhance the representative capability of the European Community. Pressure for decentralisation within member states, and not least the UK, will continue to build. The regional dimension is manifested in many different ways in the EC, but Maastricht's new Committee will help to postulate the emergence of 'Europe of the Regions'.

THE SOCIAL PROTOCOL

The social policy provisions of the Single Act remained substantively unchanged by Maastricht.[26] Eleven member states, however, were sufficiently frustrated at this lack of progress to devise a supplementary Agreement containing their more ambitious agenda.[27] Most surprisingly, the Eleven managed to persuade their twelfth partner, the UK, to allow them to proceed without it.[28] The conventional EC institutions with their normal administrative budget are to be used by the Eleven, presumably with the British representatives keeping quiet or leaving the room.[29] In addition, however, the Eleven also chose to elevate the role of the social partners at EC level. (Originally, this was a ruse proposed by the Dutch presidency to bypass British obstruction, but it remained within the final Agreement.) In some circumstances, the Eleven promise to rely on the social partners (again, presumably, without CBI or TUC involvement) to implement certain Directives; in others collective agreements between management and labour may be awarded contractual status. The Commission now has the unenviable duty to monitor and appraise the representative capability of UNICE and the ETUC – in itself a radical departure from their hitherto rather complacent tripartite relationship.

Without regard to the substantive arguments about European social and competition policies, the Social Protocol has important institutional consequences for the EC. It is the first serious example in the history of the Community of a Treaty derogation from one of the objectives of the Treaty. It gives practical expression to a willingness by a member state to be left out of integration. Conversely, it demonstrates that a majority of member states are willing to develop the *acquis communautaire* even in the absence of consensus. Whereas it is practicable for the EC to adopt from time to time a multi-speed approach to integration, for example the Treaty's phased approach to Emu, there is no precedent for the multi-tier EC created at a stroke by the Social Protocol. This is Europe à la carte – introduced as a panic measure in the middle of the night at Maastricht.

Nobody knows how the Social Protocol will work in practice. For the Commission, which has to initiate policy, there are important questions of cohesion. How provocative will it be to deploy the Agreement of the Eleven to force through legislation, such as the Works Council Directive? For the British predicament is real. Despite the obstinacy of the Tory government on these matters, the UK will not become an exclusion zone for EC social policy. UK firms operating elsewhere in the EC are bound by EC law *à Onze*, and will be unlikely to try to adopt markedly different management strategies within the same corporate regime. For the Court of Justice there are equally tricky issues. It cannot be long before carefully contrived litigation is brought against the UK government for alleged infringement of an EC social policy provision. The Court of Justice will be bound to seek to protect the integrity of the single market. For all the institutions, not excluding the Parliament and Commission or Ecosoc and the Committee of the Regions, there are questions of protocol concerning UK participation to be resolved.

DYNAMICS OF REFORM

Article N of the Treaty of Maastricht lays down that there shall be an intergovernmental conference in 1996 leading to possible revision of the Treaty. Despite the fact that Article N requires unanimity at all stages, this commitment to further reform is manifestly as major a feature of the Maastricht Treaty as a similar clause had proved to be for the Single Act. There, a minor commitment to look again at European Political Cooperation became the pretext for the wholesale revision of the Treaty.

We have suggested above that the Social Protocol is unfortunate in that it establishes a derogatory system of European integration, built on opt-outs and cop-outs. Certainly the British precedent was soon followed by Denmark, which extracted from the Edinburgh European Council in December 1992 its own derogation from Stage Three of Emu and the single currency.[30] Denmark also opted out of the defence activities of the Union.

While it is clear that these derogations caused much disappointment to integrationists, Maastricht has opened up a debate about whether it is possible to build an enlarged, multi-tiered but still functional European Community. Variable geometry already existed outside the EC treaty framework, for example with Benelux or the Schengen Agreement. WEU, the defence arm of Maastricht, comprises only ten of the twelve member states of the Community. If future European unification is not always to proceed at the speed of the slowest partner or only at the behest of the most reluctant member state, some flexibility in the institutional arrangements is inevitable. Perhaps the next IGC will consider how to build ladders between the outer and inner tier of the EC in social, monetary and defence policy. How does a member state change gear to catch up with others far ahead?

We have highlighted above some of the areas where future reform is either required specifically under the terms of Maastricht or is highly probable. This dynamism for internal reform is motivated by various external and internal causes which are likely to increase in force over the next decade. An additional driving force, of course, is enlargement.[31]

Maastricht has also introduced some institutional innovations, such as citizenship, co-decision and the Committee of the Regions, that are likely to be lasting features of the constitutional development of the Union. Other actors, notably national parliaments, left aside by Maastricht, may need now to stake a claim in any further reform.[32] All this will depend very much on the application of the principle of subsidiarity – and in particular, whether confidence can be built up to allow the EC itself to handle the appropriate aspects of the security dimension. If so, the cumbersome three-pillared structure of Maastricht is unlikely to survive intact for long. The question of opt-outs and derogations must also be tackled incisively. If the European Union shows itself to be ever more inventive, it can continue to adapt and refine its institutions to cater for a much larger membership than twelve.

3

THE TREATY NEGOTIATIONS

Roy Pryce

The first steps towards a new treaty were taken at a meeting of the European Council in Hanover in June 1988. The political map of the continent was then still essentially the same as it had been for over forty years since the aftermath of the Second World War. But in the autumn of 1989 the old order melted away. Its chief symbol, the Berlin Wall, was hacked down. In the following tumultuous months the regime that had sheltered behind it fell apart, as did the other communist regimes in Central and Eastern Europe. The contagion was so powerful that very soon the Soviet Union itself began to disintegrate. And hard on the heels of the dissolution of the old order came the reunification of Germany, achieved at breakneck speed by October 1990.

These extraordinary events had a significant effect on the negotiations for the Union. Nevertheless the pressures which gave birth to the negotiations had been generated long before, as a result of both the long-term dynamic of the process of integration and, more recently, the thrusting development of the Community in the second half of the 1980s. Similarly, the ideas and strategies of integration which provided the substance of the negotiations also derived from the EC's past experience – as did the tensions and unresolved problems in the relationships between its member states. The past weighed heavily, in both positive and negative ways, as they confronted the looming problems of a new Europe.

ECONOMIC AND MONETARY UNION

In 1988 the Community was in a confident mood. It had recovered from the 'Eurosclerosis' of the opening years of the decade and was making good progress with the programme of reforms designed to remove the remaining barriers to a genuine single market, free of restrictions on the movement of goods, labour, capital and services by the end of 1992. This objective, incorporated in the Single European Act of February 1986, had provided a point of convergence for all the member governments,

36

including that of Mrs Thatcher who, while being a fierce critic of the Community, was strongly committed to a market economy with its emphasis on open markets, deregulation and increased competition. The 1992 programme also harnessed the active support of industrial, business and financial leaders.

Fortified by this new wave of enthusiasm, and led by Jacques Delors, President of the Commission, pressure now began to build up in favour of a new attempt to move to Economic and Monetary Union. This had been a declared aim of the member states since the Hague Summit of December 1969, and although attempts to move in that direction in the early 1970s had failed, the success of the European Monetary System established in 1979 had revived pressures to go further. The 1992 programme added to these presssures. It was argued that Emu was needed both to underpin and ensure maximum benefit from the single market. Two of the 1992 measures also provided an important part of its infrastructure: the freeing of capital movements by July 1990, and a single market for financial services by the end of 1992.

The growing mood of confidence was further strengthened by the successful completion in February 1988 of negotiations on a series of measures (the 'Delors I package') to increase the financial resources – and the budgetary discipline – of the EC and to provide it with budgetary guidelines for the next five years. It was recognised, however, that the negotiation of an agreement on Emu would nevertheless require a major act of political will. The French government was strongly in favour because it would imply collective control, rather than that of the Bundesbank, over monetary policy. But in the Federal Republic there were widespread fears about a European central bank and a common currency. The first would mean a downgrading of the role and independence of the Bundesbank which was regarded as the country's bastion against any return of the inflation which in the past had brought the Nazis to power. The second would mean the loss of the Deutschmark, a symbol of stability as well as national identity.

The poorer countries of the Community had their own concerns about the impact of Emu. But it was only the British who were expected to be absolutely opposed; and it was thought that ultimately Mrs Thatcher would have to give way if her partners in the Community were determined to press ahead. She was also under pressure in her own cabinet not to allow Britain to be isolated. These calculations appeared to be borne out when in June 1988 the European Council agreed to a proposal put forward by Delors for a new study on Emu. Thatcher succeeded only in deleting any mention in its terms of reference to a European central bank, which was promptly (and correctly) dismissed as a Pyrrhic victory.

Subsequently the Prime Minister was forced by a revolt in her own cabinet to moderate her opposition to British membership of the ERM of the European Monetary System, and at the European Council at Strasbourg in December 1989 to accept a majority decision to convene an Intergovernmental Conference to draw up, on the basis of the Delors Committee report, a treaty on Economic and Monetary Union. But in September 1989 she had taken the opportunity of a speech at the College of Europe in Bruges to reassert, in characteristically trenchant terms, her belief in the virtues of 'independent, sovereign states' and to attack closer integration which in her view would inevitably lead to a centralised superstate. So it was clear that a fierce battle with the British lay ahead.

POLITICAL UNION

It was only at a later stage that 'Political Union' was added to the agenda for negotiation. This was seen as a necessary part of the creation of a European Union to which the member states had been committed since 1972.[1] Its two most important components were reform of the institutions to make them more efficient and democratic, and a common foreign and security policy. Some progress towards these goals had been made in the Single Act, notably through the introduction of qualified majority voting for much of the internal market legislation and a 'cooperation procedure' giving the European Parliament more influence over it. But the Parliament remained very dissatisfied and had continued to press for more reform, including that of co-decision with the Council over all legislation.[2]

These and related issues were however added to the agenda for a new treaty only as a direct result of German unification. The decisive pressure came from Chancellor Kohl and President Mitterrand. Both believed it essential to strengthen the Community politically in order to anchor the new Germany firmly within it. In April 1990 they sent a joint letter to the Irish presidency urging that a second intergovernmental conference be convened, in parallel with that for Emu, to accelerate the political construction of Europe. The time had now come, they said, to realise the European Union to which its members were committed.

This proposal was agreed by the European Council at its meeting in Dublin in June 1990, again in the face of Mrs Thatcher's scorn and opposition. But on some of the issues that had to be tackled by this IGC there were, as the negotiations leading to the Single Act had shown, some significant differences between Paris and Bonn, as well as between other members of the Community. This late addition to the agenda therefore threatened to make the negotiations considerably more complex and difficult.

THE NEGOTIATIONS: METHOD AND SUBSTANCE

Many criticisms have been levelled in retrospect at the way the Treaty was negotiated. It is argued that the negotiations were conducted by bureaucrats, in secret, and in a way that was oblivious to the likely impact of the outcome on public opinion in the member countries. There is no doubt that the document which emerged from the negotiations is an inelegant, complex and messy affair which is quite unintelligible to anyone not well versed in the history, institutions and policies of the Community. The responsibility for this, however, lies not with some group of faceless bureaucrats but squarely with the governments and ministers who negotiated and signed the Treaty. They could, and indeed should, have paid far more attention to the need to produce a text that could be readily understood by the citizens in whose name they were acting. They could, and should, also have found ways of distinguishing clearly between what was important and matters of detail.

But the main reasons for the unsatisfactory nature of the outcome lie elsewhere. One is the technical complexity of the issues which had to be faced in the course of the Emu negotiations. Another is the sprawling and heterogeneous nature of the Political Union agenda, which involved many additions and amendments to the Community Treaties in addition to the two intergovernmental agreements. But the most important was the lack of agreement on many basic issues. The consensus which had underpinned the 1992 programme and the Single Act did not exend to Emu and Political Union. Agreement was now possible only through a series of fudges and low-level compromises, accompanied by a rash of exceptions, opt-outs and waivers.

The most serious differences that had to be overcome in both sets of negotiations were those between Britain and its partners. The fall of Thatcher on the eve of the formal negotiations undoubtedly facilitated an agreement, but her successor John Major had to draw deeply on Britain's remaining credit with its partners to achieve a deal. There were also significant differences between Paris and Bonn (as well as between other member countries on specific issues), but the close understanding between Kohl and Mitterrand overcame these and provided the framework for an agreement: once again the Paris–Bonn relationship proved crucial.

The division of the negotiations between two parallel IGCs marked a departure from the method followed in the negotiations leading to the Single Act, where a single IGC had dealt with both treaty revisions and foreign policy cooperation. The new procedure certainly did not help the task of arriving, at the end of the day, at a single document. But the central difficulty lay elsewhere. Once again, it was a matter of substance rather than procedure: that is, a profound disagreement about the overall architecture of European Union. This was an issue on which the UK was the chief protagonist of a minority view, determined to oppose the majority who saw the gradual extension of the scope of the Community as the essence of the future Union. The British government insisted that, on the contrary, the development of the EC should be contained and ring-fenced by the development alongside it of areas of intergovernmental cooperation. It was this which contributed a great deal to making the outcome so complicated and unsatisfactory.

In other respects, the procedures employed during the negotiations were much the same as those used in earlier major negotiations, like those leading to the Rome Treaties and the Single Act. The member governments were firmly in control from beginning to end. It was the European Council, consisting of the heads of government and the President of the Commission, which formally decided to launch the negotiations by convening the two IGCs on the basis of Article 236 of the EEC Treaty. The European Council also set the agenda for them, took some important preliminary decisions before they met, monitored their progress, brokered the final agreement, and approved the signature of the resulting Treaty. Under its authority, the country holding the presidency of the Community (Luxembourg in the first half of 1991, the Netherlands in the second half) organised the negotiations, and presided over them at ministerial and official level. National governments also contributed a plethora of proposals both before and during the IGCs.[3]

In both sets of negotiations ministerial meetings were held at roughly monthly intervals: these were supplemented by one or two more informal meetings and by more intensive negotiations as the end of 1991 approached. To prepare the ministerial sessions, two groups of senior officials acting as the ministers' 'Personal Representatives' met much more frequently, often each week. The Commission was represented at ministerial and official level in both IGCs. In the case of the Emu negotiations, some of the more technical issues were entrusted to the Monetary Committee of senior officials from the member states, or to the Committee of Central Bank Governors.

Although all these bodies met in private throughout the period of negotiation, which lasted for twelve months, their work was not kept secret. Detailed, blow-by-blow accounts were published by the Brussels-based news agency *Agence Europe* (which also reproduced the texts of the main documents as they were considered), and journalists had no serious difficulty in following the course of the negotiations. In addition, regular reports on progress were made by the presidency to plenary sessions of the Parliament, whose members were also briefed by their national authorities. National ministers also reported to their own parliaments after European Council and ministerial meetings. In short, there was no lack of information for anyone who wished to find out.

There were also rather more occasions than in the past for the European Parliament to make its views known to the negotiators. Its Institutional Committee produced a series of carefully considered reports setting out the Parliament's own position and demands which, once approved in plenary, were transmitted to the Commission and Council. Regular debates followed the presidency's reports, to which the President of the Commission also contributed. In addition, following pressure from the Parliament, an Interinstitutional Committee was created specifically to provide a forum for discussion between the three institutions. This met regularly during the negotiations in advance of ministerial meetings. Although its proceedings consisted mainly of a series of monologues rather than a dialogue and proved frustrating to the parliamentary participants, it did nevertheless mark some advance on previous practice.

Similarly, and again through the initiative of the European Parliament, national parliaments were on this occasion involved in Community level discussions bearing on the negotiations. Two new channels were created. The first consisted of meetings which the Parliament organised with members of the committees of national parliaments specialising in Community affairs. More significantly, the Parliament also promoted the creation of a new and larger forum – the Conference of Parliaments of the Community or Assizes. This met in Rome in November 1990, attended by some 250 parliamentarians (two-thirds from national parliaments, one-third MEPs). The occasion provided an additional and novel occasion for EC parliamentarians to make their views known, and resulted in a general endorsement of the European Parliament's own aims in the negotiations. Its enthusiasm for regular meetings of this sort quickly cooled however when the French government proposed that they should be given a formal role in the Community's already complex institutional structure – a proposal which also failed to find favour among a majority of governments. Moreover, some national parliamentarians, especially from Britain, were infuriated to find that they had been bounced into subscribing to the European Parliament's well-prepared views on the IGCs.[4] The Roman experiment seems unlikely to be repeated.

PREPARATORY NEGOTIATIONS: EMU

There were important differences between the two sets of negotiations, well characterised by one of the participants, Sir John Kerr, the UK Permanent Representative. 'The monetary union negotiation', he said, 'was a polite and professorial negotiation, like a university senior common room; the political union negotiation was neither polite nor professorial.' In his view the major reason for this was that the negotiations on Emu were well prepared, unlike those on political union.[5]

This was undoubtedly the case. Sustained thought had been given to Emu over many years, before and after the Werner Report of 1970 which had provided the basis for the first abortive attempt at it.[6] The report of the Delors committee, published in April 1989, updated its work, and provided a basis for formal negotiations as the Spaak Report had done for the Rome Treaties and the Dooge Report for the Single Act. The fact that the governors of all the national banks sat on the committee also gave its findings great authority. The report came out unanimously and powerfully in favour of a commitment to Emu, a federal-type European System of Central Banks, and a single currency. Like the Werner Report it suggested a three-stage approach to the final goal, stressing that a decision to enter on the first stage should be a 'decision to embark on the entire process'. It then argued that an early start should be made no later than 1 July 1990 but in a politically astute move it detached this initial, but crucial, decision from the process of treaty revision which would be necessary for Stages Two and Three. The timing and duration of the three stages were, however, left to the politicians. So too were decisions on issues which the committee had discussed but not been able to resolve.

At the Madrid meeting of the European Council held in June 1989 a number of preliminary decisions based on the report were taken. The intention of moving towards Emu was reaffirmed; 1 July 1990 was set for the opening of Stage One; and it was agreed to begin preparations for an IGC to revise the Treaties in preparation for Stages Two and Three. Shortly afterwards, Mitterrand announced that he would take advantage of the French presidency in the second half of the year to convene the IGC so that it could begin its work immediately after July 1990. At the meeting, Thatcher was isolated not only among the other heads of government, but in her own delegation. It was in these circumstances that she was forced to temporise, spelling out the conditions under which Britain would join the ERM in order to show that she was not against all forms of closer monetary cooperation, and in the hope of staving off an early move towards full Emu. She had to acknowledge, however, that she could not prevent the calling of an IGC on Emu if the others insisted.[7]

Subsequently, during the autumn, the British government launched a counter-attack. At an informal meeting of economic and finance ministers in Antibes the Chancellor of the Exchequer, Nigel Lawson, put forward a plan for free competition between currencies, which he said would be a better way to move towards monetary union than the Delors plan. But the plot had been hastily prepared, and his colleagues, it was reported, were 'bemused by Mr Lawson's sketchy account of British thinking'. It signally failed to impress them.[8]

German hesitations were quite a different matter. In the autumn of 1989 domestic opposition to the Delors Report began to surface: at the same time dramatic events in Berlin and elsewhere claimed attention. From early November Kohl began to drag his feet, and briefly sought to back away from fixing a date for the IGC.[9] But when the French reacted strongly, he gave way, Mitterrand having agreed that the actual beginning of negotiations should be postponed until late 1990. This was underpinned by an undertaking on the part of the French to support Kohl on his plans for German unification, in return for a German commitment to respect the Oder–Neisse frontier with Poland. At the Strasbourg summit in December 1989 the agreement to convene an IGC on Emu was duly consummated with the support of all members except Thatcher. Her brief hopes of an alliance with Kohl had been dashed: she was now more than ever an isolated figure – one French newspaper heading its report 'L'éternelle solitude de la Dame de Fer'.[10]

In the following twelve months both the succeeding presidencies actively pressed forward with work on Emu, spurred on by the general conviction of the need to strengthen the Community as rapidly as possible, especially in the light of rapid German reunification. Preparations for the IGC were pushed forward in parallel in several different bodies: the Ecofin Council worked its way through major issues raised by the Delors Report; the Committee of Bank Governors set about drawing up draft statutes for the proposed new European Central Bank system; and the Commission set to work on a draft treaty. At the conclusion of the Irish presidency in late June 1990 dates were agreed for the opening of the Intergovernmental Conferences in mid-December, and by the summer recess most of the technical preparation for the IGC had been completed. The Italians, however, were anxious to get agreement on the date for the opening of Stage Two before the IGC began, and this they succeeded in doing at a special summit they called in Rome on 27–28 October. Chancellor Kohl then put an end to a long period of German indecision and opted for 1 January 1994.

Prime Minister Thatcher was incandescent. She had recently been pushed by her cabinet into membership of the ERM, announced on 5 October. She had hoped that this gesture would gain German support for the 'hard Ecu' parallel currency plan which the British had put forward as an alternative to Delors in June. Now she vented her spleen against both Kohl and Mitterrand, and described the Emu project as 'cloud cuckoo land'. But when she repeated similar sentiments in the House of Commons on her return she precipitated the resignation of her deputy, the long-suffering Sir Geoffrey Howe, and the train of events which speedily led to her own resignation on 22 November. By the time the IGC on Emu was formally opened in Rome on 15 December, therefore, its most vocal and determined opponent had been forced to leave the field of battle. It was not clear how far her successor John Major would change not only the style but the substance of her policies. But the others were now well on the way to a detailed agreement, and were determined to go ahead, whatever the British decided to do.

PREPARATORY NEGOTIATIONS: POLITICAL UNION

In sharp contrast little progress had been made with the discussions on Political Union in advance of the opening of the IGC in December 1990.[11] Following the Kohl–Mitterrand letter, a decision was taken at the meeting of the European Council in Dublin on 28 April 1990 to ask the foreign ministers to consider the matter. But when the first informal discussion was held the following month at Parknasilla in Ireland it confirmed the difficulty of making any big advance. On institutional issues there was a consensus that the Council should continue to be the central decision-making body, but disagreement about extending the use of qualified majority voting and also about strengthening the role of the Parliament. A majority, including Germany, Belgium and Italy, were in favour of some form of legislative co-decision, but this was opposed by the UK. It favoured increasing the Parliament's powers of investigation and scrutiny. France, for its part, was more interested in increasing the role of the European Council and building representation of national parliaments into the Community framework.

On foreign and security matters the line-up was rather different. There was general agreement that cooperation should be improved, but equally that unanimity should continue to be required. 'No country', said Roland Dumas, the French foreign minister, 'is yet ready to surrender sovereignty over foreign policy or security policy.'[12] Several countries, including Belgium and Italy, nevertheless thought that both should be brought within the ambit of the EC institutions – unlike Britain and France. But the British disagreed with the French proposal that cooperation should also be extended to defence, arguing that this should continue to be dealt with in an Atlantic framework. In this they were supported by Portugal and Denmark, and also, because of its traditional neutral stance, by Ireland.

In the light of these various cross-currents, and also Maragaret Thatcher's continued hostility to the whole agenda of Political Union, there was a general air of caution. The *Guardian* reported the proceedings under the headline 'Ministers scupper a federal Europe'. Douglas Hurd was said not to have disguised his pleasure at the turn taken by the debate.[13] Nevertheless, the work of defining the agenda went on, and in

July the Parliament put forward its own proposals, including a demand for legislative co-decision. The decision to convene a second IGC was taken at the Dublin summit of 25–26 June 1990, which also agreed on the list of issues to be tackled. But these were only procedural decisions. On matters of substance it was clear that there were wide differences of opinion.

No attempt was made to overcome these at the Rome summit of December, the first to be attended by Major as prime minister. A 'framework declaration' was agreed as a mandate for the IGC on Political Union, which reviewed the issues to be tackled and the state of play with regard to them, without emphasising that most countries took a different view from the United Kingdom. A breathing space had been offered: much now depended on how far John Major was willing or able to modify the positions taken up by his predecessor.

THE IGC NEGOTIATIONS: EMU

The Intergovernmental Conference on Emu got off to a flying start in December on the basis of a draft treaty prepared by the Commission. But while there was, apart from the British, a substantial consensus on the main features of Emu, many details still had to be settled, and behind their apparent technicality frequently lurked important political issues. One such case was the timing of the setting up of the Central Bank. In late February, to the concern of the French and Delors who feared that Bonn might be getting cold feet, the Germans proposed that this should be postponed to the third stage. Bilateral Franco-German talks on the issue followed, but that matter was not settled until the autumn. A compromise was then put forward by the Dutch presidency, which took up a Belgian proposal for a European Monetary Institute in Stage Two as a precursor to the fully fledged central bank system. It was this compromise which was eventually incorporated in the Treaty. The conditions to be fulfilled to allow transition to Stage Two also gave rise to lengthy discussion: that matter was eventually resolved by a verbal sleight of hand proposed by the Luxembourg presidency.[14]

There was also much discussion about the duration and content of the second stage. Delors, supported by the French and Belgian governments, argued that it should be as short as possible, essentially in order to reduce uncertainty. The Germans, on the other hand, insisted on the need for a set of stringent conditions to be fulfilled in order to avoid later difficulties.[15] Intertwined with these issues was that of the future role of the Ecu. In the early months of the negotiation, the UK was still insisting that monetary integration could be better achieved through the development of a parallel currency in the form of a 'hard Ecu' than by the introduction of a common currency. But as opinion hardened against this, and the final European Council of the Luxembourg presidency loomed towards the end of June, the British began to change their negotiating stance.

Delors had already suggested at an informal meeting of Ecofin ministers in May a formula to deal with the British: that is, that while no country should be allowed to prevent others proceeding to Emu, equally it should not itself be coerced into joining them.[16] While the UK continued to oppose this – with its implication of its own exclusion – it had to recognise the strength of the determination of the others to press ahead. At the June meeting of Ecofin, the UK indicated that it would not seek to veto an agreement, and at the Luxembourg summit John Major abandoned the hard Ecu plan. These concessions were part of a deal struck between him and Kohl that the latter and his allies would not press at that meeting for any final decisions.

After the summer break the official-level meetings resumed in the first week of September under the Dutch presidency. Discussion increasingly centred on the conditions to be fulfilled for transition to Stage Three, cohesion, and the terms of a possible 'opt-out' provision for the British. The latter were now supporting the Germans in arguing for a set of strict conditions for entry into Stage Three, no doubt in the hope that if these were accepted this would delay or postpone indefinitely the transition to Stage Three and hence the moment of decision for the UK. But other countries, like Belgium and Italy, feared that too draconian a set of conditions might exclude them from Stage Three, and relegate them to second division membership of the future Union. A major step forward to allay fears about a two-speed Europe was taken at an informal Ecofin meeting at Apeldoorn in late September. It was then agreed that the new Treaty would be signed by all twelve members, and that all would also take part in the decision to move to Stage Three, even if some were not able to qualify for making that move immediately. There was, however, continuing disagreement about an opt-out provision. The UK wanted a general clause to avoid being singled out: the majority resisted this for fear that it might weaken the general resolve and offer a temptation to others.

A new phase of the negotiations was opened in late October with the presentation by the Dutch presidency of a revised draft of the Treaty. This contained a good number of items in square brackets which were still to be decided, but in the following six weeks good progress was made by dint of stepping up the rhythm of both official and ministerial meetings. By early December there were only four major outstanding issues to be settled at the Maastricht summit: the terms of an opt-out clause for Britain; certain aspects of the transition to Stage Three (in particular the voting arrangements); cohesion, on which Spain and its allies were demanding firmer guarantees than those currently on offer even if the financial arrangements were left (as Delors proposed) for a later settlement; and some institutional issues. Following consultation with the heads of government, the Emu dossier was put first on the Maastricht agenda in the belief that an agreement could be reached, and thus provide an early success for the meeting.[17]

THE IGC NEGOTIATIONS:
POLITICAL UNION

Unlike the negotiations on Emu, those on Political Union got off to a stuttering start, and little progress had been made by the March minis-terial meeting: Jacques Delors emerged from that in a morose mood. The Luxembourg presidency nevertheless pressed on with the prep-aration of a first draft of a Treaty of Union covering most of the issues under discussion, which was circulated in early April in the form of a 'non-paper' to test reactions. This marked an important new stage in the negotiations. It was a well-judged package deal which provided a firm framework for future negotiations and determined the shape and much of the content of the eventual Treaty. But at the time several countries, including France, Germany, Belgium and Spain, thought it embodied too minimalist an approach. This view was shared by the Commission and the Parliament which passed a resolution in April threatening to reject it unless it was greatly improved. A central issue for all these critics was the proposed three-pillar structure for the Union. The fear was that the intergovernmental element would predominate, and over time diminish the significance of the *acquis communautaire* and the role of Community institutions. This emerged as the majority view when Delors led a counter-attack at an informal meeting of foreign ministers in Dresden at the beginning of June, which put strong pressure on the presidency to revise its draft.

  The British, on the other hand, very much approved of the three-pillar concept. But for them the Luxembourg draft in other respects went too far on many points: for instance, on co-decision for the Parliament, voting rights for non-nationals in local and European elections, social policy, and also the proposed closer defence coop-eration in WEU. While some countries shared UK reservations on individual issues, the British were essentially alone in their system-atically negative posture. A new Luxembourg draft circulated in mid-June made a number of concessions to the majority view. It also filled out the presidency's original proposals, notably by suggesting that when dealing with Community business the Council should take most of its decisions by qualified majority vote. Even more provocative from the British point of view was the addition of a new sentence to the opening article which declared that the Treaty 'marks a new stage in a process leading gradually to a Union with a federal goal'. This created immediate uproar in certain parts of the British press, and among Thatcher supporters.[18]

A clash, however, was avoided at the concluding summit of the Luxembourg presidency held at the end of June by the deal between Major and Kohl not to force the pace on outstanding issues. Major had asked for more time: his partners were willing to agree in the hope that this would lead to a more positive UK position. In any case the Twelve by then were deeply embroiled in trying to mediate between the warring republics of Yugoslavia: it was this which dominated the discussions at the European Council.

The same crisis also put a heavy burden on the incoming Dutch presidency which took over in July. This was one of the reasons, together with the habitual summer break, which delayed the subsequent resumption of the work of the IGC. But more important than either of these was a decision in The Hague to introduce a substantial number of amendments into the Luxembourg draft. The preparations of these turned into a lengthy affair, complicated both by inter-departmental and personal differences of opinion at ministerial level. It was not until the second week of September that a 'non-paper' (that is, an informal proposal) was circulated incorporating the outcome.

Several different, and in part contradictory, pressures were reflected in the new text. One was to regroup everything within the ambit of the Community, and strengthen the role of the European Parliament. Another was to keep the British on board: as a major concession to them the creation of a Union was to be postponed until some later date. At the same time, with regard to defence, the Dutch text dropped the reference to WEU and emphasised the continuing importance of Nato. But, taken as a whole, this approach appeared to go back on agreements already reached, and fell disastrously between several different stools. To add to the general confusion, the first two scheduled negotiating sessions were cancelled at short notice because the revised text was not ready. When at last the Personal Representatives met on 26 September they were in a very bad mood, irritated by the long delay and most of them fiercely critical of the new draft. The chairman had to cut the discussion short. And when the ministers themselves met on 30 September ('Black Monday') they flatly refused to negotiate on the basis of the Dutch text, which then had to be withdrawn.[19]

The immediate effect of this debacle was to cast doubt on the capacity of the Dutch presidency successfully to conclude the negotiations. For a time there was a real risk of the French and the Germans negotiating a separate deal on security and defence with like-minded member states. But the Dutch swallowed their pride, relaunched the negotiations on the basis of the Luxembourg draft, and sought to regain lost time with a very intensive timetable of meetings for the remaining ten weeks to the Maastricht summit. They were greatly assisted in this task by the fact that all except one member state were anxious to reach an agreement; and the exception, Britain, knew it could not afford to be left out if one were reached. Major undoubtedly benefited from much more goodwill than Thatcher, but this was stretched to the limits by a British negotiating strategy which aimed to extract the maximum advantage from it. It was only gradually that London gave way on a number of issues so that it could concentrate on the most important.

On defence policy, for instance, a deal was done with the Italians about the future role of WEU which resulted in a joint proposal to counter the Franco-German position.[20] On co-decision another bargain was struck. In exchange for dropping the phrase the UK was willing by mid-November to agree to its substance, though reserving its position on how wide a use should be made of the new procedure. And, in a tactic usually imputed to the French, it first proposed an opt-out clause from the commitment to a CFSP should a country believe that a 'vital national interest' was at stake – and then withdrew it as part of a wider bargain.

Similar flexibility on the part of others meant that in the run-up to Maastricht a number of issues which had previously given trouble were also resolved. These included provisions relating to citizenship, subsidiarity, and the appointment of the Commission. But the number of issues under discussion remained very extensive and it was clear that on some an agreement could only be reached, if at all, at the European Council itself. Greater help for the poorer countries ('cohesion' in the jargon) was one of these, on which Spain led the battle supported by Portugal, Greece and Ireland. Britain had its own list of sticking points, including the use of the word 'federal' to describe the goal of the Union; social policy; and majority voting on foreign and security policy. So, as the Dutch Prime Minister, Ruud Lubbers, began a series of bilateral meetings in preparation for the summit, it was still far from certain if final agreement could be reached at Maastricht.

THE MAASTRICHT EUROPEAN COUNCIL, DECEMBER 1991

The European Council was opened on the morning of Monday 9 December 1991 by Lubbers. In the two days and nights of hard negotiations which followed he and Nils Ersbøll (Secretary General of the Council) were the central dealers and brokers, the other main protagonists being Kohl and Major. The latter adopted a much less aggressive style than his predecessor but was equally determined, well briefed and attentive to detail: 'Mrs Thatcher without the handbag' according to Lubbers.[21] In contrast, Mitterrand – who many thought was showing the signs of advancing years – contributed little beyond generalised rhetoric, and was visibly uninterested in the small print.

Lubbers's main concern was to arrive at a successful conclusion and a new Treaty: that aim was shared by all his colleagues. But whereas Kohl was determined to achieve decisions which would make progress towards Emu as automatic and irreversible as possible, and to achieve as much as possible for the European Parliament, Major's overriding objective was to avoid any commitments which were likely to create trouble in his party, particularly within a few months of a general election. In the course of the first *tour de table* Major began by offering or confirming a number of concessions over a range of issues which the British had decided were of minor importance, including an extension of qualified majority voting in the Council and limited new powers for the Parliament. He also indicated support for the pet projects of some of the other leaders. It was a well-judged package of mainly cosmetic concessions, and it was rewarded by an early (if reluctant) agreement to the presidency's proposal to withdraw the phrase 'federal destiny' from the opening article of the new Treaty.

As the day wore on, agreement was reached without great difficulty on outstanding issues relating to the new provisions on foreign, security and defence policy. While unanimity was maintained for all major decisions, some qualified majority voting was admitted for the implementation of joint actions. A careful verbal formula was also found to deal with the future roles of both WEU and Nato to square both the Franco-German and Anglo-Italian points of view. Agreement was also reached on the two major outstanding issues relating to Emu. The first concerned arrangements for the transition to the third (and final) stage of Emu. France was determined that this should be achieved as soon and as certainly as possible, while Kohl, though equally concerned about irreversibility, was also insisting on rigorous entry conditions. It was finally agreed that the third stage would start in any case in 1999 with as many members as were then deemed to have satisfied the convergence criteria. But it could be sooner if at the end of 1996 the Council decided that a majority of member states were already in that position.

As part of the package deal an Emu agreement was also reached on a special Protocol for Britain. In return for a commitment that Britain would not seek to block others moving forward to Stage Three, this stated that the UK 'shall not be obliged or committed to move to the third stage of Emu without a separate decision to do so by its government and parliament'. This 'opt-out' provision enabled Major (who preferred to refer to it as an 'opt-in' clause) to claim that British parliamentary sovereignty remained intact. A somewhat similar Protocol was also agreed for Denmark. Late on the Monday evening the summit tackled the issue of cohesion which, though difficult, proved a less intractable issue than the inclusion in the EC Treaty of a series of new social policy provisions. Here Major's determination to resist these, on both ideological and political grounds, ran into equally determined resistance from a very powerful coalition of both Christian Democrats and Socialists, led by Kohl and Delors.

The initial British strategy was to water down the provisions so that they became innocuous. But although the Dutch presidency was willing to be helpful, it proved impossible to find a compromise acceptable to both sides. At the same time there was also strong resistance on the part of a majority to a second opt-out clause for Britain. Tempers became frayed as an impasse was reached on the evening of the second day of the summit. 'It's like street fighting in there,' remarked one Dutch diplomat.[22] The matter was only settled in a trilateral meeting between Major, Lubbers and Kohl when the latter proposed a different and unprecedented type of compromise. Instead of including the new social policy provisions in the revised EC Treaty these were now transformed into an Agreement between the Eleven annexed to the Treaty and accompanied by a Protocol to which all Twelve subscribed, allowing the Eleven to use the EC institutions to carry out their Agreement. In this contorted way both sides were satisfied, though at the expense of setting a precedent and a procedure which threatens to become a source of institutional and legal wrangling.

It was this deal which cleared away the last major obstacle to an overall agreement on the new Treaty. But the bargaining continued into the final session when various loose ends were being tidied up. Through his attention to detail Major then succeeded in blocking an item which would have meant large retrospective payments to pensioners by British companies, and in maintaining unanimity for decisions on research and development programmes.[23]

When finally it was all over, everyone claimed victory. Led by Chancellor Kohl most of the Community's leaders hailed the result as a great leap forward for the process of integration, stressing in particular the new commitment and detailed arrangements to move to Emu. They played down the concessions made to Britain, while Major on the other hand returned claiming 'game, set and match!'. The boast was rather misplaced for a country which had tried, but failed, to prevent a great deal of what was now incorporated in the new Treaty – and in the process had been mainly responsible for the complicated set of compromises stitched together to form it.

In spite of its length and complexity it was nevertheless a major achievement, as ambitious in its commitments as the Rome Treaties.

Like those, however, its real significance remained dependent on the extent to which its signatories would be able to fulfil those commitments. The first step along that path was the need to secure ratification by the member states: as subsequent developments were quickly to demonstrate, that in itself was to be no easy task.

4

RATIFICATION

Andrew Duff

The Treaty of Maastricht concludes by providing that it shall be ratified by all member states 'in accordance with their respective constitutional requirements'.[1] The Treaty was scheduled to enter into force on 1 January 1993 or, failing that, on the first day of the month following the deposit by the last member state of its instrument of ratification with (following tradition since the Rome Treaties) the Italian government. In the event, the Treaty came into force eleven months late, on 1 November 1993. In the two years since the Maastricht European Council, much had changed in Europe. The Treaty on European Union contributed to that change, and was itself changed by it.

After the draft Treaty was initialled by the heads of government at Maastricht, the document was put into the hands of the *juriste-linguistes*. They were charged to iron out technical irregularities. They were not instructed to produce a consolidated text of Maastricht and the Treaty of Rome. Instead, therefore, of one revised Treaty being made available for public and parliamentary consumption, Maastricht was left as a complicated jumble of titles, chapters, articles, protocols and declarations classified in sequence by letters and numbers. The new Treaty as published cannot be understood without reference to the old EC Treaties as amended most recently by the Single Act. This unnecessary confusion was the work of an obscurantist Community, and was a tactical error. The impression was given that the ratification of the Treaty could be taken for granted.

It appeared, moreover, that the EC's agenda had already moved beyond Maastricht to other pressing matters: the completion of the Single Market, the new financial 'perspectives' of the Community and the creation, with Efta, of the European Economic Area. Externally, the instability in the former USSR dominated the headlines. Furthermore, in the early New Year there were signs that some of the ingenious package agreed at the Maastricht summit would unravel. The Dutch, in particular, wanted a renegotiation of the Social Protocol. There were, in fact, some quite significant modifications made to the text after 12

December, and in order to prevent many more, the signing ceremony, again at Maastricht, was brought forward to 7 February.[2] The tortuous ratification process got underway.

DENMARK REJECTS THE UNION

Denmark was first into the breach – some thought unwisely. In its referendum on 2 June 1992 Denmark, a small and patriotic country, voted 'no' to Maastricht by 50.7 per cent to 49.3 per cent, a difference of some 47,000 votes. The Danish refusal hit the Community like a seismic shock. Only the French rejection of the European Defence Community project in 1954 and de Gaulle's veto of UK accession in 1963 were comparable. Hopes raised by the signature of this problematical Treaty were immediately dashed. Moreover, it was not only the future of the Treaty that was now jeopardized, but the credibility of the Danish political system. All mainstream parties had campaigned for a 'yes' vote. A huge gulf had suddenly opened up between the ambitions of the politicians and the inhibitions of the people.

The UK and Denmark were always going to be the most difficult countries to persuade of the virtues of Maastricht. In both countries, since their late accession in 1973, politicians had tended to accentuate the economic aspects of EC membership and to downplay the political consequences. Both governments suffered from weak representative capability: the British because of the non-proportional 'winner-takes-all' electoral system, and the Danish because of the slender parliamentary majority of the coalition. Alone of EC governments, both had been elected by a minority of the popular vote. Both countries were led by Conservative prime ministers, John Major and Poul Schlüter, who were not men of palpable European conviction, and whose campaigns in favour of the Treaty were at best defensive and at worst downright apologetic. Both men had in the Intergovernmental Conferences worked to dilute the force of various proposals, to delete others and, eventually, to place a reserve on the central goal of the Treaty, Emu. And, at least partly as a result of the ambiguous performance of their political class, in both countries a sizeable public hostility to European integration continues to exist. Most survey research shows the Danes 20 per cent behind the EC average of support for the general idea of further development of the European Community, with the British 10 per cent adrift.

John Major's position was strengthened by his surprise victory in the general election of 9 April 1992. The Treaty of Maastricht had not featured much as an issue in the election campaign because all three major parties were committed to its ratification. On 21 May the House of Commons gave the relevant Bill a Second Reading by 336 votes to 92.

Similarly, the Danish Folketing had approved of the Treaty by 130 votes to 25 on 12 May. Unlike the UK, however, where among the pro-European politicians only Paddy Ashdown, the Liberal Democrat leader, argued for a referendum, Danish ratification was subject under the constitution to a popular vote.[3]

The referendum campaign exposed deep divisions about Europe within the ranks of the Danish political parties, as well as some latent ill-feeling about Germany. Farmers and women were held to be especially hostile to the Community. Opinion polls suggested that there was widespread antipathy to the idea of being governed from Brussels. Only Venstre, the Liberal Party, under the leadership of the charismatic but controversial Foreign Minister Uffe Elleman-Jensen, made a concerted effort to sell the Treaty. The campaign was joined by several British nationalists who used Denmark as a surrogate, and was enlivened by the leak to the British populist press of an internal Commission document that contained the truism that small countries in a future-enlarged EC would play a diminished role. This was a *gaucherie* of the Delors Commission that, in the aftermath of Maastricht, appeared somewhat petulant about the Treaty – and the exposure much annoyed the two master Danish tacticians in Brussels, Vice-President of the Commission Henning Christophersen (also a member of Venstre) and Niels Ersbøll, Secretary-General of the Council.

The Anglo-Danish analogy must not be drawn too closely. At least some of the Danish opposition to Maastricht was founded on the suspicion that high Danish social and environmental standards would have to fall as a result of Maastricht: a consideration that had no relevance in the UK. Nevertheless, the narrow Danish defeat for Maastricht sapped the UK government's already weak political will to campaign for it. British popular sentiment seemed to be on the side of 'plucky little Denmark'. The passage of the Maastricht Bill at Westminster was halted in its tracks for five months.

On the day after the Danish referendum the foreign ministers happened to be meeting on other business in Oslo. At an emergency Council meeting they categorically ruled out any renegotiation of the Treaty. They confirmed their allegiance to the schedule for ratification, and agreed that 'the door should be left open for Denmark to participate in the Union'.[4] In public, at least, the Council conveniently ignored the dilemma that the Treaty signed at Maastricht could only come into force if it was ratified by all twelve signatories to it. Behind closed doors, however, there was very great consternation at the legal predicament into which the Danes had plunged the Community.

FROM LISBON TO EDINBURGH, VIA BIRMINGHAM

Ideally, no doubt, the ratification of the Treaty of Maastricht needed the full concentration of member governments if it was to be completed on time. In reality, as we have noted, the EC became quickly distracted by other things, some of which, notably the Balkan crisis and the Gatt negotiations, put the mutual relations of the EC partners under some strain. Enlargement of the EC to include some Efta countries was already pressing, and was intended to be the main point of debate at the European Council under the Portuguese presidency. In the event, however, it was the Danish 'no' that dominated the Lisbon summit at the end of June. The leaders decided to advance and broaden the debate about subsidiarity in the hope that the public could be won round to supporting a less remote and more open system of EC government. The Commission and Council were instructed to produce solutions, but the European Council decided to meet again, in Birmingham in October, to review progress and to make a rhetorical declaration about transparency: *A Community close to its citizens.*

Meanwhile, the Commission had been working hard to produce, on 27 October, its influential communication on the application of the principle of subsidiarity. Despite alternative and contrary proposals, it was this Commission document that formed the basis of the agreement reached eventually at the Edinburgh European Council.[5] What was achieved was in some ways remarkable. The link between democracy, openness and subsidiarity, ruptured at the behest of the UK during the Maastricht IGC, was firmly re-established.

The objective was to reassure the citizens that decisions are being taken as closely as possible to them without sacrificing the advantages which they receive from common action at European level, and without destroying the delicate balance between the EC institutions. Subsidiarity as defined by the EC during 1992 is a dynamic concept, to be applied pragmatically according to inevitably changing circumstances. The application of the principle of subsidiarity will not share out competences precisely between the EC and national levels of government, but it does suggest how those competences are exercised and policies formulated and implemented. Subsidiarity in a federal context (such as Germany) means the devolution of powers to subnational, regional or local authorities as well as to supranational, European institutions. Subsidiarity in the context of a unitary, centralised state (such as the UK) can only refer to the division of powers between the state and the European Community. Residual power in all cases lies at the lowest sovereign level, that is the Länder in Germany and the Whitehall government (or strictly speaking 'Crown in Parliament') in the UK.

In practice, the problem is to interpret together both Article A of the Treaty of Maastricht – closeness to the citizen – and Article 3b – comparative efficiency. In areas of exclusive competence, such as trade policy, subsidiarity cannot serve to weaken the powers of the institutions. In areas of shared competence discretion, and often self-restraint, are needed. The *Edinburgh Annex*, which is like a manual to the machinery of EC government, laid down four guidelines for the application of subsidiarity to new legislation. Simply, these require:

- a clear legal base for any proposed measure is established;
- transnational aspects are involved;
- non-action will harm EC interests;
- action will establish clear benefits.

At Edinburgh, the UK government's attempt to use subsidiarity as a means to claw back powers passed to Brussels was unsuccessful. On the contrary, it was agreed that subsidiarity will be considered as one of several factors as a matter of course within the law-making process of the Community. There will be no special preliminary mechanism to rule out Commission initiatives on grounds of subsidiarity. The Court of Justice will rule as necessary, and presumably as rarely as possible, only once a challenge is made to EC legislation in force. The Commission, which played a most skilful game in the subsidiarity debate, is reviewing some former legislation and is making proposals to amend or delete law that does not conform to the Edinburgh guidelines.

The agreement on subsidiarity and on a package of measures to placate Danish political opinion were veritable achievements for the Edinburgh Council. While the Treaty was not yet saved, it was given at Edinburgh another chance to live. The European Council also agreed to the setting up of the Cohesion Fund and on the 'Delors II' financial package, that is, on the resources it wished to allocate to the Community in the medium term, and on the broad breakdown of expenditure. The leaders decided that the annual ceiling on resources would rise from 1.20 per cent of EC GNP in 1993 to 1.27 per cent in 1999 and fixed the breakdown among main items of expenditure. That decision, which was taken without the cooperation of the European Parliament, the other arm of the budgetary authority, also took no account of enlargement or of the swing of the Ecu against the dollar. In the light of the loosening of ERM discipline forced on the Community in August 1993, the Edinbugh financing package will surely prove to be unworkable because of the cost of the 'green currencies' (Monetary Compensation Amounts) used for crossborder transactions under the CAP.

The European Council at Edinburgh, which took place on 11–12 December 1992, took decisive action towards bringing the Maastricht Treaty into force and represents a significant increase in power of the

European Council itself over both the political direction and the institutional development of the Community and the Union.

THE FIRST THREE RATIFY – AND FRANCE

Several member states had complicated constitutional changes to steer through national procedures before their ratification of the Treaty could take effect. Some of these constitutional revisions stemmed from the establishment of European citizenship; some from the new security dimension of the Union; and others from the extension of EC competences to areas that affected the internal disposition of member states between national and provincial authorities. They all contributed to delay the coming into force of the Treaty and had a marked spillover effect. Unlike the experience of the Single Act, member states watched the tortuous progress of national ratification throughout the Community with fascination.

Only nine of the twelve member states managed to complete their ratification procedures on time, within 1992. For the Irish, the ratification process, which included a constitutional revision, was deceptively simple. A referendum that had focused on Irish neutrality had stalled the ratification of the Single Act. This time the politicians were better prepared despite a strong opposition campaign, backed by the Church hierarchy, that was predicated on the notion that European integration jeopardised Ireland's very conservative laws on divorce, abortion, contraception and homosexuality. The government had even extracted at Maastricht a protocol guaranteeing a provision in Ireland's constitution protecting the Irish from freedom of information about abortion services in the UK.[6] The campaign in favour of the Treaty, however, was based on even more basic sentiments: that for every £1 the Irish put into the Community, they got £7 back. On 18 June the Irish voted 69.05 per cent yes to 30.95 per cent no. Jacques Delors welcomed the fact that Ireland had 'opted for active participation in the construction of Europe, rather than isolation and an empty future'.[7]

Luxembourg followed on 2 July, with a positive vote in the Chamber of Deputies of 51 to 6. As one of the EC's original Six and the only member state currently to fulfil the Emu convergence criteria of Maastricht, it would have been inconceivable for Luxembourg to have acted otherwise. On 31 July, by an even larger parliamentary vote of 286 to 8, Greece ratified the Treaty. The usual partisan nature of Greek politics was suspended for the debate on Maastricht. Greece shares with Ireland an irresistible financial incentive to continue with its membership of the EC, but supplements that by being much attracted to the new security dimension of a European Union that excludes Turkey.

It was inevitable that German unification would alarm many French

58

men and women. The German factor was coupled with the creation by Maastricht of the EC citizen-elector: a particularly important question for France because mayors play an important part in the electoral college of the Senate and the French constitution had to be revised to conform with a widening of the franchise. These two issues helped to revive the debate in France about the process of European unification that had, at least since the demise of Pompidou, been scarcely perceptible. Nevertheless, ratification of the Treaty in France was never short of a parliamentary majority, culminating in a grand congress of Senate and Assembly at Versailles on 23 June. But the debate opened up major divisions inside the Gaullist RPR and even some dissent within the UDF forces of Valéry Giscard d'Estaing. The temptation to exploit a divided opposition was too much for President Mitterrand. He called a referendum for 20 September, hoping not only to profit domestically, but to relaunch Europe after the Danish shock. A resounding French 'yes' would indeed have done so. Unfortunately, however, as the summer campaign wore on, many French voters began to see the referendum as a vote of confidence in Mitterrand himself, and in the unpopular socialist government of Pierre Bérégovoy. The opposition was skilfully led by Philippe Séguin, who earned for himself the Presidency of the National Assembly after the following spring's parliamentary elections. The result was positive, but only just, with 51.05 per cent in favour and 48.95 per cent against.

This was hardly the result to relaunch the Treaty. Indeed, the uncertainty surrounding the French referendum contributed heavily to the financial speculation that put intolerable strains on the ERM. On 13 September the Italian lira devalued within the ERM by 3.5 per cent. On 16 September, 'Black Wednesday', sterling crashed through the floor of the ERM, the peseta was devalued by 5 per cent and the lira was suspended. Delors, while expressing heartfelt relief at the *petit oui*, added that 'by voting "no", many French citizens have expressed anxiety. It is our duty to respond both at national and at European level by consolidating the democratic process'.[8]

FOUR MORE RATIFY ON TIME

After the dramatic events of the French referendum, Italy was next to ratify. There were big majorities for Maastricht in both Houses of Parliament, with a final vote of 423 to 46 in the Chamber of Deputies on 29 October. Facing a constitutional crisis of its own, Italy was in no mood to trifle with the Maastricht project. Indeed, the prospect of European integration offered a way forward for Italians, despite the undoubted difficulty Italy will experience in conforming to the convergence criteria of Emu. One important side-effect of Maastricht for Italy was the requirement to make its central bank independent of the government. In an interesting role reversal, when Carlo Azeglio Ciampi, the Governor of the Bank of Italy, became prime minister in May 1993, his government deliberately sought to compensate for its lack of economic credibility by reasserting Italy's traditionally strong support for European federalism.

Another member state experiencing domestic constitutional difficulties was Belgium. Its ratification process was prolonged by the need to manoeuvre the Treaty not only through the national parliament, but through the three linguistic communities. This provided a foretaste of how Belgium's new complex internal disposition will affect the conduct of its EC affairs. It was, however, encouraging that in July the Belgian Chamber of Deputies, which has the closest working relationship with the EC institutions, approved the Treaty by the wide margin of 143 votes to 33, as, on 4 November, did the Senate by 115 to 26.

The Spanish Cortès gave the greatest of all votes of confidence in the Treaty: in the Chamber of Deputies by 314 votes to 3 in October, and in the Senate by 222 votes to 0 on 25 November. This level of support was explained by the strong emphasis placed by the Spanish government on the new Cohesion Fund, which, with the concept of European citizenship, was attributable largely to the negotiating skills of Felipe Gonzalez. Similarly, on 11 December, the Portuguese Assembly of the Republic assented by 200 votes to 21. Although ratification was never in doubt, the Dutch parliament conducted a more searching debate. Doubts were expressed about the democratic deficiencies of Maastricht, and, as in Britain and Germany, there was much talk of a referendum. The Dutch presidency's disappointments in the IGC seemed to have been vindicated by the wave of popular dissent in the process of integration by stealth. Nevertheless, the Netherlands in due course ratified the Treaty: in the Second Chamber on 12 November by 137 votes to 13, and in the First on 15 December *nemine contradicente*.

A PROBLEM IN GERMANY

In 1992, despite the personal investment of Chancellor Kohl in Maastricht, Germany was more preoccupied by German than European unification. Parliamentarians from the eastern Länder, especially, began to resent any distraction from efforts to resolve the undeniably serious predicament of their own constituents. Amendments to German Basic Law were required to give effect to EC citizenship, to allow the transfer of sovereignty from the Bundesbank to a European Central Bank and, above all, to safeguard the sovereign position of the Länder and their national parliamentary chamber, the Bundesrat. In the Bundestag, as in The Hague, concern was voiced about the relative weakness of the

Treaty with regard to political integration – before assent was voted by
543 to 17 on 2 December. The application of subsidiarity appealed most
to the Bundesrat, which passed the Treaty by 68 votes to 0 on 18
December. The Bundesbank kept its own counsel, although rumours
were widespread that several governors had acquired strong misgivings
about the sacrifice of the Deutschmark for the Ecu. The Bundestag
attached a resolution to the ratification of the Treaty intended to ensure
the scrupulous application of the Emu convergence criteria. The Ecu
must be able to prove itself at least as stable as the mark before Stage
Three is to be embarked upon. The federal government accepted the
Bundestag's demand for a positive vote of assent to Stage Three at the
appropriate moment.

Germany's ratification of the Treaty, however, was impeded by a legal
challenge brought before the Constitutional Court at Karlsruhe by,
among others, a rogue Liberal politician, Manfred Brunner.[9] The litigation sought to prevent the President of the Republic from signing the
instrument of ratification on the grounds that Maastricht infringed
German Basic Law, despite the fact that that constitution had been duly
amended to take account of the new Treaty. Revised Article 23, for
example, allows for Germany to 'participate in the development of the
European Union, which is committed to principles of democracy and the
rule of law, social and federal principles and the principle of subsidiarity
and guarantees a protection of basic rights substantially comparable with
this Basic Law'. The appeal claimed, however, that these principles were
violated by Maastricht.

A lengthy and complicated judgement was eventually delivered on 12
October 1993. The Court found against the appellants on all counts. In
particular, the judges refuted the allegation of the appellants that Article
F.3 of Maastricht endows the European Union with a power of general
competence. Certainly the new Treaty gives important new competences
to the EC, but these were held by the Court to be strictly ordained to
fulfil the clearly defined objectives of the Treaty and, furthermore, to be
in accordance with democratic principles. The German Court talked of
the importance of its own cooperative relationship with the European
Court of Justice, and stressed that EC law and German constitutional
rights are protected by an effective partnership between the two jurisdictions. The Karlsruhe judges characterised the European Union as a
Staatenverbund, or 'league of states', which involves Germany in membership of supranational organisations but not the membership of a
European state. In the eyes of the Court, the Union itself, unlike the EC,
is not a legal entity.

To complement this, there is the question of popular sovereignty and
democratic accountability. European integration must be accompanied
by the democratisation of the Community. Indeed, the Court saw the
'decisive factor' as being the 'achievement of an adequately effective

amount of democratic authorisation'.[10] Most of this popular legitimation was still to be exercised by national parliaments, although the European Parliament was an important supplementary sanction, whose respectability would be further enhanced by the introduction of a uniform electoral procedure as required by the Treaty.[11] Union citizenship forms a 'legal connection' between the nationals of member states which expresses a communality of democratic interest.

The German Court welcomed the recent moves to greater openness and clarity among the EC institutions. In future, it ruled, it will be crucial that democracy and integration should grow together at the European level. German citizens have legal redress in case of an infringement by the German government or the EC institutions of the Treaty of Maastricht. The German parliament should maintain a lively interest in the affairs of the European Union, and will retain substantial duties. The German government must continue to exercise discretion about the transfer of sovereignty to the European Union, and the European Council is there to see that it is the member states who 'remain in charge of the Treaties and their further development'. But the Maastricht Treaty provides adequate checks and balances, and the Bundestag continues to hold the federal government accountable for its actions in the European dimension. The explicit introduction of the principle of subsidiarity is regarded by the German Court as a highly significant guarantee against the emergence of an overmighty European Union.

With regard to Emu, the Bundestag should hold fast to the convergence criteria leading to price stability, but the timetable, although desirable, is a 'projection' and not mandatory. The Council, moreover, cannot soften the convergence criteria without the express approval of the Bundestag. Emu is not automatic, however. Integration can only proceed either on the basis of already anticipated agreements, in other words the Maastricht Treaty, or of future intergovernmental agreements requiring the sanction of the German parliament. If Emu is relaxed and leads to inflation, the Bundestag need not regard Germany as bound to uphold it.

In summary, the German Court insisted that democracy and efficiency in the European dimension must go hand in hand. In the development of the Union, democracy must be enhanced at the same pace as integration and, at the same time, a living democracy must be retained within the member states. This means, in effect, that the growth of European federal democracy is a constitutional imperative for Germany: a fact that no government can ignore in the run up to the next IGC in 1996.

SECOND THOUGHTS FOR BRITAIN AND DENMARK

The Danish opposition parties, including the small left-wing Socialist People's Party which had supported a 'no' vote in June 1992, presented the government with a 'National Compromise' on 30 October. This laid out the terms on which the government was obliged to try to acquire the consent of its eleven partners. Although they included much rhetorical commitment to openness and subsidiarity, to which the EC had no difficulty in agreeing, other terms were precise demands for permanent Danish derogations from the Treaty. This presented Denmark's EC partners with a great problem as their inclination to indulge in a renegotiation of the Treaty was zero. One fortuitous advantage was that the British President-in-office of the Council was naturally sympathetic to Denmark. But agreement could not have been reached at Edinburgh unless the other Ten had been prepared to compromise on the substance of the Treaty with regard to defence and Emu, and the Danish ministers had been prepared to risk the National Compromise by agreeing that their EC package would be up for renegotiation at the next IGC in 1996. (To what extent this crucial Danish concession was ever publicised at home remains unclear.)

The Decision of the European Council on the Danish 'set of arrangements' took note of the National Compromise.[12] It stated that Union citizenship does not 'in any way take the place of national citizenship'. It accepted that Denmark 'has given notification that it will not participate in the third stage' of Emu, and therefore in the single currency. The heads of government noted, too, that 'Denmark does not participate in the elaboration and the implementation of decisions and actions of the Union which have defence implications'. The document concludes by noting that Denmark may at any time decide 'that it no longer wishes to avail itself of all or part of this decision', but that its duration shall in any case be governed by the IGC of 1996.

Armed with the Edinburgh agreement the Danish political parties embarked on their second campaign. Again, Elleman-Jensen was in the forefront of the debate, but he and Schlüter had fallen from office in January, and the new coalition government, led by the Social Democrat Poul Rasmussen, was quietly influential. In the second referendum, on 18 May 1993, the Danish people voted 'yes' by 56.8 per cent on a turnout of 86.2 per cent. The Maastricht Treaty was saved again. Welcoming the result, Jacques Delors added that the vote 'may also help the Community to lift itself out of the current lethargy and despondency, at a time when a great tragedy is being played out on the continent of Europe and the Community is beset by its own internal problems, most notably economic stagnation and rising unemployment'.[13]

In Britain, however, the Edinburgh Council produced no clear cut political solution to the Maastricht problem. John Major failed to convince Conservative nationalists that he had vanquished federalism. The passage of the Maastricht Bill through the House of Commons was gruelling. The measure itself was problematical as it sought to incorporate into UK domestic law only those substantive amendments to the EC Treaties that appeared in Titles II, III and IV of the Maastricht Treaty; the second and third pillars of Maastricht and the whole structure of the new Union itself were simply ratified by the government without recourse to parliamentary legislation. Many in the Commons and outside felt cheated. On 4 November 1992 the measure was only saved in what amounted to a second second reading by four Liberal Democrat votes. Failure at this point would have dashed the Treaty not only for Britain but for all Europe. The subsequent 'committee stage' of the Bill lasted until the following spring, with leading Tory nationalist Bill Cash speaking for a total of 583 minutes and the Foreign Office minister Tristan Garel-Jones for 443. Unfortunately none of the debate was very rewarding: there were few heroes. The government's lukewarm position was exposed uncomfortably. The damage to the unity of the Conservative party and to Major's leadership was very great. The damage to the reputation of the Commons was grave, and as the backstairs deals at Westminster mounted, public support for a referendum grew. The final *coup de théâtre* was a vote on the Social Protocol on 23 July 1993, which united all the government's opponents including the Tory right wing, and led to its defeat. A vote of 'no confidence' the following day was, however, roundly defeated as Tory instincts for self-preservation surfaced.

The House of Lords gave a third reading to the Bill on 20 July, and following the rejection by the High Court of a claim by a maverick Tory peer (Lord Rees-Mogg) that the ratification procedure was unconstitutional, the UK deposited its instruments of ratification in Rome on 2 August.[14]

The Belgians summoned a summit meeting in Brussels at the end of October to mark the completion of the ratification process. This was a modest, even humble occasion – but it did manage to settle the vexed question of the seats of various EC agencies, notably the European Environment Agency (Copenhagen), the European Foundation for Training (Turin), the European Observatory for Drugs (Lisbon), Europol (The Hague), the Office of Harmonisation (Bilbao), the European Agency for the Evaluation of Medicinal Products (London) and the Agency for Health and Safety at the Workplace (Alicante). The European Council's main decision was to site the European Monetary Institute at Frankfurt, an unsurprising conclusion to a long tussle involving *inter alia* London and Amsterdam. In view of the UK's coldness to the Emu project, and to Maastricht generally, London was hardly a credible venue for its institutions.

The allegiance of both Britain and Denmark to the European Union remains tentative. In a telling article in *The Economist*, John Major laid out his vision of a wider but less integrated Europe.[15] He would make the Commission subordinate to the European Council and the European Parliament to national parliaments. He claimed:

> Britain successfully used the Maastricht negotiations to reassert the authority of national governments. It is clear now that the Community will remain a union of sovereign national states. That is what its peoples want: to take decisions through their own parliaments. ... If anyone still thinks the Commission's first Maastricht blueprint was the way to go, they will have learnt nothing from experience. And they are closing their minds to the future.

Major was caustic about the Emu programme in the Treaty he had negotiated at Maastricht:

> While I always believed Europe's ambition for monetary union later this decade was unrealistic – by now the folly of the artificial timetable has become glaringly apparent to many across Europe. The plain fact is that Emu is not realisable in present circumstances and therefore not relevant to our economic difficulties.

For as long as Britain and Denmark continue to compete with one another for the minimalist position on European integration, they may be able to determine the pace and the style of the Union's future development. In *The Economist* John Major insisted that the Danes 'wanted the safeguards for Denmark that I had secured for Britain'. Both, indeed, are culpable for having lumbered Europe with a derogatory style of cooperation in contradiction to integration of a federal type.

SEMI-DETACHED: THE EUROPEAN PARLIAMENT

The European Parliament had been actively though not obsessively involved in the drafting of the Treaty. It had produced five reports in the course of 1990 that had formed much of the agenda of the interinstitutional talks with the Luxembourg and Dutch presidencies. The Parliament's rapporteurs were David Martin on institutional developments, Maurice Duverger on the role of national parliaments, Emilio Colombo on federal union, Fernand Herman on Emu and Valéry Giscard d'Estaing on subsidiarity. Although Parliament had become excited by the Dutch draft treaty of September 1991, which offered it comprehensive legislative responsibility as well as a role in CFSP, the tone of its final declarations on the IGCs was pessimistic. It rejected a revised Dutch proposal for a congress of national and European parliamentarians; it affirmed its opposition to the three pillar structure; it reasserted its own role in Emu; and it threatened to reject the final results of the conference at Maastricht.

The following month, and in a much more conciliatory mood after hearing well-judged presentations of the Maastricht conclusions by Lubbers and Delors, the Parliament softened its position. After a study of the new Treaty led by Martin, Parliament eventually reached its considered conclusions in a long resolution on 7 April 1992.[16] Lacking any formal powers of ratification itself, the European Parliament could only urge national parliaments to ratify the Treaty. Earlier there had been bold talk of linking its own approval of the Treaty to the formal assent of certain national (notably, the Italian and Belgian) parliaments. The European Parliament's early approval of the Treaty was alleged to give the green light to the others.

Parliament's approval was, however, muted. It blamed the three-pillar structure for allowing the exercise of internal and external security policy to evade parliamentary and judicial control, as well as the reliance on WEU. Among many complaints, it criticised the co-decision procedure (Article 189b) for being insufficiently balanced or comprehensive; it deplored the failure to extend the right of assent to future treaty changes, revision of the EC's own financial resources or the development of citizenship (hopefully based on its own declaration of April 1989). It blamed the Council for still refusing to accept qualified majority voting over a 'very wide range' of issues; it criticised the lack of simplicity, clarity and transparency in EC procedures, especially those of the Council, and argued again for a clear legislative hierarchy. While welcoming the willingness of the Eleven to proceed in social policy matters farther than the UK, Parliament regretted its own exclusion from the new procedures involving the social partners. With regard to the UK, Parliament 'expects that the opt-out clause regarding Emu will, in practice, never be used and considers that the derogation from parts of social policy is not sustainable and should be rectified as soon as possible'.

The convergence criteria of Emu, in the Parliament's opinion, were exclusively geared to stability and paid no regard to the need for 'responsible growth and a high level of employment and social protection'. Parliament drew attention to the increased democratic deficit created by the transfer of economic and monetary powers from national governments and parliaments to an EC Council left unaccountable. Accordingly, Parliament called for a new interinstitutional agreement to embrace decisions on economic policy guidelines, the penalties imposed on errant member states, safeguard measures against third countries, the transfer of resources between member states and the appointment of the Executive Board of the European Central Bank.

The Parliament's prescriptions, which centred on the continuing lack of real federal democracy, were linked to the next IGC of 1996 and to the imminent enlargement negotiations. In the latter case, at least, the Parliament has a real blocking power (under Article O), and in January 1993, Parliament passed an ambitious report on the institutional implications of enlargement in which it demanded a drastic reform of the Council, including its meeting in public when passing laws. But in the event the European Parliament did not use its power of dissent to block the Efta enlargement.

The negotiations about the new interinstitutional agreements proved to be long and difficult, not only concerning the new agreements consequential on Maastricht (where the Parliament demanded a say in Emu and CFSP as well as EC law-making), but the renewal of the 1988 five-year agreement on the financing of the EC budget. The Danish referendum and subsequent events left Parliament on the sidelines. During late 1992 and 1993 a certain peevishness, born of frustration, crept into the Parliament's pronouncements on the monetary and political crises in the Community. The European Council's decision to reappoint Jacques Delors for a final two-year term (1993–94) could only be endorsed by MEPs: the Maastricht provisions for full consultation and assent about the choice of Commission President did not yet apply. The postponement of the coming into force of the Treaty also meant that the introduction of co-decision, the setting up of the Ombudsman and the ability to hold enquiries were all delayed. Besides the agreement on the interpretation of subsidiarity, the Edinburgh European Council took peremptory decisions about the increase in the size of the Parliament, with which MEPs could only acquiesce, and about where the Parliament should sit, about which MEPs could only protest. The Edinburgh decision about the 'Delors II' financing package was also reached without much regard (if any) to the Parliament's own views on this matter. Parliament reacted critically to these events, but for the most part was obliged merely to repeat its earlier demands.[17] With regard to subsidiarity, it was clear that Parliament would have to continue to fight hard to make its voice heard in the reform of EC legislation and to protect its own position within the institutional balance. Negotiations over the Ombudsman proved particularly difficult, with the Council insisting on withholding certain information on the grounds of secrecy and confidentiality. The Commission weighed into the quarrel over open government on the side of the Parliament.[18]

Gradually the spirit of interinstitutional cooperation improved as it dawned on all parties, firstly, that the wrangling was reducing further the public standing of the Community and, secondly, that this complicated and problematical Treaty was only going to be made operable if compromise and conciliation between them prevailed. In April 1993

Parliament and the Commission were able to agree an important joint declaration on how to manage the annual legislative programme.[19] And in September Parliament agreed controversial changes in its own rules of procedure to take account of its new responsibilities under Maastricht, notably in the field of CFSP and the external relations of the Community, but also with regard to enlargement, co-decision and con-ciliation. Reflecting the growing size and predominance of the two large groups, the Socialists and European People's Party, the executive of the Parliament – the enlarged bureau – was replaced by one committee of party group leaders (with votes weighted according to size) and another of committee chairmen.

By October interinstitutional agreements on the Ombudsman, on subsidiarity, on transparency and on the Article 189b procedure were ready for signing. Compromise was reached on the question of confi-dentiality of documents; but the Council insisted on remaining secretive about its votes. Parliament gave the agreements only a qualified wel-come.[20] Despite continuing controversy over exemptions for Luxem-bourg, MEPs also gave their assent to the Commission's proposals to extend voting rights to EC citizens in time for the 1994 elections.

Towards the end of 1993 Parliament's hostility to the Maastricht process was superseded by a more favourable reaction to the work of the Belgian presidency of the Council in preparing the ground for Stage Two of Emu, including the appointment of Alexandre Lamfalussy as the first President of the European Monetary Institute. MEPs themselves began to turn their attention to re-election or retirement, as the case may be, in June 1994. The Commission excelled itself in producing, against the odds, its long-awaited White Paper on economic recovery, and in persuading the second Brussels European Council to back it.[21] The prospect that an improved quality of public policy flowing out of the European Union would redeem its tattered reputation gave general encouragement. The more optimistic note was reinforced by Ecofin which, following instructions from the December Brussels summit, actu-ally beefed up (instead of watering down) the Commission's first-ever draft Recommendation under Article 103(2) of the Treaty on the broad guidelines of the economic policies of the member states and of the Community.[22] Better progress on the enlargement negotiations and, at last, the conclusion of the Uruguay Round of Gatt completed the picture. The need now was to consolidate the Treaty of Maastricht: to continue to justify it and to exploit it.

Part II

POLICIES AND POWERS OF THE UNION

5

FISCAL AND MONETARY POLICY IN ECONOMIC AND MONETARY UNION

Christopher Johnson

The two crises in the Exchange Rate Mechanism in September 1992 and August 1993 have led many people to think wrongly that the prospects for Economic and Monetary Union have become much more distant than when the Maastricht Treaty was signed. On the contrary, they have shown that premature exchange rate fixity, as well as being wrong in itself, was not the best or quickest road to full monetary union. They have also brought a number of benefits.

Exchange rates have behaved quite stably within the new 15 per cent bands, in some cases returning *de facto* within the old 2.25 per cent bands. Realignments are off the agenda, because the wider bands allow more flexibility when it is needed. The speculators no longer have a one-way bet on offer, and the central banks are no longer involved in intervening to throw good money after bad, because they have refused to restore formally the old narrow bands. The new set of exchange rates is a better basis for fair competitive conditions within an eventual Emu than the old. Countries which have left the ERM or devalued have in most cases been able to lead recovery, thanks to lower interest rates and better export performance. In fact, the ERM crises have left Europe as a whole about 15 per cent more competitive against the USA, Japan and other major trading partners.

The truth, moreover, is that neither economic nor monetary union has a clear and agreed definition. In the 1989 report of the Delors Committee, economic union is held to consist of four main components: the single market, competition policy, regional and structural policy, and macroeconomic policy coordination, including budgetary matters.[1] All four go back to the Rome Treaty, enhanced by the Single European Act and then by the Maastricht Treaty. The most significant developments in economic union foreseen by the Maastricht Treaty are in the area of fiscal policy coordination. These are arguably less important and far reaching than the Treaty's monetary union provisions, notably the establishment of a European Central Bank, with responsibility for a

71

single monetary policy. Monetary union can exist in a weak version, consisting of irrevocably fixed exchange rates, or a strong version, consisting of a single currency. The Treaty chose the strong version. An account of the Treaty's provisions for Emu is given in Chapter Two (pp. 20–23).

It is a matter for debate how far Emu covers policies outside a narrow definition, such as social, industrial, or environment policies, which might be considered as part of the wider concept of European Union. The key feature of Emu as envisaged by the Maastricht Treaty is that fiscal and monetary policy are closely linked, yet assigned to different institutions of the Union, the Economic and Financial Council (Ecofin) and Committee, and the European Central Bank. The division of powers is not clear-cut, particularly in exchange rate policy covering external exchange rate policy and, during Stage Two at least, internal exchange rate policy as well.

The August 1993 crisis in the ERM resulted in some switch of emphasis from monetary to economic policy within Emu. With 15 per cent exchange rate bands, monetary policy will be less constrained. On the other hand, the general rise in government deficits to well above the Treaty limits made it more important to seek a coordinated consolidation of fiscal positions. In addition, high unemployment in most EC countries convinced supporters of Emu that labour market measures would be needed to make the new monetary and fiscal disciplines acceptable to public and parliamentary opinion.

CENTRALISATION AND DECENTRALISATION

Both Ecofin and the European Central Bank embody a balance of centralised and decentralised powers. Ecofin is more confederal, since it is composed of representatives of the twelve member governments, but generally voting by majority and working through central institutions such as the European Commission and whatever permanent central staff organisation it may need to set up to supplement the existing Council staff. The Bank is more federal, since it controls a European System of Central Banks, in which the power of the six permanent governors will be balanced by that of the twelve (or however many more or fewer it turns out to be) national central bank governors.

As a simplification, let us assume that monetary policy is effectively run from the centre by the European Central Bank, with limited powers of implementation delegated to national central banks, while fiscal policy continues to be run by national governments, subject to the agreed central constraints and to the process of coordination and mutual surveillance. In both cases, we have examples of the operation of the principle of subsidiarity, by which only what cannot be sufficiently achieved by member states becomes the subject of Community action. Monetary policy will require more Community action, fiscal policy less, according to the judgement of the authors of the Maastricht Treaty.

There is, however, no general agreement among economists as to how far fiscal policy can be safely left to national governments, or how much of the implementation of monetary policy can be delegated by the Central Bank to national central banks. It is nevertheless clear that monetary policy is to be run on a more centralised, and fiscal policy on a more decentralised basis. It is less clear how much of a say the Central Bank will have in deciding, as opposed to the implementation of, exchange rate policy, and how much autonomy national central banks will have in devising and issuing bank notes and coins each within its own territory.

The peculiar institutional structure laid down, like that of the European Community itself, is the result of the greater weight of the member states in contrast with that of the centre in existing federations. The principle of central bank independence already adopted in Germany and, to a lesser degree, in other countries provides a route to a single monetary policy without a single government. The European Central Bank will have greater independence of action than any independent national central bank, because it will be independent of twelve (or whatever the number is) governments with different views rather than one government with one view, and its powers will be subject to amendment only by changing a treaty rather than an ordinary national law. The hopes of some countries, such as France, that Ecofin will have more influence over the European Bank than it now has over the Bundesbank may be justified; but Ecofin will have less influence over the European Central Bank than the German government now has over the Bundesbank.

When it comes to fiscal policy, Ecofin will not only not be independent of national governments, but may be paralysed by differences between them reflected in its ranks. There will not be a central political authority sufficiently strong to pit its views against those of the Central Bank or to carry out whatever central fiscal policy is required to complement the Bank's central monetary policy. (The small size of the EC's budget is consistent with the lack of central political authority.) Opinions differ as to whether this combination of strong monetary and weak fiscal policy is viable as a permanent arrangement, or whether it will lead, for good or for ill, to an inevitable centralisation of economic as well as monetary policy.

INTERFACE BETWEEN FISCAL AND MONETARY POLICY

Authorities such as the Delors Committee and Lamfalussy have mapped the links between monetary and fiscal policy in Emu.[2] There is a clear connection in the limited sense that wrong fiscal policies can sabotage the right monetary policy. Excessive fiscal deficits can lead either to monetisation or to bail-outs by partners, and bring about the twin dangers of inflation through excess money creation or stagnation through high long-term interest rates on public debt. Furthermore, in an Emu it takes only one country to be in excessive deficit for all to suffer the consequences. The members of the Delors Committee followed the example of central bankers at all times and places by prescribing to governments the fiscal rectitude lying outside their own sphere of responsibility.

The fiscal policy of Emu as a whole has a wider significance, and that is its contribution to economic stabilisation. The sum of fiscal decisions by individual governments cannot guarantee a collective fiscal stance that is optimal from the point of view of the Union as a whole. If the policy mix between fiscal and monetary policy is a matter of indifference, then governments could perhaps be trusted to offset a tight monetary policy on the part of the Central Bank with a sufficiently loose set of fiscal policies to counter its adverse effects on output and employment. The danger would be that loose fiscal policy would not merely offset but undermine tight monetary policy, and become counter-productive by raising long- as well as short-term interest rates, thus depressing rather than stimulating economic activity.

The danger in this situation would be that the Central Bank would in its turn tighten monetary policy further to offset any loosening of fiscal policy, so that the policy mix could not reach a stable equilibrium. There may not be a unique optimal equilibrium for the Europe-wide policy mix, but the viable range of policy combinations may be quite limited. The drafters of Maastricht appear to have started from the opposite end of the argument, trying to impose sufficiently tight fiscal policy on governments to allow the Central Bank's monetary policy to be reasonably moderate, with a view to keeping down the real level of both short- and long-term interest rates. The single market in financial services is also designed to lower interest rates by competition, and would be set back if the result of Emu was to raise interest rates in order to achieve price stability.

Germany, the key country in Emu, exemplifies within its own borders the pernicious combination of tight monetary and loose fiscal policy which should be avoided at European level. Since other ERM countries were forced to follow the Bundesbank's monetary policy, they were also led into fiscal deficits higher than the Maastricht minimum of 3 per cent of GDP. High interest rates, by depressing the economy, make fiscal deficits worse, as the 'automatic stabilisers' of lower tax revenues and higher welfare payments come into play.

If the policy mix is to be optimal for the whole Emu, then it is likely to be different for each member state. Given the same monetary policy and the same short-term interest rates (subject only to credit risk premia) in each country, fiscal policy will have to differ from country to country for the same total effect on the economy. Each country's fiscal stance will be determined by the given central monetary policy and the total policy mix requirement, but the results will be far from uniform across countries, if only because of divergent private and external financial balances. Countries will still have a good deal of national autonomy in deciding levels of taxation and public expenditure to strike a largely predetermined fiscal deficit or surplus, and in settling the composition of total tax revenue and government spending.

MONETARY POLICY AND CENTRAL BANK INDEPENDENCE

If the central bank's objective is price stability, can it achieve this more effectively if it is independent of the government, or if it is closely integrated with the finance or economics ministry? This is a question that can be asked both at national and at European level. An independent central bank is supposed to be less subject than its government to short-term political pressures, but if it is independent and unelected, it may not be able to carry through unpopular policies, particularly if the government is opposed to them.

The evidence is that, where price stability has been achieved, central bank independence, and monetary policy in general, has been only one of a number of contributory factors, and only in some instances and not in others. Central bank independence has been helped in Germany by responsible trade union behaviour, which is not guaranteed to continue. Lack of central bank independence, however, has not prevented France or Japan from achieving even greater price stability than Germany. Blake and Westaway suggest that an independent central bank is most effective when its objectives are in close agreement with those of the economics and finance ministry.[3] This criterion will be difficult for the European Central Bank to fulfil in the absence of a single European economics and finance ministry.

Independence of the national central bank is often combined with a belief in monetarism, or the imposition of a monetary rule on an inflation-prone government. As such it may be seen by some countries – Germany and the UK, for example – as an alternative to the independence of the European Central Bank rather than a preparation for it as envisaged in Article 108 of the Maastricht Treaty. Independence of the

European Central Bank can also be combined with European monetarism; but if monetary targets are set at a European level, they will be difficult to reconcile with autonomous national target-setting. National central bank governors of the European Bank will presumably bargain with each other on the allocation of national targets within the total European monetary aggregate; their reputations may depend on this being a 'Dutch' auction in which they bid for targets as low rather than as high as possible.

National governments are in many cases reluctant to surrender sovereignty to independent national central banks, and may *a fortiori* be even more reluctant to surrender it to the European Central Bank. However, the absence for the foreseeable future of a European government in charge of economic policy will make the proposed Central Bank by far the most coherent policy-making organ at European level. There will be no European government with which the Bank can have a relationship of dependence or independence. Its accountability to the European Parliament is likely to constrain it even less than that of the US Federal Reserve to Congress. The fact that central bank governors are not democratically elected makes it easier for them to work together at European level than for finance and economics ministers, each responsible to a different national electorate. The unification of monetary policy at European level is therefore set to precede that of fiscal and other economic policy. The presence of national central bank governors on the governing council of the Central Bank gives each country some say in European monetary policy, but the six members comprising the executive board, including the president, will have no national allegiances, and will command a majority with the addition of only one-third of twelve national governors, or only one-quarter of eight national governors.

ISSUES IN THE SINGLE MONETARY POLICY

It will be the task of the Central Bank to carry out a single European monetary policy. This requires a number of key issues, including the following, to be settled one way or the other.

Monetary aggregates

A common definition of EC money supply rather than the widely varying national definitions is needed if targets are to be considered. Will the Central Bank target a broad monetary aggregate, like the Bundesbank, or a narrow one, as the Bank of England has done? (The equal status accorded to narrow M0 and broad M4 as 'monitoring ranges' in the 1993 UK Budget can be seen as a step towards compromise.)

Monetary targets

Will monetary aggregates or short-term interest rates be the main policy instrument? One alternative would be a credit target, such as domestic credit expansion (DCE) or total bank credit (TBC). It seems unlikely that the exchange rate (of the Ecu against the dollar and/or the yen) will be a monetary policy target, because exchange rate policy will be outside the Central Bank's remit. The Ecu exchange rate might, however, form part of a 'monetary conditions' target, including both interest rates and external exchange rates.

Minimum reserve requirements

Will commercial banks have to have quite large non-interest-bearing reserves, as in Germany and most other countries, or minimal working balances at the central bank, as in the UK? Reserves are a kind of tax on banking, and need to be uniform if the playing field is to be level. It is doubtful whether they give a central bank more control over monetary targets than interest rates alone; if there are no monetary targets the question is academic. One compromise is to have reserves paying market rates of interest; another is to have zero reserve requirements – not as vacuous as it sounds, because it prevents banks borrowing from the central bank. If the Central Bank follows the line of the Bank for International Settlements in adopting a gross rather than a net settlement system for banking payments, this in itself might require banks to hold reserves at the Bank as collateral.

Banking supervision

The Maastricht Treaty leaves this fairly open. Should the central bank be responsible for banking supervision, as in the UK, or should there be a separate supervisory organ, as in Germany? The two policy objectives of supplying liquidity to the banking system (central banking), and deciding whether a bank is well enough managed to be worth rescuing (supervision), are connected, but it does not follow that they must be carried out under the same roof. The damage to central bank reputations from such supervisory problems as the scandal over the Bank of Credit and Commerce International (BCCI) leads to the conclusion that the European Central Bank should not risk sullying the prestige it needs to achieve its main aim of price stability by becoming involved in other, secondary objectives. The failure of national authorities adequately to supervise international fraud – BCCI again – indicates that there should be a European Office of Banking Supervision, separate from but working closely with the Central Bank, on the model of the German Aufsichtsamt für Kreditwesen.

Market intervention

Should intervention be partly in commercial bills, as in the UK, or entirely in government paper, as in other countries, and what techniques should be used? Should it be continuous during the day, as in the UK, or carried out once or twice a week, as in Germany? Should it be done through intermediaries such as discount houses, or by direct dealings between central banks and commercial banks? The wide variety of central bank techniques in different countries outlined by Padoa-Schioppa can be overcome only to the extent that financial instruments converge and become closer substitutes. Some degree of decentralisation in the execution of monetary policy seems inevitable, although both the European Bank and national central banks might at different times intervene in the markets.[4]

CONSTRAINTS ON FISCAL POLICY

There is a policy paradox at the heart of the Maastricht Treaty. It removes, over a period, most of the national freedom of decision in monetary policy. This means that, depending on circumstances, national governments may need to make greater use of fiscal policy in order to achieve their objectives for output and employment. Yet they may be prevented from doing so by the fiscal constraints of the Treaty, which could come into operation well before the point at which fiscal policy becomes so loose as to cause monetary policy to tighten undesirably. Buiter has ridiculed what he calls the 'fiscal numerology of Maastricht' with impeccable economic logic.[5]

The solution to the paradox lies in the nature of the fiscal constraints. They are both asymmetrical and flexible. They set upper but not lower reference values for government deficits and debts. They are also tempered by important loopholes and possibilities of interpretation. Countries whose budgetary position normally lies within the reference values will thus be able to use fiscal policy more flexibly than those whose budgetary position normally lies outside them. It is indeed the latter group of countries, those who commit 'gross errors', in the words of the Treaty, at whom the fiscal constraints are mainly aimed. Unfortunately, every EC country except Luxembourg had by 1993 moved into this position.

Before analysing the Emu Treaty provisions, we should recall that fiscal constraints are already explicit or implicit in the Single European Act. The 1992 programme laid particular emphasis on the harmonisation of indirect taxation. This has led to general acceptance of a 15 per cent lower limit on the standard rate of VAT, and a 5 per cent lower limit on the lower rate. This does not prevent increases in the higher rate, such as that by the UK in 1991, and the general need to raise more tax revenue in a number of EC countries suggests that the danger of competition for international trade by lowering VAT rates is not very great.

Other forms of tax harmonisation have been advocated, but little progress has been made. Excise duties, corporation tax, income tax and social security tax all diverge widely among EC members in ways that are held to distort location decisions and competition. The Ruding Committee (chaired by the former Dutch Finance Minister) proposed to harmonise corporation tax, but there seems at present to be little political will to implement its recommendations. There are the most glaring discrepancies in national rates of employers' social security contributions, which have a direct impact on unit labour costs. The Social Chapter does not propose to rectify them, but governments are themselves taking action to reduce rates that are outstandingly high, as in the French case.

THE MAASTRICHT CRITERIA

The main constraint of the Treaty is that in Stage Three 'Member States shall avoid excessive government deficits' (Article 104c(1)). It is already one of the convergence criteria in Stage Two, started on 1 January 1994, that members must avoid excessive deficits, although they only had to 'endeavour' to do so at that stage (Articles 109e(4) and 109j(1)). Unlike the other convergence conditions, this has permanent application in Stage Three. (It is assumed that the other convergence conditions, concerning exchange rates, long-term interest rates, and inflation rates, will *ipso facto* be achieved as a necessary consequence of full monetary union.)

The criteria for judging whether deficits are excessive are that they should not be more than 3 per cent of GDP, and that general government gross debt should not be more than 60 per cent of GDP. Deficits can exceed 3 per cent only if 'the ratio has declined substantially and continuously and reached a level that comes close to the reference value, or, alternatively, the excess over the reference value is only exceptional and temporary and the ratio remains close to the reference value'. The debt:GDP ratio can exceed 60 per cent only 'if the ratio is sufficiently diminishing and approaching the reference value at a satisfactory pace'.

Any interpretation of the fiscal provisions of Emu depends on a political judgement about how the Commission and the Council themselves will choose to apply them. A strict interpretation would exclude most members (see Table 5.1), and a loose one include most of them. Because of the recession of the early 1990s, even the few countries which looked like passing the deficit criterion of 3 per cent of GDP have risen

Table 5.1 Convergence tests for EC countries

	Consumer price inflation December 1993	*Govt long-term interest rate Jan 1994*	*Forecast govt deficit/GDP 1994*	*Forecast govt debt/GDP 1993*	*Govt debt ratio trend 1988–93*
Belgium	2.5	6.5	5.6*	121*	rising
Denmark	1.5	5.9	4.2*	71*	rising
France	2.1	5.6	5.9*	53	rising
Germany	3.6*	5.6	3.5*	43	rising
Greece	14.3*	20.3*	13.3*	109*	rising
Ireland	2.0	7.3	3.8*	96*	falling
Italy	4.0*	8.5*	9.2*	115*	rising
Lux'bg	3.6*	6.8	0.1	6	falling
Netherlands	1.7	5.5	3.9*	79*	rising
Portugal	6.3*	10.5*	5.4*	64*	stable
Spain	4.9*	7.9	7.1*	48	rising
UK	1.9	6.4	7.4*	35	rising
EC12	4.1	8.1	5.8		
Average of best three	1.7	5.9+			
Limit	3.2	7.9	3.0	60	

Source: IMF *World Economic Outlook*, October 1993; *The Economist*, 22 January 1994.

Notes: All figures are percentages. * = fails test; + average interest rates of the three states with lowest inflation.

above it – the UK to an astonishing 8.6 per cent forecast for 1993 – and the majority of countries have a rising debt:GDP ratio, which is particularly serious for those above the 60 per cent benchmark. If the objective is debt sustainability, as argued by Caporale, then most countries have far to go before their debt:GDP ratios level out at less than 60 per cent.[6]

FISCAL STABILISATION WITHOUT CENTRALISATION

The fiscal constraints of Maastricht will have to be rethought if fiscal policy is to be allowed to play a stabilising role. This holds whether there is a general symmetric shock, requiring a fiscal stimulus for Emu as a whole, such as another oil shock, or a particular asymmetric shock in one national region, such as German unification. There is a dilemma here. Either member states will have to accept constraints on their budget deficits (like most US states, which have to balance their budgets), and the EC central institutions will have to abandon their own balanced budget constraint in order to stabilise activity in the states (running a US-type federal deficit); or member states will have to continue allowing the automatic stabilisers to push them into cyclical deficits, while the EC itself continues to run a small balanced budget.

MacDougall and others have drawn attention to his 1977 report proposing quite modest, but still politically unacceptable, increases in the size of the EC budget.[7] He points out that the 1.35 per cent of GDP represented by the EC budget still falls far short of his suggested 5 per cent, or the 20–25 per cent average of federal states. The structural funds embodied in Maastricht are there more to redistribute income to the poorer states than to achieve stabilisation, which is a requirement for any state irrespective of its relative income level. Much economic literature, notably Goodhart, casts doubt on the ability of national fiscal policies to achieve stabilisation without substantial supranational transfers.[8]

The opposite view is more consistent with the decentralised approach to fiscal policy adopted for Emu. If member states allow the automatic stabilisers to operate, then those suffering a loss of economic activity will pay less tax to their national treasuries just as they would pay less tax to the federal treasury under a centrally taxing federal system; only if member governments raise taxes against the cycle will the stabilisation mechanism fail to take effect. Similarly, member states will automatically pay more welfare benefits to the unemployed; here the parallel with the USA is even closer, since most welfare is paid by the states and not by the federal government.

If the stabilisation mechanism breaks down in a decentralised Emu, it will be because the member states are panicked into raising taxes and cutting expenditure to balance budgets in a recession. This would happen only if the Maastricht fiscal criteria were applied willy-nilly. The advent of monetary union, particularly a single currency, will make it easier for member states to finance deficits in a unified European bond market. The main difference between European Emu and some federal systems will be in the smaller scale of concessionary grant-type finance from the centre to offset regional deficits, which will be limited to the structural funds for poorer countries. The flows of banking and investment funds should, however, make up for this, given exchange rate stability, as they do between regions of a single country.

The thesis is often advanced that fiscal deficits in an integrated area do not help stabilisation, because of spillovers of the extra demand into imports from other states in the area. As the Commission pointed out, the economic arguments run both ways, and it is hard to say a priori whether a fiscal stimulus will have more impact on domestic or on imported output; much depends on the exact form the fiscal measures take.[9] If the objective is to maintain incomes rather than output, the argument is in any case irrelevant. Factor movements of capital into, and labour out of, the deficit area should eventually restore equilibrium.

Fiscal deficits sometimes do and sometimes do not give rise to matching balance of payments deficits or spillovers; if they do, then capital inflows simultaneously finance both deficits.

There is a case for closer coordination of national fiscal policies, even if it is possible to dispense with federal fiscal policy. This case applies both globally within the Group of Seven, and to Ecofin. The case is that a relatively small fiscal stimulus coordinated by a number of interlinked countries will, thanks to spillovers and multipliers, yield a better pay-off in terms of economic activity than a larger stimulus in only one country. Some pooling of sovereignty in this area will make national fiscal policies more cost-effective.

THE OUTLOOK

The crises in the ERM in September 1992 and August 1993 have cast doubt on whether the second stage of Emu, which started on 1 January 1994, will see a return to fixed nominal exchange rates remaining within narrow bands. Other ways of proceeding to Stage Three, and monetary union, may nevertheless emerge. The Maastricht Treaty criteria for Stage Three could still be met by a bare majority of countries in 1996 – the first decision date laid down – or by a larger majority in 1998, the date of the final decision to begin Stage Three even if there is no majority. Nominal exchange rate convergence will be achieved relatively easily if the bands remain wider than the 2.25 per cent originally envisaged. Many countries had already achieved inflation convergence by 1993, or were quite close to it, and were expected to achieve it by 1994. Long-term interest rate convergence had been achieved by a substantial majority by autumn 1993. The main hurdle will be fiscal convergence, which has deteriorated. Economic recovery, combined with fiscal consolidation, could nevertheless be enough to deal with the majority of excessive deficits by 1996 or 1998. The UK and Italy are in danger of being disqualified as long as they do not rejoin the ERM, however, and the UK and Denmark have not yet decided whether to opt in to Stage Three on political as opposed to economic grounds.

Emu could thus take place in the first instance for a limited number of EC countries, but if it is successful, the others will probably want to join later. New EC members could in some cases, notably Austria, be part of the first group to enter Emu, but the Scandinavian members may want to bide their time, along with the UK and Denmark, after the failure of earlier attempts to peg their currencies to the Ecu. Future candidates for EC membership in Central Europe may make a first approach to Emu by means of a fixed but adjustable peg to the Ecu in a new broader and more flexible exchange rate mechanism. One thing is certain. The Emu project has been part of the EC agenda since 1970, and it will not quietly fade away, in spite of its ups and downs. As the EC moves closer to a prosperous single market, Emu will become more attractive, more feasible and more urgent to the great majority of member countries.

In conclusion, it is clear how monetary and fiscal policy are intricately linked in Emu. Monetary policy will be centralised through the European Central Bank, while fiscal policy will remain in the hands of national governments working together through Ecofin. National fiscal stances, while differing both in detail and in size and sign of change, will be largely determined by the requirements of a policy mix in which the monetary component is already given. The European Central Bank will have greater power in monetary policy than will Ecofin in fiscal policy, but its independence will be more successful in stabilising prices if it gains political acceptance. The Maastricht constraints on fiscal policy are an understandable adjunct to monetary policy, but if too literally interpreted could give rise to a system of federal deficit financing which is not needed for economic stabilisation. National fiscal regimes, if properly coordinated, should be as capable of stabilising the Emu economy as a federal system, provided that the automatic stabilisers are allowed to operate, and private financial flows are stimulated by the reassurance of stable exchange rates or a single currency.

6

COMMON FOREIGN AND SECURITY POLICY

Geoffrey Edwards and *Simon Nuttall*[1]

The cataclysmic changes that took place in Central and Eastern Europe inevitably changed the face of politics in Europe and in the Western world as a whole. The policies of the Community and its member states towards the reunification of Germany and its eastern neighbours in Europe at a time of such change may well have been the most important that they had to formulate for many decades. Certainly, in the various papers that circulated before the Intergovernmental Conference on Political Union (such as that of the Belgians) as well as in the letter of Chancellor Kohl and President Mitterrand in April 1990, which led to the Conference, the developments in Eastern Europe were identified as a challenge that illustrated the limitations of the existing machinery of European Political Cooperation.[2] Reactions to the Gulf War revealed the continued differences of member states, between those who queried whether improvements, especially in terms of a security identity, were possible and those who believed improvements to be absolutely necess-ary.[3] However, when set against the changes in Europe – and German unification, above all – the need for greater convergence of policy was accepted and compromise therefore made possible on defining a com-mon foreign and security policy and the ways in which it might be implemented.

The provisions on a Common Foreign and Security Policy that evolved in the course of the IGC are for the most part contained in Title V of the Maastricht Treaty. They largely succeed those in Title III of the Single European Act, which for the first time put the hitherto informal mechanisms of EPC on a treaty basis. They therefore represent a further stage in the development of a European policy, which, in terms of foreign policy, began with the adoption of the Luxembourg Report of 1970, but which in political and security terms harks back to the debates of the 1950s over the European Defence Community.

The concept of a foreign and security policy has been plagued with ambiguity and the debate about it riddled with inconsistency. Very often member states have agreed on the end but have been unable to reach consensus on the means. Yearning for a strong Europe able to make its voice heard in the world has been combined with, on the one hand, a determination to preserve national bureaucratic prerogatives and, on the other, a cautiousness lest the United States be alienated from its strategic guarantees and support. Both have sometimes proved inconsistent with the efficient and coherent pursuit of the declared objectives. The result has been successive formulations of the aim, initially only of a common foreign policy through EPC, but, as outlined in the Maastricht Treaty, a common foreign and security policy. Procedures, however, have remained intergovernmental and thus better suited to the continued coordination of national policies than to the stated purpose of a common policy.

It would be misleading, though, to give the impression that EPC has been purely intergovernmental, as the emphasis on coordination of policies might have led one to expect. Important elements of integrationist procedure have been introduced over the years. The Maastricht debate, like those which preceded it, was about the extent to which these elements should be incorporated into the official description of foreign policy mechanisms, and built on in a radically different international environment. Some elements were introduced at Maastricht, including majority voting even if within the restrictive context of Article J.3, but they were not enough to satisfy the champions of the integrationist approach. Certainly, the highly conditional language of J.4, introducing the possibility of 'the eventual framing of a common defence policy, which might in time lead to a common defence', tended to inspire little immediate excitement. It was in the hope of remedying what was seen as deficiencies in such respects that the integrationist school secured agreement on a review conference in 1996, *inter alia*, on the provisions of Title V.[4]

EPC had been marked from the start by a trade off between the dogmatic and the pragmatic. Even the agreement to set it up was a compromise. Previous attempts to found a political union had failed, whether led by the integrationists (the European Defence Community) or the intergovernmentalists (the Fouchet Plans). The deal concluded at The Hague Summit in 1969 included features to appeal to both schools. Progress towards Political Union was to be made first of all in the foreign policy field, and the language of the Luxembourg Report was sufficiently ambitious to satisfy the integrationists, despite some initial misgivings. France, in the forefront of the intergovernmentalist school, secured procedures for what was to become EPC which were derived from work done on the Fouchet Plans during the 1960s.

The purely intergovernmental nature of EPC could not last for long, nor could its remit be limited simply to diplomatic declarations and *démarches*. Involvement of the Community institutions had to be accepted at an early stage, and recourse was increasingly made to Community instruments for the implementation of policy. Three broad stages in this process can be distinguished: more frequent presence of Commission representatives at EPC meetings (1970–81); use by EPC of EC trade and aid policy instruments – sanctions and special aid programmes (1982–89); and a fuller policy and institutional interaction between EC and EPC following the collapse of the Communist regimes in Central and Eastern Europe (1989 to date).

The use of sanctions, especially against the Soviet Union (in 1980 in the aftermath of the invasion of Afghanistan and after the imposition of martial law in Poland in the same year) and the growing divergences of opinion between (perhaps most) Europeans and the United States, whether over security in Europe or policy in the Middle East and Central America, indicated an increasing awareness of the need for a wider discussion of security issues within EPC. They also revealed some of the difficulties of doing so. Of course, security in the sense of confidence building measures within the framework of a coordinated position in the Conference on Security and Cooperation in Europe (CSCE) or arms control and disarmament in the UN framework had long been a subject for discussion within EPC. But there was an ambivalence, amounting almost to schizophrenia, over quite where the dividing line between foreign policy, security and defence could be drawn. The 'revival' of WEU in 1984 was both a reflection of the limits of agreement within EPC over 'proper' boundaries and a symptom of the pressures making for a new element to 'Europe's' identity.

The developments in EPC itself were codified at intervals when member states found it convenient to mark the progress which EPC had made. This was the case with the Copenhagen (1973) and London (1981) Reports, as well as with the Solemn Declaration of Stuttgart (1983). The Single European Act of 1987 marked a new stage, in that for the first time the provisions regulating EPC were given treaty form shared with the European Communities. The original idea of the UK, which had launched the exercise, had been to conclude a separate agreement. The fact that the EPC provisions were incorporated into a Community treaty was regarded as a victory for the integrationist school. This same school secured agreement to review Title III of the Single Act five years after its entry into force, that is in 1992, but failed to have it specified that the review would be within a general framework of further rapprochement between the EC and the EPC machinery.

ORIGINS OF THE IGC ON POLITICAL UNION

The original intention of the Intergovernmental Conferences convened in December 1990 (well ahead of the Single Act schedule) had been to progress towards Economic and Monetary Union, as a natural consequence of the single market. This had been the purpose of the European Council in Hanover (June 1988) when it set up the Delors Committee to study how this could be done. But the events of the following year in Eastern and Central Europe were of such potential magnitude that, faced with the collapse of the Communist regimes and the prospect of German unification (which came about with bewildering speed by October 1990), a rapid rethinking was necessary to meet the radically changed situation. What became particularly clear to Chancellor Kohl and President Mitterrand was that the EC and its member states were institutionally ill equipped to meet the challenge. Of particular concern was the reflex attitude, on the part not simply of the public but of many within governments, that a larger and more powerful Germany would be tempted or simply be drawn into resuming its pre-war role as an autonomous Central European power. The policy followed by all governments of the Federal Republic of deep integration within Western Europe, as embodied by the Community, would, it was feared, become progressively less attractive to their successors. Kohl was also anxious to give a political dimension to the otherwise technical Emu in order to secure the support of the German people for the latter by increasing democratic control within the Community. Hence the letter sent by the Chancellor, together with Mitterrand, to the Irish President of the Council, Charles Haughey, on 19 April 1990, which called for a second IGC on Political Union, among whose objectives was agreement on a common foreign and security policy.

POSITIONS OF MEMBER STATES AND PROGRESS OF THE NEGOTIATIONS

An initiative of such political weight, launched in such circumstances, could scarcely be ignored, but neither could its concrete implications be easily understood. At the European Council in Dublin in April 1990, Margaret Thatcher remarked with some justification that the authors of the Kohl–Mitterrand letter did not know themselves what they meant by 'political union'. As far as the CFSP was concerned, this lack of clarity led to a confusing mass of proposals and counter-proposals from the various member states and the Commission, as well as the European Parliament. Both during the preparatory period and after the formal convening of the IGCs in Rome on 15 December 1990, the different contributions were aimed at differing and for the most part unformulated objectives. Their vagueness sometimes allowed for some interesting coalitions to form, such as that of the British and Italians, before member states reverted to positions determined more by the type of Europe they wanted than with the purpose and scope of a European foreign policy. It meant, especially when combined with the UK's rejection in principle of the very concept of a common foreign and security policy until the change of government in November 1990, that even after the formal negotiations had started concrete suggestions about how the CFSP might be made to work were few and far between.

The participants in the IGC were divided into two camps. On the question of a common foreign policy, the camp led by the UK, and which included Denmark, Greece and Portugal, was prepared to cooperate in the improvement of EPC on existing lines, but was reluctant to see any further dilution of its intergovernmental procedures by bringing it closer to the Community. The opposing camp was led by France and Germany, which favoured a strong common policy of the Union. They were supported by the Benelux countries, Italy and the Commission. The line-up was somewhat different when it came to security and defence. Here the broad split was between the Atlanticists (the UK, the Netherlands and Portugal) and the rest, led by France, with Denmark, Ireland and Greece adopting distinctive national policies.

Such divisions inevitably disguise significant nuances of approach within the different camps towards both foreign policy and security. Greece, for example, was more prepared to consider moves to bring EPC and the Community closer together than was the United Kingdom. Belgium, the Netherlands and the Commission wanted a Community-based foreign policy whereas France wanted one centred on the European Council, mirroring France's own constitutional arrangements. All the member states were prepared to upgrade the role of WEU but, as Jacques Delors pointed out, member states differed:

> Should it be a forum for increased cooperation between the countries of Europe, a bridge to the Atlantic Alliance, or should it be a melting-pot for a European defence embedded in the Community, the second pillar of the Atlantic Alliance?[5]

The negotiations within the IGC were for the most part not much influenced by outside events. Its origins may have been in the great events unfolding in Central and Eastern Europe, but by the time the formal negotiations began, the Community had already established a *modus vivendi*, if not yet a fully defined policy, and the new situation seemed less frightening as it became more familiar. The collapse and dissolution of the Soviet Union was not to occur until the second half of 1991, when the IGC was engaged in the final arbitrages between already fixed positions. Similarly, Yugoslavia first impinged on the collective consciousness of the Community and its member states only from June 1991. For the next six months, at least, the response of the EC Twelve was adequate and even inventive, to the extent that there was little pressure for drastic change in the Community's foreign policy procedures.

The exception to this was the Gulf War. The response of the Twelve when Saddam Hussein invaded Kuwait in August 1990 was firm and rapid. During the autumn, cracks began to appear, over responses to the US position and over the Iraqi leader's seizure of hostages. The failure of the Twelve to have anything like a coordinated position when the fighting broke out in January 1991, still less their ability to have anything but a minimal coordinated naval effort through the WEU, impelled the IGC to devote attention to the question of a common security policy. Their dependence on the US for military leadership in the Gulf not only complicated the debate over a European role in 'out-of-area' conflicts but also, inevitably, the potential Union's security and defence policy in Europe, given the concurrent review of the role of Nato and the US contribution to it.

If the Gulf War had acted as a catalyst to several member governments to do something about the limitations of EPC, the influence of the United States during the IGC negotiations was aimed largely in the opposite direction of ensuring its successor was limited in its scope. Washington was far from sanguine about the prospect of a European defence organisation that might rival that of Nato or might at least reduce Nato's status from being *the* defence organisation to being merely one of several. There were plenty of indications of American concern and even exasperation with its allies, especially after the Franco-German announcement of their proposal to up-grade their joint brigade to a Eurocorps in October, from President Bush (at the Nato summit in Rome) down.[6] Such moves inevitably reinforced the views of the minimalists such as the UK, but they may also have had an effect in restraining others.

But in the absence of other major external pressures, confusion about the objectives to be pursued and disagreement on the modalities to be followed, it is not surprising that the provisions of Title V seem scarcely adequate to achieve the stated aims of the Treaty. After all, the aim was not only to enable the Union and its member states to 'define and implement a common foreign and security policy, governed by the provisions of this Title and covering all areas of foreign and security policy'.[7] It was also the declared purpose, even with all its qualifications and conditional clauses, that it should lead to 'a common defence'.[8]

TREATY PROVISIONS

The main elements of the Treaty have already been outlined in Chapter Two (pp. 23–25). Here the emphasis is on those provisions which are new, are of institutional importance or have wider implications, either for the balance between the integrationists and intergovernmentalists or for the Union's capacity to act in the international system.

Consistency

Developing the practice begun in the Single Act, the CFSP becomes a policy of the Union while retaining its intergovernmental procedures. In the language of the negotiations, the 'three-pillar temple' approach prevailed. Decisions will be taken therefore not by an EPC-type minister-ial meeting but by the Council.[9] The Community institutions in general enjoy only that status which is specifically conferred on them in Title V, and this remains limited. The jurisdiction of the Court of Justice, for example, does not extend to the CFSP.[10]

The counterpart to this is the confirmation that the new 'pillars' cannot impair the operation of the existing Communities. Article M provides that 'nothing in this Treaty shall affect the Treaties establishing the European Communities or the subsequent Treaties and Acts modi-fying or supplementing them'. The Court of Justice is empowered to rule on any infringement of this Article. In principle therefore the Court could be drawn into questions relating to several of those instru-ments of policy that have played an increasing role in the Twelve's external and foreign relations, such as trade sanctions, which come within the Community's competence. It would be a matter of some political sensitivity if the Commission or a member state brought another member state to Court for failing to implement a Community policy made in pursuit of a CFSP decision, and possibly counter-productive in the longer term despite the obvious immediate inconsistency.

Consistency between the CFSP and the EC should, of course, flow from the fact that at heads of government and ministerial levels the same bodies (the European Council and General Affairs Council, the latter since adopting the title of the Council of the Union) deal with questions regardless of the 'pillar' from which they originate. In addition, specific provision is made to ensure consistency through Article C, which pro-vides that 'the Union shall in particular ensure the consistency of its external activities as a whole in the context of its external relations, security, economic and development policies'. Responsibility for ensur-ing such consistency lies with the Council and the Commission.[11]

Means of action

The CFSP pursues its objectives through common positions and joint actions.[12] By and large, the 'common positions' correspond to the cur-rent practices of EPC, systematic cooperation on most and potentially any matter of foreign and security policy of general interest. 'Joint actions', which may be implemented 'in areas in which the Member States have important interests in common', are decided on only by a very much more complicated process as set out in Article J.3. This involves guidelines from the European Council and decisions taken unanimously by the Council which define the matters on which subsequent decisions can be taken by qualified majority (from which decisions with defence implications are excluded).[13]

Other elements of significance include the representation of the Union by the presidency (the Commission had hoped to extend its representative role beyond external economic issues), the extension to the Commission of a (non-exclusive) right of initiative in all CFSP matters, and the undertaking by the member states which are members of the UN Security Council that they will concert and keep the other member states fully informed. The Permanent Members will also ensure the defence of the positions and interests of the Union without prejudice to their responsibilities under the UN Charter, an important innovation.[14]

Article J.4 provides for the extension of the CFSP to all questions relating to security, including the possible evolution of a common defence policy and a common defence. The Union is enabled 'to request' WEU 'to elaborate and implement decisions and actions of the Union which have defence implications'.[15] It also continues to reflect the differences among the member states, recognising, for example, the need to respect the obligations of those that are signatories to the North Atlantic Treaty, while allowing for the bilateral development of closer cooperation among two or more of the member states.[16] The Declaration attached to the Treaty, submitted on behalf of the then nine members of WEU, throughout matches mention of a common defence or a defence component with references to the Atlantic Alliance.[17] The Declaration also suggests means of synchronising procedures, structures and venues between WEU and the European Union and 'where necessary' with the Alliance. It calls, further, for the strengthening of the operational role of WEU, with a review of all the provisions of Title V to take place in 1996.

It should be emphasised that the provisions of Title V apply only to the strictly circumscribed field of CFSP. The powers of the EC in the field of external relations remain untouched, at any rate as far as the letter of the law is concerned. The third pillar – cooperation in the fields of justice and internal affairs – covers some areas with external implications, like immigration policy. These are dealt with under the machinery set up under Title VI, not by the Political Committee and its attendant Working Groups. It has its own joint positions and joint actions, with a procedure for adopting measures implementing joint actions more transparent than that foreseen in the CFSP.[18] It also has a provision for conduct within international organisations and at international conferences.[19] The common visa policy does not fall under this section, but is an EC policy following normal Community procedures, with qualified majority voting from 1996.[20]

Of even greater potential importance, the Emu, with its significant implications for external policy, has provisions and mechanisms of its own which are connected neither with the arrangements for other parts of the Community's external relations nor with the CFSP.[21] Only the Council and the Commission have a general duty to ensure consistency under Article C.

Faced with a mass of procedural detail, it is not always easy to see to what extent the Maastricht Treaty will bring about a common policy in the fields of foreign policy and security. Our comments here are divided into three sections: organisational measures to bring EPC and EC closer together, the voting procedure, and the provisions for security and defence.

Measures to bring EPC and EC closer together

The gradual blurring of the distinctions between the integration and the intergovernmental approaches has continued. There had already been agreement on three measures to bring the EPC and EC machinery closer together in the preparatory negotiations before the IGC began its work, and these survived intact in the Treaty. Agreement had been reached, for example, on abandoning the distinction between the General Affairs Council and the EPC ministerial meetings, on the grounds that it had become increasingly artificial. The same ministers took part in both, and the questions they dealt with overlapped more and more. Under the Irish presidency in the first half of 1990, the ministers meeting in the Council had a common agenda in which EPC and EC points were present together, and it was no longer necessary to decamp from one meeting room in the Council building to another and sit in a different order around the table in order to discuss EPC points. The complete abolition of the EPC ministerial meetings meant that the two meetings a year which had taken place in the capital of the presidency disappear. This has the disadvantage of losing visibility on the national scene for the European foreign policy process, although the informal Gymnich-type meetings of foreign ministers will continue in the country of the presidency and these have often taken on a high profile.

The procedural change may seem no more than a minor contribution to greater efficiency, but its wider significance should not be underestimated. During the negotiations on Title III of the Single Act, a similar proposal by Italy had been successfully resisted. The fact that only five years later it was no longer contentious is a measure of how much attitudes towards EC–EPC convergence had evolved.

The change nevertheless leaves several questions unresolved. Although ministers deal with EPC and EC questions indifferently in the same setting, the questions themselves are prepared in separate frameworks. EPC questions are submitted by the Political Committee according to intergovernmental procedures, and EC questions by Coreper according to Community procedures, including the making of a proposal by the Commission and preparation with a view to a decision by qualified majority vote where the Treaty so provides. The IGC was aware that more work needed to be done on the further integration of EPC and EC procedures below the level of ministers, and adopted Declaration No. 28 on the matter.[22] Discussion about the division of work between the Political Committee and Coreper has not been wholly smooth. It has been agreed that since Coreper is the body which prepares the agenda of the General Affairs Council, and since the agenda includes both EPC and EC points, then Coreper should check on the EPC points as well as the EC ones, even if they have been substantially prepared already in the EPC/CFSP framework. This provides an additional opportunity to ensure that policies are consistent.

But this begs the question of what happens if Coreper and the Political Committee disagree. Neither has institutional primacy over the other, and few if any procedural formulas at the Union level are likely easily to resolve the problem. To some extent since Permanent Representatives are rarely subordinate to Political Directors in their national hierarchies, consistency will depend on coordination at the national level. In the past, EPC has had only a limited impact on national decison-making, once foreign policy coordination was retained very largely in the hands of foreign ministries. The increased use of Community instruments, such as sanctions, has inevitably challenged internal competences, and blurring the competences within the Union's policies may further question the autonomy of foreign policy.

The second area of agreement was on merging the EPC secretariat with the general secretariat of the Council. The EPC secretariat had been set up in accordance with the Single Act to provide a more permanent nucleus and institutional memory for the EPC than the peripatetic support team that had preceded it had been able to do. The setting up of a secretariat at all was a considerable achievement. Previous efforts had been blocked by the more 'integrationist' member states because they were redolent of the Fouchet approach. It was only after France had accepted that the secretariat would serve EPC, not the European Council, and had allayed any suspicions that France still hankered after an autonomous secretariat in Paris, that agreement became possible. The secretariat was established in Brussels and occupied a wing of one floor of the Council building, but many of the member states insisted that it retain as much independence from the

Council secretariat as was consistent with operational efficiency and keeping costs to a minimum. It was staffed by diplomats seconded from their national services, but relied on the Council secretariat for all office services, and had no budget of its own. It was only a matter of time before the inevitable absorption into the Council secretariat took place. That the change came about after five years was indicative of how attitudes had evolved. The change was made easier because the member states had denied the secretariat any autonomous intellectual function in the EPC process.

The merger of the EPC secretariat with the Council secretariat has taken place following discussions held in compliance with Declaration No. 28. Inevitably delayed by the slow progress of ratification, the existing secretariat is to be expanded to twelve diplomatic grade officials, one from each of the member states, matched by an equal number of permanent officials from the Council secretariat.

The third area of importance that goes beyond simply procedural change was the non-exclusive right of initiative of the Commission. In a sense this is no more than the recognition of an existing practice, for the Commission has rarely hesitated to give its views on matters under discussion and to table papers when appropriate ever since it was fully associated with EPC in 1981, and even before. To begin with it was discreet in its use of this possibility, confining its remarks to areas for which it was competent. After 1989 it grew bolder, not only because it was directly involved in many of the policies the member states wished to pursue, particularly in Central and Eastern Europe, but because the presence of the Commission was no longer the taboo it once had been, as recollections of the period before 1981 faded.

The non-exclusive right of initiative is, of course, quite different from the exclusive right which the Commission enjoys in the EC framework. The latter allows the Commission to play a decisive role in the framing of policy and provides an institutional forward planning function. The former does not. The significance of the new powers will depend on the use the Commission makes of them. If it tables proposals clearly designed to represent the interest of the Union, and does so in a manner that recognises the susceptibilities of the member states, which remain obliged by the logic of their own position to table proposals representing only their national interest, then over time the Commission may come to enjoy influence which more nearly resembles that which would flow from an exclusive right of initiative, without amendment of the formal text.

It has been argued that the Commission would not in any case be able to undertake such a formal responsibility because it has neither the diplomatic know-how in Brussels nor an adequate diplomatic network world-wide. Both are held to be essential for the formulation and

94

implementation of foreign policy. These arguments do not withstand close examination. The Commission has perforce built up considerable experience in the conduct of trade policy as it implemented Article 113 of the EEC Treaty. Moreover, the Commission has now over 100 diplomatic missions and is opening new ones in the republics of the former Soviet Union. It is a network more extensive than that of many member states, several of whom have been seeking ways of reducing at least the costs and in some cases the size of their diplomatic services. The network has provided useful support for the growing role of the Commission and particularly the Commission President. Hence the hopes of the Commission that it would be given a greater representative role in the Maastricht Treaty. However, the Treaty gives the presidency of the Council the responsibility both for representing the Union and the implementation of common measures, assisted by the troika, which includes the preceding and succeeding presidencies, and with the Commission only associated with these tasks.[23]

None the less, for its part, the Commission which took office in January 1993 decided on a number of internal reforms to prepare itself better to carry out its responsibilities under Maastricht. It began by dividing responsibility for external relations among its members. In particular, one Commissioner (Hans van den Broek, who moved to the Commission from having been Dutch foreign minister) was given responsibility for external political relations, while external economic relations were divided between Sir Leon Brittan, for the developed world, and Manuel Marin, for the developing world. The Commission's new foreign policy role was underpinned by setting up a new directorate general (DG I.A) for external political affairs.[24]

The voting procedure

That there are provisions for taking some decisions by qualified majority voting in the Treaty at all is a tribute to the persistence of those member states determined to retain some trace at least of a move towards a more integrationist foreign policy against the attacks of the intergovernmentalists. The provisions, set out in Article J.3, are, however, far from transparent and give rise to grave doubts about their practicability. The first difficulty arises because their field of applicability is unclear. Except for issues having defence implications, voting may take place to adopt certain decisions regarding joint actions but, surprisingly for a legal instrument, the concept of 'joint action' is nowhere defined. It is clear that it is different from a 'common position', and also that it is different from an action taken by the Community. So what is it? An example sometimes cited is the EC Monitoring Mission in the former Yugoslavia, which is certainly an action and not a position, and equally certainly does not fall under the field of action of the Community Treaties. But what aspects of the action could have been decided by majority voting, had the Maastricht Treaty been in force? The answer is not clear, and can become so only through experience.

Finally, majority voting is so hedged about with conditions that it seems unlikely the opportunity to take a decision by this means will ever arise. The procedure can be caricatured as deciding unanimously to decide by majority vote, and is unlikely, as a senior official involved in EPC has said, to enable the Union to achieve the objective laid down in Article B. It is arguable that Declaration No. 27 on voting in the field of the CFSP ('The Conference agrees that, with regard to Council decisions requiring unanimity, Member States will, to the extent possible, avoid preventing a unanimous decision where a qualified majority exists in favour of that decision') will, if respected, prove more beneficial to the decision-making process.

At any rate, at its special meeting in Brussels on 29 October 1993 the European Council took tentative first steps in common foreign policy by requesting the Council to define the conditions and procedures for joint action with regard to Central and Eastern Europe, the Middle East, South Africa, former Yugoslavia and Russia.

Provisions for security and defence

The provisions for security and defence are potentially of much greater significance. Certainly in procedural terms they mark a change in the traditional way EPC had developed. Whereas in EPC advances were made on a pragmatic basis and then periodically were codified and labelled progress, the Maastricht provisions provide a framework within which the Union can, if it chooses, make significant policy decisions. But the provisions do not in themselves necessarily constitute a dynamic for progress; since the divisions on the substance of any European defence or security identity were deep, the member states were able to agree only on procedure which left open the distribution of the work of elaborating and implementing decisions between the European Union and the WEU. The then nine members of WEU (Greece and Denmark were invited to join but only Greece has done so, Denmark preferring to remain 'semi-detached', along with Ireland, as observers) were somewhat chary of laying down any strict timetable – the security and defence identity being pursued only 'through a gradual process involving successive stages'.[25]

They showed somewhat greater precision about the means of bringing about a closer working relationship with the Union and its institutions and set out a list of six measures (including the creation of a planning cell) for further examination in the interest of strengthening WEU's operational role as the defence component of the Union and as the European pillar of the Atlantic Alliance. This duality – some might prefer ambiguity – in WEU's role was subsequently enhanced by the rival positions taken over 'double-hatting' Nato forces for WEU/European Union purposes and developing the largely Franco-German 'Eurocorps' to become the basis for Union forces. Progress on the European security and defence identity thus depends entirely on ulterior political determination; under the Treaty, the common security policy of the Union was a blank canvas, on which the member states could paint whatever pictures they chose.

However, two important events, positive for the integrationists, need to be noted. First, the Treaty provisions finally eliminate the semantic limitation of EPC's agenda, which had persisted up to and included the Single Act. The London Report had admitted the discussion of certain political aspects of security; the Stuttgart Solemn Declaration extended this to political and economic aspects of security and this had been confirmed by the Single Act. With Maastricht, there is no longer any 'no go' area. But the move shows, too, that a member state could join the CFSP and still maintain its policy of neutrality, which was important for Ireland and which may be equally important for future members such as Sweden, Austria and possibly Switzerland.

The second important feature of the security provisions is that the Commission is just as fully associated with them as with other parts of the CFSP.[26] This includes the non-exclusive right of initiative. The overlapping of this right with the task assigned to the WEU to 'elaborate and implement decisions and actions of the Union which have defence implications' has not been defined.[27] The Commission will at least have to forge close links with the WEU in order to achieve consistency. The move of the WEU secretariat to Brussels may help logistically.

THE FUTURE DEBATE

The revision of the Maastricht Treaty in 1996 to which the member states are committed was primarily foreseen in order to review the provisions on security and defence, bearing in mind the possibility of withdrawal from the Brussels Treaty in 1998.[28] Amendments to the CFSP are incidental to this.[29] The discussion on security and defence is likely to continue to be intense and difficult. Much will continue to depend on the evolution of the approach of the United States and its continued role in Europe through Nato and the CSCE. It will also be influenced by considerations of success and failure in meeting existing challenges, such as that of the former Yugoslavia and especially that in Bosnia. US positions on the peace proposals put forward by Cyrus Vance and David Owen, on the use or non-use of US forces and the rearmament of the Bosnian Moslems, have suggested to some in Europe, not least in France, that there are clearly situations where European and American interests diverge and that Europe therefore needs an operational capacity of its own if it is to gain any credibility. Others, such as the British and the Dutch, continue to give every appearance that they remain reluctant to envisage WEU as anything but a complementary body to Nato. The German position seems to be somewhere between the two – gaining French acceptance for example for the Eurocorps to be available to Nato – but complicated by a constitutional ambiguity that limits its use of force to the Nato area and perhaps to a peace-keeping role under UN auspices.

But it is not only the present limitations in Bosnia, nor even perceptions of future challenges which the Union may be called upon to face, whether in Europe or further afield, that cause divisions among member states of the Union. If the timetable for new admissions is adhered to, the security debate must also necessarily involve any new members. It has been suggested above that in so far as Ireland has signed the Maastricht Treaty, neutrality as such, or at least being militarily neutral, need not necessarily be a bar to membership of the Union. Since the provisions on voting do not apply to defence aspects of CFSP, the opposition of one member state will presumably be enough to prevent the Union from pursuing any particular policy. But the possibility of a number of (new) member states, concerned to match their declared commitment to the Union and the *acquis politique* with the prospective demands of their electorates to maintain what has hitherto been as vital an element of their national identity as of their foreign policy, raises obvious potential difficulties. Moreover, those difficulties will be complicated by the need to take some cognisance of the views of other prospective new members of the Union or at least the possible implications of their membership. The debates within both Nato and WEU over extending security guarantees to the Visegrad Four have already revealed ambiguities that have satisfied few in Central and Eastern Europe, while at the same time causing deep unease in military circles in Russia. The closer involvement of those countries, including the further evolution of their association agreements towards membership at some point in the future, heightens those difficulties.

THE OBJECTIVE OF THE CFSP PROCESS

Speculation about the course of the discussion between Maastricht and the 1996 review necessarily involves a high degree of prediction. A number of fundamental questions including several of those hinted at above underlie the whole CFSP approach even if they are unlikely to be discussed explicitly. First among these is whether the underlying aim has been the coordination of national policies or a truly integrated single European policy.

The objective of a European foreign policy has always been expressed on paper in grandiose terms, and Maastricht is no exception. Yet the procedures followed so far have been designed to bring about coordination of the policies of the member states rather than a truly integrated European policy. Maastricht does not significantly change this. There is, of course, nothing wrong with setting coordination of policies as an objective, and continuously improving procedures to make it ever more effective. The difficulty arises when the participating governments or their publics either become frustrated by the limitations of the approach, as in the case of the former Yugoslavia, or want for reasons of principle – such as support for full European Union – to adopt a different type of structure. Opponents of such a European Union can easily fight the battle on theoretical grounds but their position becomes more difficult when they attempt to defend both the existing procedures and the objective of an effective European foreign policy.

There are several features of the present arrangements which would need to be altered if European foreign policy is to achieve greater effectiveness, but it is doubtful if great store can be set by extending decision-making by qualified majority voting. It has been one of the strengths of EPC arrangements that once positions were arrived at by consensus, they tended then to be loyally defended. The system under the CFSP will continue to rely on its participants, national diplomats in foreign ministries and posts overseas, for the defence of common positions and the implementation of joint actions, at least until such time as there is a single European foreign ministry. This seems somewhat unlikely in the immediate future. Pending this transformation, the abandonment of the principle of consensus might only impair the effectiveness of the current system.

This does not imply that all decisions must be taken unanimously. On the contrary, the present system has had sufficient inner strength to produce a consensus even when one seemed unlikely at the outset of discussions and a 'lowest common denominator' result might have been expected. Declaration No.27 suggests how past practice may be systematised for the future. But it needs also to be recalled that EPC/CFSP relies to a considerable extent on Community instruments for the execution of its policies. As has been shown above, the Maastricht Treaty makes it plain that nothing it contains affects the EC Treaties, including, presumably, taking decisions by qualified majority vote where the Treaties so provide. It would clearly be an abuse of procedure for a requirement to decide by unanimity in EPC/CFSP to override a requirement to decide a Community measure by qualified majority vote, even when it might be subsidiary to an overall political framework. Such abuses of procedure may well occur; it will require considerable political nerve to oppose on procedural grounds decisions on whose substance all are agreed.

A feature of the existing arrangements which does need attention is that of the representation of the Union. Under Article J.5.1, the Union is represented by the presidency for matters coming within the CFSP, assisted when the need arises by the troika, with which the Commission is fully associated. This arrangement presents practical difficulties because of the pressure of work and the shortness of the duration of the Council presidency. Representing the Union is a full-time job. The relative success of EPC has imposed an increasing burden on the presidency, because of the interest of third countries in receiving early information about foreign policy positions and decisions, and their desire to be seen in formal political dialogue with the EC. Some presidencies are better equipped than others in dealing with the pressure of work, and it has not always been the larger countries that have been most successful. Smaller countries have to all intents and purposes shelved their national foreign policy responsibilities for the six-month duration of the Presidency, while a large country cannot afford such luxury. With larger countries there is always greater scope for confusion between what is national policy and what is the position of the Union.

Finally, the increasing interval between presidencies as more and more countries join the Union (every three years in 1970 with six members, every six years in 1993 with twelve members, with a Union of at least sixteen and probably more members looming after further enlargement) means that the member states lose the habit of holding the presidency and have to learn the skills afresh each time round. Some administrative assistance is available from the EPC secretariat, and the situation should improve with the enlargement of the secretariat and its incorporation into the Council secretariat, but member states hitherto have been reluctant to grant the secretariat any representational function and this may well continue as long as the CFSP is run on intergovernmental lines.

A second feature which requires attention is the lack of a forward planning function in CFSP. There exists a working group of national policy planners which meets under each presidency, but this does not serve an integral planning function within the system. What is lacking is the localisation of responsibility for setting the agenda and formulating the Union interest in the longer term. There is no guiding hand for ordering business in the present system. Agendas are compiled by the presidency, which adds items at the request of any member state. Likewise, any participant may circulate a paper for discussion. The extent to which the presidency can guide the discussion depends on the quality of the paper itself (with which the secretariat can be of considerable assistance), but the process suffers from lack of continuity inherent in the nature of the rotational system. This reflects the problems inherent in the foreign policies of many Western liberal democracies, that they inevitably react to new foreign policy problems and try to treat them only after they have occurred, usually amid considerable publicity and criticism that they should have had contingency plans for such an event. The primacy given to gaining common positions among twelve member states, on whom the problem may well bear very differently, has meant that EPC has been obliged to wait for problems to arise before dealing with them. The non-exclusive right of initiative of the Commission may help to provide a greater degree of forward planning, but will not produce the same effect of detecting the long-term common interest as does the Commission's exclusive right of initiative in the Community.

These two failings must be addressed by those who wish to put in place a more effective foreign policy. In remedying them, however, care has to be taken not to divorce the European foreign policy mechanism from the national ones. Reference has been made above to the valuable contribution made by national foreign ministries and diplomatic services to the success of European foreign policy in any currently conceivable institutional set-up and care will have to be taken not to impair this.

SUBSIDIARITY AND COMMITMENT

The principle of subsidiarity is applicable to all parts of the Maastricht Treaty. On the face of it, the CFSP is a prime candidate for the application of this principle, which would result in most foreign policy decisions being taken at the level of the Union. The original impetus for foreign policy cooperation given by The Hague Summit in 1969 came from the need for Europe to speak with one voice in the world, in order to strengthen its influence over events, and this has consistently been a declared aim. This implies that decisions taken at national level, to the extent to which they impair the effectiveness of European action, are not consistent with the principle of subsidiarity.

The political reality is otherwise. As suggested above, the likelihood of exclusive foreign policy powers being granted to the Union is remote. The immediate question to be settled is the extent to which national foreign policies may diverge from the policies agreed in CFSP. The matter is touched on in several provisions of the Maastricht Treaty. Article J.1.4 provides that:

> The Member States shall support the Union's external and security policy actively and unreservedly in a spirit of loyalty and mutual solidarity. They shall refrain from any action which is contrary to the interests of the Union or likely to impair its effectiveness as a

cohesive force in international relations. The Council shall ensure that these principles are complied with.

Article J.3.4 provides that: 'Joint actions shall commit the Member States in the positions they adopt and in the conduct of their activity'. Article J.3.6 provides for derogations from this obligation in cases of imperative need. In the area of security and defence, Articles J.4.4 and 5 provide for cooperation within Nato and bilaterally. The provisions of Article J.5.4 regarding the Security Council have been referred to above.

Curiously, the apparently more binding commitments contained in the Single Act were not taken up in the Maastricht Treaty. For example, Article 30.2(c) of the Single Act provides that:

In adopting its positions and in its national measures each High Contracting Party shall take full account of the positions of the other partners and shall give due consideration to the desirability of adopting and implementing common European positions.

It provides further that the 'determination of common positions shall constitute a point of reference for the policies of the High Contracting Parties'. Admittedly, the absence of any provisions to ensure compliance with these undertakings considerably reduced their force, but the absence of a corresponding definition in the Maastricht Treaty of the relationship between national foreign policies and the CFSP is surprising. If not revised in the 1996 IGC, it will impair the effectiveness of the CFSP.

LEGITIMACY

Foreign policy has traditionally been formulated and conducted in conditions of extreme secrecy. In national terms, this has usually been acceptable because governments have themselves been subject to democratic control. Governments could if necessary make their handling of a foreign policy issue a question of confidence. But the situation is very different in the case of EPC/CFSP. Article J.7 provides that the European Parliament is consulted on 'the main aspects and basic choices of the CFSP' and its views are 'duly taken into consideration', but the mechanisms foreseen for this are weak and have not in the past given the Parliament a chance to have an effective overview of the activities of EPC.

The purpose here is not to claim that this situation constitutes part of the 'democratic deficit' of the Union, but rather to point to its disadvantages for the effectiveness of ECP/CFSP. For foreign policy to be effective, not only must the executive body enjoy legitimacy, but the policies themselves must enjoy popular support. This will increasingly be the case as the CFSP extends beyond the arcana of habitual diplomatic intercourse to the great issues which concern the public seated before their television screens. At present, the activities of CFSP enjoy neither popular understanding nor popular support. A prime example is the case of Yugoslavia. This situation will need to be remedied if the CFSP is to be an effective European foreign policy.

7

EUROPEAN CITIZENSHIP AND COOPERATION IN JUSTICE AND HOME AFFAIRS

Malcolm Anderson, Monica den Boer
and *Gary Miller*[1]

Among the Maastricht reforms the introduction of 'citizenship' seemed to be one of the most radical, for until the signing of the Treaty this was an idea which only had substance in the context of the nation state. In accepting this reform, the member states followed a Community tradition of attaching grand concepts like 'union' to the integration process, which has often tended to raise both hopes and fears that turn out to be unfounded once the substance behind the rhetoric is revealed. The same will probably be true of the new citizenship: this chapter in fact argues that it changed very little. Whether it has much practical effect will depend on how it is further developed, for it was constructed in such a way that it was doubtful whether it could function effectively even in its own modest terms. The most telling feature was not what was included in the citizenship provisions in the new version of Article 8 in the Treaty of Rome, but what was considered so sensitive that it had to be handled completely differently. These sensitive issues were grouped together under the heading 'Cooperation in the fields of Justice and Home Affairs' and placed in a separate 'pillar' of the Treaty (Title VI or Article K). Because the citizenship part of the Treaty and this inter-governmental pillar are so closely interlinked, they can only be fully evaluated if they are considered together.

The Treaty concept of citizenship is based on the existing principle, as interpreted by the Court of Justice, that nationals of member states have certain rights in some circumstances to move freely across national borders in the common market. The problem is that key preconditions for the successful exercise of these rights are dealt with under the justice and home affairs pillar, the most crucial being the removal of border controls on persons. The creation of a single market as a 'space without internal frontiers' was first laid down in the Single European Act. Since then the member states have struggled to achieve this objective and have quarrelled about its meaning. Most took it to imply the abolition of controls on people crossing their mutual borders, which thereby implied the shifting of such controls to a common external frontier with non-EC countries. This in turn implied the development of common policies about people coming from third countries including rules about visas, asylum-seekers and refugees.

Indeed, the development of these policies originally formed part of the normal single market programme under which it fell to the Commission to make proposals, which it dutifully began to do.[2] But they proved to be too controversial for agreement to be reached easily and it quickly became clear that no progress would be made under the normal processes of EC decision-making. A group of member states had meanwhile decided under the Schengen Agreement of 1985 to go ahead alone to try to formulate such rules for themselves.[3] Schengen was designed to be a laboratory for developing practical experience which could later be transferred to the Community; the arrangements remained a purely intergovernmental affair.

Ultimately, and in parallel to Schengen, the same intergovernmental method had to be used for those aspects of a 'space without internal frontiers' which were too controversial for normal single market decisions. Thus, the External Frontiers Convention and the Dublin Asylum Convention were negotiated between the twelve national administrations as international agreements between sovereign states.[4] The fact that by the end of 1993 they still remained to be ratified reflected the continuing sensitivity of the issues involved in the establishment of a common citizenship based on the removal of internal border controls.

It was this intergovernmental approach which was retained when it came to the attempt at Maastricht to incorporate into the EC Treaties comprehensive provisions on all matters related to the abolition of internal border controls. The existing conventions were retained and together with all other related issues (except visa policy) they were now to be governed by procedures and institutions laid down in the Provisions on Cooperation on Justice and Home Affairs. This part of the Treaty will profoundly affect the way in which the citizenship provisions operate. Citizenship 'proper' comprised amendments to the EEC Treaty and thus falls under the normal Treaty structures and procedures, which means, most importantly, that the rights comprising citizenship will be enforceable by citizens before the courts. But the key condition for the exercise of these rights will be the ability to cross borders between member states unhindered: this is what formally triggers the operation of European citizenship and provides for its trouble-free operation. At the time of writing, this condition is far from being fulfilled, with controls still in place at many internal borders. Britain continues to refuse to contemplate their removal and even the Schengen group of countries cannot adhere to their timetable for suppressing controls, particularly at international airports. Progress will depend on decisions in the intergovernmental sphere on the whole range of policy issues arising from the removal of controls. If citizens' rights are infringed by measures taken – or not taken – under Title VI of the Treaty there is not the same scope for enforcing rights before the courts as under the citizenship provisions in Title II. Decisions taken in this area of cooperation will not be taken in the form of EC laws which the Court of Justice can be asked to scrutinise for their legality. This seems to make a mockery of the freedom of movement that is supposed to be at the core of EC citizenship.

ORIGINS OF EC CITIZENSHIP

Concern with citizenship and citizens has a long pedigree in EC affairs, the first mention in official texts being as early as 1961–62.[5] This seems to have had at least three distinct motivations. First there was the need to make European integration more relevant to ordinary people – a need clearly perceived by Schuman and Monnet as they sought to go beyond cooperation between states to unite the people of Europe. More recently, similar concerns were evident in the 1974 Paris Summit and the resulting Tindemans report on European Union, in President Mitterrand's attempted *relance* of the Community at the Fontainebleau European Council in June 1984 and in the subsequent work of the Adonnino Committee which gave rise to the various Citizens' Europe initiatives and campaigns from 1985 onwards.[6] This strand of development may be characterised as the 'socio-political', for it involved Community elites worrying about the degree of public support for their policies and popular identification with European institutions. Pronouncements on this subject over the years tended to repeat themselves blandly, and the post-Maastricht preoccupation with 'closeness', subsidiarity and transparency has added little new. The European Council at Edinburgh echoed almost verbatim Tindemans's plea in 1975 for Europe to be close to its citizens.[7]

In practice it has always proved difficult to interest the public in an elite-driven process of functional integration focusing largely on economic activities and governed by opaque procedures of intergovernmental decision-making. Measured against the adverse public reactions to the Maastricht Treaty, attempts at European consciousness-raising in the 1980s, such as the European flag, passport and anthem, may seem clumsy and naive. That same aspiration to mobilise popular identification with Europe was a motive for the Maastricht concept of citizenship, although its capacity to do this was severely restricted.

A second strand in the developing EC interest in citizenship was linked to the single market, where it was thought that relations between the citizen and the Community would need up-grading in two important areas: freedom of movement and social rights. It was always envisaged that the single market, establishing thorough-going freedom of movement for business by liberalising national regulations, would need at least some minimum complement of social protection for workers. This was certainly the belief of the Delors Commission, and led to the adoption of the Social Charter in 1989 and the subsequent legislative measures contained in the social action programme. Most European welfare states have some conception of citizenship involving ties of mutual solidarity and minimum levels of social protection, and it was natural to seek to reflect this dimension at the EC level. The aim of creating a single market without internal frontiers laid down in the Single Act and in the Commission's 1985 White Paper on *Completing the Internal Market* implied that the Treaty's provisions on freedom of movement should apply to all individuals and not just to certain categories of the economically active. It was this development, coupled with the Court of Justice's expansive interpretation of freedom of movement, which more than anything else provided the basis for the Maastricht citizenship.

A third strand in the development of EC citizenship, much strengthened by the direct election of the European Parliament in 1979, linked the concept to the democratic deficit. With the growth of supranational elements in the EC such as its own financial resources and the beginnings of co-decision between Parliament and Council, it became possible to think of citizenship at the European level in terms of democratic participation and popular sovereignty. Thus, the Parliament's Draft Treaty on European Union of 1984 conceived of a citizenship identical in structure to the Maastricht version, with access to it determined by nationality, but used the language of citizenship more systematically to indicate clearly the democratic basis of the Union and the central role played in it by a unified citizenry and its representatives.[8] These ideas were taken up prior to the IGC by Spain, and to a lesser extent by the Commission. In April 1989 Parliament adopted a Declaration of Fundamental Rights and Freedoms and demanded that a similar document be adopted by the IGC.[9] However, as the course of the negotiations demonstrated, the more limited concept of a citizenship based on freedom of movement was the one around which a consensus could in the end coalesce.

CITIZENSHIP IN THE IGC

The provisions on citizenship formed one of the less controversial topics for negotiation in the Intergovernmental Conference, for at least three main reasons. To begin with, no state or institution chose to make the topic into a central plank of its negotiating position or to declare the subject to be among its vital interests in the IGC, either in a positive or negative sense. Although Spain had made citizenship one of the key elements of its submissions to the IGCs, clearly its interests in the negotiations lay elsewhere, for in the end it did not insist on the more ambitious scope of its original proposals.[10] Conversely, states which may have been expected to oppose the introduction of the concept, such as Denmark and the UK, chose other areas of the negotiations in which to make a stand over principles. Others, like France and Germany, pre-occupied in other areas, did not give citizenship the attention that it perhaps deserved.

The same applied to the institutions. In its submissions to the IGC the Commission did not depart substantially from the emerging consensus on what could and could not be included in an acceptable citizenship package, judging its priorities to lie in other reforms.[11] The bare bones of what would be in the eventual Treaty could already be discerned in the Belgian memorandum on Political Union presented in early 1990.[12] Parliament, while it did go further in its citizenship proposals than the Commission, clearly saw its priority to be the traditional demand for legislative co-decision with the Council.[13] Certain aspects of a putative common citizenship with a particular bearing on Parliament's effective-ness, such as a uniform voting system for its elections, did not figure prominently in its attempts to influence the IGC, while others, such as a parliamentary ombudsman to investigate citizens' complaints, did not result from its initiatives.[14]

The second reason for the uncontroversial nature of the citizenship dossier was that it was deliberately kept that way. There was an early consensus among the negotiators that a series of more sensitive issues, including border controls and internal security, should be deliberately excluded from its terms of reference and relegated to the separate pillar. It was undoubtedly this strategy of separation which made it possible for the British, among others, eventually to accept citizenship.

In the Spanish proposals, first put forward by Prime Minister Gonzalez at the Madrid European Council in June 1989, citizenship was made into one of three fundamental 'pillars of reform' together with Emu and foreign policy.[15] In practice citizenship was used as code for all reforms aimed at overcoming the democratic deficit, including legislative co-decision for Parliament. The subsequent consensus deliberately avoided any notion of a common citizenship involving generalised democratic rights for individuals as participants in EC decision-making. Instead it favoured the more familiar and more re-strictive notion of citizenship based on freedom of movement which affected only those citizens who actually exercised their right to move to another member state to live and work. Equally, social rights, although linked to citizenship in the proposals of Spain, the Commission, the Parliament and even in the conclusions of European Council meetings, were too explosive an issue in the negotiations to be upgraded by linking them explicitly with citizenship in a Treaty text, to which there was both national and ideological opposition.[16]

Another factor in making the subject of citizenship more palatable to the member states was the tacit agreement to avoid any notion of 'fundamental rights'. This had two different aspects. The first was the omission in the citizenship provisions of any reference to human rights. The incorporation of the European Convention on Human Rights (ECHR) into Treaty law, which had been proposed in the IGC submissions of both the Parliament and the Commission, was deliberately avoided, partly because it could have meant the extension of rights to individuals from non-EC countries.[17] In the second place, the Treaty avoids any presentation of citizenship rights in a formal document like a charter addressed directly to the citizen. Most national citizenships base themselves on a statement of fundamental rights similar to the ECHR, in which some rights are universal and others reserved to citizens. The IGC, however, was opposed to framing the new citizenship in a formal charter or bill of rights, such as Parliament's 1989 Declaration of Fundamental Rights. This would have been a much stronger legal form, giving individuals more accessible protection.

CITIZENSHIP IN THE MAASTRICHT TREATY

Citizenship proved to be relatively uncontroversial because its provisions were not over-ambitious in scope when viewed against developments already underway in this field before the IGC was launched. The texts on citizenship which emerged from Maastricht represented a codification of existing trends in both jurisprudence and legislation which added little to what was already in the pipeline or being practised. In effect the member states preferred to use the occasion of constitutional change as a means of ending a period of uncertainty and disagreement in the normal process of EC decision-making rather than fundamentally altering the constitution by adding new objectives, policy content or procedures – even in some areas where a fresh policy response was badly needed.

Even Article 8c, apparently a genuine innovation establishing consular assistance for EC citizens by the diplomatic representations of other member states in third countries where their own state is not represented, had been many years in preparation within the framework of European Political Cooperation. Such assistance is already established practice to some extent, often on a bilateral basis between certain member states, and occurs on a large scale during emergencies like the Gulf

War or in dealings with difficult regimes. The rights that made up the new citizenship were given a prominent position at the beginning of Title II in a revamped and expanded Article 8. Reference to the ECHR was made, but tucked away in the Common Provisions which form the *chapeau* of the three-pillared Treaty. The content of this reference was already present in a 1977 Joint Declaration on Fundamental Rights or in the preamble of the Single Act.[18] Moreover, by declaring that the Union should respect fundamental rights 'as they result from the constitutional traditions common to the Member States, as general principles of law' it merely codified long-standing jurisprudence of the Court of Justice and did not give the Court any more leeway for applying the Convention in EC law than it had already acquired.[19]

Nevertheless, the inscription of formal rights to free movement and residence in Article 8a is certainly welcome and should help citizens to enforce their rights more effectively. Giving these rights general application to all individuals irrespective of their economic function will also go some way to clarifying a legal situation left unclear by the Court's piecemeal extension of Treaty rights before Maastricht. Although freedom of movement under the Treaty of Rome applied in theory only to certain economic categories of persons – workers, the self-employed and providers of services – these categories were expanded by the Court in its judgements over the years to ever greater number of activities and circumstances.[20] The category 'worker' was enlarged to include those looking for work while the freedom to provide services was extended to include the freedom to receive services as well.[21]

Much legal uncertainty remains, however, as to how far the Court's concept of freedom of movement can extend. In addition, apart from procedural improvements the existing provisions detailing freedom of movement are left unchanged, implying that certain restrictions they place on the exercise of this freedom will be maintained unaffected by the apparently wider scope of Article 8a. By making the right to free movement and residence subject to the rest of the Treaty – notably the justice and home affairs pillar – and existing legislation, the seemingly general and unlimited scope of the new rights is in fact substantially circumscribed.

Furthermore, installing rights of residence and political rights in the Treaty merely confirmed existing (and problematic) legislation in the case of the former, although in the case of the latter it unblocked legislative proposals which had been languishing for years in the doldrums of the EC decision-making process.[22] The directives on right of residence impose the condition that the persons exercising the right must have sufficient resources in order not to place a financial burden on the state in which they are residing. This is problematic because it seems to run counter to judgements by the Court which rule that such

110

restrictions are illegal. Instead of taking the opportunity to remove this dubious financial precondition, the IGC took fright at the prospect of the harmonisation of social assistance, on the grounds that people would be keen to move into member states with the highest welfare payments.

The component of the Treaty on political rights was based on existing legislative proposals which had proven too difficult to adopt in Council. The Commission brought forward new proposals in the latter half of 1993 in a successful attempt to adopt legislation in time for the European Parliament elections of 1994.[23] National elections were excluded by the Treaty text just as they had been in the proposed legislation. Some expected the Treaty to be more ambitious, and proposals from the Spanish and others did call for the right to vote and stand for election in national elections.[24] They argued that citizens who are long-term residents in a member state of which they are not nationals should eventually be given equal rights to participate in national votes. The Maastricht ratification process showed, however, that this area is a political minefield, for the fact that the Treaty gave voting rights to 'foreigners' was one of the most potent weapons its opponents could mobilise against it.

Member governments made much of the fact that they were able to include a right to petition the European Parliament in the Treaty and the creation of a parliamentary ombudsman to investigate complaints about maladministration by EC institutions.[25] The UK in particular praised these innovations and claimed they originated in its own campaign to rein in the Commission. Especially when combined with the new power of the Parliament to institute committees of enquiry (see Chapter Thirteen) these provisions do strengthen parliamentary scrutiny in the Community. However, the Parliament on its own initiative had accepted the right of individuals to petition it since its own inception in 1953.[26]

As for the parliamentary Ombudsman, this may be a desirable but not a sufficient innovation. The Ombudsman was seen by the British government as a stick with which to beat the Commission. But the nub of most complaints by the public seems to concern the implementation of EC policy by national authorities, and not the substance of the policy itself. This is particularly true in cases concerning the treatment of EC citizens by national immigration authorities: an area of fundamental importance to the exercise of European citizenship itself. Here there is a real need for some kind of EC-based procedure offering citizens a means of redress. Article 138e, on the contrary, seems to restrict the Ombudsman's powers of enquiry to maladministration by the Community institutions. It is also not clear that setting up one central office to investigate all complaints throughout the Community is the best approach. A more decentralised, nationally based system may have proven more effective, particularly in investigating maladministration by the member states, and would have been more in keeping with the principle of subsidiarity.

The saving grace of the citizenship provisions of Maastricht is that they allow for their further development by the Community institutions (but only by the Council acting unanimously after consulting the Parliament). This possibility is separate from the revision of the Treaty foreseen for 1996, which could also have consequences for citizenship and particularly for its relationship with the justice and home affairs pillar.

COOPERATION IN JUSTICE AND HOME AFFAIRS: A SECURITY DILEMMA

The central preoccupation of Title VI of the Treaty is the internal security of the Union. The campaign to abolish European Community border controls soon became entwined around consideration of the common policies on third-country nationals, asylum-seekers, visas and illegal immigrants which would be needed to create a common external frontier for the single market. The potential benefits of the latter for EC citizens and residents were in practice submerged by a preoccupation with the more negative issues raised by the former.

Cooperation in justice and home affairs was in a general sense analogous to cooperation in defence, and placed member states in a similar dilemma. Governments felt compelled to cooperate to counter a perceived threat, and to the extent that cooperation meant a loss of national control, their sense of insecurity increased. They viewed the impending loss of their ability to make checks at their mutual borders as increasing the potential of international crime, including terrorism, drug trafficking, money laundering, insider dealing as well as fraud against the EC itself, organised crime, and public order offences such as football hooliganism and violent political demonstrations. Clearly, greater cooperation between national police and security forces would be necessary. An additional threat was perceived in the loss of the ability to control immigration. Here again, the need for closer cooperation was accepted, for migratory flows were already a growing international problem affecting all member states. This had taken on the dimensions of a pan-European crisis as the number of asylum-seekers and illegal immigrants grew during the years preceding Maastricht.

EC governments bundled together all these types of cross-border crime along with illegal immigration into a general internal security threat which would justify very close police cooperation and would lead them even to accept a European police agency or authority. Concern about the degree of cooperation needed to cope with these problems came to override all other considerations and, in the end, to hamper the achievement of free movement of persons. Governments did not welcome the prospect of giving up their own policies while common EC measures were not yet agreed or in force. Yet it was their reluctance to give up national control of these policy areas which made it more difficult to agree on the common measures. Only in certain matters of 'administrative policing' did it prove possible to adopt some of the required measures in the normal way, producing, for example, EC directives on firearms and ammunition, money laundering, insider dealing and data protection as well as an EC regulation to discourage the use of certain substances.[27] But member governments generally preferred intergovernmental cooperation to deal with the more sensitive issues.

COOPERATION BEFORE MAASTRICHT

Cooperation in justice and police matters was already well established on an *ad hoc basis* before Maastricht. Internal security cooperation took place on several levels ranging from the global (UN, Interpol) to the regional (Council of Europe) and the bilateral. The legal basis for this activity was always slight and often chaotic: Interpol, for example, has no international treaty framework. This was partly explained by the fact that cooperation usually took the form of the informal exchange of, sometimes sensitive, information. This was the method to which officials were accustomed, and it was not surprising that they sought to continue in the same fashion under Maastricht.

The first initiatives had been taken in the context of European Political Cooperation during the 1970s, which served as a model for internal security cooperation until its codification in the Maastricht Treaty. The European Council created the 'Trevi' group in 1975 as a framework for internal security cooperation, particularly against terrorism. These meetings of justice and interior ministers and their officials eventually expanded in scope to include illegal immigration, organised crime, preparations for the completion of the internal market and, more recently, preparations for the establishment of Europol. Activities decided within the Trevi framework were supervised by senior officials from the twelve interior ministries and by Working Group meetings held twice a year.[28] Another significant forum in the EC context became the Ad Hoc Group on Immigration, set up in 1986 under Trevi to deal with immigration issues arising from the relaxation of border controls. It was assisted by the Rhodes Group of Coordinators (so-called because it was set up by the Rhodes European Council in December 1988), which made the first systematic attempt to list the measures that would compensate for the internal security and immigration problems caused by the abolition of border controls. It laid out a timetable for the completion of the single market and the realisation of free movement of people.

The Ad Hoc Group was responsible for the drafting of both the Dublin Asylum Convention and the External Borders Convention, which were to form the major legal instruments on which the external frontier of the Union would rest. The External Borders Convention, modelled on the Schengen Agreement, would define the notion of the EC external border and ruled that persons crossing the external border at any point other than authorised crossing points should be liable to sanctions. The Convention would also determine what would constitute 'effective surveillance', the competent authorities for the exercise of controls, the criteria for allowing entry, the identity documents required, the drawing up of a computerised list of persons to be refused entry, carrier liability sanctions, and the common list of countries whose nationals would require a visa for entry.

The degree of cooperation and implied loss of national control that was acceptable varied from state to state, which accounted for the growth of 'variable geometry' in this area. Although the Schengen Agreement could only be acceded to by EC member states, its provisions were held to be compatible with EC legislation and it was intended to serve as a testing ground for measures that could be adopted later by the EC, not all member states joined. It went too far for some countries, by including provisions for such things as cross-border surveillance and hot pursuit, and the exchange of information through the Schengen Information System. The signatories agreed to dismantle their border controls as from 1 December 1993 but the group of countries which had acceded to Schengen at a later stage (Italy, Spain and Portugal) were unable to satisfy all the necessary conditions by that date. Furthermore, the new government in France, one of the original five signatories, also had reservations, and implementation was postponed at first until February 1994 and then indefinitely. Meanwhile there seems no likelihood that the three non-signatories, the UK, Ireland and Denmark, will agree to abolish their border controls. The delays in the signing and ratification of Schengen and the Conventions of the Twelve are sometimes blamed on technical problems, arising for example from the setting up of an international data exchange system, or on legal problems, for example the constitutional changes necessitated in both Germany and France. However, political concern about the impact of immigration and other internal security problems seems to be the more dominant factor.

AMBIGUITIES OF THE MAASTRICHT TREATY

The Maastricht Treaty provisions are an uneasy compromise between the need to cooperate and a reluctance to give up controls and share burdens. The uneasiness is reflected in the preamble to the Treaty, in which the signatories reaffirm 'their objective to facilitate the freedom of movement of persons while ensuring the safety and security of their peoples'. At the two extremes of this compromise were the UK, whose island-state is not much threatened, and Germany, which is open and exposed at the crossroads of a continent. In the IGC, the UK was in the forefront of wanting to continue with primarily intergovernmental methods. Only visa policy, at the insistence of the Germans, was successfully tacked on to the EC pillar. And, again largely due to German pressure, a half-hearted attempt was made to lay down a stricter time-table for the introduction of a common asylum policy in a Treaty Declaration.

Member states were clearly not ready to view the European Union as a 'regional model for the development of supranational criminal justice' capable of policing a common external frontier.[29] Opposition to the transfer of sovereignty in these fields was very pronounced among national delegations.[30] The officials involved in internal security were less familiar with European integration than their foreign ministry colleagues. Moreover, Denmark feared it would be dominated by the larger states if common policies were developed by supranational methods. And after admitting the failure of its attempts to deal with some of these issues as normal single market measures, the Commission also accepted that the intergovernmental method was the only way to deal with this area of policy.[31]

Nevertheless, the fact remains that in the Treaty criminal and police matters as well as immigration and policies towards third-country nationals are recognised for the first time as a legitimate area in which to have a joint policy. Under Maastricht, cooperation in this field was indeed brought closer to the Community framework. The scope of cooperation outlined in Article K.1 is comprehensive, embracing almost the whole panoply of national policies in this field. And it has to be acknowledged that even if the general political objection to the transfer of sovereignty to the EC were swept aside it would remain technically very difficult to integrate police and home affairs. It would imply the harmonisation of criminal law, criminal law procedure and law enforcement: a formidable proposition. (As we see in Chapter 14, the scrupulous application of the principle of subsidiarity to further integration in the problematical area of individual rights under the rule of EC law is of paramount importance.)

The Maastricht solution may best be described as hybrid: essentially

115

intergovernmental but with a dash of the supranational, mainly pooling sovereignty but also partly transferring it. The extent to which the Community method prevails will depend on how these ambiguities are resolved. The inclusion of these matters in the Treaty succeeded in formalising existing cooperation and in streamlining existing procedures. Article K.3 states that the member states 'shall inform and consult one another within the Council' with a view to coordinating policies. This provides a legal basis for the existing networking between the EC ministries of justice and interior. But the procedures do not completely follow the normal Community pattern. The key lies in calling the existing ministerial meetings 'the Council'. The Commission and the European Parliament are, however, still in a fairly weak position.

Only visa policy, obviously one of the key elements of a common external frontier, is made subject to normal EC legislative procedure, albeit initially in its weakest form with unanimity required in Council, and Parliament only consulted.[32] In addition, the Commission's normally exclusive right of initiative seems qualified by Article 100c(4), which obliges it to consider requests from member states to make proposals. Although in some ways visa policy remains intimately linked with the justice and home affairs pillar, a disjunction is created between it and the other policies which could cause confusion. The national approach to these matters tends to treat visas routinely as part of general immigration policy. But in other respects, Article 100c is comprehensive: it lays down the responsibility of the Council for deciding on the list of third states whose nationals will require a visa to enter the Union, and it provides for a Community response to emergencies in other countries causing a sudden influx of people (in which case the Council could decide to re-impose visas).

On the intergovernmental side, for some policies the Commission is given a right of initiative, and these can in the future become integrated in the legal and institutional framework of the EC, becoming subject to the same procedures as visa policy.[33] This applies to asylum, border controls, immigration, drugs, fraud and judicial cooperation in civil matters. For other policies, the Commission does not have the right to make proposals and the policies concerned may not in future be transferred to the Community framework.[34] This applies to cooperation in criminal matters, customs and police cooperation.

So far, so clear: a firm distinction seems to have been made between those areas partly elevated into the Community sphere of competence, those which can be elevated at some future date and those which are far from being so elevated. Yet, as in areas of 'administrative policing', the boundaries between different types of EC competence are beginning to erode.[35] This is the justification for giving the Commission a shared right of initiative in some areas. For example, the fight against EC budgetary fraud is one instance of an area of law enforcement already subject to EC competence.[36] Another policy already present within the Community framework is the combating of drug addiction. The European Parliament and the Commission in particular have already been working in this important area, which has strong connections with the health and social policies pursued by the Community.[37] For these reasons it was perhaps surprising to see it brought under the inter-governmental pillar.

In Article K.1 (7–9), on the other hand, the justification for not giving the Commission the power of proposal is that the EC had no competence. Yet customs cooperation is included here despite the fact that a customs union lies at the heart of the original common market, and the Commission has been running a customs information exchange programme for years. It remains to be seen whether customs agencies can sort out for which activities they are covered by EC or Title VI procedures. Indeed, it is one of the advantages of using the EC framework that the purposes and scope of a policy have to be spelt out quite precisely. The fact that the scope of the policies subject to intergovernmental procedures is not specified in detail allows much room for conflict between institutions and member states and will doubtless lead to confusion. This is most serious in sensitive areas like criminal justice and terrorism, where some of the potential issues, such as extradition, are so contentious that member governments are probably happy not to be specific.

One of the most deliberate and significant institutional ambiguities is the role of the new Coordinating Committee 'consisting of senior officials' set up by Article K.4. The various existing intergovernmental fora such as Trevi, the Ad Hoc Group on Immigration and the Mutual Assistance Group will henceforth be coordinated by this over-arching committee. This marks the demise of the Trevi Group, and inasmuch as the committee can successfully coordinate and serve the Council like a specialised Coreper it will be a step towards greater efficiency and formality. But to the extent that the K4 Committee performs the preparatory legislative functions of Coreper in relation to Council it fails to build on the experience of the Community institutions and lessens the significance of calling the meetings of justice and interior ministers 'the Council'. The K4 Committee is likely to be made up of national officials visiting Brussels to represent their own departments, whereas Coreper consists of national officials based in Brussels with general responsibilities and a tendency to be more inclined to identify common interests than their domestic colleagues. The new committee may even prejudice Coreper's role in the one area of justice and home affairs to be brought under the EC Treaties: visa policy.

Also problematic is the coordinating committee's relationship with the

Commission, for the committee has a mixture of consultative and advisory tasks, including to 'give opinions for the attention of Council, either at the Council's request or at its own initiative'. This seems to imply that it will have an executive input into the drafting of measures to be adopted by Council, thereby encroaching further on the Commission's already restricted right of initiative under Article K.1. The Commission can perhaps exercise influence through the provision that it is to be 'fully associated' with the work done in this pillar. This implies that the Commission will not have to ask permission to be informed or to give its own opinions about the work of the K4 Committee and the various other intergovernmental fora. But the normal functions of the Commission are restricted in their application to Title VI by the terms of Article K.8(1), which ensures that the Commission's responsibility under Article 155 to ensure the application of the Treaty and to guarantee its right to participate 'in the formulation of the acts of the Council' does not apply to Title VI. These are serious limitations on the Commission's influence in policy formation.

DEMOCRATIC AND JUDICIAL CONTROL

It is clear that the role of the Court of Justice and the European Parliament is going to be less important for the evolution of the third pillar than that of the Commission. The key battleground for the delivery of policy will be in the relations between Council, Commission, K4 Committee and Coreper. But from the point of view of the citizen, the principal drawback of Title VI is that it is deliberately insulated from democratic control by the Parliament and from judicial review by the Court.

The exclusion of the Court from justice and home affairs policy is decreed partly by Treaty provision and partly by decision-making procedures. Article L of the Treaty ensures that the powers of the Court will not apply to Title VI. Interestingly, however, they will apply to Article L itself and thus the Court can be called upon to deliver judgement on the legality of its exclusion from Title VI. The other problem is that decisions taken under Article K do not need to take the form of a Community legal act, such as regulations or directives. Its principal measures are to be adopted as agreements between member states along the lines of the conventions or as implementing measures adopted under conventions. Article K.3(2)c does allow such conventions to stipulate that they fall under the jurisdiction of the Court, and this is the case with the Schengen Agreement. Apart from complaints brought by one EC institution against another, it is difficult to see how individual citizens can bring complaints before the Court for an infringement of rights – for example, in respect of border controls – by national authorities acting under a convention. However, the jurisdiction of the Court has always tended to expand. There was a considerable legal debate prior to Maastricht about the extent to which certain sectors of national jurisdiction could remain closed to the influence of EC law. The case law of the Court demonstrates increasingly that the strict separation of criminal law from EC law is wearing thin and criminal law is not immune to Community intrusion. It is not unlikely, especially under the institutional provisions of the Treaty, that the Court will in future gain marginal jurisdiction over Title VI.[38]

The marginalisation of the Court is more significant given that matters touched upon by Title VI will often have an impact on civil liberties: the External Borders Convention, for example, provides for the introduction of a fingerprint index and a joint list of undesirable aliens. Article K.2 rules that all matters of justice and home affairs cooperation must be dealt with in compliance with the European Convention on Human Rights. Although this recalls the provision elsewhere in the Treaty that the Union in general would respect the principles of the ECHR, a number of questions remain about the practical scope of the protection offered. First, the situation as to which courts and procedures are open to receive complaints is confused. Some member states have incorporated the ECHR into national law, others have not. It is also unclear if the new Treaty provisions go further than existing jurisprudence of the Court of Justice or merely confirm it as regards the degree to which the ECHR can be applied within EC law. The responsibility of national courts is also left vague in respect of their obligation to refer any matter concerning interpretation of the Treaties to the Court of Justice. In the kind of hypothetical case which might become commonplace, for example a Dutch national being arrested by French police officers on the basis of incorrect Spanish data, it would be unclear where, when and how an appeal could be made.

A second pressing question is the manner in which third-country nationals will be protected against discriminatory behaviour by law enforcement officials, especially in the light of increased internal controls, on-the-spot identity checks and the international compilation and exchange of data on asylum-seekers and illegal immigrants. Thirdly, although this Title is designed not to affect the responsibilities of member states in the maintenance of law and order and the safeguarding of internal security, there is some question as to whether the same protection of individual rights will apply when member states exercise their right to invoke these exceptions. As became apparent with the political interpretation of Article 8a EEC internal security considerations may in some cases be allowed to override the principle of free movement of people, thus giving rise to legal challenges.

The potential threat to fundamental rights was of course a significant risk in the choice of the intergovernmental method, and it was here that normative concerns about legal remedies and democratic accountability overlapped.[39] Before the Treaty was ratified few people predicted how much the lack of involvement of ordinary citizens in Community procedures would make Europe seem remote and threatening, and cause many of them to reject Maastricht. This was particularly the case with the matters covered by Title VI. Whereas Parliament's role in respect of the new citizenship in Article 8 was enhanced, like that of the Court of Justice, the member states hoped to keep it excluded from Title VI. Not following the normal legislative method means that Parliament cannot propose amendments, but is merely to be kept informed and consulted on principal aspects of policy, and Council is to take its views into consideration. The lack of accountability and transparency under this Title seem set to become a problem once cooperation, particularly between police forces, becomes day-to-day routine.[40] Some national parliaments, including those of the Netherlands and Denmark, are sufficiently wary of the possibility of their governments evading scrutiny in this sphere that they have expressed considerable reservations about the Title VI procedures and demanded, and sometimes received, new procedures to compensate.

This lack of democratic scrutiny may also be relevant in relation to the new international policing institution foreseen by the Treaty (Europol). The clear intention behind this innovation is to have a body better able to meet the particular needs of the Union than Interpol's European secretariat. Europol's remit is thus wider and it has the potential to develop executive powers. Some member states may see in it the embryo of a future FBI for Europe. The extent to which it will be embedded in the institutional system of the EC and placed under democratic supervision by Parliament remains to be settled by a special convention, which itself falls outside the range of legal acts which Parliament can influence. The relationships between Europol, Interpol and other law enforcement agencies, such as the Drug Enforcement Agency, as well as its relationship with Schengen and the External Borders Convention remain a matter for speculation. It is as yet unclear how Europol will relate to the new K4 Committee or to other existing arrangements for sharing information.

THE FUTURE OF TITLE VI

The Treaty's provisions on cooperation in justice and home affairs leave the impression of being very much a temporary arrangement, shaped by the same teleological spirit that characterises the mainstream EC institutions. They are not a permanent end in themselves but are geared to the achievement of fixed objectives, possessing a certain dynamic quality with deadlines and the possibility of institutional reform. At the 1996

IGC there will be a decision about whether or not Title VI should be transferred to the EC, and whether or not the European Parliament should have more influence in matters concerning justice and home affairs.[41]

How far and how fast this tier becomes integrated with normal EC Treaties will be affected by the determination of the Commission to implement Article 7a of the Treaty concerning the free movement of persons.[42] The Commission has come under considerable pressure from Parliament, which adopted a resolution in July 1993 blaming it for failure to take the necessary steps to ensure free movement of persons within the Community, on which basis Parliament has proceeded to take the Commission before the Court of Justice alleging failure to fulfil its obligations under the Treaty. Moreover, notwithstanding the slowness of their ratification, there are considerable similarities between the Schengen Agreements and the External Borders Convention and so it might only be a matter of time before Schengen will be superseded by a Community instrument adopted by all twelve member states.

WHAT FUTURE FOR THE EUROPEAN CITIZEN?

For those who believe that the Community should become a federal union, the creation of a citizenship, and the pooling of responsibilities for the whole range of related policies on non-citizens, indicate the importance of the Treaty of Maastricht – despite the fact that most of the related policies on non-citizens are put in an intergovernmental pillar. Although the description 'federal' was rejected by the IGC, the inclusion of citizenship may ultimately prove to be more radical, and it gives federalists something positive on which they might build in future. For those opposed to the Treaty, citizenship and cooperation in justice and home affairs appear as worrying confirmation that the EC does indeed threaten to become some kind of large state which will obliterate national sovereignty and identity. For them, the Union's encroachment on such intimate areas of national life as citizenship and immigration is anathema.

The reality lies somewhere in between. It was indeed encouraging for federalists that the concept of citizenship should have been attached to a Community whose core function at the time was still the single market; and the inclusion of 'political rights' in that citizenship was yet more encouraging. But, as in other areas of the Treaty, there was a big gap between its rhetoric and substance. In the case of citizenship, member states experienced great difficulty in giving practical expression to their ambitions almost immediately after they had signed at Maastricht. The ratification process, particularly in France and Denmark, suggested that citizenship was among those parts of the Treaty to which public opinion

reacted with greatest sensitivity. Since it necessitated specific constitutional or legal changes in all countries, opponents had ample opportunity to express their dislike of the reform and to play on the fears it
generated. In this sense, the anti-federalists proved to be right about the
controversial nature of European citizenship.

The potential contribution of the Maastricht Treaty provisions for
citizenship to the further development of European Union should not
be overestimated. For one thing, because it must rely on measures taken
in the intergovernmental pillar for its success, national control in this
area will remain strong. Nor should one exaggerate the degree to which
this form of citizenship represents an extension of EC powers and an
erosion of national sovereignty. In substance it consists of a series of
minor changes which were already on the horizon in 1990 and might
have been introduced sooner or later whether the Maastricht Treaty had
come along or not. It affects directly only a certain number of citizens
and applies mainly to their relationship with the member state in which
they reside. This already modest, partial citizenship was rendered even
less significant by its entanglement with the provisions on intergovernmental cooperation in justice and home affairs; and its future will be
linked with the fate of that ambiguous pillar.

A more comprehensive citizenship could have contained enumerated
political and social rights in relation to the European institutions as well
as the member states. Moreover, it could have bestowed rights on
everyone within the Union and not just those who make use of freedom
of movement and residence. That would have been a truly radical
innovation pointing clearly in the direction of a federal future for
Europe. So far, there is no consensus for such a citizenship.

8

OLD POLICIES AND
NEW COMPETENCES

Alan Butt Philip

The Maastricht Treaty is often represented as the development of a wholly new level and intensity of integration in the European Community. The commitment to Economic and Monetary Union is certainly an important qualitative leap. But while the intergovernmental systems for foreign and security policy and for cooperation on home and judicial affairs are fleshed out and made more visible, they are an evolutionary progression of existing commitments, policies, practices and procedures; and the same applies to many of the amendments to the existing EC Treaties. The consolidation of past policies and agreements into treaty-based commitments of the new European Union is indeed one of the most striking yet least recognised features of the Maastricht Treaty. This becomes very evident when the Treaty is read as a whole and when it is asked how the Treaty affects the existing policies of the Union. The Treaty is as much about consolidating the *acquis communautaire* and the *de facto* institutional arrangements as it is about innovation through policies and structures.

The Treaty does specify some competences to which the earlier Treaties did not refer. In addition to the commitment to develop and administer Emu there is, for example, the common visa policy; and partial competences are stipulated in the fields of public health, education, youth, culture, industrial policy and transport infrastructure, where previously the Community's activities were based on other Treaty articles and were thus somewhat tentative. The new treaty articles therefore confer upon the EU, and especially the Commission as the prime initiator in the decision-making system, a more certain foundation upon which to build up a policy portfolio, should this be desired. The exercise of concurrent powers is normal in any federal system of government where decision-making is shared and the structure of political institutions is balanced. In the quasi-federal system that is the European Union, the concept of the Union holding partial (in effect concurrent, but limited) competences should occasion few surprises. Few indeed would wish to see a remorseless accumulation of powers in the hands of the central government of the EU based in Brussels. Thus, the more decision-making shifts to Brussels, usually for eminently practical reasons, the more likely it is that partial rather than exclusive competences are given to the European Union. Where competence is shared between the EU and the member states then, of course, under Article 3b, the test of subsidiarity has to be applied.

It is possible, in any event, to attach too much significance to Treaty amendments as far as policies are concerned. Key changes of policy and approach have more often occurred by the new use of existing powers by existing Community institutions. It was by just such means that the EC developed its regional and environmental policies from the early 1970s (using Article 235 of the EEC Treaty) and that the Court of Justice has developed policies such as mutual recognition of standards through interpretation of the Treaties. To an important extent the Single European Act as well as the Maastricht Treaty served to codify and to set a seal on developments and decisions which had already taken place. Thus the Treaty records changes in the fields of activity of the Community which predate its signature in 1992 in the areas of public health, education and culture, consumer protection, industrial policy and the development of trans-European networks.

COST AND IMPLEMENTATION

The logic of the single market has also pointed in the direction of expanding the competences of the Community. A series of spill-over effects have been evident in the inclusion of fields of policy such as health, industrial competitiveness, immigration, refugees and asylum, air and sea transport, secondary and higher education (as opposed to vocational training) and infrastructure. There has also been a marked increase in interest in the implementation, monitoring and evaluation of the Community's policies and policy instruments. The notion of, at last, establishing a level playing field for the whole of the single market has proved to be a powerful motive for developing its powers, and especially those of the Commission, to ensure that the rules of the market are applied consistently and equitably and that the taxes levied in the member states to speed the process of European integration are properly controlled and give value for money. The applications of EC competition law, especially in relation to state aids, are an important example of this trend, as is the emphasis in the fourth and fifth environmental action programmes on stronger implementation and enforcement of EC environmental laws. There has likewise been growing emphasis on monitoring and evaluation of the impact of EC-funded programmes of regional development.

The Maastricht Treaty takes this approach two stages further, first by specifying that one of the aims of the new Cohesion Fund is to assist poorer member states with the costs of implementing EC environmental standards and, secondly, by providing in Article 171 that the Court of Justice may fine member states for not implementing EC laws.

In any development of the competences of the EU one should not assume that there is a well-founded rationale at work separating out those areas of policy which require further extensions of the Union treaty base from those where no change is required. The real impetus for extensions of competence has come from political pressures from within the EC institutions and within particular member states. There was no overriding logic in the choice of agriculture and transport as the first two common sectoral policies in the original EEC Treaty: these happened to be the subjects that founder members required to be covered, and where they thought there were distinct advantages to be gained from setting policy at the Community level. Agriculture is untouched by the Maastricht Treaty, when a substantial revision would have been in order; and the coverage of transport is only a by-product of the commitment to the development of the trans-European networks and the new Cohesion Fund for the poorest regions, although there is a good case for revising the Treaty provisions on transport in the light of judgements in the Court of Justice from 1985 onwards and the great extension of scope of the transport policy that has arisen. Instead, other sectors have been included in the Treaty on European Union which seem not to have needed to be: for example, public health and consumer protection. Political pressures account for the somewhat random distribution of gifts from the Maastricht Christmas tree. Some fields, such as the energy market and public sector monopolies, where there was a real need for a new treaty framework for policy development, have not been touched at all.

A consequence of the new policies and prominence attached to several existing Community activities had been the relative downgrading of the Common Agricultural Policy, which has moved from the centre of EC policy-making as attention has focused on the single market, the structural funds and Emu. The less sacrosanct the CAP, the easier it has been to press for its reform and to constrain its development financially. Yet the clash between CAP and other sectoral interests over the Gatt negotiations in 1992–93 shows how important agriculture remains politically despite the decline in its share of GNP.

It is also useful to analyse the distinction between those of the EU's policies which are expenditure-driven and those which are not. Some of the most important of the EU's powers do not impose direct costs on the Union's budget, other than costs of administration. These include the commercial policy and competition policy where the EU has exclusive competence, but where little budgetary expenditure is called for. On the other hand, the regional policy in the EU is almost wholly based on expenditure, with a serious interest in a common regional policy only developing on the back of the single market programme adopted in 1985. Even in the 1990s, the main effort of the Community in regional policy has been to find ever larger sums of money for the structural funds, the new Cohesion Fund and the European Investment Bank so as to defend its impact upon regional development.

In effect the same point applies in the area of social policy, although the Commission's intentions have been different. For years, the EC was able to find limited funds for vocational training through the Social Fund but was unable to agree much legislation. The ambitions of the Commission to redress this imbalance were rekindled in the late 1980s and made some headway in the Social Charter of 1989 and the social action programme of the same year, but with very limited results to date. The Maastricht Treaty now greatly extends the scope of the EU's remit in legislating on social policy although still mainly in the field of employment law. In some other policy areas such as transport and the environment where early EEC activities have been regulatory rather than financial, the new Treaty occasions further EU expenditure programmes for building trans-European networks and implementing the Union's environmental standards. In general, however, the Maastricht Treaty develops policy commitments and competences, such as Emu, the CFSP, and judicial and home affairs, where relatively few extra burdens will fall upon the budget of the Union directly. If there are financial costs arising from the implementation of these policies they will be met almost wholly by the member states.

The Maastricht Treaty reflects the EU's growing concern for a broadly even level of implementation, application and enforcement of the Union's laws in order to secure the 'level playing field'. The specific elements in the Treaty touching upon this subject have been dealt with above. But since the late 1980s there has been a growing appreciation of the need for EU-wide monitoring, evaluation and possible enforcement agencies to oversee the way the rules of the Union and its single market are implemented. This poses something of an institutional dilemma for the Commission, for whereas under the founding Treaties it could legitimately be entrusted directly with such functions, there is a practical limit to how much it can in its present form do, and a political limit to what the member states are prepared to allow it to do. The result so far has been that the Commission is not being entrusted with new powers, resources or functions to cover this aspect of policy administration, and the Commission itself has proposed that new Union-wide specialist agencies should be set up for this purpose: thus, for example, environmental standards, medicine evaluation, testing and certification for satisfaction of European technical standards, health and safety in the workplace, and veterinary inspection have been suggested as suitable candidates for such agencies. The justification for EU-wide agencies is mainly that the functions of inspection and control in such areas are very properly national or local in their organisation, but consistency of application and the generation of mutual trust between the various responsible national authorities requires some overarching European supervision, even if this is a relatively 'light touch' affair. The Council of ministers is clearly having difficulty agreeing to such proposals, for example in the field of health and safety, and is in no mood to agree to consistency of penalties to be imposed at national level for breaches of Union rules. Thus the devolutionary side of subsidiarity has so far proved dominant even if it is undermining the foundations of the single market.

Yet to achieve an appropriate perspective on the development by the Maastricht Treaty of the policies and competences of the European Union, it is worth recalling that the critical competences originally conferred upon the EEC remain central and critical in the 1990s: the common market, the common agricultural policy and the common commercial policy (covering external trade). To these three the Treaty has added a fourth key competence, monetary policy. In addition, the Treaty represents a decision by member governments that the Union should embrace several measures of positive integration, notably a single currency and trans-European networks. A programme of negative integration, such as the 1985 White Paper on the single market, cannot alone deliver all the benefits of integration that it appeared to promise.

SUBSIDIARITY

One of the features of the Maastricht Treaty most commented upon has been the 'subsidiarity' principle. This has now become a litmus test to which all new Community initiatives will be subjected, and some parts of the *acquis communautaire* may be subjected to the same test also.

Subsidiarity means different things to different people and to different political and ethical traditions. The original idea of a social and political order where public and private interests are in a balanced and protected relationship one with another has been replaced in Article 3b of the Treaty by a much narrower concept relating to the division of powers between the Community and the member states, whereby the Community 'shall take action . . . only if and in so far as the objectives of the proposed action cannot be sufficiently achieved by the Member States and can therefore, by reason of the scale or effects of the proposed action, be better achieved by the Community'. This Article incorporates for wide application a principle which was introduced by the Single Act for use in the field of environmental policy alone, where Article 130R(4) stated that the Community 'shall take action relating to the environment to the extent to which the (environmental policy) objectives . . . can be attained better at Community level than at the level of individual Member States. Without prejudice to certain measures of a Community nature, the Member States shall finance and implement the other measures.'

The impact of this last Treaty provision will be discussed in the section dealing with environmental policy (pp. 133–5). The Maastricht Treaty now erases this 1986 subsidiarity formulation by the wording of Article 3b, but there are some interesting points of difference. First, the test of attaining a policy objective better by Community action rather than national action is substituted by a test that demands that Community action be initiated only if national action is judged insufficient for the attainment of Community purposes *and* Community action is likely to be more efficacious. Second, the last sentence of Article 130R(4) deals with the financing of environmental policy measures making it clear that this will largely fall upon national governments. Interestingly, the Maastricht Treaty does not extend the use of this rather insubstantial form of words, and it is even discarded from the new environment policy articles in Title II.[1]

One of the most important qualifications to the application of the re-stated subsidiarity principle is that which limits its use to those areas that do not fall within the exclusive competence of the Community. The Maastricht Treaty is silent upon the point of the definition of those matters which are within the exclusive competence of the Community, but it makes clear that many of the new competences written into the Treaty (such as culture, public health, consumer protection and industry policy) are to be exercised concurrently with the member states. Clearly there are the makings of some interesting cases to be sent to the Court of Justice in order to discover just how wide is the Community's exclusive competence. It might be suggested that this would encompass the common policies of agriculture, cross-border transport, the common commercial policy, the management of the single currency, the development of the single market, and the organisation of the customs union. Even if this list gives the broad limits of the exclusive competence, the grey area of what is not within the exclusive competence but where Community action might be justified is still large. At worst, this grey area could fail to be defined by case upon case being sent for adjudication to the Court, especially if, as seems all too likely, member states are not agreed among themselves about what is legitimate Community-level action.

However, a more immediate outcome of the subsidiarity provisions of Maastricht is that the Council will start to apply the test of subsidiarity across a whole range of proposals as they are presented for discussion, and application of such a test will become a matter of political judgement reflecting the balance of political traditions represented in the Council. Nor will the Council be the only EC institution making such judgements; the Parliament and the Commission will also be considering the same points. Indeed, during 1992–93, even before the new Treaty came into force, the Commission began to exercise self-censorship in re-examining the appropriateness of proposed Community legislation, and in withdrawing certain other draft directives and regulations. The Commission, alongside the Council, has been chastened by the difficulty of getting public approval of the new Treaty and is signalling that it intends to exercise its rights of initiative more modestly in future, even if the scope of the Community's competence has been significantly widened.

SOCIAL POLICY

The founders of the ECSC and EEC understood that the economic restructuring expected to be triggered by the establishment of a common market needed to be supported by a social policy that encouraged mobility of labour, the creation of a skilled labour force and acceptance by labour of the contraction as well as the expansion of job opportunities that would be brought about by the liberalisation of markets. The history of social policy development in the EC has been chequered, however, and particularly lacklustre in terms of legislation by the Council. President Delors sought to establish a social dimension to the emerging single market which underscored the original Community concerns for continual social harmony and dialogue. The result was the Commission's Social Charter, which was accepted in watered-down form by eleven of the twelve member states at the European Council at Strasbourg in December 1989. Margaret Thatcher rejected it.

While the new European Social Charter offered hope and encouragement to organised labour and other social groups, earning the strong endorsement of public opinion throughout the Community (Britain included), the realisation of its aims has proved problematical. The Commission deftly linked the agreement on the Social Charter to the publication of its own social action programme, requiring the EC to agree almost 50 legislative measures as well as action to be taken separately by each member state. Major elements in this social action programme encountered stiff opposition within the Council, and not just from the UK. For example, proposed directives on employment benefits accruing to part-time workers, working hours and maternity leave have all been strongly contested, with arguments developing about the legal base under which they were proposed (carrying crucial implications for the type of majority required in the Council to obtain approval) as well as about the advisability of increasing non-wage costs facing employers at a time of rising unemployment and declining European competitiveness.

The 'social chapter' of the Treaty of Maastricht (strictly speaking an Agreement on social policy among all the EC member states apart from the United Kingdom) is the product of the log-jam in the Council of ministers caused by the difficulties in realising the aims of the 1989 Social Charter through the social action programme. Similarly, the Social Protocol, to which the Agreement is appended, and which allows the EC institutions to be used for certain social policy decisions even though the UK has excluded itself from their field of application, reflects the continuing disagreement between member states.

The position the United Kingdom has adopted on EC social policy since the mid-1980s has been complex and not entirely consistent. The UK agreed to the introduction by the Single Act of qualified majority voting for decisions about health and safety at work, and to a clause enabling the Commission to facilitate a dialogue leading to possible agreements between the social partners.[2] By the time of the Maastricht IGC important sections of the Conservative Party had become aware of the implications of European integration in the social policy field and were fiercely opposed to any further development in it. In an attempt to preserve the unity of the government party, British ministers demanded an opt-out from the social chapter and obtained just that, thereby allowing the newly selected prime minister, John Major, to return home triumphant. The UK opt-out, however, created the precedent for the set of agreements conceded to Denmark at the Edinburgh meeting of the European Council in December 1992, and it was also interpreted (within Britain and, more widely, elsewhere) as at best a Pyrrhic victory, and at worst a self-inflicted wound for Britain that damaged the new European Union too.

In the short term, the opt-out on social policy may have bought vital time for Major but in the end it added greatly to the government's difficulties in securing the ratification of the Maastricht Treaty by the House of Commons: its defeat in the vote on the Social Protocol in March 1993, until it could be reversed in a vote of confidence, damaged the government's credibility further. By demanding an opt-out, the UK has also made it easier for the other member states to press ahead with new social policy legislation. This will inevitably have an impact upon British companies with operations in other EU states, but such companies will no longer be able to be represented by the UK government in the Council when the provisions of the Agreement are invoked. These legal and political difficulties are likely to add to the pressures already facing such companies to conform to the EC norm if they are not to deny to their British workers the social benefits and protection that they offer to their employees elsewhere in the Union.

A more elegant and probably more effective answer to British concerns would have been for the UK to have agreed to the social chapter on condition that decisions taken under it should all be made unanimously. Britain could then have controlled the pace of progress on social policy throughout the EU. In the event, the Agreement as drafted allows the Eleven to agree to directives on the basis of qualified majority voting in the fields of health and safety at work, working conditions, the information and consultation of workers, equality between men and women, and the long-term unemployed.[3] The Eleven may also agree to measures, but only if unanimous, concerning social security and the protection of workers and redundant workers, the representation and collective defence of workers' and employers' interests, conditions of employment for third-country nationals, and financial support for employment promotion and creation.[4] Many of those topics featured in the original list of social policy concerns to be found in Article 118 of the EEC Treaty, but the earlier Treaty did not specifically give the Commission the right to propose legislation in most of these areas. Even so, if the social partners so wish, and the Council approves, the making and implementation of social policy in the manner described above can be replaced by contractual Community-wide agreements between management and labour.[5]

Apart from the importance of securing the support of the Conservative party for Maastricht, the UK government's main worry about the expansion of EC social policy legislation concerned the growth of non-wage costs and its adverse consequences for competitiveness and unemployment. The Eleven's Agreement shares these concerns, although they have become much more prominent since the Maastricht Treaty was signed as the recession has deepened.[6] It may even transpire that the provisions of the Social Protocol will be used sparingly precisely because the UK's early reservations are now held more generally.

The compromise at Maastricht on social policy presents the Commission with a continuing difficulty over the choice of legal base for future social policy initiatives. The Commission seems likely to try to legislate for all member states if at all possible, and only to use the Agreement of the Eleven in the last resort. Other institutional complexities introduced by the Agreement (such as the role of MEPs from the UK in the decision-making of the European Parliament on such issues) may also evoke legal wrangles over its interpretation, scope and applicability.

A further factor likely to influence the debate on future European social policy is the desire to achieve a level playing field for competing firms in the single market: this point could be exploited by employers seeking to deregulate the labour market especially in the states that have high non-wage costs, but also (and more commonly) by trade unions wishing to spread across the EC the highest achievable levels of social protection. Yet the regulation of social policy across the internal frontiers of the Union inevitably conflicts with the preservation of distinctive labour market practices and cultures in accordance with the principle of subsidiarity. This conflict between the logic of the single market and the desire to limit the influence of the EC institutions is likely to continue throughout the 1990s and beyond. There is evidence to suggest that in the field of social policy the logic of the single market is likely to prevail. If so, then the British government, so long as it is in Conservative hands, will want to make use of the opt-out gained at Maastricht: it has already indicated as much with regard to the European Works Council Directive applicable to large firms with operations in more than one EU state.[7]

TRANSPORT POLICY

The Maastricht Treaty is formally silent on the subject of transport policy, as was the Single Act. The common transport policy heralded in the EEC Treaty showed little sign of appearing until landmark judgements handed down by the Court of Justice in the mid-1980s broke the log-jam of indecision in the Council. The new Treaty does, however, commit the EC to support the development of trans-European networks (covering transport, telecommunications and energy infrastructure), and this commitment reflects the acceptance by member governments that positive as well as negative measures of harmonisation are necessary if European integration is to become a reality. Integration is much more difficult to achieve when infrastructures are not interlinked.

The new Articles establish that the purpose of any EC intervention to develop trans-European networks is to promote 'the interconnection and interoperability of national networks as well as access to such networks'.[8] This intervention will include the preparation of guidelines to cover the objectives and priorities of measures envisaged by the Community; specific actions to ensure interoperability of networks, especially in the field of technical harmonisation; and financial support for projects of common interest. The Commission is given permission to take any useful initiative to promote coordination of policies between individual member states.

The bid to achieve a more coordinated and better-developed set of infrastructures for the Union as a whole is being crucially underpinned by finance, in both grant and loan form. Substantial funds are being placed at the disposal of the European Investment Bank for this purpose, but the new Cohesion Fund will also contribute to the cost of transport infrastructure development in the four poorest member states (Spain, Portugal, Greece and Ireland). The increases in the structural funds agreed at the Edinburgh Summit in December 1992 should, on their own, more than compensate for the phasing out of the transport

132

infrastructure fund at the end of 1993, bearing in mind that historically the European Regional Development Fund has been dedicated to transport projects, at a level of around 40 per cent of the total monies at its disposal.

Transport policy has received more attention from Brussels because of several institutional and policy developments, rather than because of a change in the treaty base. Not only has the Court of Justice been influential (for example, in holding that air and maritime transport are subject to the full rigours of the competition policy), but the expanding remit of legislation governing the single market, environmental and regional policy has drawn several aspects of transport into the limelight and suggested a need for further technical and fiscal harmonisation, the reduction of state aids to airlines and railway operators (usually controlled by the public sector) and the cartelisation of the shipping industry. This is also a policy area where the uneven implementation of existing EC regulations and the lack of harmonisation of penalties, set at national level, for non-compliance with existing EC laws in the member states is a cause of friction between governments and firms.

Meanwhile, it is evident that the Union is in some ways not an appropriate geographical entity for a common transport policy and the establishment of 'trans-European' transport networks. The critical location of Switzerland and Austria, for example, has enabled these two non-EU countries to reduce the effectiveness of harmonised standards in the commercial road transport sector for EU states by imposing more exacting standards (and even traffic quotas) in order to protect their hard-pressed Alpine environment. The improvement of transport links to Greece will depend on the resolution of the conflict in former Yugoslavia. The enlargement of the European Union and intensified cooperation between it and Central and Eastern Europe will have a big impact upon the shape of its emerging transport policy.

ENVIRONMENTAL POLICY

The new Treaty states that the Community now has a duty to promote 'sustainable and non-inflationary growth respecting the environment'.[9] Environmental action by the EC, the term first used in Article 130R of the Single Act, is now upgraded to environmental policy, but no major development of the scope of such policy is promised. The objectives of environmental policy are once more listed as protecting human health; preserving, protecting and improving the quality of the environment; and the prudent and rational utilisation of natural resources.[10] International action, at regional or world-wide levels, is now also made an objective of the Community's policy. The need for environmental policy to adopt the precautionary principle is enshrined for the first time in the

Treaty, and a stronger requirement is laid upon the EC to integrate all of its policies that bear upon the environment.

The decision-making structure for determining the EC's environment policy is greatly altered, as most environmental policy decisions will now be made using the cooperation procedure.[11] General action programmes setting out priority objectives to be attained by the EC can be settled by the new co-decision system, although unanimity in the Council is retained for decisions primarily of a fiscal nature, most detailed planning and land use matters, water resources management, and major energy issues with significant impacts upon individual member states. Given that the EC has already adopted over two hundred environmental measures under conditions where unanimity was required, the significance of this change in the decision-making rules may be less than it seems. However, with further enlargement in sight and more disparate interests to be accommodated, the change is still significant.

Although the Maastricht Treaty removes the subsidiarity principle from Article 130R of the Single Act, concerning the environment alone, into the wider remit of Article 3b, it is pertinent to observe that, in so far as these matters can be known, the principle of Article 130R was not invoked in discussions within the Council prior to 1992, nor has any challenge to the competence of the EC to act on environmental concerns ever been made to the Court of Justice on the grounds of disrespect for the subsidiarity principle.

The search for subsidiarity is leading the debate on environmental policy in the Community in some strange directions. The newly approved regulation on eco-audits for companies is sometimes cited as a good example of subsidiarity in action, as participation in the EC scheme is voluntary and each member state is left to manage the scheme in its own way. It is particularly ironic that a regulation rather than the more flexible legal instrument of the directive has been used for this purpose. Even more significant was the offer made by President Delors early in 1992 to devolve much of the administration and monitoring of EC environmental regulations to the member states. This offer was not taken up by the Edinburgh European Council. Although the UK presidency approved, numerous business and green organisations protested at Delors's suggestion and begged the EC institutions to keep control in this policy area, their main fear being the application of different (and lower) standards in some member states, and the gradual disintegration of a consistent EC-wide environment policy. The need for the single market with a level playing field can sit uncomfortably alongside demands for subsidiarity. The drive for more even implementation and enforcement of EC environmental laws reflected in the objectives of the fourth and fifth action programmes for environmental policy will be strengthened by the amended Article 171 enabling the Court of Justice to fine member states for non-compliance.

Despite the assertion in the Maastricht Treaty that member states remain responsible for financing environmental policy, the arrangements for the new Cohesion Fund suggest otherwise: the cost of meeting EC environmental standards borne by the four poorest member states will be shared by the new Fund. Indeed all governments are beginning to examine more closely the costs of implementation of environmental law, much of which had not been enforced properly, and this is the motive behind the Anglo-French initiative to review some of the legislation on water quality already adopted by the Community, for example the Directive on urban waste water. It is notable that the costs to member states of implementing higher social regulatory standards have not been put in the same bracket as environmental standards, in terms of the remit of the Cohesion Fund.

REGIONAL POLICY AND THE STRUCTURAL FUNDS

The central commitment of the Treaty to establish Emu by 1999 has greatly increased the role and significance of the Union's regional policy and its structural funds. Even if Emu does not in fact occur on time, the expansion of the structural funds planned for the 1990s is set to take place, just as the earlier European Regional Development Fund survived the demise of the Werner plan in the mid-1970s. There is in fact little in the Maastricht Treaty which directly refers to the regional policy of the Union, the Single Act and subsequent regulations for the three structural funds (Regional Development Fund, Social Fund and Agricultural Guidance Fund) being the formative documents. However, just as the Brussels special meeting of the European Council in February 1988 proved to be the essential financial counterpart to the Single Act, so the conclusions of the Edinburgh European Council in December 1992 on the future structure of the budget of the Union must be seen as the essential financial underpinning of the Maastricht Treaty.

The Treaty itself does, however, set up a new Cohesion Fund whose purposes are to contribute to the finance of trans-European networks (initially only transport infrastructure) and to the cost of meeting EC environmental standards. The Cohesion Fund will, however, be available only to member states with a GNP per head of less than 90 per cent of the EC average in 1992, eligibility to be reviewed in 1996. Such states must also have adopted a programme to achieve the conditions of economic convergence set out in Article 104c of the Maastricht Treaty. The first round beneficiaries of this Fund will be Spain, Portugal, Greece and Ireland. The sums allocated to it amount to Ecu 1.5 billion in 1993, rising to Ecu 2.6 billion in 1999, and the Union will be prepared to offer co-financing of between 80 and 85 per cent of each programme's cost.[12] Nevertheless, the other structural funds and operations will have at their disposal more than ten times the amounts made available to the Cohesion Fund each year, starting at Ecu 19.8 billion in 1993, rising to Ecu 27.4 billion in 1999. Thus by the end of the decade some 35 per cent of the EU budget will be assigned to the various funds and instruments intended to facilitate structural adjustment and regional development in the Union.

The new Treaty also establishes a 189-member Committee of the Regions which is purely advisory and yet has the right to give opinions on its own initiative. The new Committee is the outcome of a very long battle by regional and local authorities to achieve institutional representation and recognition similar to that given to the social partners especially in regard to the European Social Fund. The Committee of the Regions is a pale shadow of the Social Fund committee but it has a wider remit, and may in time develop into a much more powerful body. In the meantime it will seek to establish its own authority and profile in the EC decision-making process, an ambition that cannot have been helped by the delays and disputes caused by the need for member governments to choose the members of this Committee. What may be more significant is the way in which the EC is influenced by the need to consider employment in its treatment of regional aids and the environment in its policy on structural funds.

The greater the financial commitment of the Union to the structural funds, the more concerned member states and MEPs are likely to become about the effectiveness and value of such expenditure. Thus we can expect further battles between the Commission and member governments to ensure that grants from these funds are effectively additional monies to what would have been spent in each country in their absence: in other words, the principle of 'additionality' must be respected. The Edinburgh European Council reinforced a growing emphasis in the EC institutions upon the desirability of stronger *ex ante* appraisal, monitoring and *ex post* evaluation procedures governing the spending of the structural funds. The EC has not found this an easy task over the last decade, and its realisation could well imply more bureaucracy and interference from Brussels than hitherto, the opposite of what the principle of subsidiarity is meant to lead to. The strengthening of EC regional policy has already shown the tension between meeting the key regional needs of member states to ensure convergence and the principle of subsidiarity. The EC has been financing, for example, a major expansion of the Portuguese secondary and higher education systems at a time when the EC had no formal competence to intervene in such policy areas. The notion of subsidiarity could, however, be applied if more private sector finance were able to be attracted to EC and national public sector-funded schemes, or if more effort were made to channel funds through block grants to regional development agencies to be spent on locally determined programmes whose eligibility for EC funding was decided by reference to existing procedures for agreeing Community support between the Commission and member governments.

NEW COMPETENCES

The new competences added by the Maastricht Treaty to those already in the EC Treaties included, in particular, public health, education, culture, industry policy, consumer protection and visa policy. The 'newness' of these dispositions is, as indicated above, in most cases more apparent than real, as the Community has, for some years, been slowly acquiring a presence in these fields under other Treaty articles.

Public health is a good example of an area of policy where joint decision-making between national governments and the EC has been quietly developing over time. The Single Act led to an expansion of the EC's activity in the area of health and safety at work, while also relating the remit of environment policy to the protection of human health. The new Treaty now calls upon member states to coordinate their public health policies with the help of the Commission and permits the EC to take 'incentive measures and supportive actions'.[13] In effect the new Article records what the EC has been doing in joint actions on cancer, AIDS, drug and alcohol abuse. Financial constraints will probably prevent much expansion of EC activity, but the Commission will be under pressure from health professionals and MEPs to push for more Union-coordinated work on basic health-care research, preventative measures and epidemiological research.

Article 126 on *education* and Article 128 on *culture* seek to limit EC involvement in policy areas which are highly sensitive. In education Community action is to promote student mobility, educational cooperation and exchanges, foreign language skills, and distance learning. The Community is also to be encouraged to take part in wider international cooperation in the educational field, particularly through the Council of Europe. A much stronger remit concerning vocational training had already been established in the early years of the Community but this is now clarified in amended Article 127. On cultural issues, the EC's role is to supplement national-level initiatives and to promote transnational cooperation, but action in the fields of cultural exchanges, conservation, dissemination of knowledge about European cultures and history, and artistic and literary creation (including the audio-visual sector) are specifically mentioned.

A new section on *industrial policy* in the Maastricht Treaty might signal an end to a long series of battles over whether the EC should have one.

Back-door sectoral policies, mainly under the guise of regional, competition or trade policies, have been in operation for nearly two decades. The real change of mood occurred when the Single Act set out to promote industrial collaboration and cooperation in research and development. The new provision in Article 130 represents a very limited advance upon the Single Act by enabling the EC, if the Council unanimously approves, to take general measures for realising a 'system of open and competitive markets' in which structural change in industry is facilitated, and a favourable environment created for industrial initiatives, small businesses, and industrial collaboration. Minor amendments to the *competition policy* provisions of the EC Treaty were also made at Maastricht: these enable the Commission to be more flexible in allowing state aids for cultural projects and give the European Parliament a say in any regulation applying EC competition policy rules. A new Article 129c spells out a Community responsibility for *consumer protection* previously covered by Article 100a or Article 235. The EC is entitled now to support and supplement national policies with regard to the health, safety and economic interests of its consumers. Member states remain entitled to maintain or introduce more stringent protective measures, as with the national environmental standards safeguard clause in Article 130T of the Single Act. Both safeguards, however, represent significant exceptions to the concept of a single market, whose impact is yet to be fully appreciated.

The wider context in which the EC has been endowed with the right to settle a *common visa policy* is discussed in Chapter Seven. It is significant that an amendment to the EC Treaty (new Article 100c) has been used to introduce this policy rather than a new sub-section in Title VI on Cooperation in the fields of Justice and Home Affairs.[14] This represents a compromise between very divergent views in the Council on the desirability of an EC-wide immigration policy, Germany taking a maximalist and Britain taking a minimalist position. Visa policy at any rate is now governed by the full EC institutional panoply, with decisions to be taken at first by unanimity in the Council, but by qualified majority voting after January 1996. The format of visas may be agreed by this voting method from November 1993.

Given that there has been no consensus to date among member states upon which countries' nationals should provide a visa to ensure entry into the Community, each individual member state having between 60 and 120 on its own list, the price of agreeing a common visa policy is likely to be a longer list of countries than many EC states currently maintain; thus many Commonwealth countries may appear on the EC list, even though they may not have been on the UK's own list. A provision in Article K.9 will permit more justice and home affairs issues to be determined by use of Article 100c of the Treaty (a *'passerelle'* provision linking Title VI to the EC) if the Council is unanimous in wanting to legislate in this way. However, the declaration made by the Danish government at the Edinburgh Summit creates such significant hurdles before any present or future Danish government could agree to such a process that it is unlikely that the *passerelle* will be used in the foreseeable future. Even so, the adoption of a common visa policy is a landmark in the development of the Community, a practical measure to smooth the workings of the common external frontier and a real step along the road to Union citizenship.

Other genuine new EC competences which were considered by the IGC but were not agreed at Maastricht include tourism policy, civil protection, energy policy and the direct taxation of businesses. These may well figure in the discussions of the new IGC scheduled for 1996.

The Treaty on European Union adds greatly to the complexity of the treaty base and particularly of the decision-making processes of the Union, making these anything but transparent even within a given field. This is a recipe for delay in making decisions and an invitation to intermediaries, such as consultants and lobbyists, to exploit the arcane character of the system, as well as a source of confusion for the citizens. The Treaty has endowed the Community pillar with few really new competences, and most of these are partial, running concurrently with those retained by the member states. Even where there may be an objective case for new competences, the political climate which grew up around the ratification of the Maastricht Treaty will make it hard to secure agreement on them for some time to come.

9

THE PUBLIC FINANCES
OF THE UNION

Dieter Biehl

We examine here whether it is possible to define a number of requirements, notably cohesion and accountability, that a public finance system
ought to fulfil in order to be compatible with European Union. This
implies first a theoretical and conceptual exercise to identify possible
major criteria or principles; second, to apply them to existing EU financing systems; and, third, to develop a reform strategy if and to the extent
that compatibility is not sufficiently guaranteed. In this respect, the
chapter represents a follow-up of the MacDougall Report of 1977 that
studied, at the request of the Commission, *The Role of Public Finance in
European Integration*.[1]

This report was based on the idea that something can be learned from
analysing how regional economies have been integrated to realise a
national economic and monetary union and, as we can add today, a
public finance union. The latter term was not used in the report
although it dealt with some major issues of such a union. Public Finance
Union (PFU) can roughly be characterised as covering those aspects of
integration that are closely linked with taxation and spending. The
MacDougall Report already demonstrated the importance of what we
call today 'cohesion' and the contribution of PFU to that goal.

These matters were addressed piecemeal in the Maastricht Treaty.
There was some strengthening of the Commission's accountability to the
European Parliament with respect to budgetary expenditure (see
Chapter 13, pp. 215–16). The Cohesion Fund was established (Article
130d) to contribute to 'projects in the fields of environment and trans-
European networks in the area of transport infrastructure'. A Protocol
on Economic and Social Cohesion stipulated that the projects were to
benefit member states whose GNP per head is less than 90 per cent of
the Community average and which have 'a programme leading to fulfil-
ment of the conditions of economic convergence' required for the
Economic and Monetary Union. Following agreement at Maastricht on
the principle that the funds for cohesion would be substantially
increased, the member states that would benefit, led by Spain, managed

at the European Council meeting in December 1992 to secure an increase of two-fifths in the appropriations for Structural Funds, now to include the Cohesion Fund, over the period 1993–99.

Despite this additional measure of redistribution on the expenditure side, the Union's fiscal system remains on the whole regressive. The Protocol also registered the intention that the Union would take 'greater account of the contributive capacity of individual Member States' and would 'examine means of correcting, for the less prosperous Member States, regressive elements existing in the present own resources system'. This chapter considers how the Union might move towards a system of public finance that better respects the principle of equity as well as accountability.

EUROPEAN INTEGRATION, PUBLIC FINANCE UNION, AND COHESION

When European integration started in 1952 with the European Coal and Steel Community, the six member states decided to finance its activities with a production levy.[2] This first European tax did not, however, serve as a model for the other two European Communities founded in 1957, the EEC and Euratom; their financing was based on national government contributions. In 1970 it was decided to replace these national contributions by a system of 'own resources', although this was achieved only in 1979. These are revenues from the common customs tariff, from agricultural levies and from a sharing of VAT receipts. In 1988 a new fourth revenue category based on national GNP was added to the system of 'own resources'.[3]

These modifications of the revenue side reflect both a large increase of total expenditure and a substantial change in its composition.[4] Whereas in 1961 the expenditure of the three Communities represented only 0.04 per cent of the GNP of the then six member states, this increased to 0.45 per cent in 1971, to 0.81 per cent in 1981 and was budgeted to reach 1.22 per cent in 1993 for the Community of twelve, equivalent to Ecu 195 per head. In relation to the sum of national budgets, this amounts to roughly 2.4 per cent. The financial perspective decided by the Edinburgh European Council in December 1992 provided for a further increase to 1.26 per cent of GNP by 1999. Agricultural guarantee expenditure started with a share of 8.5 per cent of total EC expenditure in 1965, rose to 72.8 per cent in 1971, then fell to 59.7 per cent in 1981 and 51.6 per cent in 1993. Structural spending rose from 4.9 per cent in 1971 to 19.2 per cent in 1981 and to 30.5 per cent in the budget for 1993. Both the increases and the changes in composition mirror the transformation of a budget dominated by agriculture into a multipurpose one with a strong commitment to cohesion.

Cohesion was also one of the main issues dealt with in the MacDougall Report, (although the term was not yet used). The report demonstrated that national public finance systems in both federal and unitary states act as interregional 'redistributors' in so far as they transfer funds from more developed regions to less developed ones, thereby contributing to what is now called 'cohesion'. Cohesion was explicitly introduced into the EC legal framework by the Single Act of 1986, although the creation of the Regional Fund in 1975 already foreshadowed that development.

Interregional transfers within a national public finance system are not, however, purely altruistic. In general, rich regions profit from the fact that the poorer regions in a national market are not allowed to protect their markets against the more competitive enterprises located in the more developed areas – which thus get a high share of the gains from interregional trade. In addition, the headquarters of multiregional and multinational enterprises are frequently located in rich regions, with the consequence that income and corporation tax revenues in particular, derived from activities outside the region of residence and establishment, are statistically reported as 'own' receipts. In this perspective, rich regions transfer through the national public finance system a part of their gains from trade and taxes to those regions where they have their origin. As a result, they are in general at the same time net exporters and net contributors in national public finance systems, whereas poorer regions represent net importers and net receivers.

The contribution of a national public finance system to interregional cohesion depends on the progressivity of both the revenue and expenditure: the higher tax progressivity, the more rich regions contribute to overall national revenues per head; the lower expenditure per head in rich and the higher in poor regions, the greater will be the net payer position of the former and the net receiver position of the latter. Admittedly, redistributive equity cannot be the only goal of fiscal and expenditure policies; there is also allocative efficiency as well as stabilisation to be taken into account. But whatever weights for equity and efficiency are implied, when decisions on tax and expenditure policies are made, these decisions always result in implicit transfers of tax and expenditure, so they will necessarily affect the net positions of the rich compared with the poorer regions. In addition, federal countries in particular apply systems of explicit regional tax sharing and transfers.

Unfortunately, the European budget, in particular its financing, is rather regressive: poorer regions and member states tend to pay more in relation to their incomes per head than richer ones. The regressivity argument was already developed in the MacDougall Report and later recognised by the EC in that the share of VAT revenue was fixed at 1.4 per cent of national bases, which were 'capped' at 55 per cent of national

GDP for 1988–92, and a new fourth revenue in the form of a GNP levy was created.[5]

In establishing the Cohesion Fund the Maastricht Treaty introduces a new instrument for expenditure to improve cohesion, but does not provide a new instrument on the revenue side. The preference for expenditure instruments has a long tradition since the creation of the ECSC Social Fund in 1952. However, owing to the small size of the European budget, the expenditure side can provide only a limited degree of cohesion.[6] In addition, there are the problems of efficient administration and even fraud, for example, in agricultural and structural spending, and also doubts as to whether an exclusively expenditure-oriented cohesion policy does not weaken efficiency incentives.[7]

In particular the experience of the doubling of the structural funds has demonstrated that there is a considerable risk that these increased transfers are not always used efficiently by the receiving member states and their regions, and that efficiency incentives are too weak if the subsidy element is too high. A condition of successful cohesion over the long term seems to be that recipient countries improve their overall economic framework by deregulating sufficiently to become attractive for private investment, and also to improve infrastructure. It also seems reasonable to insist on an adequate share of national funding of regional development projects in the sense of 'additionality', in order to keep national, regional and local governments interested in planning and administering them efficiently. National co-financing would be easier for the less prosperous countries if the Community's fiscal system were sufficiently progressive, because they would then have to contribute less to the EC budget and could use these funds to finance their own programmes. Explicit expenditure transfers to these countries could then be lower. At the same time the richer member countries, in contributing progressively more to the EC budget, would realise a more just net payer position without being restricted to specific expenditure programmes with high subsidy rates.

Such a strategy could also help to ease the long and bitter dispute between Britain and the other member states concerning the UK 'rebate', because it would become clear that the issue is not to maintain a special treatment for the UK but to apply a principle which would also benefit the less rich member states.[8] Unfortunately, despite the fact that the MacDougall Report had already in 1977 suggested that a progressive key be applied to the VAT contributors, that the Spinelli Report of the European Parliament in 1980 also proposed a new progressive financing instrument, and that the Commission in its original proposals for dealing with the financial crisis of the early 1980s included an indirectly progressive instrument, the Council in 1988 decided only to reduce the regressivity of VAT and to introduce a new neutral fourth resource, but not to create a progressive instrument.[9] Nor did the Edinburgh European Council of 1992, when deciding the medium financial perspective up to 1997, take up explicitly the question of a new progressive source of revenue.[10]

It seems plausible to assume that the weight attached to the question of progressivity depends on the size of the European budget on the one hand and the size of the distributional effects between member states and their regions on the other. As the EU budget will continue to increase, it is only a matter of time before the majority of member states will no longer be satisfied with the distribution of the financial burden. It is therefore useful to consider possible future solutions and to prepare the ground for a well-balanced decision.

The search for a progressive source of revenue is not, however, the only question to be discussed. There is also the institutional framework. Does it matter whether it is national politicians or Union politicians, and within which institutions, who decide on EU revenues and expenditure? To what extent is the present EU framework compatible with accountability and budgetary discipline and, if not, what can be an appropriate remedy? From an economic point of view, to answer these and other related questions requires an analytical method that enables us to identify the costs that are caused by the existing institutional framework and those that would result from changing it. The next section presents the key elements of such an analysis to be applied to evaluating the existing EU framework and to designing a strategy for reform.

A REFERENCE SYSTEM FOR A EUROPEAN PUBLIC FINANCE UNION

Traditional public finance theory, like traditional economic theory, is based on what may be called 'resource cost'. It seeks to assess the implications of scarcity, when resources to provide public services are no longer available for the satisfaction of private needs, and vice versa. This understanding of opportunity cost remains valid, but it has to be supplemented by an assessment of the benefits that can be obtained from a well-designed, efficient and equitable system of public institutions. It was the theory of property rights and of transaction costs, to which both neoclassical and other authors contributed, that helped us understand that a market system can function efficiently only if the public sector provides and guarantees private property rights and minimises private transaction costs.[11] This approach will have to be extended in order to include 'public' property rights or 'competences'.

However, with resource cost alone, a number of important issues in the context of institutions and political decision-making cannot be fully understood; a second major cost category has to be introduced. This is the 'frustration' or 'preference' cost. 'Frustration' arises, for example, when a defeated minority has to accept a majority decision or even to contribute to policies that are not in line with its system of values. It is the loss in terms of preferences and not only of resources that has to be considered in any economic assessment of political decision-making. Buchanan and Tullock developed the basic idea in 1962.[12] The resource cost function is to be understood as the cost involved in an institutional political decision-making system: the higher the number of the members of a society that participate in political decision-making, the higher the resource cost. The minimum resource cost is in the case of a single decision-maker or 'dictator'. If all political decisions are left to him, no other members of society will have to devote time or effort to political business, thereby using their full capacities for profitable market activities. However, frustration costs will at the same time be at a maximum, as all the other members of that society are deprived of political participation with the consequence that they have to accept decisions that may not be in line with their own preferences. The more people are authorised to take part in political decisions, the greater the probability that these decisions reflect the different individual values. With a unanimous vote, preference costs can even be zero. If it is assumed that the countervailing resources and preference costs can be aggregated, the total costs can be minimised by a system of taking political decisions that allows substantial expression of individual preferences without raising the costs of the political process unduly. This leads to the conclusion that a representative democratic system minimises cost.

This basic cost calculus can be applied to many other constitutional issues. The well-known principle of separation of powers can, for example, be explained as being the outcome of a trade-off between efficiency (minimising resource cost by concentrating political decision-making power within one single governmental institution) and equity (minimising frustration caused by a government potentially abusing its power). As a result, the three main functions (legislative, executive, juridical) are entrusted to three different institutions that control each other.[13]

PRINCIPLES FOR PUBLIC FINANCE UNIONS

The institutional implications of the approach outlined above can be summarised in the following eight main principles.

1. *Optimal assignment of competences*. The basic idea is to assign a competence to the level of government that can provide a service or apply a tax at lowest resource cost. As services and taxes differ in their spatial dimensions, there should be congruence of the servicing or tax area and

the competence area or 'territory' of a government: those services and taxes with a smaller servicing area or less mobile tax bases are to be allocated to local governments, larger ones to regional and national levels, and those of a European dimension to the EU level. In addition, there should be a certain balance between expenditure and revenue competences, in order to guarantee adequate autonomy for the governments or institutions at each level.

2. *Optimal differentiation of competences*. First, competences can be assigned as full competence with respect to a given function, or split up and distributed as partial ones to different levels of government; second, they can be exclusive or concurrent. Assigning full competences strengthens the autonomy of the governments concerned and tends toward competitive PFUs; splitting up creates a tendency towards cooperative forms of PFUs as no single level of government disposes of all competences needed to provide the service concerned. Tax legislative authority can, for example, be given to the highest level in order to avoid differences in regional tax rates, whereas in order to guarantee financial autonomy to the other levels, the distribution of tax revenues would have to be fixed by assigning to them specific taxation authority in the constitution. Classifying a competence as concurrent allows another specified level of government (in general a higher one) to take over that competence under certain conditions, but without formally modifying the constitution; the costs of constitutional change are reduced.

3. *Optimal separation of powers*. Concentrating all competences in one single powerful institution incurs the risk that these competences can be abused. The resulting potential preference cost can be reduced if authority is split up so that legislative, executive and judicial powers are entrusted to different institutions that control each other. Horizontal separation of powers can be supplemented by vertical separation, that is, by dividing the highest level of government into a federal one and a state one. Both unitary and federal systems often also split up legislative authority into two chambers. The assumption is that the preference for separation of powers is the stronger, the more it is feared that an abuse of powers may affect the freedom and dignity of the citizens and the autonomy of the different levels of government.

4. *Optimal combination of competences and merging of institutions*. It can be argued that monofunctional organisations like James Buchanan's 'clubs' are appropriate institutions for providing public goods.[14] However, a 'club' would be needed for each public good provided and to the extent that the principle of the optimal separation of powers (see 3 above) applies, each 'club' would need a more or less large and differentiated institutional capacity, causing high resource costs. In order to minimise resource cost, an optimal number of competences would have to be assigned to each club, or a club's institutional capacity increased until it

can deal with those competences for which, according to principle 1, servicing area and competence area are congruent. Multifunctional spatial organisations like local, regional, national and European governments are, of course, the normal form of club which reduces resource costs by spreading them over a number of competences.

5. *Subsidiarity.* Like separation of powers, subsidiarity is based on preference cost. It implies on the one hand that the individual or the family is given a certain priority compared with society, and that on the other hand smaller or lower levels of government are given a certain priority compared with larger or higher levels of government.[15] The economic rationale is that preference costs are minimised and welfare is increased if political decisions are taken by the citizens concerned or as close to them as possible. This implies that certain competences remain with member states, or with a lower level of government, even if it could be proved that in terms of resource cost, a higher level of government is more efficient in providing the service in question.[16]

6. *Optimal representation of payers and beneficiaries ('correspondence').* The purpose of this principle is to avoid over-supply and under-supply of public goods.[17] Over-supply and excessive spending result if the beneficiaries dominate in the decision-making institutions and are capable of shifting the tax burden on to others; under-supply and too low a level of spending are the outcome of decision-making if the taxpayers dominate the decision-making and do not profit adequately from services financed with their taxes.

7. *Fair burden-sharing.* This principle is fundamental for distributing the burden of financing public expenditure among individuals. Fair burden-sharing ranges from benefit finance in the form of prices in case of private goods, to ability-to-pay finance in the form of taxes for public goods. The more public the nature of goods, the more markets will fail in providing them on a price basis, and the more they will have to be financed from taxes or levies. Whereas prices are more or less in line with the benefits a consumer can derive from private goods, taxes have no systematic link with benefits received, but with income, consumption and wealth as indicators of ability to pay. In developed democratic countries, the distribution of the tax burden is considered to be fair if it is more or less progressive.

8. *Fair fiscal equalisation.* The principle of fair burden-sharing can also be applied to systems of multi-level governments or institutions where not individuals but governments or similar organisations are members. If the financial burden is distributed taking into account differences in average income or tax capacity per head, fiscal equalisation can be qualified as being 'fair'. If, for example, the objective is to enable a local or a regional government to provide a minimum level of service per inhabitant independently of its local or regional tax capacity, the

financially weaker ones need explicit or implicit transfers from the stronger ones. As a result, the former become net receivers and the latter net payers. These transfers can take many forms, depending *inter alia* on homogeneity of solidarity preferences in the community concerned.

DEFICIENCIES OF THE PRESENT EUROPEAN PUBLIC FINANCE UNION

In this section, the principles presented above will be applied to the European Union in order to identify possible deficiencies that cause unnecessarily high cost. As will be seen, some arrangements and rules represent a violation not just of a single principle, but of a combination of them.

1. The principle of *optimal assignment of competences* seems to have been partially violated in the first years of European integration as the number of competences assigned to the EC was small compared with the decision-making capacity created. The structure of this capacity followed relatively closely the principle of separation of powers, making the Community an entity *sui generis* that differs considerably from a traditional international organisation. This in turn implied that the 'fixed' cost of this institutional capacity was relatively high. If only a small number of competences with a Europe-wide servicing area are assigned to the new decision-making level, the costs per competence are high, too. At the same time, this means that the decision-making capacity was under-utilised, so that, later on, new competences could be transferred to the EC and existing competences enlarged at relatively low resource cost. Thus the overall long-term balance need not necessarily be negative.

2. The principle of *optimal assignment of competences* is clearly violated as far as the assignment of tax competences to the EC and the relationship between expenditure and revenue competences are concerned. Despite the fact that the total 1993 budget amounted to 1.22 per cent of EC GNP with approximately Ecu 68 billion, the Union does not dispose of an adequate system of revenues, and above all, of a true legislative tax authority based on responsibility and accountability to the European citizens.[18] Tariffs and agricultural levies cannot be considered to represent truly satisfactory revenue sources as they can hardly be modified in order to correspond to the revenue required; they are determined mainly through international agreements like Gatt, or by the difference between agricultural prices on world markets and within the Union. The financing from VAT represents a form of revenue-sharing, which can be an element of any financing system. Evaluation of it depends, therefore, on other criteria, such as the degree of regressivity which violates the principle of fair burden-sharing (see 7). The fourth revenue,

the GNP levy, has only a very weak 'own resource' character. Moreover, every major change of the revenue system requires ratification by national parliaments. As a consequence, the revenue autonomy of the EU is low. Admittedly, it can be argued that member states wish to maintain this low degree of autonomy. But this would not be in line with so many summit declarations and extensions of the original Treaties, and could have been realised with much less preference and resource cost.

3. Partly different, partly similar conclusions apply to the principle of *optimal differentiation of competences.* Like foreign trade policy, the Common Agricultural Policy is an example of a full and almost exclusive competence; in most other cases, the competences are partial and concurrent ones. This alone need not represent a violation of one of the principles; it depends on combinations with the other rules. As will be argued below (see 6), it was the full and exclusive CAP competence combined with the violation of the correspondence principle that was responsible for the strong increase in agricultural and, through this, total Union expenditure.

4. The principle of *vertical differentiation of competences* is violated as the EU has only a limited competence to tax, but no legislative tax authority on which democratic responsibility and accountability of politicians at European level could be based. The authority to tax in the form of a production levy was granted to the ECSC (Article 49), but not extended to the EEC. The latter was originally financed by national contributions, the normal instrument for international organisations. Nor did the system of 'own resources' of 1970–79 include a true tax authority. No wonder that owing to violation of the correspondence principle (see 5 and 6 below) the Community experienced many financial crises; they were ended in 1988 with the substantial reform proposed by President Delors and adopted in a modified form by the Brussels European Council under German presidency. However, this reform consisted mainly of introducing new restrictions in the form of binding upper expenditure limits: a bundle of measures that reduced the autonomy of the Community and did not solve the responsibility issue. From the point of view of the majority of member states, the time was not yet ripe for a transfer of true tax authority to the EC; and this implies that preference cost still seems to have been perceived by them as being too high, as tax authority is considered to be one of the major expressions of national sovereignty. But this appears to be a one-sided and partial evaluation, as some important cost elements have not been taken into account.

5. The distinction between compulsory and non-compulsory expenditure in conjunction with the maximum rate of increase rule causes important violations of the *correspondence principle.*

As far as the expenditure competences are concerned, the budget has to be balanced; debt financing is excluded (Article 189). The expenditure competences are assigned to the budgetary authority, the Council and the European Parliament; the Commission acts partly as an executive government that has to prepare and submit its budget to the two 'arms' of the budgetary authority. A closer inspection shows, however, that the two-armed budgetary authority is not equivalent to a two-chamber system such as exists in many states. The major reason for this is the splitting up of the budget into two parts, the so-called 'compulsory' and 'non-compulsory' expenditure categories.[19] According to a complex Interinstitutional Agreement, the Council has the last say on compulsory expenditure, and the Parliament on non-compulsory expenditure.[20] At first sight, this distinction seems to be plausible if one reads that compulsory expenditure is defined as 'such expenditure as the budgetary authority is obliged to enter in the budget to enable the Community to meet its obligations'.[21] However, a large part of non-compulsory expenditure is also in line with this definition so that the Commission qualifies this distinction as 'essentially political'.[22] The other peculiar rule is the maximum rate of increase for the non-compulsory expenditure.[23] It limits the power of the Parliament to increase its part of the budget to the extent that it would exceed real GNP growth of the Community, the average variation in member states' budgets, and the rise in the cost of living during the previous financial year.

These two rules violate the correspondence principle: owing to the deficient tax legislation authority, the decision-makers in the Parliament and Council are representatives mainly not of taxpayers, but of expenditure beneficiaries, with the consequence that there is a high risk of excessive spending. In order to reduce this risk, the Treaties fixed these two rules as a sort of artificial substitute for the normal democratic way for securing budgetary discipline, which is to oblige politicians to decide simultaneously on expenditure and taxes.

6. Another violation of the *correspondence principle* explains the extremely strong increase in agricultural spending which made the EC budget grow so fast up to the end of the 1980s. One of the main reasons seems to have been the practice, based on the full and exclusive CAP competence, to leave it to the ministers of agriculture to decide on all important agricultural issues, especially those that created financial obligations. At the beginning, the ministers of finance were present in the Agricultural Council meetings; later, they seem to have left the field to a group of politicians who have to be understood as being largely committed to serving their clientele. As a consequence, taxpayer interests were for a long time not adequately represented. It was only in the context of the budgetary reform of 1988 that the growth of agricultural spending was limited to 74 per cent of that of EC GNP. In addition, the Council

provided for a special meeting to be attended by both groups of ministers when expenditure is rising too fast.

7. The principle of *fair burden-sharing* is also among those violated. The largest part of the total revenues, in particular agricultural levies and VAT revenues, is regressive: its relative burden increases with decreasing income per head. On average only about half of all the revenue in the member states is of an indirect and therefore mainly regressive nature; the other half consists of direct and more or less progressive sources of revenue. From this point of view, the structure of EU revenue and the distribution of the tax burden are not in line with revealed preferences in the member states.

8. *Fiscal equalisation*, or fair burden-sharing among member states, implies that countries with high incomes per head due partly to the gains from intra-Union trade should contribute relatively more to Union financing and benefit relatively less from Union expenditure. As a consequence, the richer countries should be net payers, the poorer ones net receivers. Unfortunately, this is not always the case as the British example in particular shows: the UK was for a long time the second largest net payer after Germany, despite its considerably lower income per head, whereas some other richer countries profited substantially as net receivers. After two earlier correction mechanisms, since 1986 the UK's VAT base is reduced by two-thirds of the difference between its VAT share and the EC expenditure allocated to it. Germany accepted the role of the major net payer, but insisted that its contribution to the UK rebate be reduced to two-thirds of the normal VAT share applied to all other member states in order to finance the British compensation.

In countries with federal governments, the implicit fiscal equalisation is supplemented by an explicit one. But this presupposes a substantial homogeneity of preferences and a common constitution which guarantees that those who pay transfers can be sure that they are in accordance with generally accepted and enforceable rules. Both conditions are not (yet) realised in the EU so that it can be argued from the point of view of the potential payers that the preference costs for a typical explicit equalisation scheme are still too high. The EU disposes, however, of some instruments of implicit equalisation that come close to explicit equalisation. Thus, according to the new regulation for the Regional Fund of 1989, the major part of this Fund goes to regions that are less developed by European, and no longer by national, criteria. As poorer member states have more of those regions than richer ones, they also obtain higher transfers. The two other Structural Funds (Social Fund, Guidance section of the Agricultural Fund) have similar rules so that a large part of what amounts to about 28 per cent of total EU expenditure contributes to implicit fiscal equalisation. However, given the high share of agricultural market spending that is not in line with equalisation because it is determined by other factors, the positive contribution of the Structural Funds to cohesion is counterbalanced by the partly negative contribution of CAP. It is exactly this mechanism that is also partly responsible for the British net-payer position: the UK does not participate proportionately in CAP expenditure because of its small agricultural sector and owing to its large imports of farm products from outside the EU.

The preceding analysis demonstrates that there are a number of serious deficiencies in the European Public Finance Union as it stands today. Some of them relate to the CAP and its high share of expenditure, and cannot be modified substantially in the medium term. Reforming the regressive financing system is, however, a task that can, and should, be taken up without delay. The reform cannot consist only of endowing the EU with a progressive type of revenue but must be supplemented by additional measures that help to improve the institutional system and the decision-making procedures of the EU.

A PROPOSAL FOR REFORM OF THE PUBLIC FINANCE UNION

On the basis of what has been shown in the previous section, it seems reasonable to propose a European income and corporation tax in order to make the financing system of the EU more progressive. However, the cost criteria and the principles that are based on them should also be applied to any reform proposal. If this is done, it becomes obvious that to proceed in this way would be rather cost-maximising: if, despite more than 40 years of European integration, national income and corporation taxes are still so different, this implies that there are still substantial differences between member states as to the conception of a 'good' tax on the one hand, and as to the economic framework conditions (for example, level of development, tax mentalities, administrative capabilities) on the other. To introduce a uniform European tax under these conditions would clearly cause both high preference and resource costs.

It is therefore necessary to seek a second-best solution. This could consist of a two-stage progressive surcharge to the existing national income and corporation taxes. In the first stage, as with a system of national contributions, member states are considered to be contributors. Their contributions are fixed in a progressive way by taking account of the differences in incomes per head from the EU average. As member states obtain on average half of their revenues from direct/progressive taxes and half from indirect/regressive taxes, one could envisage at first financing only the expenditure increases and finally financing half of EU revenues from this new progressive source. In the second stage, the national contributions are redistributed among national income and/or

152

corporation taxpayers with the aid of a uniform surcharge percentage to be applied to the individual tax amounts to be paid according to national tax laws. This surcharge is to be explicitly shown on each national tax invoice so that the taxpayers know their direct EU tax burden.

The question as to the desirable degree of progressivity cannot be answered a priori, as it depends on the preference costs implied; these preference costs have to be expressed through the political decision-making process within an optimal institutional structure. It is naturally reasonable to present some scenarios based on different progressivity keys in order to see the implications of choosing a higher or lower progressivity.

This proposal has the following advantages. It avoids all the costs that would be caused by introducing a new European tax that must necessarily deviate to a large extent from the existing national taxes. Due to its progressivity, it is in line with the principle of fair burden-sharing. It contributes to a fair system of implicit fiscal equalisation as richer member states would have to pay relatively more than poorer ones. The violations of the principles of optimal assignment, optimal differentiation, and optimal combination of competences are eliminated or at least reduced by endowing the EU with a legislative tax authority. The correspondence principle is realised as European decision-makers are both allowed and obliged to decide simultaneously on expenditure and on taxes to finance it.

The distinction between compulsory and non-compulsory expenditure and the rule on maximum rate of increase can be abolished, budgetary discipline and accountability being now guaranteed by normal democratic procedures. This implies, however, that the principle of optimal separation of powers is more fully realised, requiring the two-armed character of the present budgetary authority to be transformed into a consistent bicameral system where the Council and Parliament assume jointly full responsibility for the EU level. The principle of subsidiarity can be taken into account if the decisions relating to the first stage are taken at the EU level, whereas the subsequent fixing of surcharge percentages is done at the level of member states.

With the aid of these proposals the European Union would be endowed with a sufficiently progressive tax competence, its institutional structure improved, and some of the existing disincentives that have been responsible in the past for many problems eliminated. In addition, these proposals would represent a significant step forward towards a full political union.

Part III

THE GOVERNMENT OF THE UNION

10

PROBLEMS OF GOVERNANCE IN THE UNION

David Coombes

Any expectation that the 1990–91 Intergovernmental Conference of the European Community's member states might design a political union with its own government was bound for disappointment. The *angst* affecting the conference on the subject of federalism has been well publicised. A big majority of member states' representatives favoured a decisive and unanimous act to formalise by treaty the separate projects of Emu, common foreign and security policy and enhanced cooperation in justice and home affairs (effectively, police). But faced as they were with British and Danish reluctance to accept anything that might be seen as leading to a comprehensive constitutional settlement, they came to a decision that some treaty was better than none.

In fact, the agreement reached at Maastricht in December 1991 dealt primarily with policy, and above all with *policy* as a series of common promissory objectives, to which the twelve member states had in one way or another, implicitly or explicitly, already given some commitment. As in previous interstate agreements to legitimate integration in new spheres of public policy, the institutional changes were essentially secondary to the policy objectives themselves.

Nevertheless, the resulting Treaty on European Union made several important revisions and additions to the Community's established legal framework. These, too, did not go much beyond what had been condoned in principle and in many vital respects already practised. But the Community's institutions and member states increasingly admit that European integration, both in theory and in practice, gives rise to new problems of governance. There seems to be general understanding not only that those problems are exceptionally difficult (compared to policy, which is difficult enough) but that they will one day before too long have to be resolved more thoroughly than they have been up to now. Indeed, the Treaty provides for its own major revision by 1996, precisely with respect to the most problematical aspect of all: Political Union.

With that prospective in mind, I shall in this chapter deal far more ruthlessly and frankly than the Community's member states have so far been willing to do collectively, with the question of how a European Union could and should be provided with its own government. There are fundamental issues that the institutions and member states ought to have addressed in the Maastricht exercise, but did not and possibly could not address. I shall not attempt here to offer pragmatic solutions. The following analysis and recommendation deal with principles and do so deliberately, because it is precisely with respect to the principles of good government that the Maastricht Treaty, like all its predecessors, is most unsatisfactory.

In short, I shall argue that the objectives of public policy enshrined in the Maastricht Treaty demand in principle that European Union be founded with its own *government*. The values and interests prevailing among the present member states of the Union seem to require no less, while the same states have expressed openly their common determination to prescribe for others outside the Union, in Europe and elsewhere, not only the practice of 'good governance' but also general respect for human and civic rights, including democracy.

As an introduction it will help to explain why, nevertheless, at no stage so far have sufficient member states of the European Community been willing to make their consent to further integration conditional on the entrenchment of similar principles in a suitably constitutional form, and also why, on the other hand, an indeterminate number of people throughout Community Europe have continued to view certain principles of constitutional government as a necessary means and end of European economic, social and political integration.

HISTORICAL BACKGROUND

There have previously been only two significant attempts in the framework of the EC to make a genuine constitutional settlement between the member states, that is, one intended both to guarantee the comprehensive rule of law over the use of public power and to provide for legitimate and effective government. The first of these was the ill-fated draft treaty for a political community, proposed in connection with the Treaty establishing a European Defence Community of 1952, which was never fully ratified. The second was the Draft Treaty to establish a European Union, adopted by the European Parliament in 1984, which was, in effect, superseded by the Single European Act of 1986. Both these initiatives came from representative parliamentary institutions established under Community Treaties; neither obtained the support of sufficient states' governments at the time to become the actual basis of a revision or replacement of existing Treaties; and neither was effectively put before the citizens of Europe for popular approval or rejection.

Despite major political setbacks in 1954 and 1965, both of which occurred as negative reactions (primarily in France) to initiatives intended to treat the Community as an essentially political undertaking, the founding Treaties were successfully implemented up to the end of the 1960s on the basis of their primarily economic principles and objectives, which the six original member states sought to realise by means of a limited transfer of legal authority. In fact, the powers transferred by Treaty to the common institutions resembled those typically delegated to the executive branch of government in those same states, which normally exercised similar powers in accordance with established codes and customs of administrative law.

The parliamentary organ, with consultative and supervisory powers, was included among the common institutions almost as an afterthought – the *coiffure parlementaire*. For many of the legally binding acts authorised at an EC level, the formal consultation of organised economic and social interest groups was considered at least as relevant as the intervention of political representatives. It seemed as if the chief function of both kinds of consultation, parliamentary and corporatist, was to inform deliberation within the states themselves. The activities of both European Parliament and Economic and Social Committee would, in other words, help corresponding organs within the states to hold accountable ministerial representatives in the Community's Council, while also affecting them with a more European perspective (through overlapping memberships).

Just as, in this respect, national institutions were left with responsibility for ensuring democracy and accountability, so national executives and judiciaries were left with the main task of applying legally binding acts made in accordance with the Treaties, and providing for their enforcement. The founding Treaties did not correspond fully to a constitutional act; in view of their specifically functional scope, arguably they did not need to do so.

THE RISE AND DECLINE OF FUNCTIONALISM

The functionalist approach to European integration was partly inspired at first by a desire to shift the emphasis from legal constitutionalism to economic and social objectives. Functionalism is the theory that international cooperation, especially when pursued without a direct challenge to state sovereignty, will lead to incremental improvements to welfare and promote the peaceful resolution of international conflict. The functionalist method generally leads to increased international organisation and may result in a proliferation of 'international regimes', but it is designed to avoid the establishment of a new overarching sovereignty, as has occurred in most federations of states. Although the functionalist approach has been widely applied in Europe since the end of the Second World War, the experience of the European Community, in particular, has demonstrated that it is subject to major and fundamental limitations.

First, the successful establishment of the ECSC and especially later of the EEC, together with their subsequent enlargement of membership, owed much to the willingness of certain states (including eventually all the major states of Western Europe) to depart from pure functionalism by founding a new 'supranational' legal order with structures that are in many respects more intrusive on national sovereignty than those implied by a mere international regime. The concept of 'supranational' has remained ambiguous both in theory and in practice, and has been persistently disputed. The results of economic integration by the Community method are disputable in terms of improved welfare, especially when considerations of equity are applied. Nevertheless, what benefits may have been obtained, and especially in terms of equity, clearly could not have been achieved without the special structures that differentiate the Community from ordinary international organisations: in particular the legislative, executive and judicial powers transferred to the common institutions established by treaty.

Second, the Community method also owed its success to a deviation from functionalism by dealing with integration on a regional rather than a global scale. By establishing a customs union and common agricultural policy, and operating a common commercial policy, as well as by the later development of the European Monetary System and further progress towards a common legal framework in economic affairs, the Community has evolved into a distinctive regional economic entity of major significance in its own right in relation to the wider global economy. At the same time, the EC's member states have increasingly regarded economic union both as a reason and as a necessary basis for political union, which they have also pursued as a distinctive regional grouping, so far confined to Western Europe and, within that increasingly questionable definition, even excluding some states previously reluctant to seek membership on political as well as economic grounds. Again, though the EC has confronted a perpetual crisis of identity and been severely strained by pressures for territorial enlargement, it is highly improbable that integration would have proceeded as far as it has unless the Community's membership had been restricted and extended, when it was, only according to strict economic and political conditions.

Third, functionalist methods did not succeed in supplanting, within their fields of competence, the bureaucratic apparatus of the national state, nor established forms of political authority. Ever since the end of the war, European integration has been obstructed by national policies as defined and defended by states. National governments continue to intervene substantially in the management and organisation of economic activity, both to promote welfare goals and to pursue mercantilist aims, albeit subject to new kinds of collective international obligation.

Fourth, functional integration, even as modified by the Community method, did not prevent either greater or lesser European powers from resorting to conventional diplomacy as a way of managing their relations with each other and with third countries. Since the early 1970s the Community states re-asserted the primacy of foreign policy over welfare and technical functions by means of European Political Cooperation. Despite the progress of economic and legal integration on a regional basis, national security throughout the region continued to be determined by relationships with the North Atlantic military alliance, whether positive, negative or neutral. Most European states retained, and some significantly extended (by means of nuclear armament), their own capacity to pursue national objectives by military means, albeit with varying degrees of credibility in terms of defence against external attack.

On account of these limitations of pure functionalism, the EC states have increasingly wanted to define their relations with each other and with the outside in political as well as merely functional terms. They have tended to do so by retaining the principle of state sovereignty on which the modern international system is still founded. Neither on a global nor on a regional basis, therefore, has functional integration led automatically to political integration. Indeed, in view of the continued primacy and ubiquity of the political realm, and with it state sovereignty as the unique and universal foundation of political authority, functionalism has probably lost any relevance it might have had as a distinct approach to global or European integration.

THE FEDERAL VOCATION

The founding treaties and their subsequent development, as well as the consequent actions of the Community's institutions themselves, were in part inspired by a federal vocation. That vocation, already embodied in the transfer of legal authority itself, was sustained throughout by the Commission, European Parliament and Court of Justice. All the institutions, including the Council, were to some extent deliberately designed in accordance with federalist principles, while some states' governments have always been willing and able to assert a federalist approach.

As a political doctrine federalism has become closely associated with constitutionalism, almost to the extent that the two are theoretically, and even practically, inseparable. In the context of European integration federalism may be best defined as an attempt to extend to the relations between political communities organised as states principles of constitutional government similar to those normally observed in most

European states themselves or, at least, derived from the various European constitutional traditions (which have, of course, been subject historically to deviation and are maintained only with aberrations and imperfections in contemporary conditions).

In this context, therefore, federalism may be understood as prescribing four main general principles of good conduct in the relations between political communities organised as states and in the collective use of public power by states:

- each state should remain autonomous, except in matters that concern other states or the union as a whole (*subsidiarity principle*);
- states should act, individually or collectively, in matters of mutual or common concern only subject to a common legislative and judicial authority (*rule of law*);
- the conditions of membership of the union apply equally to all states willing to observe the rule of law as established by the union, which may be empowered to act on behalf of all by the vote of a majority (*majority principle*);
- the union recognises and guarantees inalienable and universal rights of common citizenship, including that of direct political representation at all levels of government (*citizens' rights principle*).

Although the Community's member states have never agreed to establish a union among themselves by means of a genuinely constitutional act, the advocates of federal union can claim some important advances:

- the Court of Justice successfully established the orthodox doctrines of direct effect and precedence of EC law and that institution's preeminence as the ultimate arbiter of the law prescribed by the Treaties, over any national authority, be it legislative, executive or judicial, is rightly celebrated;
- the Community system of common institutions has survived with its attribution of powers more or less intact, at least within the EC's established legal framework, in spite of successive political onslaughts by member states;
- the EEC was eventually attributed its own financial resources and empowered to determine its own budget;
- the European Parliament became directly elected and achieved an incremental enlargement of its powers, especially in relation to the Community's use of its own financial resources.

Despite these advances, the federal vocation has had disappointing results overall; arguably, it has suffered several major reverses, culminating in the Maastricht Agreement of December 1991, which, in effect, rejected a constitutional settlement and confirmed that the Community's legal framework would not extend to crucial aspects of policy, including external and internal security and even public finance and social affairs in the broader sense. Indeed, the prevailing doctrine seems to condone the cumulatively joint or collusive exercise of functions of public policy by states' governments without a concomitant transfer of political, or even legal, authority.

The European Union now proposed seems to be a sub-species of confederation, itself a species of international relations (that is, a system founded on state sovereignty). While it may be a kind of international regime in which the states involved have made a substantial application of federalist principles, most federalists would argue that the states concerned have not gone far enough in this respect, and ought to go further. However, European federalists need not, and ought not, to adopt the extreme position that the federalist principles would be satisfactorily applied only by the establishment of a new federation or sovereign state. Indeed, the case for federalism in Europe since 1945 has been closely associated with political doctrines that are sceptical of state sovereignty and seek to replace it with an alternative basis of political order both within and between political communities.

The real issue for the government of European Union, from this point of view, though one that is rarely addressed as such, is the value of sovereignty. Whether federalism makes sense as an alternative to state sovereignty, or whether such an alternative is possible at all, remain difficult questions of academic discourse, though with great bearing on practical affairs. There is now a considerable school of academic doctrine willing to argue that the search for an alternative to state sovereignty is vital to the survival of the human species on a global scale.[1] European federalism could be seen as closely related to this trend of political and social thought.

When evaluating the performance of the European Community in terms of political criteria such as 'good governance', therefore, it is not enough to understand the Community's development as a special kind of international relations. The 'neo-functionalism' of the EC method has proved to be a poor alternative to federalism. The inefficiency and inequity of economic integration by the Community method, with its reliance on bureaucratic and corporatist structures, and the 'democratic deficit' induced by the inevitable, if unintended, political consequences of economic integration are notorious. Habitual resort to intergovernmental mechanisms like the European Council and EPC has further weakened parliamentary accountability and the rule of law at both national and European levels. Meanwhile, the progressive transfer of specialised functions of public policy to a European level is of limited value on its own for welfare objectives, often impairs efficiency, and undermines democracy. To the extent that it has increasingly been condoned outside the EC's legal framework, it also undermines the rule of law. The vocation to extend constitutionalism to a regional European scale seems as relevant fifty years on from the Second World War as it has ever been.

THE RELEVANCE OF CONSTITUTIONALISM

The most obvious reason why European states should want to conduct their relations with each other and with peoples elsewhere as far as possible in accordance with principles of constitutional government is that virtually all states geographically and historically definable as European profess to such principles. Indeed, the Treaty on European Union, in Article F, now stipulates by implication that the member states shall both have systems of government founded on the principles of democracy and be assumed to respect fundamental rights. What is more, the Community's member states have, since at least the late 1970s, prescribed similar principles of human and civil rights and democracy for the rest of the world.

The same Article F (incidentally so lettered) stipulates certain principles of federalism: that the Union 'shall respect the national identities of its Member States'; that it, too, shall respect fundamental rights; and that it 'shall provide itself with the means necessary to attain its objectives and carry through its policies'. It might be argued that these provisions can be reasonably applied only if the Union is furnished with a government. As is so often the case, the matter is by no means as simple in practice as it might seem in political or legal theory, and the new Treaty fails to fulfil the intention, implied in its own preamble and Title I on common provisions, to found the Union on a clear constitutional basis with democratic institutions.

Even so, there are in the present conjuncture a number of significant reasons for believing that the intentions are fully justified and the failure to fulfil them is reprehensible in terms both of political values and of the efficiency with which the states' declared common objectives of security and welfare can be pursued, as well as, indeed, of the viability of the project of European Union itself.

NEW THREATS TO PEACE

From its initiation in 1950 the Community method was confined to economic integration. Most European states were able to rely for their collective security on Nato and the preservation of a global and a regional balance of power. The security thus provided was inadequate and costly, requiring nuclear deterrence and subordination of European interests to those of the superpowers. The situation following the demise of the Warsaw Treaty and the collapse of the USSR is, however, far more unstable and revives a number of threats to peace in Europe and the world that may be geopolitically endemic but were previously easier to ignore. The unification of Germany revives a traditional threat to the regional balance of power and increases the urgency of finding a durable political solution to the inevitable material superiority of a national German state. The collapse of Soviet-style communism once more exposes the related problem of conflicting national interests in Central and Eastern Europe. And the end of the cold war reduces the USA's commitment to assume responsibility for protecting the common interests of West Europeans both in neighbouring regions of strategic importance (such as the Middle East) and farther afield.

Meanwhile, the secular decline of European power in relative global terms (of demography, economic performance, political and cultural influence) is henceforth less likely to be compensated or checked as a result of the desire to sustain West European autonomy as a defence against international communism. In general, Europeans are obliged more than ever before since the Second World War to assume responsibility both for their own internal relationships and for their common interests beyond Europe.

This situation must remain highly dangerous for peace throughout the world so long as individual European states can continue legitimately to claim the right to determine and implement in the last resort their own national foreign and security policies, but also so long as they, and especially the larger and more militarised states, are allowed to develop further cooperation in foreign and security policy outside a properly constituted system of democratic government.

A federal union, on the contrary, would offer a unique solution to certain major current threats to peace:

- by allowing diverse national identities and structures within Europe to coexist in a common political framework, guaranteeing basic rights of citizenship and interests of security and welfare, including those of more recent immigrant peoples;
- by protecting the security and welfare of less populated and materially weaker communities against cultural, economic or political dominance;
- by discouraging European states, individually or in confederation, from seeking to dominate other regions, from adventurism in foreign affairs, and from pursuing separate national interests under the guise of common interests;
- by applying criteria for membership that emphasise political values rather than economic performance, racial or religious identity, and strategic interest.

EFFICIENCY AND EQUITY

Theoretically, integration (even, and in some respects especially, on a regional European basis) offers economic advantages in terms of both efficiency and equity. Experience with the EEC, however, confirms that those advantages will not accrue without a measure of centralised control of the use of public power, especially to limit the tendency for organised sectional interests to exploit increased economic integration to their own ends, including the manipulation of new kinds of state intervention (non-tariff barriers).

The European Community has, in effect, tended to pursue integration and manage its consequences by deliberately provoking an iterative resettlement of competing organised sectional interests (the 'dynamics' of integration). Since organised economic interests rely everywhere on the concerted use of public power by states, the process inevitably requires the reconciliaton of national interests *as defined by states*. The process of integration has, therefore, been continuously threatened with paralysis or dissolution from the conflict of national interests so defined. The temptation to invoke the political authority of national governments has become ever more irresistible, but at the same time progressively less effectual, as a way of guaranteeing the genuine freedom of economic activity.

Despite the provision for a uniform legal order, the EC also failed to control the use of public power adequately for purposes of supplying public goods, such as social, environmental and consumer protection. States give every sign of being increasingly reluctant to transfer sufficient powers in these respects. Consequently, integration has made it more difficult for economically vulnerable groups to defend their own interests. As economic growth has become less viable, or even desirable, on ecological and social grounds, the need to supplement the Community with adequate political institutions becomes correspondingly greater.

The protracted, if not endemic, disputation over the role of public finance in the Community offers a typical and crucial example. The Community has been given responsibility for a limited redistributive function as well as for management of the CAP (which is regressive in its redistributive effects), but not for the efficient and equitable deployment of public finance, either in macroeconomic or microeconomic terms. Since fiscal power has remained with the member states, while the EC's capacity to authorise expenditure has been enlarged, a genuine problem of social redistribution has been exacerbated. The real desideratum is a common policy for the use of fiscal power, which for obvious reasons is impossible without political institutions.

Monetary union has been proposed as the alternative to fiscal union (and the political institutions the latter would entail). But recent experience in the first stage of Emu demonstrates the high risks of relying on monetary policy as a means of governing a common market, especially when it includes the imposition of dues or fees for membership (as it may inevitably do, in the absence of a full economic union). Since there may be no manageable path to monetary union *per se*, without fiscal union (and without, therefore, the institutional prerequisites), economic integration itself, including the free movement of capital, may well prove unsustainable.

PLURALISM AND DEMOCRACY

The European Community's constant resort to treaty-making by more or less conventional procedures of international relations is symptomatic of its failure to resolve crises without invoking the sovereignty of its member states. This same deficiency of governance also explains why it is so difficult to apply the simple rule of subsidiarity in contemporary European affairs.

Although the rule of subsidiarity is simple, it works both ways: it is not, as it tends to have become in current usage, simply a justification for retaining state sovereignty. On the contrary the rule is intended, and makes sense only, as a guide to the assignment of powers and functions between various levels of government in a federal union. As such it needs to be applied with due regard for the requirements of public policy in any given time and place; as part of its simplicity, the rule does not contain within itself instruction as to how it should be applied in any given case. Consequently, subsidiarity makes sense only in the framework of a properly constituted federal union, that is, one providing institutional mechanisms for resolving disputed assignments of public powers and functions (and not only through judicial structures).

Nevertheless, subsidiarity is essential to federal union. It underlies the principle that public power should be used only with the consent of a majority of the people and in accordance with the rule of law both at the level of states and at that of the union. An assignment of powers that offends the rule of subsidiarity also offends the fundamental majority principle: either may be breached as much by an excessive decentralisation as by overcentralisation. Two current developments demonstrate why the rule of subsidiarity is so vital in this sense, not only for the realisation of universal virtues of political rule, but also for attaining the EC's economic and strategic objectives, as redefined in the Treaty.

First, member states seem less able than before to commit themselves even to obligations explicitly defined in the treaties, on account of domestic political opposition or political uncertainty. The difficulties encountered in ratification of the Maastricht Treaty provide a poignant illustration. Despite the confidence of all governments that were signatories to that Treaty, four were only able to ratify up to a year beyond the agreed date, and three of these by dint of extreme political subterfuge and manipulation (effectively, the proposal was adopted without adequate popular support in both Denmark and France, and probably in the UK, too). The myriad exceptions and loopholes written into the Maastricht Agreement in December 1991, and subsequently, present those responsible for applying and administering its provisions with an awesome, if not ultimately impossible, task.

Second, however, this apparent revival of pluralism does not indicate a renewed or strengthened attachment to the national state or its institutions. On the contrary, increased centrifugalism weakens the national state as much as, if not more than, it impedes the supranational structures of the Community. Indeed, it is not only theoretically reasonable to expect that the transfer of powers to a supranational level (especially for the financial support of public works and services directly benefiting local communities within states) will tend to weaken the dependence of groups on national states. In practice, organised sectional interests and local authorities have increasingly sought direct access to the Commission and Parliament of the Community, while there is some evidence that certain economic interests and prominent territorially based political movements have been encouraged in the pursuit of autonomy by the opportunity to invoke supranational authority.

On the other hand, this coalition of transnational or subnational forces with supranational authority is much more patchy and unreliable than the neo-functionalist theorists predicted it would be. The Community's member states have on the whole successfully resisted the transfer of more than partial responsibility for crucial functions of public provision, as well as that of the main responsibility for public finance. Consequently, the more dependent groups, socially and territorially defined, still depend primarily on the national state, rather than on supranational authority. At the same time, the states have obstructed access by subnational authorities and private bodies to the Community's institutions beyond purely consultative, not to say, cooptative, procedures (such as Ecosoc, the new consultative committee for regional and local authorities, and even the Parliament itself). National executives remain the preponderant agencies of representation from civil society to the EC, as well as to ordinary international organisations.

Where the Community is concerned, the direct influence of economic corporations, particularly multinational firms, seems to have actually superseded that of European interest groups like the employers' organisation, UNICE, and its sectoral counterparts and affiliates. Despite the widely publicised efforts of the Commission, Parliament and European interest groups and political groups themselves, civil society is still over-

168

whelmingly organised throughout Europe in relation to states: even non-governmental organisations have to be defined as such, as if to emphasise the normality of governmental organisation, rather than as social movements and interests that naturally transcend the established political boundaries of states. Trade unions and other organisations qualified to represent the public, as opposed to sectional, interests are still much less influential and efficient on a European or international scale than the representatives and the corporate managers of capital.

Although this is not the place to speculate adequately on the relationship between internationalism and pluralism (albeit that the topic is quintessentially the subject-matter of federalism, as already indicated above), it is vital to recognise that opposition to Maastricht, as well as the more secular centrifugalism in Europe, do not imply a rejection of federal union. As much as anything else, it is a reaction to the effects of both internationalism and nationalism, which are different sides of the same coin. Correspondingly, it must be acknowledged that social integration, on an economic and on a political dimension, cannot come about without disintegration. In one sense the contemporary European states are, indeed, not sufficiently empowered to effect a genuine federal union: their dislocation from civil society is too great. But in another sense they are expected to do too much, so that federal union is impossible until a much greater detachment has occurred between the existing state structures and the social forces they are still designed, almost uniquely, to control.

Specifically, part of the problem lies in the inadequacy of parliamentary and other representative institutions within the member states, which is perfectly consistent, of course, with the main argument here that the problem is essentially one of constitutionalism and political values. But partly it is also a separate problem of subsidiarity or the assignment of powers. If national representative institutions are inadequate, it is partly because powers and functions have been inappropriately assigned to a national level rather than to a subnational or European level. Only by the provision of federally representative institutions (with appropriately assigned powers) could the plurality of opinions and interests that transcend nationality and state find adequate expression and be satisfactorily mediated.

THE GOVERNMENT OF EUROPEAN UNION

The main and prior issue to have been addressed at Maastricht should have been how the proposed European Union is to be governed. That necessarily constitutional matter was addressed by the European Parliament in its own Draft Treaty of 1984 and was pressed by Parliament again during the deliberations of 1990 and 1991. The

Commission also did much to try to frame those deliberations in terms of a genuinely constitution-making exercise, as did some member states' governments (most notably, Belgium, Germany, Italy and the Netherlands). If the whole project of European integration is not abandoned, the task will have to be taken up again and earnestly, in preparation for renewed deliberations on political union in 1996.

So far, with the notable exception of the European Parliament's contribution, the issue of the government of European Union has been treated, if at all, far too discretely, disjointedly and incrementally. There has been an awful lot of legalistic attention to detail, within the terms of the Community's present legal framework, and of pragmatic, but over-elaborate, improvisation, intended mainly to reconcile the desire of governments to cooperate formally in a wider range of fields (but especially defence and police) with the minimum respect for administrative propriety and political realism. The detailed legal incrementalism, the results of which are invariably just tedious, and the pragmatic improvisation, the results of which are often simply bizarre, are actually less important than the principles at stake. But those are rarely, if ever, pronounced, at least parsimoniously and directly, by either practitioners or academics.

One obvious excuse is that some governments, possibly most, do not believe that European Union should have a government at all, and some states (Britain and Denmark particularly, along with others still outside the EC) have never envisaged the Union as more than an association of sovereign states. Since that belief and that view are incompatible with other professed aims of the same governments and states, it is important to assert here what the principles of government should be in a European Union.

THE SEPARATION OF POWERS

In one form or another, the doctrine of the separation of powers has influenced all living examples of constitutional government in Europe and North America, and by derivation and imitation also those in other regions, especially where the foundation of modern sovereign states succeeded British or French colonial rule. The structural separation of legislative, executive and judicial powers is recommended both for the protection of fundamental civic rights and freedoms, by entrenching the rule of law and preventing the concentration of public power in a single institution, and for the greater efficiency of public administration, by permitting a specialisation of functions and allowing sufficient discretion for executive action.

The institutions of the European Community already partly reflect this doctrine in their own structures, as provided by the founding treaties. For example:

- each of the institutions is separately endowed by treaty with its own rights and obligations;
- the Commission is clearly established as an executive organ in its own right, empowered by the treaties to exercise its own power of decision, which may be legally binding in accordance with substantive provisions of the treaties or with acts of the Council in implementation of such provisions;
- the Court of Justice is clearly established as a judicial organ in its own right, making final decisions regarding the interpretation of the law established by the treaties and arbitration of disputes either between private citizens and public authorities performing obligations imposed by EC law or between different public authorities.

As in all living forms of constitutional government, the separation of powers between the EC's institutions is far from perfect and has to be. For example:

- each of the institutions is authorised to take some part in the due process of passing legally binding acts into justiciable Community law and most important acts require the participation of more than one institution;
- the Commission is accountable for the exercise of its executive and other powers to Parliament, which by passing a motion of censure can oblige the Commission's entire membership to resign and which now has a role in the appointment of the Commission's president and that of its other members;
- the Commission exercises a number of important quasi-judicial functions (for example, surveillance of member states under Article 189 EC);
- budgetary authority is shared between Council and Parliament, and also necessarily involves the Commission for its effective exercise.

However, the assignment of powers to the European Community is so equivocal with respect to legislative and executive powers as to deviate from the norm of constitutional government in an altogether exceptional and exceptionable way. In effect, neither of those fundamental powers of governance is clearly or reliably established in the Community's institutions at all. Both are, therefore, at best vaguely and inadequately provided so far in the governance of European Union. The position of judicial power has remained more or less secure, though in this respect too the recent expansion of functions exercised legitimately at Union level without a concomitant enlargement of the jurisdiction of the EC Court puts the rule of law in doubt.

LEGISLATIVE POWER

The IGC rejected a recommendation of the Commission to include a categorical and hierarchical classification of legislative powers in the new Treaty, which does not refer to the Community's having *law* or *legislative power* as such. (A similar classification was, however, provided in the Parliament's own Draft Treaty of 1984.)

The enactment of legally binding provisions by the Community's institutions, in accordance with the Treaties, still, therefore, seems to be confined to a kind of 'secondary' or 'delegated' legislation, even though the substance of such provisions may be of general and direct effect and concern major aspects of public policy (as it has always done in practice), and even though the significance and frequency of the application of 'open-ended' provisions like Articles 100 and 100a of the EC Treaty have been increased, while the number and import of enactments adopted by majority vote in Council have also greatly increased. Furthermore, the status and legal effect of acts taken in accordance with the Treaties in the sphere of CFSP and police matters remain as unclear as ever, and have possibly been made even less clear by the Maastricht Treaty.

Except for its recently acquired power to prevent Council's adoption of specified legally binding acts of a substantive nature, Parliament has no overriding legislative power, only a right to be consulted in specified cases, and sometimes a right to insist that its amendments to proposed enactments be reconsidered. There is no justification, in terms of the theory or normal practice of the separation of powers, for denying the directly elected European Parliament the right to reject ultimately any legally binding enactment that the EC is authorised to make, subject to a normal delegation of legislative power or the assignment of executive powers of decree in appropriate cases. Parliament's legislative power of rejection (and approval) is unequivocal only with respect to some parts of the Community's annual budget. In spite of its limited power of 'assent' (*avis conforme*) in specified cases, Parliament has no general power to make legislative provision with respect to foreign policy, security or police, and even has no formal consultative power with respect to the conduct of external economic relations.

The effect of the peculiar assignment of powers to the Community, as endorsed and extended by the Maastricht Treaty, is a usurpation of legislative power by the executive branches of states. But states' executives, even so, are authorised to use that power collectively, and in many crucial aspects of public policy, only when they are able to act through their representatives by unanimity. The effective transfer of law-making power to the executives of states by means of the treaties, which is potentially overriding when the states' own executive representatives can act by unanimity, makes a nonsense of the separation of powers at both national and European levels. Equally importantly, the capacity of the states' executives to assume discretion to act authoritatively outside the Community's legal framework, for example in the sphere of CFSP, or even in spheres where powers have been duly assigned to the EC, has a similar consequence.

The condition of unanimity may provide some guarantee for the rights of national parliaments, but only to the extent that the latter can exercise those powers effectively in the prevailing constitutional and political conditions at national level. However, the requirement of unanimity among states' representatives may be highly inequitable. When the states concerned are of unequal size and potency, or when some are more dependent for welfare and security on common action than others, it is inclined to favour the stronger against the weaker.

These and other shortcomings of legislative power (and the 'democratic deficit' itself) can be remedied only by a genuine assignment of legislative power to the Union, including competences both exclusive from and concurrent with those assigned to the states (or residing with the latter), and by a clear investment of that power in duly and periodically elected representatives of the peoples of the Union, deliberating in assembly, as well as in the representatives of states. Legislation by recurrent and reiterative treaty making, and by cumulative delegation to executive authorities, is a poor, and ultimately unworkable, substitute for constitutional government.

EXECUTIVE POWER

A major part of the genius of the founders of the American Union was to recognise that legislative power cannot on its own guarantee that the political community to which it belongs will be governed either efficiently or democratically. Executive power, in other words, needs to be securely established both in order to curb or resist the temptation of representatives endowed with popular mandates to respond too much to merely passionate or partisan appeals and so that collective actions projected or required in the public interest can be efficiently performed, sometimes without the possibility of prior or detailed referral to popular, or legislative, approval. The satisfactory provision of executive power is, indeed, one of the peculiar virtues of federal union, and derives essentially from its application of republican principles.

The authors of *The Federalist* explicitly referred to the need for a separate executive power (ultimately embodied in the office of president in the 1787 Constitution) as an agency of republican government designed to accomplish 'extensive and arduous enterprises for the public benefit'.[2] The presidential power of legislative veto was included in the US Constitution out of a desire to restrain the likely tendency of popular representatives in Congress to emphasise the ends of public policy at the expense of procedural and institutional forms.

It is also relevant that John Locke, when describing what has subsequently been more commonly denoted as the executive power, referred to a *federative* power, connoting in effect the whole range of functions pertaining to the security of the body politic and to its external relations beyond its own sovereign jurisdiction. It is no more possible to conceive of a body politic that is governed constitutionally without a legislative power of its own than it is to expect one to be capable of survival or coexistence with others as an integral unit without a clearly established executive, empowered among other things to represent the union in external affairs. 'For a constitutional people,' according to Harvey Mansfield, 'nothing is more necessary than to define what executive power is.'[3] In the European Community the definition and disposition of executive power became increasingly ambiguous, especially with the development of interstate cooperation outside the Community's legal framework, with respect both to economic policy and to external relations.

The Treaty on European Union did little to resolve that ambiguity, though it did endow the Community's institutions with important new competences in economic and, more especially, monetary policy. In its ultimate form, however, the Emu would be governed in accordance with predetermined rules implemented and applied by a system of independent central banks, including a new European Central Bank. The very inflexibility of such an arrangement explains both the decision to leave the power of public finance overwhelmingly with the states themselves and the need to make accession to the new monetary system more or less optional and conditional for individual members.

The new treaty also goes further than any previous similar act to mend the dislocation between the procedures of EPC, on the one hand, and executive responsibility for the Community's external relations, on the other. It does so chiefly by obliging the member states to 'inform and consult one another' on CFSP, when required, in the Community's own Council and by vesting Council with responsibility for defining common positions (Article J.2) and deciding that, and broadly how, a matter should be the subject of joint action, including the possibility of implementation of joint action by majority vote in Council.

However, the member states' own governments are still supreme where the political aspects of external affairs are concerned (and when are they not concerned?), reserving the right to set 'general guidelines' in their own European Council. Although the Treaty confirms the practice of using the Community's own powers in external economic relations to pursue political objectives determined by states' governments, and also empowers Council to charge operational expenditure for similar ends to the Community's own budget, the Commission's role in CFSP remains pretty nebulous and Parliament's merely and loosely consultative. Executive authority to represent the Union externally is divided between the presidency of Council, for CFSP, and the Commission, for matters falling within the EC's defined sphere of external economic relations.

The Union has, therefore, no single locus of responsibility with respect to economic policy, external affairs and security (including now internal police powers), executive power being deliberately divided between Council and Commission, and in some vital respects left in limbo, so that those who hold political sway in the states at the time may still decide for themselves whether the Union shall be capable of acting effectively, and whether all or only some of their own number need meet any obligations or enjoy any benefits involved. Unfortunately, phobia about the Commission seems to have prevailed over any genuine concern for either the efficiency or the accountability of the Union's governance.

The European Parliament's right to approve the appointment of the President and other members of the Commission is now confirmed and, if used appropriately, could strengthen the Commission's political authority. Conceivably, appointment as president could be reserved for an individual endorsed, prior to European elections, by one or more political groups capable of forming an absolute or two-thirds majority in Parliament, after the elections. Parliament's three main political groups have continued to evolve into organisations resembling national parties in the USA, but they are still at least as undisciplined and incoherent as Congressional parties in that country, and the European Union is nowhere near obtaining presidential parties even on the model of the French Fifth Republic or federal parties on the German model, while the Westminster model of one-party oligarchy would hardly be desired or desirable on a European scale.

The Commission, in other words, might well remain a largely bureaucratic organ, with its capacity and its competences correspondingly restricted. On the other hand, Council, with its shifting composition of states' delegations and necessarily short-term and largely mediative presidency, is inherently unsuited on both democratic and administrative grounds for the executive responsibilities for which it seems increasingly intended, if only by default.

Both those living within such a Union, and those affected beyond its borders, must consider with some trepidation the prospect of what might be attempted in its name.

JUDICIAL POWER

The European Community's member states have progressively enlarged their capacity to act confederally with respect to both internal and external economic and political objectives. But they have not correspondingly either established new constitutional foundations for the joint use of public power or enhanced the possibilities of ultimate control of their joint actions by recognised judicial authority significantly beyond what is already provided in the Community's confined legal framework. Consequently, these states claim an increased justification to combine their material capacity to make use of public power in relation to their own citizens and others, while remaining free of any ultimately overriding arbitration beyond what is already provided in international law, including the United Nations Charter.

The role of the Court of Justice in relation to the basic human and civic rights, as confirmed or extended by the new Treaty, remains equivocal, more especially as a result of the exclusion of matters defined in the sphere of 'justice and home affairs' from the Community's established legal framework. That exclusion, in effect, invites an intrusion by states' governments into matters (such as those pertaining to the free movement of persons) previously understood as belonging to the judicial competence of the Court.

The Maastricht agreement seems to have deliberately eschewed the option of entrenching a comprehensive bill of rights for the Union as well as that of defining fundamental political rights and obligations of European citizenship. Those directly affected by the Union's jurisdiction internally have no corresponding juridical entity from which they might claim protection or redress in all possible cases of abuse or misuse of public power. Those liable to suffer from action taken in the Union's name have little assurance that the action might ultimately be restrained by fundamental respect for the rule of law.

The rule of law could be effectively guaranteed only by scrapping the entire edifice presently conceived in terms of 'pillars' in favour of a comprehensive and unique constitutional settlement, similar to what was proposed by the Parliament's Draft Treaty of 1984 and making similar allowance for the provisional retention of competences by states in specified spheres of public policy.

GOOD GOVERNMENT

The preceding critique has deliberately interpreted the problems of governance in relation to European integration in terms of traditional and conservative precepts of good government, as understood by reference to characteristically European values. However, paradoxically, the major obstacle to realising a solution couched in precisely those terms seems to be the reluctance of the present members of the European Community to transpose the relevant precepts to a European, rather than a purely national, scale. The key to explaining this paradox is the concept of state sovereignty, which seems in turn to be at the heart of a crucial contradiction in the modern, rationalist exposition of liberal European values.

In terms of that exposition, democratic and republican forms of government seem to be accompanied, particularly in some of the more centralised member states, by a corresponding principle of unlimited and indivisible political authority, which is further complicated by the modernist sociological assumption that a human community can cohere sufficiently to enjoy the benefits of political rule only by adopting an exclusive principle of common national identity.

The federal vocation has, therefore, repeatedly faced resistance from those who naturally assume that constitutional government would be possible in a European Union only if accompanied by a transfer of absolute sovereignty to the Union, and even by the emergence of suffi-cient cultural homogeneity to justify some kind of pan-European nation-alism. But this is not the only explanation for the failure of the federalist project, which, when properly understood, actually implies a rejection of such sovereignty as a unique principle of political rule and assumes fundamentally that political rule need not, and ought not, be identified with nationalism.

In practice, not all, or even any, member states of the European Community may be considered capable in their present form of attain-ing the standards of good government implied by classical constitution-alism. This could be one explanation for their failure to apply those standards also on a European scale. In other words, the failure of European federalism as a contemporary project may be more closely associated than is normally imagined with a corresponding failure of the national state in its modern form. European integration may, con-sequently, have far more radical implications than its chief exponents, of either a functionalist or federalist persuasion, have been so far usually willing to admit.

Perhaps this chapter's emphasis on constitutional forms reflects an anachronistic attachment of federalist doctrine itself to political, legal and even economic relationships inherent to the embodiment of sover-eignty in the national state. Possibly the crucial challenge to exponents of federalist principles and methods remains that of explaining why apparently all previous attempts at federal union have either dissolved into a form of international relations or evolved into a new sovereign federation, equivalent in essential respects to the national state.

If Europeans could successfully develop an alternative approach to the government of political communities and the relations between them, they would not only be responding to their own needs but also providing the kind of influence, by example, that is the only truly effective way both of defending one's own enjoyment of pluralist values pertaining to a civil society and ensuring their ultimate availability to others.

11

THE EUROPEAN COMMISSION

John Fitzmaurice

However one regards the likely development of the European Union beyond Maastricht, the European Commission is of central importance. This is the case whether or not the Union achieves significant institutional deepening in a federal direction, regardless of the most important priorities of the member states, and whatever enlargement takes place due to the joining of some Efta countries and those of Central and Eastern Europe. Almost all would agree that the Commission has played a crucial role in building the Community and that without the Commission, with its unique characteristics, the European construction could hardly have come so far so fast. The Commission has a key role in whatever may be the preferred scheme for the development of the Union.

Most would accept, for example, that without the Commission, there could hardly have been the 1992 programme to create the internal market. Even those who are most critical of the Commission's activism complain paradoxically about the ineffective implementation of EC law and the corresponding unlevelling of the single market playing field. Others have often criticised the Commission for its excessive prudence, its low profile in institutional debates and its unwillingness to commit itself unequivocally to the federalist cause – or even, less ambitiously, Parliament's more moderate vision.[1] The Commission is still what it always has been, a central actor in the Community, variously solicited as an ally on all sides and blamed by all sides.

It is crucial, therefore, to incorporate the Commission into the strategic debate about the future of the Union. Nevertheless, it is important not to entertain unrealistic expectations about the Commission's future capacity. The Commission must not be overloaded with more duties than it can reasonably bear, and it should not be expected to be something it is not. Certainly, the Commission has shown in recent years a considerable capacity for adaptation to new political situations and new managerial challenges. Moreover, much criticism of the Commission is misdirected, in that it ascribes to the Commission a role that it does not

179

have. So at least one perfectly reasonable conclusion to draw from an analysis of the Commission is that it should continue to do what it already does, yet seek to be even more effective. Such a minimalist conclusion should not be written off as of no interest or value.

Much discussion about the Commission is sentimental, arguing that the Commission should merely be allowed to return to its innocent state in a former golden age. This begs the question, of course, of whether such a golden age existed and whether uncompromised innocence can be recovered. One of the essential merits of the first Delors Commission (1985–89) was that it sidestepped this unproductive nostalgic discussion by looking to the future and by seeking to make the Commission an effective political and managerial instrument for new tasks, in a new situation.

So, what is the Commission? What can it reasonably become? Can it adapt? How far should it adapt? One thing is clear. What the Commission becomes depends only partially on the Commission itself. If it does not develop into something closer to a European government, that will not be the fault of the Commission. It is only given to the Commission in the very narrowest sense to be the 'motor of integration', as it is often referred to in textbooks. But the Commission can fulfil quite well the strategic role assigned to it in the system if it is allowed to by member governments. This is not to belittle the Commission nor to underrate its importance, but to establish the proper yardstick by which to judge it.

PARTNER IN COMMUNITY GOVERNMENT

It is a truism to assert that the European Community is neither a state, nor an international organisation. Keohane and Nye termed it in a recent book a 'regime' whereas William Wallace has called it 'less than a federation, more than a regime'.[2] Indeed, at different times in the development of the Community, models of analysis have derived from functionalism, regime theory and cooperative federalism, and all have a relevance to understanding the Union and the Commission's role within it.

If the EC is more than an international organisation or regime, but less than a federation, it follows that the Commission is more than a secretariat and less than a government. The EC has no 'government' and yet is governed. The reality of the Community as it has developed is that it is a form of collective government in which the Commission is only one, though important, actor. The Commission exercises the governmental function together with the European Council, the Council, member states, the European Parliament and other bodies. Some may wish to see the Commission assume a much larger part of the governmental function. However, given that the Commission is unlikely to achieve such a prominent position or to hold a near monopoly of the government function in the foreseeable future, it is more relevant to examine how the Commission can best play the role currently assigned to it in what will continue to be a pluralist and collective government structure that can function only through cooperation between all its equally legitimate components.

The Commission's role within the Community system can be defined as that of animator, impresario and manager. The Commission plays for the largest stakes. Member states and citizens have a largely instrumental view of the Community. It is one way, perhaps the best, but not the only way to achieve their policy objectives. The Commission, however, stands or falls by demonstrating that the Community and only the Community can deliver. This contrast creates a constructive dialectic. Even more than the European Parliament and the political forces represented there, it falls to the Commission to manage the system as it is, and to make it work. The Commission has to be proactive; it has to bring together the component parts of the EC system and manage constructively both their cooperation and their conflicts. The Commission has to turn political principles into real and effective policy. The Commission is the 'player–manager' of the Community system.

THE SIZE AND APPOINTMENT OF THE COMMISSION

The appropriate size of the Commission is a matter of legitimate and continuing debate. The current rule is that the Commission must include at least one, but not more than two members from every member state. Conventional wisdom, which was expected to find its way into the relevant provisions of the Maastrict Treaty (Article 157), is that the size of the Commission is already, at seventeen members, too large, and that its growth should be restricted before the next enlargement by establishing the rule of one Commissioner per member state. In fact, the decision was postponed at Maastricht, and the Council was asked to dispose of the matter (acting unanimously) during 1992. In the event, the Council, too, made no change. The following year, however, a radical proposal from the CDU in the Bundestag to reduce the Commission to ten members reopened the debate.[3] This proposal has the merit of recognising that an attempted revision to one Commissioner per member state would be hardly worth the inevitable quarrel as it could only be a short-term palliative. Under such a rule, the question of the size of the Commission would have to be posed again if and when the Union enlarges to include Central European countries.

The Brussels European Council in December 1993 simply agreed on an automatic continuation of the existing practice in prescribing one

Commissioner for each of the four candidate states, but recognised that the issue is real by referring it to the 1996 IGC.

The issue of the size of the Commission should not be divorced, as it often is, from the procedure for its appointment and its relationship with the European Parliament. The Maastricht Treaty takes a significant step towards making the Commission a parliamentary executive. It provides that member governments shall consult the Parliament about their nomination as President of the Commission. The governments in consultation with the President-designate shall nominate the other Commissioners. The whole of the new Commission shall then be subject as a body to a vote of approval by the Parliament. Significantly, the terms of the Commission and the Parliament are synchronised (involving an extension from four to five years for the term of the Commission) so that the Parliament newly elected in June can influence the formation of the Commission to take office the following January.[4] This new arrangement, to be tested in 1994, should lead to a much closer relationship between Commission and Parliament. If the President-designate manages to become *de facto* if not *de jure* in charge of the selection of his or her Commission, the discussion about the size of the Commission will take on a different character. National governments, it should be remembered, rarely have a fixed size, but vary according to political and operational needs.

The argument for a size limitation is that the present Commission of seventeen, let alone a larger one, does not offer equally worthwhile portfolios to all its members. Its size is thought to create an unwieldy college, making cohesion and coordination more difficult. This has negative effects on the administration, making coordination difficult there too: it prevents consolidation of the Directorates General into a smaller number, leading to complex arrangements with several Commissioners responsible for the same Directorate General. For some federalists, the present (and future) arrangements enshrine the unwelcome principle of national representation in the Commission, despite the fact that, under the Treaty, the independence of members of the Commission is supposed to be 'beyond doubt', and that member governments undertake 'not to seek to influence the members of the Commission in the performance of their tasks'.[5]

Nevertheless, it can be argued that there are merits, at this fragile stage in European integration, in ensuring that all nationalities have a stake in the Commission. Moreover, that the larger member states have two members allows them often to appoint one each from the government and opposition parties, providing a greater political pluralism. This last point would lose its significance if the Commission changes its character and becomes a parliamentary Commission based on shifting majorities in the European Parliament (usually, in practice, a grand

Socialist–Christian Democrat coalition). There is also the need to consider how to protect the interests of small member states, an issue which may actually increase in force as the Union enlarges.

These arguments about size seem quite finely balanced.[6] One approach, equally valid for a future 'parliamentary' Commission based on the present model, would consist of fixing clearer ground rules: a maximum size could be set; no two members could come from one member state; a large/small state ratio could be established and a minimum number of nationalities could be prescribed.

From the point of view of the internal reform of the Commission, therefore, Maastricht made only one modest change. The number of Vice-Presidents was reduced from six to a maximum of two.[7] An additional proposal by the IGC for the Council to appoint (by qualified majority vote) five Deputy Commissioners was dropped by the heads of government. They would have acted like junior ministers, outside the cabinet. Certainly there will be pressure to reopen this whole debate at the next IGC in 1996, and its course will no doubt be much influenced by the successor of Jacques Delors, who is due to retire after ten years as President of the Commission in January 1995.

A 'PARLIAMENTARY' COMMISSION

The Community after Maastricht will see some subtle shifts in the triangular institutional balance between Council, Commission and Parliament. The provisions in the new treaty for parliamentary consultation on the President-designate and the requirement for an investiture vote, together with the synchronisation of the terms of office of Parliament and Commission, may prove in the long term to be one of the most significant of the institutional reforms. It could imply a more parliamentary Commission: a Commission that, in the words of a leading MEP in a recent debate on the revision of the Parliament's rules of procedure, 'could not pursue a legislative programme which does not reflect the will of Parliament'.[8]

Such a 'Parliamentary' Commission, corresponding in its composition and programme to the will of the parliamentary majority, could find itself obliged to adopt a more arms-length and even aggressive stance towards the Council. The Commission's independence has to be an independence equidistant from both institutions if it is to be credible. That is why the Commission has attached great importance to maintaining the institutional balance and, especially, in protecting its right of initiative as the pivot of that balance. Fending off attacks on the powers of the Commission was a key defensive mission for the Commission's campaign in the IGC.[9] During the process, President Delors undertook a persistent and effective effort to educate the member states in this regard, reminding them that the Commission's monopoly right of initiative, including within it the right to amend or withdraw its proposals during examination and the provision that the Commission proposal could only be amended unanimously by Council, were key elements in ensuring the success of the Community method and should not be abandoned lightly or without an alternative model being proposed. He sought to stress that 'if the Commission were to lose its initiative the system would lose its dynamism'.[10] At the Rome Assizes in November 1990 he said:

> The institutional triangle of the Rome Treaty, Council, Parliament, Commission, has worked well. The Commission has functioned well. If that was not the case how could we already have implemented two-thirds of the Single Act? How could we be so sure that we would have a single market without frontiers by the end of 1992? Ladies and Gentlemen, if one day you should decide to greatly change that institutional triangle, first ask yourself if you would be as democratic and as effective. If the answer is 'yes' then never mind the Commission, which is there to serve the process of building Europe and not the other way round. But, be sure to propose something at least as effective and coherent before jettisoning the legacy of the Founding Fathers of the Treaty of Rome.[11]

This defence was successful because the Commission has proven, contrary to much popular criticism, very adaptable. This is important. It must continue to be adaptable in the future.

AN ADAPTABLE COMMISSION

Since the mid-1980s, the Commission has done much to improve the preparation and planning of EC policy. It carried through much as planned and close to the timetable the ambitious internal market programme. It has established much more efficient internal and inter-institutional legislative planning, enabling stability and planning in Community expenditure and avoiding the previous unseemly and inefficient annual budget battles. This new approach was instrumental in obtaining the neccessary political agreement in Council to provide the stable long-term financing first of the Single Act and then of Maastricht, known as the Delors I and Delors II packages. The Commission forged the necessary political consensus.

The Commission has also begun to pay greater attention to the need to adapt its administrative structures and increase its efficiency. Faced as it often was with ill-informed and destructive criticisms of its efficiency, it had to prove that it could cope with the major new tasks to which it aspired, in particular the single market, the new structural

184

funds, new R&D policies and the coordination of aid to Central Europe. It had to adapt to modern management techniques and performance-orientated approaches to public administration. The Commission has not remained passive. It has in a quiet manner acted to increase its efficiency through greater staff flexibility and mobility, more use of outside expertise on a temporary basis, smaller and less rigid internal structures, some decentralisation of management, improved lateral inter-service coordination and, above all, adaptation to a resource environment in which new tasks cannot automatically be met by new staff, as was often the case in an earlier period. Much remains to be done, but there is definite progress.

THE COMMISSION AND SUBSIDIARITY

By far the most important adaptation, however, is the Commission's new self-denying ordinance on legislation, subsumed under the general portmanteau heading of subsidiarity (though it has several different aspects, notably transparency). Subsidiarity is now a legally binding concept, justiciable before the Court, anchored in Article 3b of the Maastricht Treaty. Yet, above all, it is a political concept, a state of mind, an approach. It may mean less and certainly different Community legislation, but it is not a one-way street, designed simply to reduce the existing competences of the EC and to deny it new ones. It can equally be the justification for new Community competence if the Community level is clearly the more appropriate.[12] Even where a clear EC competence can be demonstrated, the Commission in its document on subsidiarity has indicated that it will use further tests of proportionality and appropriateness before deciding that legislation is necessary. Beyond that, it will seek to make legislation less detailed, less complex and less intrusive, while continuing earlier new approaches, based on greater use of mutual recognition allied with minimum standards, that had been established most clearly in the Cassis de Dijon judgement of the Court of Justice in 1979.[13]

The Commission has also attempted to make the legislative process more open and accessible. The annual work programme for the coming year will be published every October and be subject to an inter-institutional debate.[14] Consultative documents will be announced in advance. Improved but regulated access by lobbies and pressure groups is to be allowed. The Commission is also encouraging the Council to open up at least part of its legislative proceedings. These measures should help to ease a critical situation which could, if not addressed seriously, paralyse the Community's legislative machine and prevent the Community fulfilling its legitimate functions. In any event, the Commission carries the blame for a perceived propensity to over-legislate, though often it is not deserved. In fact, however, a significant amount of legislation arises from requests by the Council or member states (about 21 per cent in 1991 and 15 per cent in 1992).[15] Several proposals that might now be criticised on general subsidiarity grounds, such as the Directive on time shares, originated under pressure from member states. Under 10 per cent of legislation in both 1991 and 1992 arose from spontaneous and independent Commission initiatives of the kind that is criticised by 'Euro-sceptics'. Much individual legislation also arose through the systematic implementation of programmes agreed to by all member states.

It should not be forgotten, moreover, that much of the impenetrable complexity of EC legislation arises less from the original Commission proposal than from the successive compromises in Council in the course of its enactment that undermine clarity, coherence and incisiveness. It could be said the Commission, far from being remote and insensitive, has acted to respond to those new sensitivities and, far from abusing its right of initiative, exercises it with moderation and intelligence, taking due but not slavish account of the wishes of other institutions.

In any event, now that the single market programme is almost complete, there is a tendency for less new legislation.[16] One can expect more monitoring of the implementation of EC law and of compliance with it. There will be 'care and maintenance' of the mass of internal market legislation that has been put in place. Experience of implementation and changes in technology and business practice are bound to throw up deficiencies and loopholes and necessitate routine amendments. The Commission will have to adapt to this new mode. Monitoring, investigation and collection of information will replace legislative activism. Here, too, a greater delegation of executive implementing powers to the Commission would be a helpful step forward. It may also prove necessary to strengthen staffing in these monitoring areas.

Less legislation; better legislation; less intrusive legislation; more framework legislation; better-respected legislation; legislation more openly arrived at: these are goals that the Commission is pursuing. Their accomplishment should contribute to making EC legislation more acceptable and less open to criticism and rejection. This is now a vital objective of the Commission.

THE COMMISSION AS EXECUTIVE

One of the most intractable problems facing the Community is the absence of a developing executive capacity. The EC does not have a government. Executive functions are shared between Commission, Council and member states' governments, all of which act as agents of Community policy. The Maastricht Treaty does not alter this dispersal of power. It must be a major concern of the Commission to do what it can to overcome the problems inherent in such a system, which, necessary though it may be for political reasons, leads to considerable problems of effectiveness. The Commission is the nearest that there is to an executive, but it is far from being the government of the Union.

It is most likely that the present pattern of a mixed or shared executive will continue. The Council of ministers is likely to retain its present position or something close to it. There will, therefore, continue to be a joint or a collective executive. The most important thing will be to ensure that the interrelationship operates well. The Commission must be able to provide the element of stability, coordination and coherence that an otherwise unstable system requires. It must be involved at all levels. It must be able to make the 'pillars' structure of the Maastricht Treaty less unwieldy by coordinating across the board. That was the sense of the statement by Delors in 1990, commenting on the Commission's role in Common Foreign and Security Policy:

> We have never said that the Commission should have the same powers in the area of foreign and security policy as in other matters. Simply it is unthinkable that the Commission should not take part in the process of reaching decisions and in giving impulsion to that policy that has been put in common in certain areas.[17]

It would not be wise for the Commission to play the role of a national foreign ministry; but without its involvement in ensuring overall coherence, particularly between political positions and trade and economic policies, the CFSP will not be effective. The third Delors Commission has made the preparations for such a political role. A Commissioner for political relations has been appointed and a new Directorate General IA, charged with the political aspects of external relations, has been created. The same applies in the third pillar created by Maastricht on judicial and interior affairs. Here, the Commission does have a full right of participation and a partial right of initiative, and it clearly expects to play an active role in such a way as to approximate as far as possible to normal EC business.

In both aspects, CFSP and interior affairs, the Commission has to develop a new expertise and play a proactive role in ensuring the necessary coordination between, for example, trade, human rights and immigration issues that cut across all three pillars. Only the Commission can provide the necessary overview to guarantee policy coherence. The Commission also has an important role in operating the complex procedures under Stage Two of Economic and Monetary Union. Here, within the Ecofin Council and the new European Monetary Institute, the Commission exercises not only a right of initiative but important monitoring, gate-keeping and coordination functions to ensure the overall balance and coherence of the system.

COMITOLOGY AND THE HIERARCHY OF NORMS

Both the Commission and the European Parliament, with different emphasis in detail, have argued that effective executive management in the Community requires a clarification of the present complex situation in relation to powers of execution – or what might be called delegated or secondary legislation, *'le pouvoir règlementaire'*.[18]

The present position, which was unchanged by both Maastricht and, despite some good intentions, by the Single Act, is that the Commission should exercise powers of execution but that, in exceptional cases, the Council may reserve to itself part or all of the powers of delegated rule-making under primary legislation.[19] In practice, however, this exception has become the rule. Through a complex and arcane system of committees that 'assist' the Commission, which has hardly been made simpler by the post-Single Act Regulation on Committees, the Council fetters the Commission's executive powers by giving these committees not merely reasonable advisory powers on draft rules but effective powers of veto or of referral back to the Council with suspensive effect.

The Commission argued in its Opinion for the IGC that it was urgent to resolve this complex situation, known as 'comitology', in favour of clarity and of greater effective delegation to the Commission. It followed this up by presenting as one of its earliest working papers to the IGC detailed proposals to this end.[20] This paper proposed establishing a clear 'hierarchy of norms'. In this hierarchy, the Treaty would form the apex of the Community, followed by 'laws' (new nomenclature to replace 'regulations', 'directives' and 'decisions') approved by the legislative authority (Council and Parliament on a proposal from the Commission). The corpus of EC laws would be of a framework character and would have long-term stability. Laws would be implemented as a whole or in part either by measures of member states (as directives are now) or by EC measures. In the latter case, executive measures would be adopted by the Commission subject only to an advisory committee of national officials being consulted and a residual 'right of substitution' given to the Council and Parliament, both of which would have two months to react to trigger the substitution procedure. When that happened, the Commission would adopt a new measure or a new proposal that would be subject to the full legislative (co-decision) procedures. All delegated legislation would be open to challenge in the Court by all the institutions and member states. The Commission argued that this procedure would have respected the rights of the other institutions and the principle of subsidiarity but permitted a greater clarity and efficiency of implementation. As we have seen in Chapter Two, the issue of creating a legislative hierarchy remains important unfinished business from Maastricht.

FUTURE OF THE COMMISSION

In conclusion, therefore, we can see that no matter how the Union develops beyond Maastricht, the role of the European Commission will remain crucial. In a model of development that might be described as the status quo plus or a dynamic status quo, the role of the Commission will be no less vital than in a model which expects major institutional changes. The role of the Commission is, furthermore, just as central in a Union which gives priority to widening over deepening. A wider Union enlarged to include both the Efta states that opt to join and Central European states would require more holding together than a smaller and deeper Community. It is paradoxical that a more intergovernmental Union with a more complex structure than that envisaged, for example, in the Parliament's Draft Treaty of 1984 has greater need of the Commission as the central pivot to hold the system in balance.

The Community went through a long and optimistic period of accelerating development between 1985 and 1991, culminating, or so it seemed at the time, in the signature of the Maastricht Treaty in December of that year. Since then, the Community has entered a more stormy period, beset by criticism and uncertainty. Some argue that the fault is in the process by which the Treaty was negotiated; others take the view that the Treaty itself is a mistake because it prescribes either too little integration or too much; others note the misfortune that the Treaty, like the first enlargement in 1973, coincided with a deepening economic recession in Europe; still others blame political leaders for ignoring the need to carry public opinion with them.

Few if any of these explanations can be held to be the responsibility of the Commission in any but the most indirect sense. Yet the Commission, lacking as it does its own direct political legitimacy, has been perhaps the most serious victim of this new scepticism. The Commission can do little to repair this situation or reverse the new and more difficult political atmosphere. Part of the response, however, lies in making the Union as it was forged at Maastricht work effectively to demonstrate that Europe can solve problems and can adapt to new circumstances and requirements. It is here that the European Commission can make a positive and essential contribution by holding the Union together, by minimising the dispersion caused by the institutional arrangements that derive from the Treaty and by managing effectively the new interinstitutional arrangements that derive from the co-decision procedure.

189

12

REPRESENTING THE STATES

William Nicoll

The Union of the Treaty on European Union is a union among, not of, the states. The first dozen words of the Treaty say so, unambiguously. But lest this reignite the bitter old dispute about the subordination of the state to the people, the next dozen words borrow the 1957 formula concerning a process creating an ever closer union among (not of) the peoples (plural).[1] The expression 'close union' itself comes from the Statute of the Council of Europe. According to the Schuman Declaration, the economic community was to lay the basis for a European federation, but the word was never used in a formal text until it made its brief and explosive appearance in the early draft of the Treaty on European Union. The word 'supranational' was used once, in the original version of the ECSC Treaty, to describe the functions of the members of the High Authority, but extirpated in the Merger Treaty of 1965.

What John Major has called 'national precedence' shines through the density of the Treaty.[2] The integrating remit given for the first time to the European Council (Article D), the doctrine of subsidiarity as expounded by the European Council in Edinburgh in 1992 (national action is the rule, Community action the exception), the intergovernmentalism of the second and third pillars (and, as it will be argued here, of the Council in the first pillar) and the consecration in Maastricht and in Edinburgh of variable geometry in Community legislation, all speak volumes about the priority given in the Treaty to the authority of what Margaret Thatcher (and long before her, Douglas Hurd) called the 'independent sovereign states'.

The consequence is that the Treaty reserves its most sweeping effects for the Council, that part of the structure which represents the states, and which retains and reinforces its hegemony within the institutional separation of powers.

THE SINGLE FRAMEWORK

The deepening and widening of the Council involves a certain amount of word-play. The notable example of verbal sleight of hand is the Article C evocation of a 'single institutional framework'. Closely examined, this framework reveals itself to be multiple: what is singly called 'the Council' behaves quite differently according to what it is doing. The change is in the constitutional vocabulary. The Council mandated throughout Title V, being an element of the Union, not of the Community, is what was heretofore known as 'The Ministers of Foreign Affairs meeting in the framework of Political Cooperation'. Proprietorially and presumptuously, they regularly describe their pronouncements as those of 'the Community and its Member States'. What was hitherto the 'Meeting of Ministers responsible for Immigration' becomes another Council (along with other formations involving the same Ministers and their Justice colleagues). But the third pillar Council behaves differently from the second pillar Council, and both are different from the Council of the European Community.[3]

THE INTERGOVERNMENTAL COUNCIL

All this said, the legendary singleness of the Council is more real than it is often given credit for by observers who note that there are many different Councils and that they do not always cohere, especially where spending is involved. There is another school which picks over the 'Community method' and the abandonment of it.[4] A different analysis from either of the foregoing suggests that, within the Community method of the first pillar, the Council is not immensely less intergovernmental than it is when the member states step outside the Community, but stay within what they now call the Union.

In the terms of this analysis, the Council is not especially different from the sum of its governmental parts. This is evident when it practises unanimity, as it must when the legal base of its decision so requires, or when it changes a Commission proposal.[5] Unanimity is reached through protracted intergovernmental negotiation; no power exists to impose anything on a member state against its will.[6] The Thatcher/Hurd prescription, seconded by John Major, is complied with.[7]

One ostensible snag for this triad is that the member states are not proactive: they need a Commission proposal to set them off and they are required to remain within the ambit of that proposal. But in the real Community, the Council collectively, and the member states individually, in presidency and out of it, continuously ask the Commission to make this or that proposal; and, as Chapter Eleven shows, around one-fifth of legislation arises from such requests.[8] The Council has the legal

191

right to make these requests, acting by simple majority (Article 152 EEC). The doctrine upheld by the Legal Service of the Council is that the Commission may not decline to respond to such requests, but is free as to the nature of the proposals it makes. By analogy, the same should hold for the Parliament's new power to ask for a Commission proposal under Article 138b of the Maastricht Treaty. Such requests are not considered incompatible with the self-denying ordinance of Article 157.2, under which the member states undertake not to seek to influence the members of the Commission in the performance of their tasks. They would be out of order if ever addressed to the European System of Central Banks: under Article 107 of the Treaty, the Community institutions and bodies and the governments of the member states undertake to respect the independence of the decision-taking bodies of the European Central Bank and of the national central banks in the performance of their tasks.

Because the real Council is what it is, an intergovernmental negotiating forum with the difference that some of its products pass into national law, open and public sessions cannot give an authentic picture of its work. The observer affects the phenomenon. By its nature a negotiation cannot be open to public view. The negotiator needs to be able to take positions and change them in a way which would upset particular interest groups and weaken his bargaining stance. Open sessions are for the delivery of set-piece speeches. The negotiation goes on out of view, and if pushed out of the conference room by the cameras, in the back rooms. The demonstration is in the UN. Speeches from the rostrum are for the TV 'feeds'. Open sessions of the Security Council are the manifestation of happenings elsewhere in the building.

Similarly, a wholly transparent Council would be largely ceremonial. After the bargaining round the table, and in the presidential suite where there is bilateral dealing on difficult issues, there could be, perhaps at the end of a multi-item agenda, a public session at which the Council 'legislates'. This would doubtless consist of the chairman reading out the list of decisions taken and of votes cast. Some participants might then wish to make their statements about what has been decided, corresponding to the existing but unpublished 'entries in the minutes'.[9] Publication of the results of Council votes is provided for in the October 1993 revision of the Council's rules of procedure.

The nature of the negotiation process inside the conference room means that the work of the Council is likely to remain opaque. The public knows what the Commission proposed (but not how each commissioner voted, or what compromises were struck at the preparatory meeting of *chefs de cabinet*). It knows what the Parliament suggested (but it does not know what went on in the caucus meetings at which the party groups decided on their votes, or in the intergroup meetings at which compromises are struck). It knows what the Council decided, but it does not know, except from what individual participants have to say about their achievements, how it got there.[10]

OBJECTIONS

Two objections can be put forward to the proposition that the Council of the first pillar is fundamentally intergovernmental.

What of the voting which became standard practice in the implementation of the Single European Act, and was enshrined in the Council's amended internal Regulation? A vote can impose an obligation upon an unwilling member state, theoretically up to five of them. The Council is then more than the collection of its parts. It is exercising a constitutional power which does not depend upon the willingness of (each of) the member states.[11] Moreover it is commonly suggested, for example in the European Parliament's Hänsch Report, that in an enlarged Community, it should be made more difficult to block the will of a majority of member states, and especially of the larger ones.[12]

Recourse to voting incontestably makes the Council of the first pillar less intergovernmental. But in its *modus operandi* the Council still regularly sets out to achieve the consensus which it adopted as its badge after the Luxembourg Compromise of 1966. It normally finds that there is no majority for anything and that one has to be crafted. It aims for consensus via compromise and drafting dexterity. It is only when sustained effort is exhausted that it settles for a qualified majority. The Budget Council points up the difference: it stops compromising when a qualified majority has been counted.[13] The psychology is illustrated in the 1993 transparency rules: a member state publicly records itself as abstaining. Although an abstention in qualified majority voting has the same effect as a negative vote, it signifies acquiescence. So it is that Declaration 27 of the Treaty of Maastricht enjoins upon member states to abstain when unanimity is needed and a qualified majority exists for a decision in the CFSP.

Second objection: what of co-decision? The Article 189b procedure cannot impose anything on the Council, any more than the Council can impose on the European Parliament. The Parliament can indeed prevent the Council from acting. But neither the assent powers conferred on the European Parliament in the Single European Act and in the Maastricht Treaty nor the co-decision of that Treaty (nor, for that matter, Parliament's powers as a joint budgetary authority) can oblige the Council to accept anything which it or a blocking minority of its members does not want to accept.[14]

And then there is the veto, when very important national interests are at stake. Although much discussed, but inconclusively, in the preparatory stages of the Solemn Declaration on European Union of Stuttgart in 1983, and again in the Dooge Committee in 1985, talk of veto went out of fashion after the signature of the Single Act in 1986. A version of it was dangled around by the UK in September 1993, as a possible reprisal against threats to the conclusion of the Uruguay Round, but was not taken seriously. (The main threat was of a French veto.) All that can be said is that a national veto would be regarded as anomalous in the context of most barrier-reducing legislation, and would be deployed only in a discussion of transcendental importance and after marathon sessions. The intention would be to provoke a political crisis. None the less, the veto has not definitively been laid to rest. Meanwhile, other ways have been found of appeasing or outflanking uncooperative delegations.

THE WORD AND THE FLESH

The word-play which invented the 'single institutional framework' is not, so far as the Council is concerned, entirely removed from reality, but it may not be the reality perceived by the authors of the words. The words, once pronounced, began to be fleshed out. They combine with other words, in Article 151 of the Treaty, which have a profound effect upon the Council and its bodies.

New Article 151 says that:

- the Committee of Permanent Representatives (Coreper) prepares the work of the Council (not new);
- the Council is assisted by a General Secretariat under the direction of a Secretary-General (new, taken from Article 16 of the Council's internal Rules of Procedure).

The Council being widened to appear in the second and third pillars, Article 151 applies to them. Hitherto, the Political Secretariat of European Political Co-operation was not within the General Secretariat and the Coreper was not involved. Hitherto, also, the ministers of justice met under the aegis of EPC and the ministers responsible for immigration met outside the Council framework, but with unofficial support from the Council secretariat. Ministers responsible for police cooperation (Trevi) met on their own, without the Commission and with successive presidencies providing the material underpinning. The Coreper was not involved in any of the activities which have been brought together in the third pillar.

Under Maastricht, all changes. Under the new style Council, the Coreper and the General Secretariat take over the work of Title V (Article J) and of Title VI (Article K), to which is transferred Judicial Cooperation.

ORGANISATIONAL CHANGE

The effect can be seen in the intended structures for Article K (Table 12.1). It can also be seen in the future top structure for Article J (Table 12.2): This structure serves the Committee of Permanent Representatives and the Council of the second pillar. The Political Committee (of Political Directors from national foreign offices) sheds the responsibility given it in the Single Act to 'prepare Ministers' discussions' (Article 30.10c) and will instead 'contribute to the definition of policies by delivering opinions' (Article J.8.5).

The widening of the Council to span all the pillars automatically entails the extension of the competences of Coreper, already one of the most hard-pressed entities within the system. As Brussels residents, and with cast-iron Treaty authority, they have an edge on the two groups of officials who have hitherto ruled their roosts: the Political Directors of EPC and the 'Co-ordinators' responsible to the Immigration Ministers. As officials (traditionally) of national foreign ministries, Permanent Representatives are knowledgeable in matters of foreign and security policy, and are professional colleagues of the Political Directors. But the third pillar will be new to most of them.

THE 'ECONOMIC GOVERNMENT'

One area has for long been seen as off-limits for the Coreper: the organisation of agricultural markets. By convention, meetings of the Agricultural Council (except in so far as concerns Single Market measures) have been prepared by the Special Committee for Agriculture, several of whose members are not Brussels residents. Will the Council of Economic and Finance Ministers now go the same way?

In Article 109c the Treaty installs a Monetary Committee (already extant), to be replaced at the start of the third stage of Monetary Union by an Economic and Financial Committee, predictably to be abbreviated to Ecofin Committee. (The change of name is a tactful recognition of the transfer of competence for monetary policy.) Although Coreper's responsibilities are formally saved, it is clear that the Committees will be the Ecofin Council's preferred people. The qualifications of members of the new Committees are not specified, but it is difficult to believe that senior finance ministry officials, who compose the existing Monetary Committee, will forgo the seats.

If this is the likely pattern, it illustrates a weakness in the standard analysis of the 'temple', sustained by its three pillars. Economic and Monetary Union is treated as a policy of the Community, proper to the first pillar. But the Community method does not apply to monetary

Table 12.1

Council (Ministers of Justice and Home Affairs)		
Coreper		
Coordinating Committee of Senior Officials ('K4')		
Steering Group I	*Steering Group II*	*Steering Group III*
8 sub-groups	4/5 sub-groups	judicial cooperation***
immigration subjects*	police, customs cooperation**	

Notes: * previously served by the Council Secretariat; ** previously served by rotating presidencies; *** previously served by the Political Secretariat

Table 12.2

Council Secretariat DG A	
(Secretary-General)	
Director General, DG A	
Extant	*New*
Deputy Director General	Deputy Director General
External Economic Relations	External Political Relations

union, which has its own bodies. Their interactions are not initiated by the Commission, and they act without Parliamentary consultation. As has been said above, the central bank system is insulated against intervention from outside, to the extent that the European Central Bank is even given its own powers to make regulations, binding in their entirety and directly applicable in all member states, and to impose fines.[15] This arrangement has nothing in common with the generality of the first pillar and in particular with the effort to compensate for the 'democratic deficit'. Monetary Union deserves a pillar of its own in the visual aids.

What then of Ecofin? Although the European System of Central Banks is responsible for defining and implementing the monetary policy of the Community (Article 105), it defies belief that finance ministers will wash their hands of what has been one of their preeminent concerns, and the object of national electoral controversy. The participation of the President of the European Central Bank in Ecofin meetings will not be suffered to become a one-way traffic system. In the debate televised from the Sorbonne on the eve of the French referendum in September

1992, President Mitterrand maintained that ministers establish exchange-rate policy and the European Central Bank would be the 'technocrats' who implement it. This is apparently an extrapolation from Article 109.2, which allows the Council to formulate general orientations for foreign exchange-rate policy. But it also shows the drift: the expectation that Ecofin will have a relationship with the European System of Central Banks which is not as 'hands-off' as the text of the Treaty declares. Intergovernmentalism may not disappear from the monetary union.

FURTHER REFORM

The Intergovernmental Conference on Political Union did not find it necessary or appropriate to dwell on the functioning of the Council of the first pillar. Reform, if any, is relegated to the 1996 IGC, after the next wave of enlargement. While there are changes in the interfaces with the European Parliament, notably the creation of co-decision in eleven areas and the extension of assent to eight, the inner workings of the Council went unexamined. There is also no commitment to re-examine them in 1996, but pencils are being sharpened.[16] Matters such as the voting strength of new Efta members (and whether they will have a Commissioner, and how many MEPs they will have) have already been agreed, subject to review in the next IGC. Some, such as the strong institutionalists of the Belmont European Policy Centre, justly see this sequence as back to front. The 1994 Parliament and the 1995 Commission will be in place until the end of the decade. Most would agree that if the first wave of enlargement can perhaps proceed without major institutional reform, the next waves cannot.

THE COUNCIL PRESIDENCY

One of the questions which may be studied, or not, is the role of the presidency. There are as many presidencies in the Community as there are institutions, but when used *tout court*, the Council presidency is meant.[17] The Council presidency enjoys no functions in the EEC Treaty, being mentioned only once, in connection with the rotation. But 'the Presidency' has higher profile in Title III of the Single Act, on political cooperation, where it is charged with keeping the European Parliament informed and with ensuring consistency between the EC and EPC (jointly with the Commission).

In the Stuttgart Solemn Declaration on European Union of 1983, the heads of state and government said that they would, in the light of experience of Political Cooperation, reinforce the attributions of the presidency as regards initiation, coordination and representation. The

Single Act saw to all three (Article 10b). The Maastricht Treaty reiterates that the presidency represents the Union for the CFSP.

The Treaty also provides that the presidency may participate in meetings of the Governing Council of the European Central Bank, and may 'submit a motion for deliberation' (Article 109b). It also consults and informs the European Parliament on the CFSP (Article J.7) and on Justice and Home Affairs (Article K.6) and ensures in both cases that the views of the Parliament are 'duly taken into consideration', where the word 'duly' may be unconsciously humorous. But there is much more to it than the Treaties have to say.

THE WORK OF PRESIDENCIES

Council presidencies have always been responsible for setting the agendas for their terms. Beginning with the Danish presidency of 1987, and with growing confidence, they have set out their agendas for all planned Council meetings well in advance, and after consultation (non-binding) with the Commission. While the Commission concerts its annual programme with the European Parliament (which debates and votes on it), the Council keeps a freer hand, but seeks to avoid outright conflict. It has now agreed to 'take position' when the Parliament has debated the Commission's annual programme. The Parliament continues to press for a formal tripartite agreement on the annual work programme.

Most presidencies want to make a good showing, and most succeed, if only because the other member states know that it will be their turn on average in three years. Having a good presidency includes being a source of the compromises which will command consensus, or a qualified majority. This has reached the point in, for example, the Agricultural Council and the Budget Council where the presidency compromise is awaited as the basis for the decisive stage of the discussion. The Commission is also a source of compromise between conflicting delegations and often makes the suggestion which carries or the formula which appeases. But with the European Parliament making waves, the Commission can be inhibited by the deals which it may have done with the Parliament as the latter voted on amendments to Commission proposals. In hard cases, the Commission may have lost the flexibility to change its proposal, even if it is privately persuaded that it should, in the direction of majority opinion in the Council. (This can drive the Council towards unanimity for what would otherwise be votable proposals.) In brokering solutions, the presidency can have the 'technical assistance' of the Commission (as a source of information) and the negotiating and drafting skills of the 150 committee staff of the Council Secretariat as well as the advice of its Legal Service.

COUNCIL SECRETARIAT

Some member states need or appreciate Secretariat support more than others. They (and the Commission) rightly have an ideology to guide them. The Council Secretariat does not; it is not there to second guess the Commission or to tell a presidency what 'politically' should be done. It can present options, tease out presidency thoughts and write in house style and with the degree of Community lore required the documents for the Council to peruse, and the briefs for the president to draw on. Other parts of the Council service translate them and distribute them to short deadlines. Presidencies do not want or need a Secretariat which has an agenda of its own, a legitimacy to oppose theirs, a loyalty to some cause of its own selection and a commitment to some objective which is independent of the Council and its Presidency. Proposals to give the Secretariat, or its Secretary-General, a higher profile are mis-conceived.

Given the essential Monnet principle that all member states are equal, it is difficult to see what formal powers can be vested in a presidency other than those to do with management of six months work. Its approach to this task is a blend of the advancement of national interest, uncontrollable inheritance from its predecessor(s) and search for agreement among its fellows.

Empirically, presidencies have been using their representational responsibilities to tackle the substance of interinstitutional differences on behalf of the Council, but without its prior support. This was first formalised in the budgetary Trilogue, beginning in 1982. The Trilogue brought together the three Presidents, aiming to settle budgetary disputes. The Budget Council President, whose *vis-à-vis* are more commonly the Commissioner responsible for the Budget and the Chairman of Parliament's Budget Committee, acts on his own responsibility. But he has a pretty clear idea of what he can get the Council to accept. It took time for the Trilogue to spread to other fields, but the 1993 Belgian presidency (General Affairs) used a similar informal arrangement to good effect to obtain a settlement on the post-1993 Structural Funds and on the programme for R&D. More of the same will in all likelihood be needed to make the conciliation phase of the co-decision procedure productive rather than stalemated. Out of the view of the public and of their own colleagues, representatives of the three institutions will negotiate the necessary compromises.

DEALINGS WITH THE EUROPEAN PARLIAMENT

It is precisely in its extended dealings with the European Parliament that the Council needs to learn new tricks. The co-decision procedure of

Article 189b will see in the field a Parliamentary delegation united in determination to have its way, and buttressed by hardline resolutions voted in plenary. It will know all about log-rolling, multiple level game theory and package deals. The Council delegation will normally be on the defensive and, unlike the Parliament, will have a presentational interest in making the procedure work, since it is the invention of the member states. Parliament will predictably do everything to demand, as in the past, changes in the legal base of a proposal to bring it into the ambit of co-decision. When this does not work, it will seek to blur the distinction between cooperation and co-decision by trying to import a conciliation phase into the former. It is even surprising that it did not get on to this idea sooner. A sign of the times is that in its new internal regulation on rules of procedure, adopted on 16 September 1993, the Parliament is demanding automatic acceptance by the Commission of all the amendments which it votes through.

With the assistance and advice of the Commission, already promised, the Parliament will further seek to insert itself by proxy into the second and third pillars, from which the Treaty effectively excludes it. This presages its 1996 Samsonian resolve to bring the pillars of the temple crashing down and to plant a commemorative tree on the site.

Future Commissions can likewise be expected to continue to uphold the value and virtue of the Community method and to deplore inter-governmentalism in all its forms. The present Commission has seized victory from the jaws of defeat by relishing its new non-exclusive right of initiative in the second and third pillars. It will remain opposed to comitology, which the Treaty left untouched.[18] But it is the champion of subsidiarity and is fully aware that it must apply the Edinburgh doctrine fair and square.[19] (Is it necessary? Can the result be sufficiently achieved by the member states? Is the remedy proportional?)

REPRESENTING THE COMMUNITY/UNION

Who represents the Community to the outside world? The entity which other countries can most readily get at is the Commission. But its formal competences do not embrace the whole span of matters of international discussion and negotiation. The original member states were sobered by the landmark AETR case in which the Court of Justice told them that 'each time the Community, with a view to implementing a policy envisaged by the Treaty, adopts provisions laying down common rules, whatever form these may take, the member states no longer have the right, individually or even collectively, to undertake obligations with third countries which affect these rules'.[20] They became sensitive to the creeping competence which the EC might acquire by virtue of international commitments which it might undertake. If the Community were invariably represented by the Commission the member states might find themselves ceding sovereignty where they wanted to hold on to it.

The answer to this problem was and is 'bicephalism'. Where there is exclusive Community competence, only the Commission can represent the Community. This is the case with the common commercial policy, even although the EC as such does not belong to the Gatt (and prefers to keep its twelve separate votes). Where competence is shared, as in most environmental matters, there is a double-headed leadership, shared in accordance with their competences between the Commission and the presidency on behalf of the member states. Where there is no Community competence at all, the member states act in their own names. Some of the interstices of policy give trouble. Exclusive competence, concurrent competence and reserved competence may be difficult to separate out and in any case change. A current example is the Commission's challenge to member states who think they exercise competence in international civil aviation. And even if all is reasonably clear to the insiders, third countries can be confused and uncertain who 'speaks for Europe'. It is at least unambiguous that in the CFSP, the presidency speaks for the Union.

Despite some imprecisions, there are also clear ground rules in the area of international monetary relations. Here the Council has placed itself in the forefront. It concludes any agreements to be made with third countries or international organisations, having consulted the European Central Bank and associating the Commission with the negotiations.[21] At international level it looks as if in anything to do with economic policy the Council will take the lead (Article 103); for monetary policy the Central Bank might step in – it is specifically envisaged that the European System of Central Banks should be involved in international cooperation.[22] The Commission does not appear to have a representational role. The Council decides on Community representation and, unusually for a semi-technical decision of this kind, it needs unanimity.

THE COUNCIL, ITS MEMBER STATES AND THEIR REGIONS

The member states have another presentational interest in success. In willing the setting up of a body to represent the opinion and demands of the regions, the onus is on the same member states to show that theirs was not an empty gesture. It was a response in particular to those countries where regional government is growing in status but feels itself and its future expansion preempted by decisions taken in Brussels by national authorities.

The omens for the Committee of the Regions are not too good. The

Committee is to be served by the staff of the Economic and Social Committee, without increased provision. This is already causing the Ecosoc, the sitting tenants, anguish. The Committee of the Regions is advisory and has, like the Ecosoc, the right to issue opinions on its own initiative. But in the Community of today and tomorrow, the big legislative players are the Council and the Parliament and there is a limit to the inputs that can be accepted from elsewhere. Subsidiarity, as expressed in Article 3b, does not help the regional representatives much. Logically, if decisions are to be taken as closely as possible to the citizen, as under Article A, local and regional government should be empowered. But in the EC version of subsidiarity, the line is drawn at the member state and not at any other level of government. So far as the Treaty is concerned, a member state can organise as it will the distribution of powers between its centre and its parts. Local government cannot rely upon Article 3b to secure recognition of such rights as it may claim to legitimacy and authority. The British government has made much of the distinction between decentralisation (from Brussels, good) and devolution (from Westminster, not axiomatically good).

The Committee of the Regions faces formidable obstacles to making itself heard. Its success will depend upon the quality of its output – it not being evident that regional interests are congruent – but much more upon the clout which regional representatives have with their central authorities in domestic politics. The Commission will help: it set out in 1988 to make direct links with regional authorities in the administration of the Structural Funds. The prospect of the 'Marshall Plan times three' in the expenditure projections up to 1999 suggests that these links will be strengthened.

THE NEW EUROPEAN COUNCIL

Aside from its name, the European Council has not much in common with the Council. It grew out of the 'Summits' which had met at lengthy intervals. Its establishment was a counterweight to the discussion leading to the decision to respect the founding treaties and proceed to the election of members of the European Parliament. At their first meeting in Dublin in 1975 the heads of government (sic) preferred to call themselves a Council, but they abandoned this style at their second meeting in Brussels later in the year. At the time, however, the 'European Council', sometimes placed in quotation marks, was synonymous with a meeting of the heads of state or government (the designation which gradually established itself). They first addressed their own organisation in London in 1977. They concluded that they had two main functions: private and informal exchanges of view and decisions which set guidelines for future action. They might also settle problems unresolved at lower levels. In matters of Community competence, they would respect Community procedure. To ensure privacy, they did not want high officials to participate in their exchanges, as the high officials do in Council meetings.

Subsequently, they refrained from taking decisions as a Council, but did the next best thing. For example, they set up the European Monetary System by means of a Resolution (Brussels 1978). In doing so they charged the Council to take the flanking Community decisions. In Brussels in 1987 they took the nearest thing to a Council decision, but not in the prescribed form, when they agreed on what should be done about such matters as the system for 'switch-over' of 'artificial' monetary compensation amounts (a question beside which the status of Schleswig-Holstein is for kindergartens).

In Stuttgart in June 1983, a notoriously heavy meeting, they became a little confused. For the first time they defined the composition of the European Council as the Heads of State or Government *and* the President of the Commission. But they contradictorily envisaged that the European Council would act as a Council in matters falling under the European Communities. (They meant the national members only.)

STUTTGART AND MAASTRICHT

The easily forgotten Solemn Declaration of Stuttgart was to become the quarry for what the Treaty of Maastricht was to say about the European Council (see Table 12.3).

Some Stuttgart attributes, however, were omitted from the Treaty of Maastricht. Under the terms of the Stuttgart Declaration, the European Council:

- debates questions relating to the Union and ensures coherence;
- opens the way to cooperation in new sectors;
- solemnly expresses the common position on external relations questions.

The Maastricht Treaty escapes from confusion over the role of the heads of state or government: they, not the European Council, act as the Council in Articles 109f.1 and 109k.2.[23] With these various qualifications, the European Council is nothing like the Council. It is not an institution, even of the Union. It does not legislate. All its meetings are restricted to ministers (plus only the Secretaries-General of the Council and of the Commission). It does not deliver decisions in the due form, but customarily produces lengthy argued 'conclusions'. In future, however, its declarations on foreign policy matters will be indistinguishable in kind, although invested with more authority, from those of the Council of the second pillar.

Table 12.3

| | European Council | |
Maastricht	Stuttgart
Government leaders and Commission President, assisted by ministers of foreign affairs and a member of the Commission	The same (as also in the Single Act)
Provides the Union with the necessary impetus for its development	Gives the European construction general political impulsion
Defines general political guidelines	Gives general political guidelines
Submits a report to the European Parliament after each meeting	The same
Submits an annual report to the Parliament on progress achieved by the Union	The same
Meets at least twice a year	The same (as also in the Single Act)

THE MOTOR OF INTEGRATION

Deep textual study may tend to skip over a development of overwhelming importance. Following the Solemn Declaration, the Maastricht Treaty stipulates, for the first time in a treaty article, that the European Council shall provide the Union with the necessary impetus for its development. Conventionally, and textually elsewhere in the Solemn Declaration, the Commission was described as 'the driving force in the process of European integration'. This traditional attribute of the Commission is absent from Maastricht. It places the heads of state and government in the driving seat of the development of European Union. In doing so it reaffirms the leading role of the member states, rather than of any other institution or body. This is exactly what the Treaty says: 'the High Contracting Parties establish among themselves a European Union'. And having said it, it does it.

THE WAY AHEAD

Up to the next IGC, the Council and European Council have plenty to do to keep the presidencies of Germany and France (both beset by domestic elections), and then of Spain, at full stretch. There is still work on the completion of single market legislation, including deregulation, in the fields, among others, of financial services, data protection, free movement of people and telecommunications networks. The enlargement negotiations with Austria, Finland, Norway and Sweden having been completed, the new member states must be inducted; as a corollary a new, enlarged Commission of, unbelievably, twenty-one members has to be installed. The Commission's initiative for renewed growth, employment and competitiveness, begun in Edinburgh and in Copenhagen, was launched at Brussels in December 1993, apparently with wide divergence among the member states over what can be done on the demand side to alleviate unemployment. The principle of subsidiarity has to be applied according to the Edinburgh criteria to all legislation. The Exchange Rate Mechanism needs to be nursed and the interim European Monetary Institute needs running in. CFSP has to find ways and means of effecting political change in ex-Yugoslavia, including the gradual realisation of the potential of the commitment to a common defence policy. The European Parliament needs to be won around to giving effect to the new interinstitutional agreements on subsidiarity, the Ombudsman and the second budgetary agreement proposed in Edinburgh in December 1992. Vast problems loom in relations with Russia, with the rest of the former Soviet Union and with the countries of Central and Eastern Europe.

Another agenda will be written for the 1996 IGC. A lesson learned, it is to be hoped, from Maastricht is that careful preparation, as with Emu, makes an IGC run well. A vague remit, as with Political Union, spells trouble. In 1996 there will be a larger number of participants and one among them, the UK, promises to be more active than reactive. This IGC will have to grapple with the awesome problems of a future union possibly four times bigger than the original six states and at widely different stages of economic development, a Community obliged to act as a mechanism for planned resource transfers within tight budgetary constraints, and with member states versed in variable geometry working in over 150 language pairs round the conference-room table. This whole programme must be tackled by the Council while the two branches of the legislative authority circle warily around each other and practise their disparate versions of co-decision.

The European Parliament elected in June 1994 will show its muscle by (as it will perceive it) co-appointing the new President of the Commission. The appointment of the Commission may even have been politicised in the course of the Parliamentary electoral campaign. Strengthened by its new control over the Commission, Parliament will want to assert itself with regard to the Council. The fact that expenditure on joint CFSP actions (such as the EU observers in ex-Yugoslavia, Russia and South Africa) is to be defrayed from the 'non-obligatory' provisions of the EC budget gives Parliament an *entrée* to the sphere of the second pillar from which the Treaty of Maastricht sought to exclude it. In the third pillar, from which it is also largely excluded, Parliament can count on the Commission to keep it posted and involved in Commission initiatives. Perhaps the Parliament will also realise the potency of an instrument which it possesses but scarcely uses, namely, the appearance of Council presidencies in its committees. Traditionally, these are occasions for the riding of hobby-horses; skilfully managed, however, they could become a means of genuine interrogation and influence – in both directions. It is safe to predict, too, that Parliament will sustain its attack on the cosy comitology practised by the Council, and demand co-decision whenever the process involves new legislative or regulatory action.

For the European Parliament the business is unfinished. It will probably adopt a new draft constitution for the 1996 IGC, where the mantle of Spinelli has fallen on the redoubtable Fernand Herman. Parliament will face a Council in which there is agreement to continue the European journey whose destination is disputed – and with some of the travellers allowed to climb off when they do not like the landscape.

13

REPRESENTING THE PEOPLE

Richard Corbett

Provision for the representation of its people has always been a matter of concern in the European Community. This is because of the Community's ability, unlike traditional international organisations, to adopt binding legislation without necessarily requiring approval of all member states and because it was originally conceived as 'a first step in the federation of Europe', and any such federation of democracies would itself have to be based on democratic principles.[1] The creation of a parliamentary body among the institutions of the EC was in order to 'reflect at Community level the fundamental principle that the peoples should take part in the exercise of power through the intermediary of a representative assembly'.[2] National parliaments too play an important role in European affairs in terms of scrutiny over their respective ministers who represent their state in Council meetings, but in terms of representation at EC level, it is the European Parliament that represents the peoples directly.

In the original Community Treaties, however, the Parliament was given only consultative powers in the adoption of EC legislation and the budget, as well as some powers of scrutiny over the Commission (including a right to dismiss the Commission but not to influence the choice of its successor). These meagre powers were increased in a number of steps, notably by amendments to the Treaties signed in 1970, 1975 (the 'budget' treaties), and 1986 (Single European Act), by rulings of the Court of Justice, such as the 1980 'isoglucose' judgement, and by inter-institutional agreements.[3] These steps forward still left the European Parliament short of its aspiration for equality with Council as the two arms of the Community's legislative authority, representing respectively the member states and the electorate as a whole.

During the negotiations which led to the Maastricht Treaty, the European Parliament was heavily engaged in pressing forward proposals to increase its own powers.[4] It obtained significant changes in the two areas where it had been most pressing in its requests for change, namely in the Community's legislative procedure and as regards its involvement in the appointment of the Commission. The new Treaty also brought in a number of smaller changes which, whilst of lesser importance, none the less have significance for Parliament's powers. In addition, the Treaty contains provisions affecting other aspects of democratic accountability not specifically related to the powers of the Parliament, but fails to make changes in some important areas. Let us examine these five aspects in turn.

PARLIAMENT IN THE COMMUNITY LEGISLATIVE PROCEDURES

Co-decision procedure

The Maastricht Treaty introduces a new procedure for Parliament's participation in the adoption of Community legislation, but only for a limited area. The procedure is laid down in Article 189b and is not given a name as the UK government objected to the term 'co-decision'. Nevertheless, that term is in general use.

The field of application of the co-decision procedure is limited, but somewhat larger than seemed likely even a few weeks before the close of the IGCs. The member state most opposed to extending Parliament's powers, the UK, seemed to make concessions on this point, rather than give way on other points that were more important for it. As finally agreed, the procedure applies to some fifteen Treaty articles. It remains far from being the generalised system of co-decision sought by Parliament, but the areas that fall under its scope are significant, including most internal market legislation, public health, consumer protection, educational and cultural measures, equivalence of diplomas and qualifications, the free movement of workers, the framework programme for research, and the guidelines for trans-European networks.[5]

However, this list is not as impressive as it might seem. First, it should be noted that the framework programme for research and technological development as well as the field of culture come under the co-decision procedure, but with unanimity required in Council. Since the essence of co-decision is the negotiation of compromises between Parliament and Council, and whereas it will be extremely difficult for Council to modify its position where unanimity is required and where it may well have reached that position only with great internal difficulties, this particular requirement, again at the insistence of the UK, effectively neuters the co-decision procedure. This is likely to be an area of conflict between Parliament and Council.

Second, co-decision in certain areas is limited to the approval of general 'guidelines' or 'programmes', leaving the specific items of legislation to be approved by other procedures. In the field of research and technological development, co-decision will apply to the framework programme, but the individual programmes will be adopted by Council after consulting Parliament (previously cooperation procedure). In the field of trans-European networks, co-decision will be used to approve the general guidelines, specific items being left to the cooperation procedure. In the field of the environment, a single Treaty article (130s) will henceforth provide for three different procedures: co-decision for pluriannual programmes, cooperation procedure for most individual items of legislation, but simple consultation of Parliament (and unanimity in Council) for fiscal matters and measures affecting land use, water supply or energy.

It has also been suggested that the granting of co-decision rights regarding internal market legislation is of limited significance, given that such legislation should have been adopted by 1992 and that Articles 100a and 100b of the EEC Treaty would no longer serve a purpose after that date. This view, however, is not entirely accurate. Once in place, the Community's internal market legislation can only be modified pursuant to the same Treaty articles as those under which it was adopted. Any text which proves unsatisfactory or which, over time, becomes out of date or is no longer politically acceptable will require modification using the relevant procedure: henceforth co-decision. There are already some six hundred items of EC legislation adopted pursuant to Article 100a amounting to a huge volume of legislation which is enacted at Community level and cannot be modified by national procedures. The areas concerned are thus governed at European level and, as regards any changes to such legislation, will come under the co-decision procedure.

If the scope of co-decision is not entirely what Parliament wanted, nor is the procedure itself. The text of the new Article 189b which lays down the procedure in detail is based on the proposal initially made by the Luxembourg presidency in its draft treaty. In so far as it takes up the European Parliament's proposals of two readings in each body with a conciliation procedure to negotiate compromises that then have to be approved by both sides, the procedure is to Parliament's liking.[6] However, an additional provision allowing Council, in the absence of an agreement in the conciliation committee, to act unilaterally in a third reading by adopting a text which will become law unless the European Parliament rejects it within six weeks by a majority of its members could weaken Parliament's position. If Parliament seems unlikely to reject a text, either because it prefers a half measure to nothing at all, or because it does not wish to be perceived in a negative light as responsible for hold-ups, delays and failures in the legislative procedure, or because of the requirement for a special majority, then Council would have little incentive to go very far in negotiating compromises within the conciliation committee. This provision appears to load the procedure in favour of Council.

On the other hand, the right to say 'no' does give Parliament a bargaining position which it has hitherto lacked regarding Community legislation, and is of fundamental importance to public perceptions of Parliament's role: it can no longer be accused of lacking teeth. Furthermore, the loading of the procedure, in favour of Council described above would, to a certain extent, be true even if the extra paragraph had not been included in the procedure, and agreement between both bodies was the only way to adopt legislation. The right to say 'yes' (or not to) and the right to say 'no' (or not to) are in practice not very different. In both cases, the advantage in the negotiations will be with the institution that can make the other one chose between a half measure or nothing at all. This will usually be Council (also because of its voting provisions which make its position less flexible), but will sometimes be Parliament. This may well also change over time: at present, when the Community is legislating frequently for the first time in many areas, the national ministers in Council are often reluctant to go very far. Future Community legislation, however, will increasingly be about modifying existing EC provisions, with the pressure for change often coming from member states. Parliament will more frequently be in a position where saying 'no' will be less awkward for it than for Council.

For the time being, all this is speculation. Much will depend on how the new procedures are applied in practice. Parliament will certainly endeavour to make it unthinkable that Council should proceed unilaterally without reaching agreement with Parliament. It might, for instance, start rejecting automatically any Council text adopted unilaterally, thus hoping to teach Council that it must negotiate compromises with Parliament.

Article 189b also contains two other provisions which differ significantly from the Single Act's cooperation procedure and, indeed, from the original Luxembourg presidency proposal in the IGC. The first concerns Parliament's right to reject a text outright in second reading. Whereas in the cooperation procedure Council then has three months to overrule Parliament by unanimity, in the co-decision procedure such rejection by Parliament is absolute and cannot be overridden. It has, however, been rendered more complicated. Parliament must announce its 'intention to reject' by a majority of its members, such a statement to be followed by a conciliation procedure with Council. Following conciliation, Parliament can either proceed to rejection (causing the text to fall), or can instead propose amendments to the text (reverting to the normal procedure). Potentially, then, there are four readings: initial consultation of Parliament (followed by Council's first reading), second reading consideration of Council's position leading to an announcement of the intention to reject (followed by a conciliation meeting with Council), parliamentary consideration of the results of conciliation and adoption of amendments (followed by Council's second reading and, possibly, another conciliation) and final acceptance or rejection of text. Furthermore, under the case law of the Court of Justice, if Council intends to adopt a common position that contains new provisions not originally included in the Commission's original proposal, then Parliament must be re-consulted (in other words, a second first reading), so there are potentially even more readings in Parliament. Simplicity is not the essence of the co-decision procedure.

A second difference from the cooperation procedure concerns the second reading in Council. In the cooperation procedure, any amendments adopted by Parliament in second reading that are accepted by the Commission are incorporated into a revised Commission proposal and can be taken out or modified by Council only if the latter is unanimous, whereas a qualified majority will suffice to approve the text as a whole. (Amendments not accepted by the Commission need unanimity which, against the will of the Commission, is unlikely and they are therefore effectively dead.) Under the new co-decision procedure, Parliament's second reading amendments are not incorporated into a revised Commission proposal but are submitted individually to Council, where a qualified majority is needed to approve if the Commission accepts them, unanimity otherwise. This is a significant difference as regards those amendments that the Commission accepts (for the others, there is no change). Whereas under the cooperation procedure these were incorporated into the text automatically, requiring Council either to use unanimity to remove them or to threaten non-adoption of the text to persuade the Commission to take them out, under the co-decision procedure the onus will be on obtaining a qualified majority to support each and every one of them. The last few years have shown that Council accepts about half of the second reading amendments incorporated into the text by the Commission; with the new procedure this percentage is likely to fall. The result will be an increased number of conciliations, with a greater distance separating Parliament and Council before they enter into the negotiations.

In the months preceding the entry into force of the Maastricht Treaty, Council and Parliament negotiated an agreement on the operation of the conciliation committee, specifying that it will be co-chaired by each of their Presidents, that its venue will alternate between the premises of each, that the secretariat will be joint, that the co-Presidents may elaborate draft texts to submit to the committee and that the committee could appoint rapporteurs. Parliament also decided on the composition of its delegations, choosing a compromise between the US system (where the

211

Senate and the House of Representatives each nominate *ad hoc* delegations of expert members for each conference meeting) and the German system (where the Bundestag and Bundesrat nominate permanent members who sit on each meeting of the Vermittlungsausschuss, whatever the subject). Parliament decided that its delegation should contain three permanent members, drawn from among the Vice-Presidents of Parliament (who would gain experience in the practices, procedures and precedents), with the rest chosen in each individual case preferably from the committees concerned and including the chairman and rapporteur of the committee responsible. Within these parameters, the delegation will be appointed by the political groups in proportion to their size.

Assent procedure

Maastricht extends the assent procedure to six new areas and enlarges the category of international agreement for which Parliament's assent is required.[7] Parliament had asked for the assent procedure to be used for constitutional matters where Council acts by unanimity. Maastricht has, indeed, provided for this in three cases: the uniform electoral system, amendments to the Protocol of the European System of Central Banks and special tasks to be entrusted to the Central Bank. However, the procedure has not been extended to the inherently constitutional matters covered by Articles 236 (amendment of the Treaties), which Parliament was particularly keen on, 201 (own resources) or even 235 (extensive interpretation of the Treaty).

The new Treaty also provides for use of the assent procedure for inherently legislative matters, but where unanimity is still required in Council, namely the definition of the tasks, objectives, organisation and coordination of the structural funds; the creation of the new Cohesion Fund; and measures facilitating the right of residence and freedom of movement of Community citizens.

At the same time, the Treaty no longer specifies that a majority of members (or absolute majority, 284 votes in the new Parliament of 1994) is required in Parliament to give its assent to a measure. A simple majority of those voting will suffice, except in two cases: accession of new member states and the uniform procedure for European elections, where absolute majorities will still be needed. Thus, there now are two variants to the assent procedure.

Extension of the cooperation procedure

The cooperation procedure introduced by the Single Act (two reading procedure, but where Council has the last word if it is unanimous) is now provided for in most other areas of legislation in which Council acts by a qualified majority. The most notable exceptions are the fields of agriculture and external commerce. This is therefore a considerable extension of the cooperation procedure. Most of the areas previously subject to it will now fall under the co-decision procedure. The Treaty provides for no change to the procedure as such, and Council always acts under the traditional rules for qualified majority voting (that is, a qualified majority to accept but unanimity to amend Commission proposals).

Consultation procedure

New requirements to consult Parliament are introduced, almost entirely for new provisions added to the Treaty. They fall largely under one of four categories:

* measures where unanimity is still required in Council, but member states were unwilling to introduce the assent procedure (such as arrangements for voting rights in local and European elections, supplementary action on economic and social cohesion and industrial policy);
* measures outside the Community framework but in the Union Treaty's 'pillars' on foreign policy and on justice and home affairs;
* the decision on transition to Stage Three of Emu;
* consultation on nominations of individuals (President of Commission, President and board members of the Central Bank, President of Monetary Institute).

Besides these, the consultation procedure is introduced for secondary legislation pursuant to the statute of the System of Central Banks, for specific research programmes (previously cooperation procedure), for regulations concerning state aids and for visa policy (Article 100c).

Taken together, these changes set up the beginnings of a bicameral system in which draft legislation must overcome two hurdles to become law, needing to pass before both the Council, whose members examine texts from a national perspective, and the Parliament, whose members work from a political or ideological perspective. Between them they represent the people, directly in the case of the Parliament, and indirectly (via national governments through national parliaments) in the case of the Council.

However, and this is particularly important at a time when politicians and political structures generally stand accused of being remote from the people, it does little to make the institutions any easier to understand. There are now, besides the budgetary procedure, four different procedures for involving the European Parliament in the adoption of Community legislation, and three of these procedures have themselves two variants: the assent procedure (with majority of members in

213

Parliament required or with simple majority required), the co-decision procedure (with unanimity in Council or with qualified majority voting in Council) and the consultation procedure (with unanimity or qualified majority in Council). In terms of one important requirement for democracy – clarity and transparency of procedures – the Treaty of Maastricht clearly fails.

PARLIAMENT AND THE APPOINTMENT OF THE COMMISSION

The importance of the Commission as the Community's executive has been growing. Parliament has always enjoyed the right to dismiss the Commission by a vote of censure obtaining a two-thirds majority, but has never been formally involved in the appointment of the Commission. Parliament proposed to the IGC that the term of office of the Commission should be linked to that of Parliament and that, following each European parliamentary election, the President of the Commission should be elected by Parliament on a proposal of the European Council and, once he or she and the European Council had agreed on the rest of the college of commissioners, it should be subjected to a collective vote of confidence by Parliament before taking office.

The new Treaty takes up Parliament's proposal almost entirely. The term of office of the Commission is linked to that of Parliament and the Commission as a whole can take office only following a vote of confidence from the Parliament. However, instead of electing the President of the Commission on a proposal of the European Council, Parliament will only be 'consulted'. But 'consultation' in such circumstances, a public vote on an individual politician by an elected Parliament, is surely tantamount to an election or confirmation as it is inconceivable that any politicians would wish to proceed should Parliament reject their candidacy; and even if they did, Parliament would then be likely to reject the Commission as a whole.

A more serious departure from Parliament's original proposal is that the President-designate is not given a stronger role in the choice of commissioners. Member states will be obliged to consult the President of the Commission, but not, as Parliament proposed, to choose the rest of the Commission in agreement with the President. Such a change would have strengthened the collegiate nature of the Commission and its cohesion as a team.

This new procedure will begin after the 1994 European elections. The autumn months will be used to go through the procedures so that the new Commission takes office in January 1995 for a five-year period. Any Commission censured by the Parliament would be replaced by a new Commission which would only serve out the term of office of the previous Commission. Parliament is likely to hold public hearings with the candidates and to insist that the Commission presents a programme to Parliament prior to its debate. It remains to be seen how far the appointment of the Commission becomes an issue in the European parliamentary elections that will henceforth precede its appointment.

OTHER IMPROVEMENTS IN THE POWERS OF THE EUROPEAN PARLIAMENT

Right of initiative

Hitherto, the Commission has enjoyed a monopoly in almost all areas of the right to put forward proposals for Community legislation. The Parliament, Council, member governments, Ecosoc, social partners or whoever could all come up with ideas, but only the Commission could submit a proposal in due legal form for consideration and possible adoption through the Community's legislative procedures. The rationale behind this system was that the Commission, neutral as between member states, was best placed to draw up proposals in the interest of the EC as a whole. None the less, the European Parliament challenged this in so far as it asked for a safeguard in the cases where the Commission was unwilling to bring forward proposals where there is popular demand. Parliament asked for the right to be able to request the Commission to bring forward a proposal and, should the Commission fail to do so within a specified period, to bring forward a proposal itself.

The IGC agreed to a provision allowing Parliament to request the Commission to bring forward proposals, but not to allow Parliament to take up that right itself should the Commission fail to do so. Presumably, Parliament would have to rely on its right of censure to bring pressure on the Commission if the latter failed to respond to Parliament's requests, although it might exercise a right to take the Commission to Court, as Chapter 12 indicates the Council could already do.[8]

The powers of budgetary control

The Maastricht Treaty, in response to specific requests by Parliament, specifies that 'the Commission shall submit any necessary information to the European Parliament at the latter's request' and that 'the Commission shall take all appropriate steps to act on the observations in decisions giving discharge and on other observations by the European Parliament relating to the execution of expenditure' and that 'at the request of the European Parliament or the Council, the Commission shall report on the measures taken in light of these observations and comments, and in particular on the instructions given to the departments which are responsible'.[9] It is also specified that the Court of Auditors may issue special reports on specific questions at the request of other institutions.[10] The Court of Auditors is elevated to the rank of a 'Community institution'.[11]

Right of inquiry

In response to a specific request by Parliament, Maastricht provides that Parliament may 'set up a temporary committee of inquiry to investigate, without prejudice to the powers conferred by the treaty on other institutions or bodies, alleged contraventions or maladministration in the implementation of Community law, except where the alleged facts are being examined before a court and while the case is still subject to legal proceedings'.[12] It provides for detailed provisions governing the exercise of this right to be determined by common agreement among Parliament, Council and the Commission.

Petitioning of Parliament and Ombudsman

The European Parliament's Rules of Procedure have, for many years, allowed citizens to submit petitions on matters falling within the sphere of competence of the EC. The number of petitions received has continued to grow year after year, and Parliament has a special committee on petitions to deal with the various matters raised. Parliament had asked for this practice to be recognised in the Treaty, which would give the procedure greater legal standing, thus helping Parliament when approaching other institutions or national governments on behalf of petitioners.

The IGCs agreed to put this right of petition into the Treaty. In addition, it has been provided that the European Parliament may elect an Ombudsman to whom the Parliament or citizens can turn for help. The Ombudsman will have a renewable five-year term of office, running concurrently with that of the Parliament. The statute of the Ombudsman is laid down by Parliament with the assent of Council, the latter acting by a qualified majority.

Parliament and the European Central Bank

The new Treaty gives the Parliament the right to be consulted on the appointment of the President and the board members of the European Central Bank, as well as (during Stage Two) the President of the European Monetary Institute. Again, this consultation will involve a public vote by an elected Parliament on individuals, no doubt following a public hearing in front of a parliamentary committee, and it is surely unlikely that any candidate would wish to take office if rejected by Parliament.

The Treaty provides that the President of the Central Bank shall report to Parliament annually in plenary and attend parliamentary committee meetings upon invitation in order to give account for the policies of the Central Bank and submit to questioning.

Right to go to Court

Parliament had asked for the Treaty to recognize a right for Parliament to bring cases to the European Court against the other institutions for annulment of illegal acts. The IGC agreed to add to the Treaty provisions allowing Parliament to bring the other institutions to Court in cases where Parliament's own prerogatives have allegedly been violated. This entrenches current case law in the Treaty. Similarly, the right of other institutions or member states to bring Parliament to Court, if it is alleged that its acts violate the Treaty, has also been written into the Treaty.

OTHER NOVELTIES IN THE TREATY ENHANCING DEMOCRATIC LEGITIMACY
Role of national parliaments

The new Treaty contains in its annex a 'Declaration on the role of national parliaments in the European Union', in which governments undertake to make sure that national parliaments receive Commission proposals in good time to enable them to make their views known to their respective governments. The Declaration encourages the national parliaments and the European Parliament to cooperate with each other and another Declaration invites them to meet as a Conference of Parliaments of the European Community (or 'Assizes') on appropriate occasions to discuss the main features of European Union.

A proposal to set up a new institution, called 'Congress', bringing together members of national parliaments and the European Parliament, was not retained by the IGC. This proposal, originating mainly with members of the French parliament and taken up by the French foreign ministry with some support from Portugal and the UK, had attracted strong criticism from the European Parliament and had pointedly not been taken up in the Final Declaration of the Conference of Parliaments ('Assizes') held in Rome on the eve of the IGC in November 1990.

During the ratification process of the Treaty of Maastricht, new provisions were introduced in many member states to enhance national parliamentary scrutiny of their country's representative in Council. In

France and Germany, this went as far as introducing new provisions into the Constitution. In France, the Senate and National Assembly were granted the right to receive all proposals for Community acts containing provisions of a legislative nature and to adopt resolutions on them (a right that the French parliament enjoys in no other area of policy). In Germany, the constitutional amendments specified that further transfers of powers to the European Union will require the approval of both the Bundestag and the Bundesrat by two-thirds majorities. It obliged the government to inform the Bundestag and the Bundesrat and to allow the Bundestag to give its opinion before decisions are taken at Community level. The opinion of the Bundesrat will be required for matters affecting the Länder, and where a matter is discussed in the Council that concerns the exclusive competences of the Länder, a representative of the latter appointed by the Bundesrat will represent Germany.

In other member states, the rights of the national parliament to receive information on Community matters, and usually on individual legislative proposals, were strengthened.

Since the Maastricht Treaty was signed, no meetings of the 'Assizes' have been called, but contacts between the European Parliament and national parliaments have been increased through traditional channels, notably the annual Conference of Presidents, the biannual Conference of European Affairs Committees (CEAC, better known by its French acronym, COSAC), direct contacts between individual committees and direct contacts between equivalent political Groups. The CEAC, initiated in 1989, has become a regular feature bringing together six members from each of the specialised 'European Committees' of national parliaments with six MEPs. Its meetings regularly feature addresses by a member of the Commission and the Council presidency.

Role of European political parties

Article 138a of the Treaty refers explicitly to the importance of European political parties in developing European public opinion. This article was introduced following a letter from the presidents of the three European party political federations (Guy Spitaels for the then Confederation of Socialist Parties, Wilfried Martens for the European Peoples Party and Willy De Clercq for the European Liberals, Democrats and Reformists) addressed to Jacques Delors and European Council President Lubbers in the closing months of the IGCs. Initially, it was agreed to incorporate this into the chapter on citizenship, but it was finally placed in the chapter on the European Parliament.

The article has already had an effect on the political families. The Confederation of Socialist Parties of the EC was replaced by the new

'Party of European Socialists' at The Hague Congress of November 1992, and the liberal federation became the 'European Liberal, Democrat and Reformist Party' at Torquay in December 1993. Although the Treaty article has no direct legal consequences on the status of European political parties, its existence gives encouragement and legitimacy to the process, already underway (albeit very gradual), of strengthening the structures and procedures of transnational party political cooperation. All three main party political federations have seen the intensity of their activities increase in recent years, and the European Parliamentary elections have been a stimulus and focus for joint policy development. It remains to be seen whether the linkage created by Maastricht between the parliamentary elections and the appointment of the Commission will lead in time to the European political parties nominating or backing rival candidates for President of the Commission during the election campaign.

Right of access to information

Annexed to the new Treaty is a Declaration on the right of access to information. The Commission is asked to submit a report on measures designed to improve public access to the information available to the institutions. The Declaration emphasises the importance of transparency in the decision-making process. This issue became an important part of the Community's response to the result of the first Danish referendum on Maastricht. The Edinburgh European Council of December 1992 approved a series of measures designed to enhance transparency in the EC's decision-taking process, including the holding of certain Council meetings in public, greater access to documents and information, and the publishing of the results of votes in Council. This last point has yet to be fully implemented.

Requirement that member states be democratic

The Treaty introduces for the first time provisions which imply that member states must be democratic. This is included in Article F of the Union Treaty.

Increased majority voting in Council

The limited, but significant, increase in the scope of qualified majority voting in Council improves the efficiency of the Community's decision-taking procedures in the areas of its responsibility and at the same time ensures that the Community, in these areas, can no longer be held hostage by an individual government. Many instances have been seen in recent years of one single government blocking the development of EC action or the revision of existing EC legislation where their country might gain an advantage, at the expense of the other member states, by blocking or at least holding up decisions. The scope for minority interests blocking the views of the majority is limited by this extension of qualified majority voting. However, even a qualified majority leaves scope for minority interests as it consists of fifty-four out of the seventy-six votes in Council, that is 71 per cent. A lower threshold of a two-thirds majority is provided for certain decisions under Stage Three of Emu and some other instances.

It is also the case that the influence of the European Parliament over the content of EC legislation is always greater when Council acts by a qualified majority than when it needs to find the lowest common denominator acceptable to all. This is true whatever legislative procedure is followed in Parliament.

Strengthened powers for the Court of Justice

Democracy also requires the fair and equal application of laws that have been adopted. Until now, the Court of Justice has not been able to sanction member states failing to respect its judgements. The European Parliament requested the IGCs to include a provision in the new Treaty giving the Court such a right. The new Treaty now contains a provision allowing the Commission to propose to the Court a fine or lump sum penalty payment in cases where a member state refuses to apply Court judgements.

WHERE MAASTRICHT FAILED TO IMPROVE DEMOCRATIC ACCOUNTABILITY

The IGC failed to reach agreement, or sometimes even to address, a number of points where there had been some pressure for reform that would increase democratic accountability.

Comitology

The complex and bureaucratic procedures whereby the Council subjects the Commission's implementing powers to the supervision of a plethora of advisory, management and regulatory committees composed of national civil servants has been criticised on numerous occasions. Management and regulatory committees have the right to block Commission decisions (the former by a qualified majority, the latter if there is a blocking minority) and have them referred to Council (by-passing Parliament entirely). In practice, this happens rarely as decisions emerge from deals made between the Commission and national bureaucracies: well away from public scrutiny.

In the IGCs, the Commission put forward a proposal to introduce a hierarchy of Community acts and to allow the Commission full executive powers subject in certain circumstances to recall to the full legislative procedure involving Parliament and Council. Committees of national civil servants would only have a consultative role, leaving political accountability clearly with the Commission, except where a measure is returned to the full legislative authority. However, the IGC failed to make progress on this, leaving it for the 1996 IGC.

A battle will certainly be fought on this issue before then in the context of the first co-decision procedures, in which Council and Parliament will have to agree on implementing powers to be given to the Commission. Parliament might argue that the existing comitology system cannot be used here as it is based on a Council framework decision adopted pursuant to Article 145. This article refers to implementing acts 'which Council adopts' and makes no reference to acts adopted jointly by Parliament and Council. In any case, Parliament is certain to oppose use of the more restrictive comitology procedures.

The pillar structure

The two 'pillars' of the Maastricht Treaty on common foreign and security policy, and justice and home affairs are often described as 'intergovernmental' as they do not come under the Community legal framework. However, they were presented by the Luxembourg presidency to the IGC as a 'half-way house between intergovernmentalism and communitarisation', on the grounds that decisions will be taken by the Council (rather than a separate Conference of Foreign Ministers), the Commission has a right of initiative, Parliament must be consulted and informed, the Community budget may be used and it may be decided (unanimously) to use majority voting for implementing measures.

In terms of parliamentary scrutiny, there is certainly an improvement, especially as regards justice and home affairs which was previously dealt with in a plethora of intergovernmental *ad hoc* working parties not linked formally to the Community and where there was no obligation even to inform or consult the Parliament. Nevertheless, in areas of interest to the citizen such as internal security, or of general political importance such as CFSP, opportunities for fully involving the European Parliament are limited by the pillar structure. The IGC agreed to re-examine the pillar structure in 1996.

Uniform electoral system

The representation of the people in the European Parliament is still distorted by the absence of a uniform procedure for European elections. Although the adoption of a uniform electoral system does not itself require amendment to the Treaties, the IGC might have examined the matter as part of a package or in order to facilitate the adoption of such a procedure, for example by introducing qualified majority voting or by setting a deadline. In the end, it merely provided that Parliament must give its assent to any procedure that is adopted, but the unanimity requirement in Council makes that unlikely in the near future.

Number of MEPs per member state

The IGC had reached a provisional agreement to adjust the number of MEPs to take account of German unification (and to cut the number of Commissioners in view of future enlargement). This element fell out of the final package at Maastricht itself, where there was pressure for a more general review of the number of MEPs per member state and where, it has been suggested, France wished to link its acceptance of an increase in the number of German MEPs with the fixing of Strasbourg as the main seat of the European Parliament. It was agreed to return to the issue in the course of 1992.

At the end of 1992, the Edinburgh European Council agreed on a change in the number of MEPs (but not in the number of Commissioners) per member state. The European Council took up entirely a proposal made by the Parliament concerning its own member-ship, and the number of MEPs increased in 1994 from 518 to 587.[13]

Seat of the institutions

No attempt was made in the IGC to fix the seat of the institutions or the new bodies set up by the Treaty of Maastricht, nor to modify the provision whereby seats are fixed by the common accord of the member states. It was, however, agreed to settle the seats of the new bodies during 1992. This required a settlement of the thorny issue of the seat of the European Parliament, as France would not agree to the fixing of any new seat before that matter was settled.

Under French pressure, the Edinburgh European Council agreed to fix Strasbourg as the seat of the European Parliament where it should hold twelve monthly sessions, Luxembourg as the site of its secretariat and Brussels as the venue for committee meetings and additional plenary sessions. Parliament immediately stated that it did not feel bound by this decision, questioning its legality.[14] It scheduled only eleven part-sessions in Strasbourg for 1993 and ten for 1994, but three in Brussels in 1993 and four in 1994. A new building in Brussels, containing for the first time in that city a suitably equipped plenary chamber, became available in mid-1993. The representation of the people through the European Parliament is certainly handicapped by working in three different locations, and the issue has not been settled by Edinburgh.

Budget procedure

The IGC did not modify the budget procedure to provide for greater equality between the two arms of the budgetary authority, the Parliament and the Council. Budgetary questions generally were held over until 1992 in order to implement the increase in the Community's resources necessitated by the new policies agreed in Maastricht and the exhaustion in any case of the previous ceiling on own resources. Council eventually reached agreement on this at the Edinburgh Summit and subsequently negotiated a new interinstitutional agreement with Parliament which, without formally changing the Treaty, enhances Parliament's influence over the budget, including obligatory expenditure.

THE EUROPEAN PARLIAMENT'S FUTURE PROSPECTS

The European Union established by Maastricht is one where representation of the people directly through the European Parliament is still weaker than their representation indirectly in the Council. Even in the areas of Community legislation where the co-decision procedure applies, the onus in adopting a measure will normally be on obtaining the qualified majority (and sometimes unanimity) in Council rather than the simple majority (or non-rejection by an absolute majority) in Parliament. In other areas, Council's domination is still stronger, not least in the 'pillars' of CFSP and interior affairs.

None the less, Maastricht constitutes an important step forward, both for the European Parliament and, to a lesser degree, for the indirect channel of representation through national parliaments. The latter have seen, as a result of the ratification process, improvements in the obligation on national governments at least to inform them in good time of what is happening in the Union and even to allow national parliaments to comment directly on draft Community legislation and press their position on their government. As regards the former, the Maastricht Treaty has, as we have seen, improved its position considerably giving it, in crucial areas of legislation, a co-decision procedure the bottom line of which gives it the right to block legislation – crucial for the credibility of the Parliament. The new procedure for appointing the Commission also has considerable potential for the Parliament, which leaves the relationship between the legislature and the executive at a point somewhere between the European and the US traditions. However, despite other improvements in Parliament's position, Maastricht still falls short of providing generalised equality of power between the Parliament, as the direct representative of the peoples, and the Council, representing the member states. It also fails in terms of clarity and transparency, with a plethora of complex procedures for adopting Community legislation.

What are the prospects for the future? Clearly, the European Parliament will use the new provisions to the maximum. It is already introducing new internal rules of procedure designed to interpret the Treaty provisions to full advantage and has negotiated a series of interinstitutional agreements with the Commission and the Council to put flesh on the bones of the Treaty as regards the budget, subsidiarity, transparency, the Ombudsman, inquiry committees and the conciliation procedure.[15] But it is likely to go beyond that and press for further revisions of the Treaty. The new intergovernmental conference scheduled by the Maastricht Treaty for 1996 is to re-examine the scope of the co-decision procedure, the pillar structure of the European Union and the hierarchy of legal acts. Parliament is also pressing for some institutional reforms to be linked to the enlargement process, as the Treaties of Accession will inevitably modify some of the institutional provisions of the existing Treaties. Finally, it is preparing a draft constitution, in response to requests expressed by the 1990 Assizes with national parliaments and the referendum in 1989 in Italy, which would provide the European Union with a clearer constitutional basis than the current set of overlapping treaties. What are the points that Parliament is likely to press for on these occasions?

First, Parliament is likely to press for an extension of the co-decision procedure to cover all areas in which Council adopts legislation by a qualified majority. It is likely to press for an extension of the sphere of qualified majority voting in any case and (in the context of enlargement) a lowering of the threshold for achieving a qualified majority (currently 71 per cent of the weighted votes in Council). Where unanimity remains the order of the day, notably for 'constitutional' decisions such as revision of the Treaties and own resources, Parliament will press for the assent procedure to be used. Concerning the appointment of the Commission, Parliament will press for a stronger role for the President in choosing (jointly with the member states) the other members of the Commission and perhaps giving Parliament the right to choose the President, or at least formally to confirm him (instead of informally through what is formally a 'consultation' at present). On the budgetary side, Parliament will continue to press for an end to the distinction between obligatory and non-obligatory expenditure (the whole procedure following that currently used for non-obligatory) and for incorporating the European Development Fund into the budget. It will press for full rights to go to Court, not only to defend its own prerogatives. It will probably press for an improvement in the co-decision procedure to simplify it (if both institutions agree already at first reading, why have a second reading? Is the stage of 'intention to reject' really necessary?) and to eliminate the provision allowing Council to act unilaterally in the absence of agreement in the conciliation committee.

Others will also have their agendas as far as the parliamentary aspects of reforms are concerned. The French Parliament may press again for the establishment of a 'congress' of national parliamentarians and could again gain some support from the UK. The French government, particularly if the Gaullists are in a strong position, may try to strengthen Council's prerogatives over the Commission. The British government may seek to strengthen the intergovernmental elements in the Union. They, France and Denmark may oppose many of the items for which the European Parliament will be pressing. The WEU Assembly will be seeking to survive and, if successful, to find a role.

The outcome will no doubt be another compromise between the more federalist and the more reluctant member states, between different concepts of the integration process and between various ideas as to how the people can best be represented. One thing is certain: the issue of the representation of the people in the European Union is one that will still be with us for many years; it is far from having been resolved satisfactorily at Maastricht.

ANNEX

Legislative procedures of the European Parliament resulting from the Maastricht Treaty

1. The *assent* procedure applies to:

- measure facilitating right of residence and freedom of movement of European citizens (Article 8a);
- definition of tasks, objectives, organisation and coordination of the structural funds (Article 130d);
- creation of Cohesion Fund (Article 130d);
- uniform procedure for European elections (Article 138(3)); *
- international agreements with certain institutional, budgetary or legislative implications (Article 228(3));
- accession of new member states (Article O of Title VII); *
- amendments to the Protocol of the European System of Central Banks (Article 106(5));
- special tasks to be entrusted to the Central Bank (Article 105(6)).

[* Parliament's assent to be given by an absolute majority of its members.]

| Council
adopts position
*(unanimity) | → | **European Parliament**
approves or does not
approve proposal (simple
majority except for
accession treaties and
uniform electoral system
where majority of MEPs
must approve) | → | **Council**
adopts act only
if Parliament
has approved
it |

Figure 13.1 Assent procedure

the Council acts on a proposal of:

- the Commission (Articles 8a, 105(6), 130d, 228(3));
- the Parliament (Article 138(3));
- the Central Bank[16] or the Commission (Article 106(5));
- applicant states, after consulting the Commission (Article O).

2. The *co-decision* procedure (Article 189b) (*see* Figure 13.2) applies to:

- free movement of workers (Article 49);
- right of establishment (Article 54);
- treatment of foreign nationals (Article 56);
- mutual recognition of diplomas (Article 57(1));
- provisions for the self-employed (Article 57(2));
- services (Article 66);
- internal market harmonisation (Article 100A);
- internal market mutual recognition (Article 100B);
- education (incentive measures) (Article 126(4)); *
- trans-European network guidelines (Article 129d);
- incentive measures in field of public health (Article 129(4));
- incentive measures in field of culture (Article 128(5));
- consumer protection (Article 129a(2));
- multi-annual Framework Programme for Research & Technology (Article 130(i)); *
- environment programmes (Article 130s(3)).

[* In these areas, the Council must act unanimously.]

3. The *cooperation* procedure (Article 189c) applies to:

- rules prohibiting discrimination on grounds of nationality (Article 6);
- transport (Article 75);
- Social Fund implementing decisions (Article 125);
- other measures in field of vocational training (Article 127(4));
- trans-European networks (interoperability & finance) (Article 129d);
- Regional Fund implementing decisions (Article 130e);
- rules for participation of undertakings, research centres and universities in Community Research & Technological Development (R&TD) (Article 130j);
- rules for dissemination of results of R&TD programmes (Article 130j);
- supplementary R&TD programmes with only some member states (Article 130k);

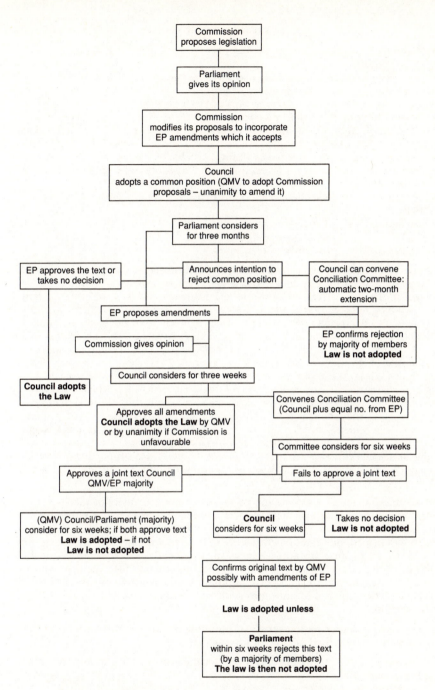

Figure 13.2 The co-decision procedure (Article 189b of the Treaty)

Source: Author's compilation
Notes: EP   =   European Parliament
        QMV =   Qualified Majority Vote

- Community participation in R&TD programmes of several member states (Article 130l);
- environment (except fiscal, land use, water & energy) (Article 130s(1));
- development policy (Article 130w);
- social policy (health and safety at work) (Article 118a);
- social policy pursued by eleven member states concerning working conditions, information and consultation of workers, equal treatment and integration into labour market (Protocol of the member states minus the UK, Art. 2 (2));
- rules on multilateral surveillance (Emu) (Article 103(5));
- definition of conditions for access to financial institutions by public authorities (Article 104a);
- definition of access to debt with central banks by public authorities (Article 104b);
- denominations and specifications of coins (Emu) (Article 108(3)).

4. The *consultation* procedure applies to the following.

Common policies: agriculture (Article 43); private sector competition (Article 87); regulations for state aids (Article 94); certain aspects of Emu (Articles 104c(14), 106(6), 109(1), 109e(6), 109e(7), 109i(2), 109i(4), 109j(2)); certain social policy matters (Articles 126 and 127); coordination of structural funds (Article 130d); specific programmes for research and development policy (Article 130i); the setting-up of joint undertakings (Article 130n); environmental policy (fiscal, land use, water and energy) (Article 130s); further measures to attain one of the Community's objectives (Article 235); abolition of restrictions on the freedom of establishment and on the provision of services (Article 63); taxation (Article 99); harmonisation of national provisions which affect the common market (Article 100); determination of which third-country nationals require visas (Article 100c(1)); uniform format visas (Article 100c(2)); international agreements other than those requiring Parliament's assent, except Article 113(3) agreements (Article 228); specific supplementary actions on economic and social cohesion (Article 130b); specific measures supporting industrial policy (Article 130(3)); and nuclear energy and radiation (11 articles in Euratom Treaty).

Institutional matters: appointment of President and members of the Board of the Central Bank (Article 109a(2)) and President of the EMI (Article 109f); framework decision on implementing powers for the Commission (Article 145, third indent); appointment of President of Commission (Article 158); setting-up of the Court of First Instance (Article 168a); amendments to Title III of the Statute of the Court of Justice (Article 188); appointment of the members of the Court of Auditors (Article 206(4)); adoption of the Staff Regulations (Article 212); and the calling of an intergovernmental conference to modify the Treaty (Article 236).

Budgetary matters: decision on the Community's own resources (Article 201); and Financial and other Regulations (Article 209).

Citizens' rights: voting in European and local elections (Article 8b); and other rights (Article 8f).

14

EUROPEAN UNION AND THE RULE OF LAW

Kieran Bradley and *Alastair Sutton*[1]

Part I: The Maastricht Treaty and the Rule of Law

The rule of law is widely accepted as a fundamental requirement of any modern system of democratic government, notwithstanding the absence of a clear consensus as to the exact content of this notion.[2] As it applies between the institutional actors of the Union, the rule of law may be taken as implying that both the member states and the institutions act in accordance with fixed and identifiable rules and principles, and that sufficient judicial remedies are available to ensure respect for these rules and principles, as authoritatively interpreted by an independent court. The proposition that the European Union should be based on the rule of law is hardly open to serious contention; not only do its member states aspire to uphold 'the principles of liberty, democracy, and respect for human rights and fundamental freedoms and the rule of law', according to the preamble of the Treaty on European Union, but the European Community, centrepiece of the Union, is founded on respect for the rule of law. The question of whether, and to what extent, the Union established by the Maastricht Treaty, as distinct from the Community, in fact complies with these basic requirements of the rule of law requires a more qualified answer.[3]

As a summary of the immanence of the rule of law in the legal order set up by the Treaty of Rome, it is hard to better the Court's own spare prose, in its first opinion on the European Economic Area (EEA) Agreement:[4]

> The EEC Treaty, albeit concluded in the form of an international agreement, none the less constitutes the constitutional charter of a Community based on the rule of law ... the Community treaties established a new legal order for the benefit of which states have limited their sovereign rights, in ever wider fields, and the subjects of which comprise not only member states but also nationals ... [T]he essential characteristics of the Community legal order which has thus been established are in particular its primacy over the law

of the member states and the direct effect of a whole series of provisions which are applicable to their nationals and to the member states themselves.[5]

While such a description might now be considered unexceptionable, the metamorphosis of the EEC Treaty from international agreement to constitutional charter is the result of a long process of incremental constitutionalisation, effected by the Court of Justice and condoned, albeit sometimes rather reluctantly, by the courts of the member states. The doctrines of the primacy and direct effect of Community law were developed in the early 1960s, though it was not until 1986 that the Court was first moved to describe the Community as being based on the rule of law, a finding it deduced from the creation by the Treaty of a 'complete system of legal remedies and procedures, designed to [ensure that] neither [the] member states nor [the] institutions can avoid a review of the question of whether the measures adopted by them are in conformity with . . . the Treaty'.[6] The system of legal remedies provided by the Treaty was, and still is, in fact somewhat short of complete, and it fell to the Court to extend its own jurisdiction both *ratione materiae*, to include respect by the institutions for fundamental rights and general legal principles, such as proportionality and equality, and *ratione personae*, to include acts of the European Parliament and acts of the other institutions susceptible to violating Parliament's prerogatives. Recent Court judgements have also strengthened the protection of individual rights, holding the member states, as well as the institutions, to be obliged to respect fundamental rights when acting within the sphere of Community law, and discovering in the scheme of the Treaty a liability in damages of the member states, in certain circumstances, for their failure properly to apply EC law.[7]

In the second part of this chapter Alastair Sutton gives a fuller account of the development of the rule of law in the Community as it has affected the rights of the individual citizen. Here we look at one aspect of the judicial resolution of disputes on the distribution of decisional powers between the Community and the member states, in legal basis cases, which may serve as a topical illustration of the application of the rule of law in the Community's legal order and the priority of the rule of law over the rule of governments. The perspective of the implementation of the constitutional principle of subsidiarity poses a specific problem for the Court in this area, that of the justiciability of Article 3b.

PROCEDURAL RULES AND POLITICAL SAFEGUARDS

Unlike most federal-type entities, the European Community does not operate under a material division of powers, such as the list-based systems in Canada or Australia, nor indeed under a series of rather open-ended criteria defining the extent of the central authority's power, such as those provided by the United States Constitution. Instead, the Treaty sets the Community a number of more or less specific objectives and tasks, and provides the institutions with the means to achieve these ends. Under such a functional distribution of powers, there is therefore no predefined core of member state powers which is 'safe' from some form of Community 'interference'.[8] The principal safeguards for the interests of the member states are twofold: in the first place, the member state governments participate directly and decisively in the Community political processes at all levels, and in the second place, they have an unrestricted right to initiate annulment proceedings before the Court of Justice, should they consider that a Community institution has acted *ultra vires*.[9]

The formal extent to which an individual member state may defend national interests in a given legislative procedure depends on whether the Council may act by a majority vote, or whether the particular enabling article of the Treaty, the 'legal basis', imposes unanimity.[10] The potential influence of the Commission and the European Parliament, representing, respectively, the interests of the Community *per se* and those of the peoples of the Community, equally varies in function of the legal basis. Apart from the few cases where it can act under autonomous legislative powers, the Commission may exert a greater degree of influence on the contents of legislation where the Council acts by a majority, whether qualified or simple; in such circumstances, the interplay of the Commission's right to modify its proposal at any time, and the requirement that the Council act unanimously in order to modify a Commission proposal, means that it is easier for the Council to adopt the Commission's proposal, modified if need be to satisfy the wishes of the relevant majority of national delegations, than any other act. Parliament can assert its views most forcibly where either the negative assent ('co-decision') or assent procedure applies.[11] To date, judicial review of the respect by the Council of the limits of its Treaty-given powers has usually not been a straightforward question of *vires*, but a strict control by the Court of the respect of the procedural rules of the Treaty, and hence of the respective prerogatives of individual member states, the Commission and Parliament.[12]

The preliminary point that, under the rule of law, the member states must fully respect and implement the Treaty, and may not therefore agree simply to bypass its provisions, however inconvenient, is illustrated by the Court's judgement in the second *Defrenne* case.[13] There the Court held that a resolution of the member states to postpone the application of a particular Treaty provision was 'ineffective to make any valid modification of the time-limit fixed by the Treaty', which could only be changed by the amendment procedure of Article 236 EEC. The generality of this obviously sound decision may have been somewhat undermined by the judgement in the *Bangladesh* cases of 30 June 1993, where the Court found that nothing in the Treaty precluded the member states conferring on the Commission the power to take decisions having legal effects outside the ambit of the Treaty's supervisory mechanisms.[14] This finding is rather difficult to reconcile with the principle of enumerated powers reflected in Article 4.1 EEC, a provision conspicuous by its absence from the text of the judgement.

That the rule of law does not permit even a unanimous decision of the member states to set aside the procedural provisions for the adoption of a particular measure which are dictated by its legal basis is illustrated by a series of cases initiated by the Commission and, latterly, by Parliament, following the institutional reforms of the Single European Act. In the first of these, the Court found that the legal basis must be identifiable from the text and be based on objective factors which are amenable to judicial review; the choice of legal basis may not depend on the necessarily subjective appreciation of the adopting institution as to the objective or objectives the measure seeks to attain.[15] The applicable procedure for the adoption of an act is therefore determined by legal criteria, rather than considerations of political opportunity.

Though it may appear a rather formalistic ritual to the outside observer, legal basis litigation is the only means the Treaty provides for resolving a struggle for influence between the Commission (and Parliament) on the one hand, and individual member states on the other, and with the coming into force of the Treaty on European Union, between Parliament and the Council where negative assent applies; as the Court noted in the *Tariff Preferences* case, '(the) choice of the legal basis could . . . affect the determination of the content of the contested (measure)'. In making such a determination, the Court has identified as the principal criterion the objective(s) the contemplated measure seeks to achieve and its material content, though the Council appears to have a strong nostalgic attachment to the 'principal objective' of the measure as the decisive criterion.[16] In principle, a specific legal basis is to be preferred to a general enabling clause, though where the Community competence to adopt a particular measure reposes on two Treaty provisions, the procedural provisions should be combined, unless this is precluded for institutional reasons. Where, on the other hand, the addition of a superfetatory legal basis does not affect choice of procedure to be applied, the measure will not be annulled for such a formal defect.

While the Court has had to rule on the extent of the Council's power to legislate by a majority vote in a number of fields of Community activity, the most controversial legal basis question to date has been that concerning the delimitation of the respective fields of application of

Articles 100a and 130s of the Treaty, for measures dealing simultaneously with internal market and environmental protection concerns. Even before the entry into force of the Maastricht Treaty, the stakes were high. Article 100a, which expressly includes a number of mechanisms to ensure the protection of the environment is not forgotten in the rush to the single market, allowed for a qualified majority in Council, and hence, theoretically, the adoption of the highest common factor of member state protection, while Article 130s provided for unanimity, thereby reducing the formal impact of both the Commission's proposal and Parliament's opinion, and presumably leading to environmental protection at the level of the lowest common denominator.[17] In a carefully selected test case, the Commission, supported by the European Parliament, challenged the Council's choice of Article 130s as the legal basis for a directive on the production of titanium dioxide, a white pigment of considerable economic importance. The directive sought to harmonize national provisions in this area, with a view to both reducing the pollution which resulted from the production processes, and equalising competitive conditions in the industry; the Commission was able to show that disparities in national regulatory measures gave producers in member states with less rigorous standards a competitive advantage of 10–15 per cent, and argued the directive was an internal market measure rather than being specifically intended to protect the environment.

In a judgement which has been heavily criticised, though not always for the right reasons, the Court found that, from its aim and material content, the directive fell simultaneously within the Community's internal market and environmental protection powers.[18] The cumulation of the unanimity requirement of Article 130s and the cooperation procedure would however, in the Court's view, undermine one of the 'essential elements' of this latter procedure. In particular, Parliament's prerogative to reject a common position, which rejection can only be overridden by a unanimous Council, would be rendered nugatory if the Council were required in any case to act unanimously throughout, and the 'very purpose of the cooperation procedure, which is to increase the involvement of the European Parliament in the legislative process of the Community would thus be jeopardized'. Having excluded the possibility of a double legal basis in this case, the Court had no difficulty in choosing Article 100a as the appropriate enabling provision. Indeed, the reasons the Court provides for its choice appear sufficient to exclude reliance on Article 130s in the first place; one might be forgiven for wondering if the case could not have been decided on the basis of the interpretation of the relevant Treaty provisions alone, without the institutional detour, however gratifying this may have been to the intervening party. It is also significant that, in what the Court took to be a fifty–fifty situation, it opted for a solution which gave priority to what it dubbed the principle of democratic participation over the right of veto individual member states enjoy under a unanimity rule.

The first 'hormones' case may serve a paradigm of the converse situation, where a member state resorts to the Court to defend its right of veto in the legislative process. Since the earliest days of the CAP, the Council had insisted on founding harmonisation directives in the field of agriculture on both Articles 43 and 100 EEC, requiring unanimity. Towards the end of 1985, a proposal for a directive prohibiting the use of certain growth-inducing hormones in meat production ran up against the firm, and well-publicised, opposition of the UK government; in order to avoid the inevitable British veto, the Council decided to base the directive on Article 43 alone, which allows qualified majority voting. In ruling on the annulment proceedings taken by the United Kingdom, the Court confirmed the appropriateness of this article for Community legislation on the production and marketing of agricultural products, including for measures which take account of considerations of human and animal health; the practice of the Council over many years of choosing a double legal basis was found not to have created a precedent binding on the institutions.[19] The directive was none the less annulled, as the Council had acted in breach of its own rules of procedure by resorting to urgent procedure when the rules required unanimity for the application of such procedure.

SUBSIDIARITY

Writing in 1990, before the IGCs leading to the Treaty on European Union had been convened, Jacqué and Weiler noted in the constitutional development of the Community 'a weakening of any workable and enforceable mechanism for allocation of jurisdiction/competences/ powers between the Community and its member states'.[20] This weakening was said to have arisen, on the one hand, from profligate legislative practices, and, on the other, from the attitude of the Court of Justice, which has interpreted extensively the reach of the Community's competences, while adopting a self-limiting approach to supervising the expansion of these competences by the political organs. In order to preempt possible 'rebellions' by national supreme courts against a perceived erosion of the powers of the member states, the authors proposed 'to grapple with what has been considered impossible: making subsidiarity justiciable'.[21]

The basic idea of subsidiarity in the political context is relatively simple and even attractive: that decision-making powers should be exercised at the lowest appropriate level of government (local, regional, provincial, national, Community, international) in the interests of efficiency and/or accountability of the deciding authority to the citizen. The Maastricht Treaty incorporates two different formulations of this principle; while the eleventh recital of the preamble and Article A refer to the creation of an 'ever closer union . . . in which decisions are taken as closely as possible to the citizen [in accordance with the principle of subsidiarity]', the new Article 3b, equally dubbed 'subsidiarity', reflects quite other concerns.

The first and third sub-paragraphs of this article declare that the Community must respect the principles of enumerated powers and proportionality. The nub of 'Community subsidiarity' is contained in the second sub-paragraph, which provides one positive and one negative condition for Community action in areas of concurrent competence:

- that the objectives of the intended action cannot be sufficiently achieved by the member states;
- that the scale and effects of the action are such that the objectives can be better achieved by the Community than the member states.

It is clear that these criteria, as amplified by European Council conclusions and the interinstitutional agreement of 25 October 1993, will be relied upon by the political institutions in assessing whether a particular Community initiative is opportune; indeed, it seems likely that similar considerations have long played some part in decisions on the exercise of legislative powers at EC level, at least in areas outside the four freedoms and the original common policies.[22] The question to which Article 3b gives rise is whether it can be said, in fact, to have made subsidiarity justiciable, in the sense that the Court would strike down a Community measure for failure to respect this Treaty provision.

On the one hand, neither the fact that Article 3b is to be found amongst the 'principles' in Part One of the Treaty, rather than its substantive provisions, nor the political implications of the decision to be taken, would preclude judicial review. The Court has derived binding constitutional obligations for the member states and the institutions from Articles 5 and 7 EEC (now Articles 5 and 6 EC), also among the 'principles' of Part One, and relied upon Articles 3 and 4 EEC as an aid to interpretation of other, more specific provisions. Equally, though framed in terms of respect for procedural rules, legal basis disputes raise issues of major political import on the respective powers of the Community and individual member states, and of the institutions *inter se*. Though Maastricht did not amend the grounds for annulment set out in Article 173 EC to include an express 'subsidiarity' ground as Jacqué and Weiler proposed, such jurisdiction could, arguably, be founded on the general ground of 'infringement of the Treaty'.

On the other hand, the criteria laid down in Article 3b do not appear to admit of any kind of useful legal appreciation. The question of whether the (presumably, EC) objectives of a particular action can be sufficiently achieved at national level is one which the member state governments and the Community's political institutions will be well placed to answer; it is rather difficult to see on what objective legal grounds the Court would be able to review the evaluation of the comparative efficiency of national and Community action adopted by the Commission and Council, or give a ruling, divorced from any situation of fact, that an applicant national government is incapable of achieving a particular objective.[23] Similarly, while an assessment of the scale and effects of a given action might be considered a relatively simple matter, the question of whether the action can 'therefore . . . be better achieved at Community level' is not one on which the Treaty provides the beginnings of a response. The comparison with legal basis disputes is instructive; there the Court can rely on the text of the enabling article in question, interpreted in the light of its context and objective(s), as well as the objectives and material content of the proposed action. All of these elements are available to the Court, which need not depend solely on the submissions of the parties. In applying Article 3b, the Court would itself be obliged to compare the objectives of the proposed action, with whatever, *ipso facto* conflicting, assessments of national and Community capacity to achieve these as have been submitted to it.

In dealing with subsidiarity, the Court will in essence have to choose between two approaches.[24] In the first scenario, it would defer to the Community legislator's judgement on the question of comparative efficiency, just as in the past it has refused to review the 'necessity' for Community action under Article 235 or to examine the expediency of a policy measure unless this is 'patently unsuitable to the objective which the competent institution seeks to pursue'.[25] If, however, the Court were to auto-limit its supervision of respect for Article 3b to cases where national action is 'patently' sufficient and Community action manifestly not 'better' for achieving Community objectives, then it seems doubtful that the justiciability of this provision would add anything to the respect for the rule of law in the EC, or the confidence of national courts that national powers are not being eroded, or any other of the obscure ends its inclusion in the EC Treaty sought to achieve.

If, on the contrary, the Court were to take a more active view of its role under Article 3b than it does at present in supervising respect for the limits of EC legislative powers under Article 173, it would be entering uncharted, and presumably troubled, political waters, without Treaty guidance as to a suitable course. In a system which seeks to ensure the defence of the various interests present primarily through procedural safeguards, it is right and proper that the Court should ensure respect both for those procedural rules and the limits on Community competence which derive from the Treaty. The case for the Court's assuming a substantive jurisdiction to evaluate the comparative efficiency of projected Community and national action is not entirely convincing, and evokes rather the spectre of a shift from the rule of law to the government of the judges.

THE SECOND PILLAR AND THE RULE OF LAW

The European Union established by Article A of Maastricht is a new entity, without separate legal personality, which operates through its component parts, the European Communities, the Common Foreign and Security Policy and Cooperation on Justice and Home Affairs, and in some cases through the member states. The rule of law in the EC has been examined above; it is proposed to consider in turn the application of this principle in the other two pillars, before suggesting some conclusions regarding its application in the Union in general.

Though cooperation between the member states on foreign policy matters dates back to 1970, it was not until the Single European Act that the substantive obligations and procedures were set out in Treaty form, as opposed to reports and declarations. Political Cooperation could be said to have been subject to fixed and identifiable rules and principles, one of the principal aspects of the rule of law, at least from 1987, if not before.[26] Article 31 of the Single Act, however, expressly removed Title III from the jurisdiction of the Court of Justice.

Title V of the Maastricht Treaty develops and adds to the substantive obligations and procedures of the Single Act; in particular, it allows the Council, acting unanimously, to decide, within the framework of joint action on a particular matter, which decisions may subsequently be taken by a qualified majority (Articles J.3.1 and J.3.2); furthermore, joint actions, including presumably decisions adopted by a majority, are said to 'commit the member states in the positions they adopt and in the conduct of their activity', while member states must ensure their national policies conform to common positions defined by the Council (Articles J.3.4 and J.2.2, respectively).

Notwithstanding the facility for majority voting, and the supposed 'single institutional framework' to serve the Union (Article C), Article L provides in effect that the Treaty provisions concerning the powers of the Court of Justice and the exercise of those powers shall not apply to Title V. Thus, the Court has no jurisdiction to rule on a complaint of the Commission or a member state that another member state has failed in its obligations under this title, or that the Council has acted in breach of this part of the Treaty; nor can the Court provide an authoritative ruling as to whether a particular matter could, by virtue of an earlier decision, be dealt with by a qualified majority vote in Council. The 'complete system of judicial remedies' the Court discerned in the legal order of the EC obviously does not obtain in the framework of foreign policy.

The incomplete application of the rule of law in this area should, however, be appreciated in the light of the particular nature of international relations; common positions and joint actions bind the Community *vis-à-vis* third states, regardless of possible legal irregularities within the Union's legal order. Furthermore, the substantive obligations of Title V are not such as to create direct rights and duties for the citizen, the characteristic of the EEC Treaty which provided the main foundation for its constitutionalisation. Article J.1.4, for example, obliges the member states to support the Union's foreign policy 'actively and unreservedly in a spirit of loyalty and mutual solidarity' and to 'refrain from any action which is contrary to the interests of the Union or likely to impair its effectiveness as a cohesive force in international relations'. While this recalls the duty of Community solidarity implicit in Article 5 EC, and could conceivably have been applied in concrete cases by the Court, in the absence of sufficiently clear and precise legal obligations, the Council is arguably the appropriate body to ensure compliance with these principles, as Article J.1.4 provides. Title V could thus be said to be subject to the rule of international, rather than constitutional law.[27]

From the overall perspective of democratic government, a number of improvements from the pre-existing situation may be noted. The CFSP numbers amongst its objectives the development and consolidation of 'democracy and the rule of law, and respect for human rights and fundamental freedoms'; if the Union seeks to promote these lofty ideals in third countries, it can hardly ignore them closer to home. The European Parliament is to be consulted on 'the main aspects and basic choices' of the CFSP, presumably before these are decided upon, and with a view to enabling Parliament to bring some influence to bear on the decisions. Information after the event, which was the extent of Parliament's formal participation in EPC, now applies to the development of the CFSP; Parliament may also ask questions of the Council – a facility not granted it by Article 140 EC, though allowed in practice since 1959 – or submit recommendations to it, and must hold an annual debate on progress in this field.[28] If the mechanisms for influencing the Council at Parliament's disposal remain somewhat underdeveloped on paper, the possibility of extensive public scrutiny may have a salutary effect on foreign policy decision-making.

THE THIRD PILLAR AND THE RULE OF LAW

Cooperation between the member states in matters of justice and home affairs is nothing new; Title VI puts this form of cooperation on a Treaty footing, as Title III of the Single Act had done for EPC. In so far as the activities of the member states in this area had heretofore been largely shrouded in obscurity, with the possible exception of the Schengen initiative, the publication of the decision-making procedures and the identification of a few substantive obligations may be said to constitute the beginnings of the application of the rule of law in this area; as with CFSP, the jurisdiction of the Court to interpret or provide judicial remedies for failure to apply Title VI is precluded by Article L.[29]

The authors of the Treaty of Maastricht were clearly conscious of the possible overlap in, or inconsistency between, the material scope of Title VI and the EC Treaty, particularly as regards measures to ensure the free movement of persons under Articles K.1.2 and 3 and Article 7a EC, respectively. To this end, the heading of Article K.1 specifies that the action of the member states in the listed areas of common interest shall be 'without prejudice to the powers of the European Community'. The exact extent of the EC's powers in relation to free movement of persons in an internal market is controversial, and is currently *sub judice*, as a result of the action for illegal failure to act commenced by the Parliament against the Commission. In any case, action taken by the member states in accordance with Title VI which infringes the Community's powers is open to judicial sanction at the suit of the Commission (Article 169 EC) or indirectly, at the suit of the citizen, in national proceedings contesting the implementation of such cooperation in individual cases (with a possible reference to the Court of Justice under Article 177 EC). Furthermore, it is clear from the *Bangladesh* cases, cited above, that the Court has jurisdiction to examine the question of whether a particular act has been adopted by the Council, and is hence amenable to judicial review within the Community framework, or constitutes a collective decision of the member states, possibly subject to judicial review in the national courts.[30]

As the matters dealt with in Title VI are such as to directly affect the rights of individual citizens, Article K.2.1 specifies that member state action must comply with the European Convention on Human Rights, the 1951 Convention on the Status of Refugees and the protection afforded under national law to political refugees. Though it is in principle beyond the jurisdiction of the Court of Justice, Title VI is subject to the rule of national and international human rights law.

TITLES I AND VII OF THE TREATY OF MAASTRICHT

The Union described in the preamble and Titles I and VII, above and beyond its constituent 'pillars', is partly aspirational in character; the Treaty is thus described as a 'new stage in the process of creating an ever closer union' (Article A, second paragraph), rather than an end point.

The task of the Union is to 'organize . . . relations between the member states and between their peoples', rather than unify them under a single system of government, such as the merger of the Federal and Democratic Republics of Germany in 1990. Though formulating a number of rules and principles for the functioning and future development of the Union, Title I does not confer upon it any decision-making powers; subject to Article M, the Court of Justice has no jurisdiction to ensure respect for the obligations and procedures set out in Title I, such as the duty of the European Council to meet at least twice a year and to report annually to the European Parliament on the progress of the Union. This is not to say that Title I cannot serve as an aid to interpretation of the other titles of the Treaty, particularly those concerning the Communities; in the EEA opinion cited above, the Court quoted Article 1 of the Single Act in identifying the objectives of the Community treaties, notwithstanding the express exclusion of its jurisdiction to ensure respect of this provision under Article 31 of the Single Act.

Title VII, on the other hand, sets out the procedures for amending the Union Treaties and for accession to the Union, repeals parts of the Merger Treaty and the Single Act, and lays down substantive provisions on the duration, ratification and entry into force of Maastricht. Significantly, these provisions are subject to the normal jurisdiction of the Court of Justice; in particular, the Court can ensure respect by the member states and the EC institutions of Article M. This provides in essence that nothing in Titles I, V and VI can be taken as affecting the EC Treaties, and, by implication, the *acquis communautaire* the Union is already bound to respect and build upon by virtue of Article C. Article M is intended to ensure that the principle of the rule of law in Community matters, so carefully nurtured over three decades by the Court of Justice, will not be eroded through the back door of the Union or its intergovernmental components.

THE LAW AND INSTITUTIONS

While the member states still appear to have certain difficulties in the matter of implementation, at least the structures and principles for the application of the rule of law are firmly in place as regards the European Community.[31] In the delicate matter of the distribution of decisional powers between the EC and the member states, the Court has played an essential arbitrating role, without being drawn into controversies it more properly falls to the political institutions to resolve, though its policy of restraint will be put to the test in applying the principle of subsidiarity as formulated in Article 3b. The legal basis cases bring to light two related aspects of the rule of law. On the one hand, the Court has generally upheld the application of the terms and underlying principles of the

Treaty over any contrary political arrangement the Council or, as in *Defrenne II*, the member states may have made. On the other hand, the procedural rights of the member states in the internal decision-making of the Council must be scrupulously respected, illustrating what Advocate General Tesauro has dubbed 'a member state's fundamental right to the observance of those procedural rules which it had previously accepted and not other rules'.[32]

Neither of the intergovernmental pillars of the Maastricht Treaty provides for review by the Court of Justice of respect for their pro-visions; though measures under Titles V and VI do not constitute Community law, in so far as they affect the rights of the citizen they are amenable to judicial review in the individual member states. Furthermore, the integrity of the Community pillar is protected by Article M, which both safeguards the *acquis communautaire* from Union erosion, and vests jurisdiction in the Court to this end. While the intergovernmental pillars are not as fully subject to the rule of law as the Communities, particularly in the matter of judicial interpretation and remedies, it would be wrong to conclude that the European Union has abandoned this basic principle.

Part II: Justice and Fair Play in the European Union[33]

For constitutional lawyers, as well as the general public, the expression 'the rule of law' has different meanings. As it applies to individuals, however, the concept is understood to imply that:

- the powers exercised by politicians and officials must have a legitimate foundation;
- they must be based on authority conferred by law; and
- the law should conform to certain minimum standards of substantive and procedural justice.

In particular, under national constitutional systems, the rule of law implies the protection of individual rights and freedoms from arbitrary action by the state. The fact that, in all Western European legal systems, general principles of law exist to this effect, is reflected in the provisions of the ECHR of 1950. These principles have been explicitly incorpor-ated into Community law in Article F of the Maastricht Treaty.

Despite this reinforcement of the rule of law in the EU system, the fact remains that, even as amended at Maastricht, the Treaties creating the Union are at best only an embryonic constitution for an entity which claims federal or confederal status. Our principal purpose here is to highlight some of the flaws in the present system, particularly from the standpoint of the private sector.

One theme which emerges from an analysis of the legal structure of the original Treaties, as well as of administrative and judicial practice in the EC over the last 40 years, is the way in which the EC's legal order has operated more to the advantage of privileged parties, such as the institutions and member states, rather than for individuals and companies. There is in fact a simple historical and legal explanation for this situation. This can be illustrated by the political and economic evolution of the Community, since its creation with the ECSC Treaty of 1951.

The crisis concerning the ratification of the Maastricht Treaty has merely highlighted the democratic deficit which has always existed between the European Community and the average European citizen. Although the political and popular dimensions of the EC were an integral part of the original Treaties, the first 35 years emphasised economic rather than political integration. The structure and goals of the ECSC, the EEC and Euratom in their early years gave pride of place to the institutions and member states, rather than to individuals and companies. It is true that the Court of Justice as early as 1962 established the principles of the supremacy and direct effect of Community law in the cases of *Van Gend en Loos* and *Costa* v. *Enel*.[34] Thus the unique supranational character of the Communities, together with the direct involvement of individuals and companies in the Community legal order, was never in doubt. On the other hand, the principal activities of the EEC between 1957 and 1968 concerned the progressive dismantling of tariffs and the creation of a customs union. Subsequently, although legislative steps towards the creation of a common market were taken, the years until 1985 were dominated by the economic downturn of the 1970s and the 'stop-go' effects on Community policies of the successive enlargements of the EC. In these circumstances, it is understandable that little controversy existed over the protection of individual and corporate rights under Community law.

Until the launch of the single market programme in 1985, the impact of EC law and policy on the private sector, and the participation of the private sector in the law-making process, were therefore relatively uncontroversial. In the early years of the Community, individuals and companies in the original six member states accepted without question the need for a new framework for European cooperation, after the destruction wrought by two world wars in 30 years. Although the first enlargement of the Community involved controversy over the effect of membership on national sovereignty, issues such as the rule of law, the democratic nature of the EC processes and the role of the individual were not of primary importance. It is true that Community membership was seen as guaranteeing parliamentary democracy in the case of Greece, Spain and Portugal, but the nature of EC decision-making and its effect on the private sector were not seriously questioned.

In essence, since its creation in the 1950s, the Community had been of primary importance to 'economic operators', rather than the private citizen. In times of relative economic prosperity, the Community was seen as contributing to growth through the promotion of economic integration. In the recession of the 1970s and early 1980s, the Community was largely seen by industry as providing more effective protection, principally against imports from Japan. The most visible aspects of Community policies until 1985 were in the field of external relations (through the implementation of the common commercial policy), competition policy and agricultural policy. Activities in these fields, together with the first legislative steps to secure the free movement of goods, the right of establishment and the free movement of workers were not of a dimension or nature as to excite opposition, at least in continental Europe. It is true that, particularly in the United Kingdom, the Community was criticised for unnecessary centralisation and harmonisation. It is also true that, throughout Europe, the policies and procedures of the Community were widely misunderstood. None the less, the democratic deficiencies of the EC came to light mainly after 1985 and, directly or indirectly, as a result of the '1992' programme.

THE LAW AND THE SINGLE MARKET

Although the EC's single market programme was launched in 1985, largely as a result of pressure from European industry, public apathy towards the Community persisted into 1986. This situation was changed by the campaign's launch – initially by President Mitterrand, Prime Minister Thatcher and the Delors Commission itself – to promote the economic benefits which could be achieved through the completion of a genuine single market in Europe.

The legislative programme and timetable for the completion of the single market, contained in the Commission's White Paper of 1985, provoked lobbying on a scale more akin to Washington than to Brussels. Ironically, the leaders in the race to influence the institutions and member states in the execution of the single market programme were companies and governments from outside the Community, especially Efta countries, the United States and Japan. In due course, however, economic policy in all member states, as well as the corporate strategies at least of larger corporations, were linked to the EC's single market 1programme. A number of factors combined, particularly between 1985 and 1989, to bring the Community and its activities to the attention of individuals and companies. These included:

- the unprecedented volume of EC legislation, particularly as regards the 'four freedoms';

- EC involvement in 'new' areas of policy such as environmental protection, transportation, telecommunications, worker consultation, protection and information, energy policy;
- a more vigorous implementation of competition and state aids policy as a corollary to the liberal economic policies upon which the single market was based;
- the increased importance given to EC financing of research and development, on the basis of a partnership and shared responsibility between the EC institutions, member states and industry;
- increased EC involvement in the economic development of less developed areas of the Community;
- Community assistance to enable small and medium enterprises to benefit from the economies of scale created within the single market.

THE LAW AND THE CITIZEN

The expression '1992' came to symbolise the Community in the years between 1985 and 1989 and, as this implies, the principal impact of European integration was still on economic operators. None the less, in parallel, the actual or potential importance of the Community to the private citizen was growing as a result of:

- the negotiation of the Single Act in 1985, which highlighted the possibility of qualified majority voting in the Council and an increased role in the formation of EC law and policy for the Parliament;
- the impact of EC law and policy on the citizen as worker, international traveller, company director, qualified professional, or simply as a voting European citizen;
- the passage of European legislation to ensure direct elections to the European Parliament;
- the proclamation of a 'Citizen's Europe';
- the extension of the free movement of workers to embrace the free movement of persons.

Certainly it is correct to highlight the role of the Court of Justice in securing the protection of individual and corporate rights and freedoms in the years leading up to 1989, but it would have been exaggerated and misleading to compare the Community at this stage with other federal or confederal entities. The contrast between the distribution of political power in the EC and the limitations of the Community's legal order with capitals such as Washington, Canberra, Ottawa, Berne or Bonn was obvious.

Although the transition in the Community legal order from that of a supranational economic institution to an embryonic European constitution was given momentum by the Maastricht Treaty, the origins of the evolution preceded it. The turning point and the true genesis of the need for a constitutional framework, providing comprehensive guarantees for the rule of law at European level, sprang from the realisation of the implications of the total abolition of internal frontiers within the Community. The far-reaching implications of a Europe without internal frontiers include the following considerations:

- in a genuine single market based on the mutual recognition of different national systems, shared trust, confidence and respect are indispensable;
- capital can move freely, thereby affecting the flow of investments and the industrial structure of the Community;
- technological changes, particularly in telecommunications and transportation, reinforce the irrelevance of conventional international frontiers;
- the link between a single market without internal frontiers and more far-reaching macroeconomic, monetary and fiscal measures to ensure that the single market is underpinned and strengthened by a single economy, comparable to that in a nation state;
- the unavoidable link between common internal policies leading to the creation of a single economy and the need for common external policies in the same fields.

If the increased volume of economic activities of the Community had highlighted the need for democracy and the rule of law, this was reinforced at political level by the events of 1989 and thereafter. The perceived success of the '1992' programme (although still largely potential) became both a model and a magnet for neighbouring countries. The Efta countries in particular moved from a policy of pragmatic economic cooperation with the EC in fields covered directly and indirectly by the single market programme, to a more structured relationship in the EEA Agreement and, finally, to applications for membership. Since 1989, too, the disintegration of the Soviet empire has led to the conclusion of Association Agreements between the EC and Hungary, Poland, Romania, Bulgaria, the Czech and Slovak Republics; the prospect of comparable agreements with the Baltic States; and negotiations for a Partnership Agreement with Russia and other CIS states.

Since the legal basis of all the Community's agreements with its neighbours in Efta countries as well as in Central and Eastern Europe is the EC legal order, problems which exist within the Community with regard to democratic control over decision-making and the rule of law may tend to be amplified in the wider framework. The EEA Agreement, which entered into force on 1 January 1994, is an example of this phenomenon, notably as a result of the relatively limited powers of democratic control which exist under the EEA Agreement for legislation passed by the EEA Council. There is, however, at least the possibility of judicial review of administrative action by the Efta Court and, ultimately, by the Court of Justice itself.

The negotiation of the Maastricht Treaty was a response to both internal and external pressures on the Community. Although imperfectly constructed and by no means a draft constitutional document, the Maastricht Treaty was much needed in order to provide a more adequate framework for internal policies in the field of justice and home affairs and to provide a more coherent framework for united Community action in foreign and security policy. Now that the Maastricht Treaty has been ratified, three important features are distinguishable.

First, the apparently limited substantive content of the Maastricht Treaty masks a more profound underlying shift in institutional and member state activity towards a greater concentration and rationalisation of activities at Community level. Second, the prominence given to the notion of subsidiarity in the debate on the Treaty obscures the fact that a considerable degree of cohesion and even centralisation is indispensable in order to manage the effective operation of a single market, not to mention a political area without internal frontiers and an evolving economic and monetary union. Third, the exercise by the Community or European Union of its enlarged powers across practically the whole spectrum of political and economic life makes it urgent to ensure a more effective protection of the individual through the rule of law. The following section illustrates some of the areas in which reforms are essential if this goal is to be achieved.

STATE COMPLIANCE WITH COMMUNITY LAW

If the benefits of the single market are to be realised by individuals and companies, it is important that relevant rules of Community law are effectively and correctly applied at national level. Although EC law is an integral part of national law, and can be enforced as such, the enforcement of Community law has traditionally been the responsibility of the Commission, acting as the 'guardian of the Treaties'. Article 169 provides that if a member state has failed to fulfil an obligation under the Treaty, the Commission shall deliver a reasoned opinion on the matter after giving the state concerned the opportunity to submit its observations. If the state does not comply with the opinion within the period laid down by the Commission, the Commission may bring the matter before the Court of Justice. Many thousands of cases have been initiated by the Commission under this article. A small proportion has been referred to the Court, leading to the development of case law on all the major principles of EC law laid down in the Treaties. The vast majority of infringement procedures started under Article 169 are settled by negotiation between the Commission and the member state concerned.

There is no doubt that the Commission's role in securing respect for Community law by member states under Article 169 has been (and still is) of critical importance in securing respect for the rule of law in the Community. None the less, although it is almost always individuals or companies who suffer the direct consequences of a member state's failure to respect Community law, these individuals or companies have very little influence (at least formally) in the conduct of infringement proceedings under Article 169. It is true that individuals and companies may have a more direct role in the enforcement of Community law by raising actions in national courts, which may obtain guidance on the interpretation of relevant rules of EC law from the Court of Justice under Article 177. In recent years, faced with a burgeoning number of complaints under Article 169, the Commission has advocated a policy of decentralisation of law enforcement within the Community, with a greater role for national courts and tribunals. Although there has been a sharp rise in the number of cases involving Community law coming before national courts and tribunals, it will take time for economic operators, legal advisors and judges throughout the EC to play their full role in securing the application of Community law. Meanwhile, particularly as a result of the publicity generated in the 1992 campaign, it is inevitable that the Commission will have to continue to act as 'guardian of the Treaties', even if this is done on a more selective basis.

Despite the efforts made by the Commission to secure more openness and transparency in its procedures, the existence of Community law and the machinery involved in its enforcement under Article 169 remain a mystery to most individuals and enterprises in the Community. Compared with the wealth of documentation on the single market or Community financing, explanatory materials on the way to secure the enforcement of EC law are few. As in many fields, the Commission has wide discretion in exercising its role as law-enforcement agency. Despite having produced a standard form for complaints from the private sector, little attempt has been made by the Commission to draw the attention of industry and commerce to its existence. Complaints on the failure of member states to respect EC law, although growing in number, reach the Commission unsystematically. In addition, the Commission may decide, in its discretion, whether to 'self-initiate' cases which come to its attention in other ways than by private sector complaint. Of increasing and welcome significance are complaints from MEPs. Each Commission service has responsibility for the prosecution of infringements in its particular field. As might be expected, the bulk of cases arise in the internal market (DG XV) and agriculture (DG VI). The environment, social affairs, customs and taxation have also become more important in recent years. None the less, the attitude of individual services and Commissioners to the rigour with which infringements should be treated varies considerably. Despite public statements in 1993 by the Commissioner for the internal market, Vanni D'Archirafi, on the need for stricter enforcement of Community law, the private sector requires the same kind of publicity now on the available means of securing redress at national and Community level for alleged breaches of EC law as was used in the 1992 programme itself.

Although most Article 169 cases are started by complaint by the private sector, complainants have no formal role in the conduct of proceedings. Thus, 'due process' is by no means assured. Once the Commission has received a complaint from the private sector, disclosing a *prima facie* breach of Community law, the case is registered by the General Secretariat and given a case number. The dossier is then examined by the relevant Commission Directorate General, in consultation with the legal service. Twice a year (or on an *ad hoc* basis in the case of urgent matters) suspected infringements are reviewed by regular meetings by *Chefs de Cabinet*, and, to the extent that agreement is not reached at this level, by the Commission itself. Decisions are then taken either to close the case, to postpone action pending further study or to decide that a formal 'letter before action' should be sent to the member state concerned. Once the 'Article 169 letter' has been sent, member states are given a period (usually two months) to reply. Extensions of time are frequently sought and granted almost automatically. If cases are not settled by negotiation or by the member state accepting the validity of the Commission's contentions, the Commission, using the same procedure as that described above for the sending of 'Article 169 letters', may decide to send a reasoned opinion to the member state concerned. The reasoned opinion is a formal statement of the Commission's legal position and, in theory, cannot be subject to negotiation with member states. Failure by member states to take the necessary action to conform to a reasoned opinion within two months may (but not must) be followed by the Commission referring the case to the Court of Justice.

Throughout this procedure, the private sector complainant plays virtually no part. Having once complained to the Commission, the complainant has no right to see the correspondence between the member state and the Commission and has no right to intervene at any stage of the proceedings, even at the level of the Court of Justice. Should the Commission, for political or economic reasons, decide not to pursue a complaint under Article 169 (even one which is well founded), the complainant has no possibility of judicial review of such a decision. Article 175 in theory offers a possibility of 'an action for inaction': in other words, litigation on the question of an alleged failure to act by the Council, Commission or Parliament. Although such actions are potentially open to individuals and companies as well as to member states and the EC institutions, such possibilities have been greatly circumscribed by the Court and never admitted in the case of Article 169 procedures.

Whether this situation is satisfactory from a constitutional point of view depends partly on one's view of the adequacy of the availability of a judicial review at member state level. In theory, it could be argued that the direct effect of many rules of Community law in national law offers a complete set of remedies to private parties. This interpretation has been reinforced by the recent rulings of the Court of Justice in the *Francovich* and *Bonafaci* cases whereby member states may in certain circumstances be liable to pay damages to individuals and companies who have suffered as a result of the failure of the member governments to implement EC directives.[35] But this is only partially true. The fact remains that, in many of its activities, the Commission is practically immune from judicial review.

The reasons why the European Community has suffered the most serious crisis of confidence in its existence over the last two or three years are complex. No doubt the perceived remoteness of the Community and its institutions from the private sector is an important contributing factor. Equally, the failure of the EC yet to deliver the vaunted benefits of the single market also diminishes the importance of the Community in public eyes. At the same time, however, the failure of the Community legal order (and its component national parts) to secure the full respect of the institutions and member states, particularly in highly visible sectors such as the free movement of goods and of persons, is equally damaging to the reputation of the EC. In this respect, the notion of the rule of law in the Community is closely identified with the way in which the Commission exercises its role as 'guardian of the Treaties'.

There are some encouraging signs that the Commission recognises the urgent need to improve law enforcement within the Community for the benefit of the private sector. As far as the effective transposition of directives is concerned, the Commission recognises that 'it is clear that people are looking to the Commission to ensure not only that this job is done, but that it is done properly'.[36] One major problem in this as in other matters concerning the administration of the single market is the fact that the Commission's resources are inadequate to the size of the task. That the Commission is apparently ready to take 'appropriate action' under Article 169 (including recourse to the provisions of Article 171 regarding the imposition of sanctions) is of small comfort to businessmen whose sales prospects may disappear in the two or three years which procedures under this Article normally take.

As regards enforcement of Community law when member states act in breach of the Treaty, the Commission recognises that enforcement must, in practice, be carried out on the basis of close cooperation and mutual assistance between the member states' authorities themselves and between them and the Commission. The Commission acknowledges that 'a major effort is needed to ensure that this happens across the board in all areas of the Internal Market', and further notes that 'in a Single Market, individuals and firms need to know that there are adequate means of redress available if they need them'. The Commission hopes that the provisions in the Maastricht Treaty on judicial cooperation will provide a valuable framework for it and member governments to act effectively together.

One major defect in the present Community legal order, which has an adverse impact on the private sector, is the mandatory use of directives as an instrument for EC legislation to implement the Treaty principles underpinning the single market. In this respect there is an antithesis between, on the one hand, the clarity and uniformity of Community law for the benefit of economic operators and, on the other, the political attitude adopted (at least publicly) by the institutions and member states regarding subsidiarity and the greater devolution of law-making authority in the Community.

The possibility of Treaty amendments to replace directives by regulations (which are, under Article 189, of general application, binding in their entirety and directly applicable in all member states) has always appeared politically unacceptable to the member states. There is little to suggest that this situation will change in time for the IGC in 1996. None the less, in present circumstances, the Commission is faced with a mountain of national implementing legislation which has to be checked for conformity with EC directives and then checked again to ensure that it is being correctly applied in practice. In order to deal with this herculean task, the Commission intends to use a combination of methods, including the comprehensive monitoring of texts by Commission staff; use of external consultants to overcome the problem of limited staff resources; multilateral and bilateral meetings with member states' officials; direct contact with economic operators; and receipt of complaints from individuals and businesses as a means of identifying problem areas.

REDRESS FOR INFRINGEMENTS OF COMMUNITY LAW

Securing rapid, inexpensive and efficient judicial redress for breaches of law is a problem endemic in modern industrialised societies. The European Union is not unique in its failure to provide citizens with a smoothly functioning system for the enforcement of legal rights. On the other hand, the novelty and unique nature of the Community legal order (as well as that established by the EEA Agreement) mean that it is particularly important for Community law to be seen to work in practice.

In fact, it is no exaggeration to say that (in contrast to the situation within national political and legal systems) the inefficiency combined with 'structural' defects in the Community legal order, particularly as regards the protection of individual and corporate interests, strikes at the very heart of the Union as a political and economic entity.

Despite the special powers of the Commission as 'guardian of the Treaties', the particular nature of Community law implies that, as a rule, the bulk of law enforcement must take place at the national level. The Commission recognises that the coming into operation of the internal market will inevitably result in an increase in the number of cases in which residents of one member state will need to claim their rights in another. Conversely, if businessmen entertain doubts about the feasibility of obtaining judicial redress in other member states, there is a significant obstacle to cross-border transactions and, therefore, to the realisation of the economic goals of the single market. Much remains to be done, mainly by the member states but also by the Commission, to remove business scepticism about the possibility of judicial redress in the single market. A key problem is to improve knowledge of EC law, on the part of economic operators and their advisers, and also of national judges.[37]

The third 'pillar' of the Treaty on European Union provides a new basis for the Commission to promote cooperation in the judicial field between itself and member states. The Court of Justice might also be involved in this cooperation, particularly as regards the promotion of a wider knowledge of the Court's case law. In this respect, the Commission has developed an action programme for the years 1994–96, comprising the wider dissemination of EC law in legal circles; encouraging recourse to the national courts; reinforcing the mutual recognition of judgements; and finding new means to resolve conflicts of law in the single market, including possible strengthening of the Rome Convention on contractual obligations.

The Commission's determination to secure the rule of law in the single market is reinforced by its work to improve the access of consumers to justice and the settlement of consumer disputes in the single market. A new Green Paper asserts the link between the rule of law in the Community context, the credibility of the EC legal order in the eyes of the citizen and economic operators, and the achievement of economic growth.[38] 'Access to justice', says the Commission, 'is at once a human right and a prerequisite for an effective legal order.' Judicial redress against the bad management of the single market matters most to the consumer who is affected directly by the free movement of goods, services and capital. The Commission recognises that judicial frontiers still endure to threaten the effective functioning of the single market and the confidence of economic operators, not least because of the multiplicity and variety of national procedures available for dispute settlement. Possible solutions to the problem include the 'free movement' of actions for an injunction; the liberalisation of legal aid; simplification of the settlement of cross-border disputes; and self-regulation of the dialogue between consumers and professionals.

The Commission, clearly, is now responding to the question of fair play in the management of the single market. There are, however, other areas where, despite the existence of a complete Community legal order, administrative discretion, particularly of the Commission, appears to be excessive and the availability of judicial review inadequate. The administration of the common commercial, or trade, policy illustrates this.

TRADE POLICY

Under Article 113 of the Treaty the Community enjoys exclusive competence in commercial policy matters. Apart from the negotiation and management of international agreements, the Commission is responsible for measures of commercial defence in the form of safeguard action and the imposition of anti-dumping and countervailing duties. Definitive action against imports is always taken by the Council, on a proposal from the Commission. The Commission itself may take time-limited provisional action. In both cases, the decisive preparatory work is conducted by the Commission's services.

Community law provides a number of procedural safeguards for industries affected by commercial defence measures, including producers (both in the EC and in the exporting country) and traders involved in exporting and importing. Although, in theory, consumer interests should also be taken into account by the Community in reaching its decisions in the field of trade policy, in practice the interests of European producers have always greatly outweighed those of the European consumer. There is little evidence, particularly in a time of deep recession and unemployment, that this trend is changing. The most important procedural safeguards guaranteed by Community law are the publication in the Official Journal of a notice announcing the opening of a procedure, the right of interested parties to make their views known to the Commission, the right to oral hearings, the right to comment on the Commission's 'disclosure' of its proposed findings and the possibility of judicial review by the Court of a final decision by the Commission or Council. Although the sharp increase in the volume of commercial defence actions launched by the Commission between 1980 and 1990 has been accompanied by an increasing number of references to the Court, in practice the Commission retains a very wide (and substantially uncontrolled) discretion in its appreciation of the economic arguments for and against the adoption of measures of protection against imports.

In the conduct of anti-dumping or safeguard actions, the Commission naturally relies heavily on information supplied by the European complainant industry. In practice, the Commission works closely with representatives of European industry to formulate complaints. Many industries, for example chemicals, electronics and automobiles, are well organised in Brussels for the presentation of complaints to the Commission on trade matters. Although the impact of the 1992 programme has been to provide new areas of activity for these trade associations, the effect of the prolonged recession and lack of competitiveness on the part of many sectors of European industry has meant that lobbying the Commission for protection remains an important activity. It is true that the Commission will not decide on the formal opening of an investigation until it is satisfied that it has 'sufficient evidence' that, for example, non-EC products are being dumped and are causing injury to European producers. On the other hand, the Commission's initial determination of dumping and injury is made without the non-EC industry and traders concerned having the right to present their views. News that a complaint on dumping, or a request for safeguard action, has been submitted to the Commission circulates by rumour only. This in itself causes uncertainty and has an adverse effect on trade.

Once a case has been opened, the non-EC industry, together with exporters and importers, is put in the position of having to rebut a presumption of unfair trade. Exporting companies and their representatives have, in the past, almost always made submissions on fact and law to the Commission in the course of its enquiry. The Commission also holds hearings at which the opposing views of European industry and non-EC producers may be heard. None the less, the calculation of dumping margins and the assessment of injury to European producers involve calculations (and, more importantly, methodology) which are not revealed in detail at any stage of the proceedings. These findings, which are often made at relatively junior level in the Commission, are subject neither to political review by the Commission itself nor to judicial review by the Court. Thus, although the Court has been willing to admonish the Commission for failing to respect minimum procedural safeguards in dumping cases, it has been unwilling to review the substance of the Commission's economic findings. Even in the Commission itself, it is doubtful whether, throughout the history of dumping cases, the 'college' of Commissioners has ever had to discuss or to review the economic merits of a particular dumping action. The assumption is that these are 'technical matters' which are best dealt with at the level of the services.

Most of those involved in trade in the Community, particularly in sensitive sectors, are now resigned to the fact that trade policy decisions are based on rules which are applied with considerable administrative discretion and which, by their nature, are difficult to subject to judicial review. In many cases, particularly those involving exports from Japan and from non-market economies, non-EC producers and their traders have reduced their efforts to cooperate with the Commission, having realised that the time and cost involved is disproportionate to the results achieved.

SAFEGUARD MEASURES

In cases involving the imposition of quantitative limits on imports through safeguard action, the rights of non-EC producers and traders are even more limited than in the case of 'unfair' trade, such as anti-dumping or anti-subsidy actions. Unlike the situation in the United States, safeguard actions are conducted almost exclusively between representatives of the Community and the foreign government concerned. There is no Community Regulation, like that in dumping, setting out procedural safeguards for the private sector interests involved. In practice, the Commission does consult the European industry concerned, particularly in order to compile relevant information on actual or threatened material injury. European producers who allege injury from foreign imports will normally have submitted a complaint and will lobby the Commission and Council throughout the procedure to ensure that action is taken. On the other hand, consumers, non-EC producers and traders have little formal possibility to make their views known. In addition, given the fact that most safeguard actions are general in scope (in other words, not directed against particular companies), the possibility of judicial review under Article 173 is even more limited in the cases of anti-dumping actions, where individual companies are frequently named and consequently can generally claim a right of judicial review under Article 173 on the basis of 'direct and individual concern'.

This situation is even more serious in the cases of 'grey zone' measures taken by the Community on 'sensitive' products imported from Japan. Since, by definition, 'grey zone' measures have no legal basis, economic operators concerned have no certainty that their rights and interests will be protected by Community law. The Community's measures on imports of cars and electronic products from Japan have been negotiated in secret; the results are leaked but not published; they are imposed (by agreement between the EC and the foreign country concerned) without any basis in Community law; notification to the Gatt and OECD is perfunctory if it occurs at all; and, finally, such measures are incapable of judicial review by the Court of Justice, and they represent perhaps the high watermark of administrative discretion in Community trade policy.

There are legal and practical limits to the extent to which this situation can be changed under the present Community institutional and legal system. First, in a recession with high unemployment and severe import competition, it is unlikely that the political will can be mustered to secure radical change. Second, it is probably unrealistic to expect the Court of Justice to review detailed findings of economic fact by the Commission. Perhaps the Court of First Instance might improve this situation when it is endowed with the jurisdiction to hear anti-dumping cases. Third, the right of recourse by individual companies to the Court is tightly circumscribed, notably under Article 173.

One solution would be to establish in Europe a specialised tribunal for the review of trade policy action by the EC. This would at least ensure a more effective separation of powers than currently exists. At present, the Commission is (or at least appears to be) simultaneously prosecutor, judge and enforcement agency. The Commission takes the lead in launching anti-dumping cases through its initial assessment of the evidence and publication of the notice of initiation in the Official Journal. The Commission assesses the evidence and frequently imposes a provisional duty. It also has to be remembered that the Commission in itself is the principal legislator of EC dumping law (particularly since its proposals are altered very little in the Council) and claims a privileged position in the interpretation and application of anti-dumping law.

As far as democratic control of decision-making in trade policy (as opposed to due process) is concerned, even under the Maastricht Treaty, the Parliament is almost wholly excluded, in a formal sense at least, from the formulation, administration and execution of EC decisions on trade. In practice, the Council frequently approves Commission proposals without radical changes. This situation is unlikely to change without a radical new initiative, such as the establishment of an independent trade commission. Such a body could, if it were independent of the Commission, ensure a more even-handed and objective review of each step of an anti-dumping or safeguard procedure, even if its powers were limited to making recommendations to the Commission and Council based on the evidence it had heard.

COMPETITION AND STATE AIDS

Apart from the decisions in the field of trade policy, there is no field of Community activity which impinges so directly upon private sector interests as that of competition policy, including state aids. Community law endows the Commission with the powers of legislator, watchdog, investigator, judge and enforcement authority. Although the Court of Justice (and, latterly, the Court of First Instance) have imposed disciplines on the Commission in its conduct of competition proceedings, the Commission none the less continues to enjoy a measure of administrative discretion unparalleled in most national jurisdictions.

Some commentators have criticised the allegedly insufficient judicial control of EC competition law enforcement.[39] Although it may well be that in competition, as in anti-dumping, cases the Court has been unwilling to review the economic judgements of the Commission, the most obvious fault in the present system lies in the cumulation (or lack of separation) of powers in one administrative body.

As far as competition policy is concerned, it is true that Regulation 17 provides a basis for quasi-judicial hearings by the Commission in antitrust cases. This at least ensures that all interested parties have a right not only to submit their views in writing, but to be heard by the Commission before a decision is made. None the less, the administrative discretion enjoyed by the Commission at all stages of proceedings, whether under Article 85 (prohibition of concerted practices in restraint of trade), Article 86 (abuse of a dominant position in the market), or the Merger Regulation, is extensive.[40] On the positive side, it can be argued with considerable justification that if the Commission had not enjoyed such wide administrative discretion in the last forty years, then Community law would never have developed to the extent that it has. It is certainly true that, by an imaginative use of its powers, particularly under Article 169 and the Treaty provisions on competitive and state aids policy, the Commission has played a critical role in the development of EC law and policy.

On the other hand, many enterprises which have been directly affected by the Commission's enforcement of competition law may well feel that its decision-making powers in this field are untransparent and unpredictable. Above all, enterprises may feel that the extent to which their views are taken into account varies considerably from case to case, depending on the individuals or departments involved. Industries may also consider that the Commission's objectivity in competition matters is affected by the fact that it plays, simultaneously, the role of prosecutor, judge and enforcement agency. The fact that the same Commission which decides competition policy cases also (perhaps even at the same session) has to formulate macroeconomic, monetary, industrial, environmental or social policies, injects an unavoidable political note into a quasi-judicial function. The fact that competition policy decisions (including the politically sensitive question of state aids) may be tempered by considerations of economic or industrial policy may well be appropriate. But in considering whether the EC's institutions take their decisions according to the rule of law, this is not the issue. The fundamental question is whether, in all cases where the Commission takes decisions by exercising its administrative discretion with an effect on the private sector, justice is seen to be done. Despite the political probity, technical expertise and good faith of the Commission and its staff, this is not the case today.

It is important to underline, in reaching this conclusion, that such a situation was probably unavoidable. The evolution of the Community's legal order and the growing role and competence of its institutions have had steadily increasing significance for companies and individuals. However, the intensification of the Community's economic role (particularly through the 1992 programme and its related policies), in addition to the rapid development of the Community's political personality in the Maastricht Treaty, has highlighted the comparative immaturity of the Community's legal order in comparison with its political and economic pretensions. As far as competition policy is concerned (though, unfortunately, not yet for trade policy questions) the creation of the Court of First Instance has been a step in the direction of ensuring more detailed scrutiny of the economic (as opposed to the procedural) grounds upon which Commission competition decisions are based. It may be that, unless or until independent tribunals are created with quasi-judicial decision-making powers in the field of trade and competition policy, the Court of First Instance will be the last bastion of protection for the individual or company against the abuse of administrative discretion by the Commission.

The Commission's discretion in competition policy is exercised at different stages of the procedure. At the very earliest stage, the Commission may select the cases it wishes to deal with; subsequently it may decide whether to accept an informal settlement; and finally it decides on remedies or sanctions to be applied in cases where there is no 'amicable settlement'.

As regards the selection of cases (whether in the field of infringements, competition or trade policy), the Commission's role is not only to decide which cases are well founded in law, but which cases are to be pursued as a matter of political preference. The fact that the Commission's services in the field of trade, competition and infringements policy (particularly as regards internal market matters) are overburdened makes selectivity inevitable. The Commission admits this situation, which is closely related to, though not entirely the cause of, its policy on the decentralisation of law enforcement. Whilst decentralisation may work well in the field of infringements policy (as discussed above), it is less obvious that cases of unfair trade or competition where the 'inter-state' or Community dimension of trade is present can be so easily dealt with by national courts and tribunals.

Refusal by the Commission to open formal proceedings, particularly in anti-trust, state aids or trade policy matters, is very difficult to contest under EC law. Article 175 allows any natural or legal person to complain to the Court of Justice that an EC institution has 'failed to address to that person any action other than a recommendation or an opinion'. An action by an enterprise or individual is only admissible if the institution concerned has first been called upon to act and, within two months, has failed to 'define its position'. In addition, the plaintiff has to demonstrate that it has been directly and individually concerned by the institution's failure to address an act to it. In practice, taking action under Article 175 may have more political than legal effects. A 'call to act' which is well prepared in fact and law, accompanied by a threat of Court proceedings, produces a response from the institution concerned. In most cases, however, particularly where enterprises are not well versed in EC law, the refusal of the Commission to take action in a particular case is effectively without judicial remedy.

The high-water mark of the Commission's administrative discretion lies in the informal settlement of cases. In the case of trade policy, informal settlement may take the form of acceptance of an 'undertaking' by the exporting company. In competition policy, informal settlement frequently consists in the Commission sending 'comfort' letters to parties to an investigation under Article 85 or the simple closure of a case, without a formal decision. Informal settlement, as a result of negotiation with member states, is also the way in which the vast bulk of Commission investigations with member states under the infringement procedure of Article 169 is settled.

There is nothing inherently wrong with the principle of informal settlement. But whatever the structure of law enforcement in the Community, those affected by decisions should know the reasons on which they are based. The accelerated enforcement of EC law which is possible through the Commission's periodic package 'negotiations' with individual member states is to be welcomed. On the other hand, in the case of unfair trade and competition matters there are frequently two or more parties with conflicting interests at stake in any given procedure. It is in these cases that greater transparency is indispensable.[41]

Clearly, the Commission has to strike a balance between maintaining business confidentiality, administrative efficiency and reasonable transparency. The Court's position on this matter, as set out in one important case, is that the 'legitimate interests of the complainants are fully protected when they are informed of the outcome of the negotiations in the light of which the Commission wishes to close the proceedings'.[42]

While that is satisfactory as an abstract statement of principle, it is important to remember that the volume of cases settled by administrative discretion compared with those which proceed to a final reasoned decision is overwhelming. In these circumstances, a more transparent system, based perhaps on American practice in anti-trust procedures, is surely overdue. Practice over the last three years under the relatively new Mergers Regulation, under which virtually the totality of cases considered by the Commission has been approved (with minimal published reasoning), tends to confirm this view. It is easy to guess why, in a period of acute recession, the Commission has been 'user-friendly' towards companies giving notice of proposed mergers under the Regulation. On the other hand, the relative absence of information setting out the legal and economic criteria on which decisions have been based makes it difficult for companies and their advisers to plan their business strategies with certainty.

One of the most painful examples for companies of the Commission's discretion is in the imposition of fines in competition cases. The only published guideline for fines is that provided by Regulation 17, which states that fines in excess of one million units of account may not exceed '10% of the turnover in the preceding business year of each of the undertakings participating in the infringement'. Although subject to judicial review like any other Commission decision, the imposition of fines is based on an arcane and undisclosed (even to other Commission services) methodology within DG IV. The fact that decisions on fines, as on many other important economic aspects of decisions in trade and competition policy, are taken at a relatively low level in the administration and barely (if at all) reviewed at the political level of cabinets in the Commission itself, only underlines the need for an independent decision-making body (or bodies) in trade and competition matters, in which evidence can be heard and assessed in a transparently fair and even-handed manner.

When Commission decisions are taken, enterprises which are directly and individually concerned can apply for judicial review under Article 173. The Court of Justice has frequently annulled Commission decisions, particularly in competition cases, but also on rarer occasions in the field of trade policy, especially on grounds of procedural irregularity or inadequate reasoning. None the less, the Court is, in general terms, reluctant to 'second-guess' the Commission in matters of economic policy.[43] Although in criminal and civil matters falling under national law, it may be possible to distinguish between issues of fact, on which a right of appeal seldom exists, and issues of law, which commonly are subject to appeal, the economic law of the EC does not admit such a clear distinction. Thus, whilst it is understandable that the Court as a matter of judicial policy would not wish systematically to put in question the economic evaluations made by the Commission in good faith and on the basis of explicit reasoning, none the less a more rigorous analysis by an independent review tribunal is indispensable. It is premature to say whether the Court of First Instance will fulfil this function or not: certainly, in two of its early cases it has taken a robust line in overturning Commission decisions.[44]

The situation in state aids investigations is even less favourable for companies than is the case with competition matters. Although, according to Article 93, all state aids are to be notified to the Commission for review under EC law before being granted, the practice of member states under this Article is patchy and inconsistent, especially where 'general' aid schemes are concerned. Individual state aids investigations are frequently launched on the basis of a complaint from the private sector. After publication of the notice of opening of the investigation in the Official Journal, the Commission's investigations are conducted more or less exclusively with the member state concerned. Although enterprises affected by the subsidy in question have a right to make their views known to the Commission, there is no right to an oral hearing, as is the case in competition matters. Given the extent to which competition is distorted by state intervention in the economy in favour of one or other company or product, there is no apparent justification for treating state aids enquiries any differently from other competition matters.

As far as judicial review by the Court of Justice of state aids decisions is concerned, this is available to the private sector on the same terms and conditions as with competition or dumping decisions. Provided a firm can establish that it was directly and individually concerned by the Commission decision approving or rejecting the aid in question, it may ask the Court to annul the Commission decision. Although criticisms may no doubt be made of Court practice in reviewing Commission state aids decisions, the real problem lies elsewhere. Companies throughout the EC are generally insufficiently aware of their rights of redress under Community law, whether before the Commission or before national courts and tribunals. The vast majority of firms in the Community probably do not know that, under EC law (as applied by the Court of Justice in the *French Salmon* case), damages can be obtained against a member government that has granted competition-distorting state aids without having notified these to the Commission for review.[45] Even if aids have been notified, however, or if the Commission investigates an alleged aid on the basis of a complaint, it is difficult or sometimes impossible (depending on the cooperative spirit of the case-workers in question) for an enterprise to participate in and thereby protect its rights and interests under present EC procedures.

IMPACT OF THE EUROPEAN ECONOMIC AREA AND ASSOCIATION AGREEMENTS

On 1 January 1994, the EEA Agreement entered into force for the Community, Austria, Finland, Iceland, Norway and Sweden. The effect of the Agreement is to transpose entire areas of EC law (known as the *acquis communautaire*) to the Efta countries. In essence, EEA law consists of EC rules on the free provision of services and the free movement of goods, capital and persons, as well as EC rules on certain 'flanking' policies such as environmental protection and social policy.

The existence of a parallel, but supposedly identical, legal order merely adds another layer of procedural difficulty as far as the protection of individual rights is concerned. All the difficulties described above which are currently inherent in the EC legal order are transferred to, and exacerbated in, the legal order of the EEA. It may, of course, be that early accession to the Community by at least some of the Efta states will rapidly render the EEA redundant. Meanwhile, however, businessmen will have to become familiar with the Efta Surveillance Authority, the Efta courts and the political institutions linking the EC to the Efta states. The Surveillance Authority and Efta Court are of primary concern to businessmen doing business in and between Efta states. On the other hand, where trade with the Community is concerned, there may well be difficulties in deciding whether Efta or EC institutions are competent to handle a particular case. Although the Agreement provides mechanisms for allocation of jurisdiction, it could be argued that this only reinforces the extent to which administrative discretion governs decision-making (and reduces transparency for business) in the EEA.

The problems of protecting individual rights and freedoms under the EEA arise because of the direct applicability throughout the EEA of the Agreement's provisions, as well as those of secondary law and the case law of the Court of Justice and of First Instance and (as far as the Efta countries are concerned) of the Efta Court. The situation is different with countries in Central and Eastern Europe which have concluded Association Agreements with the Community (such as Hungary, Poland, Romania, Bulgaria and the Czech and Slovak Republics). Unlike the EEA Agreement, the Association Agreements are comprehensive in nature, covering political and economic cooperation, as well as all other areas of EC law and policy. Apart from the creation of political institutions to manage the Association Agreement, enforcement is left to the relevant authorities in the Community on the one side and the associated states on the other. None the less, to the extent that the Association Agreements are successful in promoting economic integration between the EC and the associated states, it is likely that the EC institutions, particularly the Commission, will acquire extended powers to enforce competition policy throughout those states. Although these issues may only arise in concrete form in years to come, it is important to note now that the geographical scope of EC law, policy and institutions extends potentially well beyond the frontiers of the present-day Community. If the EC legal order, therefore, does not develop institutions which are respected in the conduct of its internal affairs, the rule of law may be undermined in the emerging legal framework for wider European integration.

INADEQUATE PROTECTION OF INDIVIDUAL RIGHTS

It may well be that the member states and peoples of the European Union are not ready for a radical overhaul of their legal structure and institutions in 1996. Radical or 'constitutional' reforms may have to wait: it is worth remembering that the ECSC Treaty is due to expire in 2001. Likewise, the fact that security (including all aspects of nuclear) policy falls within the competence of the European Union may make it appropriate to review at the end of the decade whether the provisions of the Euratom Treaty might not be better integrated into a single constitutional document for the European Union. At this time, consideration should be given to some adjustment to the jurisdictional provisions of the Treaty, particularly as regards the protection of individual rights.

In a constitutional order where all subjects of the law have equal rights under the law, it seems inequitable and wrong in principle that certain entities, the institutions and member states, should have a privileged position as regards recourse to Community justice. The inequalities which exist between the institutions and national authorities on the one hand and the private sector on the other have already been clearly illustrated in the economic field. The gap is even wider in political matters. Although this is understandable given the comparative novelty of the Community's genuine political competence, it is potentially more serious and goes to the heart of the 'democratic deficit' from which the Union currently suffers.

The procedural difficulties confronting a national political party seeking to enforce provisions of Community law in the Court of Justice, for example, were illustrated in the case of *Liberal Democrats* v. *European Parliament*.[46] Although no final decision was rendered by the Court in that case, it is likely that it would have declared the action by the Liberal Democrats inadmissible on the grounds that a national political party had no 'direct and individual concern' in the European Parliament making a proposal for a uniform electoral procedure across the Community. Such a decision would have been based on the letter of Article 175 as previously applied in economic matters. But such an outcome would not have been inevitable. Since the Court of Justice is not formally bound by its previous decisions, it could perfectly well have held that, in a constitutional legal order, justice requires that political parties and even individuals enjoy the necessary procedural possiblities to secure the enforcement and application of 'constitutional' rules. It is significant that in the case in question neither the Commission nor the Council intervened before the Court. Thus, a finding of inadmissibility by the Court of Justice would have left Article 138(3) of the Treaty unenforceable by judicial means.

It is significant that Article B of the Treaty on European Union provides that one of the objectives of the Union is to 'strengthen the protection of the rights and interests of the nationals of its member states through the introduction of a citizenship of the Union'. In addition, Article F.2 of the Treaty provides that the Union shall respect fundamental human rights as laid down in the European Convention on Human Rights and according to the common constitutional traditions of the member states as general principles of Community law. A new Article 8 enshrines the concept of citizenship of the Union in Community law. Article 8.2 provides that: 'Citizens of the Union shall enjoy the rights conferred by this Treaty and shall be subject to the duties imposed thereby.'

Simply to state that citizens 'shall enjoy the rights conferred by this Treaty' when those rights effectively mean that, in terms of access to justice at Union level, individuals are second-class citizens, is not sufficient. The core of the problem is the set of articles which confer jurisdiction on the Court of Justice and which endorse the privileged position of member states and institutions. The key provisions are Articles 173, 175 and 177 of the Treaty.

In essence, although natural and legal persons are given express rights under Articles 173 and 175 to bring actions to annul acts of Community institutions or to force them to take action, in practice these provisions have been tightly circumscribed, notably by the Court's definition of the concept of 'direct and individual concern'. Defenders of the present system might well argue that, so long as effective remedies are available under national law (backed by the 'umbrella' of preliminary rulings by the Court under Article 177) enabling natural and legal persons to secure rights conferred by Community or Union law, then there is no legal vacuum. It is certainly true that comparatively recent decisions of the Court of Justice in cases such as *Factortame*, *Francovich* and *Bonafaci* and *French Salmon* underline a member state's obligations under EC law as applied in national courts.[47] Thus, the ruling in *Factortame* was to the effect that national courts have an obligation under Community law: a revolutionary concept in the United Kingdom given the historical background of Parliamentary sovereignty. The *Francovich* and *Bonafaci* cases held that individuals who suffered damage as a result of a failure by a member state properly to implement a directive were entitled to damages. Likewise, in *French Salmon*, the Court held that individuals who had suffered as a result of a state aid which had not been notified under Article 93.3 were equally entitled to damages at national level.

Despite these rulings, it is still the case that, for the most part, the actions of the institutions of the Union are subject to judicial review as a result of action by individuals only in a very limited sense. Any constitutional reform in this field would need to strike a balance between fostering and facilitating recourse to justice at national level (which is indispensable for the smooth functioning of the bulk of the economic law of the Union) and ensuring that natural and legal persons have full rights of action against the Union institutions where this is appropriate. The history of the EC since 1952 (and particularly since the inception of the 1993 programme nearly ten years ago) shows that it is difficult to predict areas of Community or Union activity which will impinge on individuals. Only a short time ago, as a result of the almost total absence of EC secondary legislation, areas such as equal pay, pensions, retirement provision, sports, broadcasting, fisheries, telecommunications and energy distribution might well have been thought to be relevant only to governments and institutions. The exponential increase in the regulatory and decision-making powers of the institutions in these fields means that this is no longer the case.

More seriously, as far as fundamental rights and freedoms of the individual are concerned (which go to the heart of the issue of whether or not the rule of law can be said genuinely to exist in the Union legal order), the increasing activities of the Union in the fields of justice and home affairs may well highlight the inadequacy of existing remedies available to individuals under Union law against the institutions. This is particularly so given the limited jurisdiction of the Court of Justice in matters falling under the 'third pillar' of the Maastricht Treaty. On the other hand, to the extent that issues such as asylum policy, immigration policy and actions in the field of criminal law are transferred to Community competence by virtue of Article K.9, the inadequacy of the current means of redress by individuals against Union institutions will be underlined.[48]

Although the limitations on legal protection for individuals which flow from the present structure of the Treaties are serious, the rule of law in Union affairs has political as well as legal connotations for the general public. The apparent or perceived remoteness of Union institutions from Union citizens is to a certain extent inevitable. However, although the comparatively limited powers of the European Union currently mean that issues of national and local government are of more immediate significance for the citizen, this may not always be the case. Much may depend on the extent to which the abolition of internal frontiers makes inevitable a closer union of public (especially criminal) and private law, as well as the extent to which external pressures or threats force the Union to develop more operational responsibilities in the field of defence and security.

In any event, given the comprehensive scope of the current Union Treaty and its probable consolidation in a future constitutional conference, it is vital for the underlying political support for the Union that genuine improvements be made in the openness and accountability of the institutions. The provisions in the Maastricht Treaty recognising the importance of political parties at European level as a factor for integration within the Union were a step in the right direction. Equally, the fact that any citizen of the Union or any natural or legal person in a member state now has the right to address petitions to the European Parliament on a matter which comes within the Community's field of activity and which affects him, her or it directly is constructive. The right of petition is supplemented by the appointment of an Ombudsman with powers to receive complaints from any citizen of the Union or any natural or legal person residing in a member state on instances of maladministration by the EC institutions or bodies. This provision partially fills the gap which existed until now where individuals or companies felt aggrieved by officials in any of the institutions (particularly the Commission) and yet were effectively denied redress before the Court of Justice.

More recently, measures taken by the Commission to improve public access to its documents represent belated recognition of the fact that if Community policies are to have public support, then the public must be properly informed of their political scope, technical detail and practical impact. The dramatic negative effects which flow from leaving this task to the media is illustrated by the activities of the tabloid press in the United Kingdom since accession in 1973. It remains to be seen whether the new Commission policy works in practice. Early signs are not encouraging. There is a marked tendency for EC institutions (particularly the Commission and the Council) to accord privileged access to information to those considered to be 'insiders' (essentially politicians or officials from other institutions or the member states), and to regard with suspicion enquiries, expressions of interest and simple requests for information from 'outsiders'. If this is a problem for non-governmental experts concerned with EC affairs in Brussels, how much more so is the problem felt by concerned citizens elsewhere in the Union? Until citizens in the regions feel that they are relevant to the political processes of the Union, it cannot be argued that the rule of law is respected in the fullest sense.

In conclusion, ensuring respect for the rule of law in the Union legal order is as much a question of political practice as of legal or constitutional theory. The problem goes beyond the necessary reforms of the jurisdiction of the Court of Justice and Court of First Instance. Much depends on improvements to the administration of justice at national, as well as Community, level. As far as the regulatory and decision-making powers of the institutions are concerned, particularly in fields such as law enforcement, trade and competition policy, urgent consideration must be given to the need to separate the legislative, quasi-judicial and enforcement functions which are currently accumulated in the

Commission. At political level, it is an illusion to believe that transparency, accountability and respect for the rule of law in the administration of the Union can be achieved only by reforms, whether political or legal, at the centre. For this reason, in future, subsidiarity must be practised (as well as preached) not only in the regulatory field, but in the management and administration of the Union. This implies a far greater level of accountability, especially for the Commission, at national and regional level. The beginnings of a solution in this direction lie in the greater association of national parliaments, not only to the work of the European Parliament but to that of Union institutions. The newly created Committee of the Regions may also act in such a way as to surprise sceptics and to strengthen the links which exist between the centre and more peripheral regions of the Union.

The next Intergovernmental Conference, therefore, has a tough agenda if the new European Union is to become a haven of justice and fair play. The question of the separation of powers with respect to the Commission and the possibility of establishing tribunals in the fields of trade, state aids and competition policy should be addressed. European law in general has to become better explained, understood and enforced. In particular, the rule of law in the European Union has to become less remote for all its citizens.

CONCLUSION

15

BUILDING THE UNION: POLICY, REFORM, CONSTITUTION

John Pinder

The Maastricht Treaty is the most recent of a series of steps that have been taken to create a Union among European states and thus to strengthen their economies and their security. Security was the prime motive for the first step: the integration of heavy industries under the institutions established by the European Coal and Steel Community in order to ensure that France, Germany and their neighbours would never go to war with each other again. The desire to strengthen the European economy was more prominent among the motives for the second great step: the foundation of the European Economic Community, which created the common market, provided the collective power to negotiate on trade as an equal with the USA and consolidated the peaceful relations among the member states. The ensuing prosperity and security confirmed that the Community was a valid framework for dealing with the growing interdependence among them. Further steps were accordingly taken, including the direct elections, the European Monetary System, successive enlargements and the Single European Act. Thus the Community acquired a wide range of powers in the fields of the economy and environment in particular, exercised by institutions based on the rule of law, embodied in the Court of Justice, and with elements of government and democratic control through the Commission, the Council and the European Parliament. This system of institutions, with such significant responsibilities for their common affairs, contributed both to enhance the well-being of the peoples of these states and to banish the fear of war between them.

The Maastricht Treaty takes this process further by adding currency to the fields for which the Community is to have responsibility and strengthening the provision for security cooperation in what is now, incorporating the Community, called the European Union. Democratic control of the Community is improved through a somewhat stronger role for the European Parliament; and at the same time a largely intergovernmental method is applied to the Common Foreign and

Security Policy and the Cooperation in the fields of Justice and Home Affairs. Some conclusions about the merits of these two ways of handling the collective use of power are drawn below.

This latest step in developing the Union has caused unease among many people. The Maastricht Treaty has been drafted in such a way as to be largely incomprehensible to those who do not already have a detailed knowledge of the Community and how it works. Interdependence and the need to deal with it can be disturbing phenomena for people whose view of politics has been formed within the context of the nation state. The nationals of old-established states such as Britain, Denmark and France are particularly liable to feel disturbed. Recession has undermined confidence in economic prospects and the war in former Yugoslavia, together with the resurgence of nationalism elsewhere in the continent, has exacerbated the unease. The Maastricht Treaty, though intended to strengthen the capacity to deal with such matters, has also been caught up in the malaise. Many have questioned whether it was a step in the right direction.

The weight of the evidence in this book is that the Treaty will help significantly to deal with the problems of interdependence; and a failure to deal with these problems would be disastrous for the people of our countries, because the forces underlying the growth of interdependence are among the most important that determine the quality of their lives. The European Community has been the most successful response to these forces and it is reasonable to suppose that the principles on which it has been based will continue to respond successfully to them. This concluding chapter endeavours, therefore, to draw from the body of the book ideas that can help towards making the best of the opportunities offered by the Maastricht Treaty and developing the Union further in order to deal better with the problems that confront it: the recession and the weaknesses in Europe's ability to compete; the rise of insecurity in Europe and beyond; and the citizens' worries about the Union's institutions.

EMU AND ECONOMIC REGENERATION

The programme to establish the Economic and Monetary Union is the last of the steps taken by the Community to create the single market and thus enable European business to work in a context favourable for scale, specialisation and competition. Starting with the customs union, the Community went on to create the single market, including the single market for capital and financial services. The latter in particular should make an outstanding contribution to economic efficiency in the Union because the efficient allocation of capital is fundamental for the whole economy. At the same time the free movement of capital in an integrated financial market allows instability of exchange rates whenever dealers come to suspect weakness in any currency. Stability can be guaranteed by the creation of a single currency.

This is a basic motive for the Emu project to establish the single currency and the European Central Bank. It is strongly supported by business leaders in the Association for the Monetary Union of Europe, because it will not only save transaction costs but, more importantly, enable them to plan their investments with confidence and thus make European business more dynamic and competitive. It is also strongly supported by a majority of the Union's governments, led by the French, in order to gain their share in the control of monetary policy which, in the integrated capital market, has been lost partly to currency speculators but, more importantly, to the German Bundesbank. Beyond that economic motive for regaining at least a share in monetary sovereignty is the political motive to anchor Germany as firmly as possible into the system of the Union, rather than risk the instability that could result if the united and enlarged Germany has to face the problems of Central and Eastern Europe on its own. Germany's political leaders, aware of the stability that the Community has brought their country, fully concur with the aim of consolidating the Union as a safe anchorage.

German citizens are undoubtedly worried about the prospect of exchanging the Deutschmark for the Ecu. But Germany is committed to this by the Maastricht Treaty and the German government is well aware that failure to honour its obligations would place its relationship with both France and the European Union at risk. It is therefore likely that, with French and German leadership, the Emu will be established, though probably without the participation of all member states at first. When business becomes confident of this, an investment boom will follow, as it followed the launching of the customs union and the single market programmes. Beyond that, the better allocation of capital will continue to add a competitive edge to the European economy. But as Biehl reminds us, economic policy is concerned about stabilisation and distribution as well as allocation.[1] The single currency alone is not enough. It has to be accompanied by policies to provide a framework for a dynamic economy that can compete in the world markets and offer employment for all; and the economically weaker as well as the stronger regions and countries must be satisfied that they are gaining from the process of integration, or the political consent on which it has to be based will disappear.

The independent European Central Bank will be one guarantee of a stable currency. The control over member states' public deficits will also help to ensure that lax policies do not export inflation to more prudent partners and that interest rates are not driven up in the integrated capital market by excessive demands from individual states. But there will also be times, like the present, when expansionary policies are required. As Johnson points out, such policies will be more effective if undertaken in a coordinated way by member states.[2] But effective coordination among twelve – and in the future more – governments is hard to achieve. The Union's budget itself is too small to offer the potential for a significant expansionary impulse. A programme of investments in infrastructure, bringing together private with public capital as well as the Union and the member states, could however be a major source of expansion in the Union's economy.

As a recent study of the Federal Trust has shown, there is a need for massive investments in transport and communications linking the Europeans closely together, as well as for common action for a clean environment, if Europe is to offer a congenial context for business in the next century as well as to satisfy the needs of the people.[3] The funds to pay for these investments can come from the vast single capital market, boosted by the savings required to finance the pensions of an ageing population, and consolidated by the single currency. The Maastricht Treaty's trans-European networks and Cohesion Fund are building blocks for such an infrastructure programme. But the contribution of public money need be no more than is required to promote the networks as a European public good. Private investment, channelled through the financial institutions in the single capital market, would provide the lion's share. Since the programme would be designed to satisfy a long-term need and to regenerate the European economy, it would match the time-scale in which the pension and life assurance institutions must operate. It would also provide employment and sharpen European competitiveness over the medium term which is relevant to these. And its launching would give an early impulse to the recovery that Europe's economic and political circumstances so urgently require.

Such investments in infrastructure would be of particular benefit to the weaker economies of the Union, which happen also to be the peripheral ones that have most need of efficient transport and communication with the central areas. The Cohesion Fund is also intended to help them; and the Delors II budgetary package, which was a by-product of the Maastricht Treaty, considerably strengthened the Union's distribution policy that had been developed through the Structural Funds. But as Biehl observes, the Union's budget will remain regressive, taxing the poor to pay the rich, so long as its income comes from regressive taxes.[4] His proposal for a progressive surcharge on direct taxation, or a progressive key to the VAT contributions, could not only rectify this glaring injustice but also, if combined with a further shift in the balance of expenditure away from the agricultural policy, point towards a generally equitable system that could render unnecessary the special rebate to deal with Britain's particular problem. A system that is just for all would offer a more stable basis both for resolving the British problem and for the Union as a whole, by giving those against whom the budget is now biased more reason to support the Union over the longer term.

The need is, indeed, for common economic policies based on a long-term view of the single market, bolstering it with the single currency, a programme of investment in European infrastructure which is essential for a dynamic economy, and a budget sufficiently equitable to generate support throughout the Union. Maastricht should be seen as the starting point for developing policies based on that long view.

EUROPEANS AND THEIR SECURITY INTERESTS: THE CFSP

Behind the shield of American military power, the Community has given the peoples of Western Europe the framework in which they can no longer regard each other as threats to their security. But security is now threatened by instability to the East; and the United States is no longer ready to bear the burden of dealing with all of these new threats. German unification has, moreover, altered the balance among European states. The Germans' responsibilities with respect to European security will inevitably increase. The safe anchorage of Germany within the Union is, as we have seen, a prime objective of both French and German policy; and the Maastricht Treaty's provision for the CFSP is one of the results.

The institutions and instruments stipulated for the policy by the Treaty are, however, as Edwards and Nuttall observe, sufficient to encourage the coordination of the member states' policies but not to establish a common policy, although the latter is the Treaty's stated aim.[5] This may, as they put it, be enough unless one is frustrated by the results. But the results of foreign policy cooperation among the Twelve with respect to former Yugoslavia suggest that frustration may well ensue. Even if all the member states are more likely to support a policy wholeheartedly if they have all agreed to it, such a policy is only too likely to be diffuse and weak. It is reasonable to suppose that the Union will need stronger policies to meet the challenges that will confront it in Europe and the wider world. So it is worthwhile to ask whether there may be ways in which the Union can go beyond reliance on both unanimity and member states' policy instruments.

One answer comes from the experience of the Community. Acting with common policy instruments and under the procedure of proposal by the Commission and qualified majority in the Council, the Community responded to the start of transformation in Central and Eastern Europe in 1989–90 by launching its programme of trade liberalisation, aid and association agreements, which has been a considerable support to the new democracies. The Community's record in Gatt negotiations and in relations with developing countries is on the whole positive. The member states would not have served the interests of themselves and of third countries better through an intergovernmental system such as is provided for the CFSP. This external economic policy, which will be reinforced when the single currency is introduced, will be the greatest asset for the Union's foreign policy and it is essential that it should not be weakened by subordinating it to the weaker system of the CFSP. On the contrary, although defence is a field with different requirements and sensitivities, there are other fields of foreign policy that are not closely related to defence and that could appropriately be dealt with in ways similar to the external economic policy. Indeed relations with regions such as Latin America, South Asia, South East Asia and Japan, where economic rather than security interests predominate, might be dealt with in such ways. Proposals by some member states to allocate such fields to the scope of joint actions under the CFSP point in that direction.

The Commission could, as Edwards and Nuttall point out, come to play a decisive part if it makes skilful use of its right of initiative under the CFSP.[6] This would help to give coherence and continuity to the policy, despite the constant changing of presidency of the Council, and to relate it to the strong point of the external economic policy. In order to do this, the Commission needs to develop its forward planning function and the diplomatic capacity of its missions throughout the world, and to be allowed to play its due part in what Nicoll calls the 'bicephalic' representation, by the Commission and the Council presidency, of the Union in the world outside. Without such a role for the Commission, it is hard to envisage a really effective CFSP. Germany and the majority of member states wanted the CFSP to be within the scope of the Community institutions. The provision for majority voting on joint actions if there is unanimous agreement to employ it is one residue of that intention; and Declaration 27, whereby member states agree to 'avoid preventing' a unanimous decision 'where a qualified majority exists in favour of it', is another. The more the member states make use of those provisions, the more effective the CFSP will be. But although the Maastricht Treaty puts defence on the agenda of the Union, the Union's role in it is limited and member states are not likely to accept majority voting in that field in any near future. Stepping aside from decisions, as indicated by Declaration 27, is however a feasible way to prevent paralysis. The same procedure could help to make the WEU, to which the Union delegates a large part of its defence role, more effective. The Union may in any case decide, at the IGC set by the Maastricht Treaty for 1996, to bring WEU into its structure when the fifty-year term of the WEU Treaty comes to an end in 1998. While defence will, rightly, be the last of the major fields in which member states are interdependent to become subject to far-reaching integration within the Union, integration is a logical objective over the longer term. It would be dangerous to embark on it before member states are ready to accept the implications. They will require very full confidence in each other and in the Union institutions in order to do so. As is likely in the field of money, moreover, such integration may at first be limited to a core group within the Union. But while member states are not likely to be ready to set a timetable for any such process of integration, there may be proposals that at least a core group should agree upon the objective. The Eurocorps, with its French, German and Belgian participation, may be a harbinger of this.

CITIZENS AND THEIR RIGHTS

With immigration, asylum, crime and drugs, the Cooperation in Justice and Home Affairs covers some very sensitive subjects. Anderson and den Boer explain what is involved.[7] Freedom of movement across frontiers within the Union requires such cooperation. Among the most effective instruments would be efficient controls in which all member states have confidence along the whole extent of the Union's external frontier, implying a substantial degree of common organisation and supervision. But however effective the means chosen for cooperation in this field, the implications for citizens' rights will remain a source of preoccupation.

Article F.2 of the Maastricht Treaty requires the Union to respect its citizens' fundamental rights. But this is not within the jurisdiction of the Court of Justice, which is confined to the part of the Treaty that concerns the Community. The Court in fact already requires the Community institutions to respect fundamental rights, on the grounds that it has to ensure that the law of the Community is observed, and member states would not be able to observe it if it contravened the rights that are basic to their systems. But the member states, as Miller explains, refused to make this explicit in the Treaty.[8] The suspicions that such evasion may evoke among citizens could readily be dispelled by incorporating the European Convention on Human Rights into Community law as both the Commission and the Parliament proposed. Further reassurance could be offered by giving the Court the power to judge cases concerning the respect for rights by the Union's institutions too.

Article F.2 does not mention respect for fundamental rights on the part of the member states, although F.1 states that their 'systems of government are founded on the principles of democracy'. But the standing of the Union as a stronghold of rights and democracy is very important for its member states and citizens. The need to ensure that the member states all continue to respect fundamental rights will become the more pressing as new democracies accede to the Union. The IGC of 1996 offers an occasion on which this could be made explicit. The Union will, indeed, be taking a risk if it does not give the Court the power to judge whether rights are being respected by the member states as well as by the Union.

The 1996 IGC also offers the opportunity to provide for the progressive assimilation into the Community of the areas defined in Title VI on Cooperation in Justice and Home Affairs, thus making law-making more transparent and democratic as well as effective and opening up new prospects of judicial remedies for individual citizens.

DEMOCRATIC AND EFFECTIVE INSTITUTIONS

Many citizens would agree with Coombes that the EC's bureaucratic and corporatist method of integration has led to inefficiency, inequity and a democratic deficit.[9] The principles of good governance require, on the contrary, that political power such as the member states exercise collectively in the Union should be not only effective but also democratic, in the sense that it should be subject to the rule of law based on fundamental rights and controlled by representatives of the citizens as well as of the member states.

Central to the success of the Community has been its juridical system, operated mainly by the member states' courts but guided by the Court of Justice, which has earned a reputation for effective and impartial judgements. Following the logic of its duty to 'ensure . . . that the law is observed' (Article 164 EC), the Court has carried through a process of, as Bradley has expressed it, 'incremental constitutionalisation', establishing the rule of law without which the single market could be neither created nor sustained.[10] While the rule of law has been sufficiently respected to make it a reality, individuals lack, as Sutton points out, adequate means of redress if they suffer because their governments fail to respect it; and member states have tended to be dilatory in ensuring that it comes into effect.[11] This is unfair on the other member states, often placing their firms at a competitive disadvantage, and could, if not checked, lead to the disintegration of the Community. As a counter measure, Article 171 of the Maastricht Treaty provides that the Court may impose penalties on member states that fail to fulfil their obligations. While obligations relating to the CFSP and the Cooperation in Justice and Home Affairs will be in many cases less justiciable than those under the Community, failure of the member states to respect them could be equally damaging. It would be in the general interest that the Court should have the power to judge cases such as can be justiciable in these fields.

Although the Maastricht Treaty, as Corbett explains, strengthens somewhat the European Parliament's role, Community law is still mainly to be made by the Council acting behind closed doors.[12] The reason for this is understandable, when the legislative process is largely a negotiation among member states. But it remains an extraordinary departure from the normal principles of democratic government. Fitzmaurice notes that the Council has been encouraged to open 'at least part of its legislative proceedings'; and even if, as Nicoll suggests, the member states would wish to confine this to a reading out of the votes cast and of entries requested by governments in the minutes, that would be better than nothing.[13] But the fundamental reform required to make Community legislation a normal democratic process is to apply to all legislation the principle of co-decision between Council and European Parliament that has long since governed much of the Community budget and has been extended by the Maastricht Treaty to apply to some other legislation. The majority of member states, led by Germany, Italy and Belgium, wanted a wide provision for co-decision in the Treaty; and Pryce records that one of the British government's early concessions during the final negotiation of the Treaty in the European Council was to accept a limited strengthening of the Parliament's powers such as the Treaty does indeed provide.[14] Thus there is no objection of principle on the British government's part. Resistance to the extension of co-decision and thus of the significance of open debate in the Community's legislative process does not square with demands for more transparency in Community affairs. Nor does the government's insistence on eliminating the word co-decision from the Treaty, so that the procedure is officially just that of Article 189b, show much respect for the need of citizens to understand how the Community's laws are made. Co-decision is one of the subjects that Maastricht places on the agenda for the IGC in 1996. There is an opportunity to make the Community more democratic by extending the procedure to all Community legislation.

The Maastricht Treaty does provide a form of co-decision for the appointment of the Commission, in the approval by the European Parliament which is required before the Commission can take office. The British government favoured, in the Maastricht negotiations, powers for the Parliament to control expenditure and to enquire into alleged maladministration by the Commission or other institutions. It is evident that member states' parliaments cannot control the Commission, so that parliamentary control of the Community's executive must rest with the European Parliament. Accountability of the Commission to the Parliament could be much strengthened as a result of the new method of appointment. It is important that all possible be done to make this method successful.

Fitzmaurice suggests that the responsibility of the Commission to the

Parliament could be one of the most significant changes brought about by the Maastricht Treaty.[15] This would be a great improvement on the present system, in which there is no clear line of executive responsibility. The Community has, as Fitzmaurice puts it, 'a form of collective government', in which the executive function is divided between the Commission, the Council, the member states' governments and, beyond the Community itself, the CFSP and the Cooperation in Justice and Home Affairs.[16] This confusing system leads to big problems of effectiveness. The attempts of twelve governments – soon more – to keep control over the execution of Community policy are not likely to result in successful collective government. Nor is success likely without an effective Commission with clear responsibilities for execution. Now that the single market programme is virtually complete, the balance of the Commission's role is moving from the legislative process to monitoring the execution of the laws. For this task it needs adequate implementing powers, at present constrained by the committees of member states' officials that have authority to impede it on behalf of the Council, and it needs the resources, in particular staff, to do this properly. The number of Commissioners, which should clearly be related to the number of jobs to be done rather than to the number of member states, is a significant but less pressing issue. Despite the constraints placed upon it, the Commission has played an essential part not only in proposing and executing legislation, but in promoting coherence in the Community's action and animating its development.

The Maastricht Treaty assigns the role of animator, as Nicoll reminds us, to the European Council, which is to give the Union the 'necessary impetus for its development' and 'define the general political guidelines'.[17] Both the European Council and the Commission have done much to give impetus to the Community, the heads of state or government providing political authority, at least intermittently, and the Commission offering the more coherent and systematic view of the common interest that its position as a European institution, independent of the member states' governments, enables it to form. Both will doubtless continue to provide impetus for the Union. The Treaty does not bring much change to the role of the Council in the Community, save where it has to share its power more equally with the Parliament. But the extension of the Council's responsibilities in the fields of internal and external security intensifies the problems relating to the rotation of the presidency and to the weighting of the member states' votes, which gives what the larger feel to be an excessive weight to the smaller. The prospect of the forthcoming enlargements, to include mainly small new member states, will increase the pressure for a revision of the weighting. It should also precipitate a reform of the system for the presidency, which will be weakened every time that enlargement increases the number of states and hence, under the present system, the time before a state's turn comes round again. One element in any solution can be to define the role of the presidency carefully and to refrain from over-loading it with tasks. Another is to strengthen the Commission's role in representing the Community.

The inclination of intergovernmentalists is, on the contrary, to weaken the Commission by concentrating responsibility for executing Union policy, whether external or internal, in the Council, supported by hun-dreds of committees of members states' officials under Coreper. But it is not realistic to suppose that such responsibility can be effectively carried by the representatives of twelve or more separate governments, each one responding to the particular circumstances of a single member state's polity, rather than to the interest of the Union as a whole. It is hard to escape the conclusion that those governments which advocate the intergovernmental method are more concerned to keep power within their own hands than to enable the Union to work effectively in the general interest of the citizens.

The same can be said of the intergovernmentalists' preference for enacting Community legislation through negotiations undertaken by officials and ministers behind closed doors. Such a method is not designed to produce laws effectively. Still less does it respect the funda-mental principle of representative government that laws be enacted by representatives elected for that purpose by the citizens. While the minis-ters who now enact Community laws in the Council are in principle responsible to the voters of member states indirectly through their parliaments, this is an ineffective form of democratic control, for two main reasons. First, the ministers' main responsibilities lie elsewhere, in their own governments, so that the meetings of a Council which legis-lates in a given field are inevitably infrequent and short: the laws are in fact the result of deals cut by the member states' officials beforehand. Second, if each minister really was responsive to the wishes of each parliament, the legislature would in effect be the twelve different parlia-ments meeting separately, in a centrifugal system incapable of enacting legislation such as the Community requires. Unless a member state's parliament wants to make the Community so incapable, it has to forgo democratic accountability in the intergovernmental system and accept the deals that have been made. While some intergovernmentalists might be attracted by the prospect of a Community that could not enact laws, it would be a Community incapable of carrying through the single market programme and, indeed, of sustaining the rule of law among its peoples, which has provided a basis both for their mutually beneficial economic relationships and for the guarantee that there will be no more violent conflicts between them.

Intergovernmentalism is then unsatisfactory by the criteria of both

279

democracy and effectiveness. In so far as the Maastricht Treaty moves the Community's institutions further beyond the intergovernmental, it makes them more democratic and effective; and in so far as the CFSP and the Cooperation in Justice and Home Affairs rely on intergovernmental methods, they fail to apply the principles that the Community has been developing so successfully for nearly half a century.

SUBSIDIARITY

Advocates of intergovernmentalism often claim that it is the more decentralised system. But it is hard to see why decisions taken in this way should be regarded as more decentralised than those taken by the Community institutions with full participation of the Commission and Parliament. Decision through intergovernmental negotiation is, rather, likely to produce a more complicated, opaque and inefficient form of centralisation because it has to be based largely on negotiations among the bureaucracies of all the member states, which are necessarily secretive and complex, less effective without the unifying influence of a body such as the Commission, and lack the relationship with the public provided by the European Parliament and the judicial safeguards of the Court. Effective decentralisation lies elsewhere: in the juridical system that gives the bulk of the cases regarding Community law to the member states' courts; in the administrative system whereby Community policy is largely executed by the member states' bureaucracies; and, we may hope, in the principle of subsidiarity which is given prominence in the Maastricht Treaty.

Not much can be expected of the statement in Article A that 'decisions are taken as closely as possible to the citizen'. In centralised Britain, this may well be seen as Westminster and Whitehall.[18] But Article 3b EC is clearly intended to be operational, with its requirement for the Community to act only 'where the objectives of the proposed action cannot be sufficiently achieved by the Member States and can therefore, by reason of the scale or effects of the proposed action, be better achieved by the Community'. Bradley argues that these words are more amenable to political than to legal interpretation.[19] If the additional safeguard of judicial review is desired, it might be necessary to list the fields that are reserved to the member states, as the constitutions of Australia and Canada do.

Coombes affirms that the principle of subsidiarity should, as Article 3b indeed indicates, be the basis for assigning powers to the most suitable level of government, not just for preventing action by the Union; and the principle will not be respected unless the Union is given the institutions and instruments that will enable it to perform the tasks allotted to it.[20] As Article F.3 puts it: 'The Union shall provide itself with the means necessary to attain its objectives and carry through its policies.'

ENLARGEMENT

Membership of the Union is possible for all democratic European states. Wider membership will enhance Europe's prosperity and security, provided that the enlargement does not weaken the Union's ability to serve the interests of its citizens. While the inclusion of some member states from Efta may be accommodated without radical changes in the institutions, 'most would agree', as Nicoll puts it, 'that further waves of enlargement cannot proceed without major institutional reform'.[21] The greater number and diversity of member states will make unanimity harder to achieve. If the Community is not to grind to a halt, majority voting will have to become commonplace; and majority voting or stepping aside will have to become normal in the CFSP and the Cooperation in Justice and Home Affairs. In the absence of the member states' veto power, the case for democratic control by co-decision between Council and European Parliament will be strengthened. Respect for fundamental rights will have to be ensured in all the member states if those where they are respected are not to be alienated from the Union because of flagrant violations in other member states.

The Maastricht Treaty provides for derogations from adoption of the single currency on the part of member states that are not yet ready for it, and thus for two or more speeds in that field. As regards defence, not all member states are members of WEU, which is to be the defence arm of the Union. The Efta enlargement may add to the number of those that do not participate in the field of defence; and Central and East Europeans, when they enter, may not be ready to adopt the single currency. Thus enlargement may be accompanied by more recourse to variable speeds or even tiers. This will tend to weaken the Union's institutions by eroding the sense of collective responsibility and reducing the scope for the trade-offs that are an essential element in the Council's decision-making. One way to counter this danger is to confine the derogations to a transitional period, thus limiting the variability to the speed at which an objective is attained rather than the commitment to the objective itself. Another way is to provide incentives for convergence, as are offered by the Maastricht Treaty to encourage member states to converge on the conditions required for adoption of the single currency.

BRITISH POLICY

The British government has espoused the cause of intergovernmentalism. Duff, in Chapter 2, cites John Major's plea for intergovernmental cooperation, 'not under the Treaty of Rome', on the grounds that it is 'much more amenable to the institutions of this country'.[22] But it has to be asked whether, in fields where interdependence is intense, British institutions as they stand can, outside the framework of institutions such as the Community has been developing, provide the sort of government that British citizens need. Should not the principles of effective government, based on the rule of law and on control by voters' elected representatives, be applied in common institutions as well as in those of member states? It is evidently hard for people in the older nation states, and particularly for their rulers, to face up to this question. It is not altogether surprising if the governments of other states are better placed to draw the necessary consequences.

John Major added that the intergovernmental option 'is available to cover wider areas in the future'. But surely the EU already covers the areas in which interdependence gives rise to significant problems. The principle of subsidiarity could indeed require that its coverage should, at least at the margins, be reduced. The implication must be therefore that fields of competence of the Community might be returned to intergovernmentalism. While this too may be possible at the margins, any proposal for large-scale renationalisation of Community competences could only be regarded with the greatest apprehension. All the authors of this book would view any attempt to erode the Community in such a way as damaging and dangerous for both Britain and its partners. The continued growth of interdependence requires, on the contrary, a Union that is stronger and more democratic.

The British government's attempts, in the negotiations leading to Maastricht, to impede some of the principal reforms proposed, such as Emu and co-decision, made the Treaty less effective, more complicated and opaque than it would otherwise have been: less capable of dealing with problems such as monetary stability and the anchoring of Germany within the Union; less open to the democratic influence of the citizens and hence less able to win their support. This can only be to the detriment of the Union as a whole. But it is more harmful to Britain than to the rest.

From 1950 when Britain, as the most powerful state in Western Europe, stood aside from the launching of the first Community, to the present time, with the Union clearly led by Germany and France, Britain has drifted from its central role in Europe towards the margin of Community and Union development. Most other member states support the Franco-German lead because they judge that it is designed to strengthen the Union, which they see as an essential interest of European countries in the contemporary world. Attempts to promote intergovernmentalism may receive support from some of the more nationalistic politicians. But they are likely to weaken British influence, not carry weight, with the mainstream.

The British government's determination to exclude the mention of a federal aim in the Maastricht Treaty was symptomatic. Some of Britain's negotiating capital was spent in keeping it out, against the resistance of all the other member states save Denmark. One justification put forward is that whereas the word federal implies decentralisation on the Continent, it implies centralisation in English. This is not accurate. On both sides of the Channel, a federal system requires powers to be assigned according to the principle of subsidiarity: they are to be exercised in common where, as the Maastricht Treaty puts it, objectives can be better achieved by the Community. The question at issue is whether the powers are to be exercised in common by an intergovernmental system, which is both inefficient and undemocratic, or by an effective system which respects the principles of democratic government, with the rule of law based on fundamental rights and with properly representative government under which representatives of the people – together with, in federal systems, representatives of the states – enact the laws and control the executive. This system is based on British, more than on any other, political philosophy. It is very sad that British governments should oppose its application to the European Union where interdependence renders a new level of government necessary.

BEYOND MAASTRICHT: POLICY, REFORM, CONSTITUTION

The first need, after Maastricht, is to make the Treaty work as well as possible. Policies have been suggested above to regenerate the European economy: a sound macroeconomic policy, promoted by the European Monetary Institute in the perspective of the move to the single currency and European Central Bank; and a structural policy to establish not only flexible labour markets but also a great programme to give Europe the infrastructure of transport and communications that it needs for the next century. Security can be enhanced through joint actions under the CFSP and development of the role of WEU, with member states that dissent from the majority stepping aside so that actions can go ahead, and with the Commission given the resources it needs for its planning and coordinating role; and the CFSP can be strengthened by using, whenever possible, Community instruments and procedures. The institutions can be improved by ensuring that the European Parliament's role in approval of the new Commission and in co-decision with the Council is really effective.

Beyond these immediate steps, the Maastricht Treaty stipulates the holding of the Intergovernmental Conference in 1996 to review matters such as co-decision and the CFSP. The aim here should be not only to improve the working of the Union in the light of experience but also to ensure that the more-or-less concurrent accession of Efta states strengthens, not weakens the Union and to prepare the institutions so that they are sturdy enough to accommodate the further new members resulting from subsequent enlargements to Central and Eastern Europe and Mediterranean countries. Following the preceding argument, reforms that should be on the agenda at that stage include the incorporation of the European Convention on Human Rights in EC law and the requirement that it be applied in all member states; the progressive assimilation into Community competence of the fields defined for the Cooperation on Justice and Home Affairs; the general application of the principle of qualified majority voting in the Council and of co-decision with the Parliament for Community legislation; progress towards an equitable system of public finance for the Union; and moving the institutions of the CFSP closer to those of the Community.

Thus reformed, the Treaty on European Union would contain most of the elements that a solid European constitution would require: competence in the fields of trade, money, the environment and, increasingly, foreign policy and defence; a federal judiciary, the Commission as an executive responsible to the European Parliament, and the Council together with the Parliament as the legislature. To complete the process of strengthening the institutions in order to accommodate Central and East Europeans, however, and to make clear to the citizens how they are governed at the European level, the Union should then design a constitution to enter into force by the time of the next enlargement.

For effective government, such a constitution should provide for majority voting as the general rule in the Council, and the Commission would need the competences to ensure the execution of the Union's policies. For democracy, the Commission would be fully accountable to the European Parliament and the Parliament would share legislative power with the Council. The Union's powers over trade, money and the environment would remain much as stipulated by the existing Treaty. Defence and foreign policy related to it would, however, not be brought within the scope of this federal structure of institutions until member states were ready to integrate their powers in that most sensitive area of sovereignty. The constitution could state the aim, but without commitment to a date. Meanwhile there would not be a federal state, although it might be legitimate to call the EU a federal union.

Such a constitution should not be designed in a hurry. Nor should the drafting be left to diplomats, who have other skills, or ministers who have other preoccupations. The text would have to be prepared with the help of leading experts in constitutional law, to ensure that it is rooted in sound constitutional principles, and of Members of the European

Parliament and of member states' parliaments, who should be able to see that it both reflects contemporary political realities and is comprehensible to the citizens. The European Parliament already has a draft, based on the work of distinguished jurists, which can offer a starting point for the constituent process. That process would have to involve governments' representatives as well as members of the parliaments and should culminate in a constitutional convention for the adoption of the text, with thorough explanation and debate followed by referenda in all the member states.

Such a procedure is a novelty for the British. Our constitution has developed in a different way. But the exercise of political power in common with our neighbours to deal with the problems of mutual interdependence has reached a point where a constitution will be needed to ensure that it is properly controlled; and the need will become more acute as the number and diversity of member states increases. The European constitution cannot evolve over the centuries as the British one did. Nor should it be allowed to develop much further by the methods employed to negotiate the Maastricht Treaty. The Treaty is a positive achievement. But it is confusing and obscure and it has not carried the people with it. Europeans need an effective Union with a democratic structure, which must be established in a way that can secure the consent of the citizens. The full potential of Maastricht will be realised only if it is completed by a constitution established in such a way. Only thus can Europeans provide for the security, prosperity and environment that they should have in the intensely interdependent Europe of the twenty-first century.

NOTES

1 THE MAASTRICHT TREATY AND THE NEW EUROPE

1 See Andrew Duff (ed.), *Subsidiarity within the European Community*, London, Federal Trust, 1993.
2 *Eurobarometer* 39, June 1993.
3 Association or 'Europe Agreements' were first signed by the EC with Czechoslovakia, Hungary and Poland in December 1991 and subsequently with Romania and then Bulgaria.
4 'Perils of being a good guy', *Financial Times*, 14–15 August 1993.
5 Switzerland was not included in the negotiations with the other Efta countries, the Swiss having rejected in a popular referendum in December 1992 their country's proposed membership of the European Economic Area. The Swiss government has not, however, withdrawn its application to join the Union.

2 THE MAIN REFORMS

1 *The Treaty on European Union*, Article A.
2 The Treaty is completed by 17 Protocols, which are an integral part of the Treaty and are binding on all 12 member states, as well as by 33 Declarations, which may not be.
3 HC Debate, 4 November 1992, col. 288.
4 Articles 2, 3a, 4a and 102a to 109m inclusive; Protocol on the statute of the European System of Central Banks and of the European Central Bank; Protocol on the statute of the European Monetary Institute; Protocol on the excessive deficit procedure; Protocol on the convergence criteria referred to in Article 109j; Protocol on the transition to the third stage of Emu; Protocol on certain provisions relating to the UK; Protocol on certain provisions relating to Denmark.
5 Belgium and Luxembourg, of course, have a currency union.
6 EC Bulletin 12/92, I.36.
7 The UK signed up, although the then Chancellor of the Exchequer, Norman Lamont, later admitted that he had never believed that the single currency and ECB were either feasible or desirable.
8 Article 3a.
9 Article 103.
10 Articles J to J.11 inclusive; Declaration on Western European Union.
11 Article J.4.

12 Articles K to K.9 inclusive.
13 Articles C and D.
14 HC Debate, 11 March 1993, col. 1157.
15 For a fuller discussion of the theory and practice of subsidiarity, see Andrew Duff (ed.), *Subsidiarity within the European Community*, London, Federal Trust, 1993.
16 Articles A, B and 3b.
17 EC Bulletin 12/92, I.15–29.
18 Article 145.
19 Articles 8 to 8e inclusive, 138(3) and 138a to 138e inclusive.
20 Article F.
21 Article 138a.
22 Article 189b.
23 Article 158.
24 Articles 146, 198a, 198b and 198c.
25 Article 130d.
26 Articles 117 to 122.
27 Agreement on Social Policy concluded between the member states of the EC with the exception of the UK.
28 Protocol on Social Policy.
29 A qualified majority in the Council *à onze* is 44 votes.
30 Denmark and the Treaty on European Union, OJ 92/C 348 31 December 1992.
31 Article O.
32 Declaration on the role of National Parliaments in the European Union.

3   THE TREATY NEGOTIATIONS

1 See Roy Pryce (ed.), *The Dynamics of European Union*, London, Croom Helm/Routledge, 1987.
2 The European Parliament's proposals were drawn up in two reports by its Institutional Committee, whose rapporteur was the Labour MEP David Martin. See Richard Corbett, 'The Intergovernmental Conference on political union', *Journal of Common Market Studies*, September 1992.
3 For a list of proposals made by national governments, see Yves Doutriaux, *Le traité sur l'union européenne*, Paris, Armand Colin, 1992.
4 British Tory MPs and peers were particularly aggravated by being made at the outset of the Assizes to sit according to party political formation rather than by national delegation.
5 Briefing in London, 23 February 1992.
6 John Pinder, *European Community: The Building of a Union*, Oxford, OUP, 1991, ch. 7.
7 Press conference, reported in *The Guardian*, 28 June 1989.
8 *Financial Times*, 9 September; *The Guardian*, 11 September 1989. An elaborated paper, 'An evolutionary approach to economic and monetary union', was produced by the Treasury in November 1989.
9 *The Guardian*, 8 December 1989.
10 *Libération*, 8 December 1989.
11 For a detailed account, see Finn Laursen and Sophie Vanhoonacker, *The Intergovernmental Conference on Political Union*, Maastricht, European Institute of Public Administration, 1992.
12 *The Guardian*, 21 May 1990.
13 *Agence Europe*, 19 and 21 May 1990.

14 See Bernard Snoy, 'Exposé Introductif' in *Les conférences intergouvernementales au terme de la présidence luxembourgeoise*, Brussels, Institut d'études euro-péennes, 25 June 1991.
15 For the Luxembourg 'non-paper' on these issues, see *Agence Europe*, 25 April 1991.
16 Ibid., 4 May 1991.
17 Ibid., 6 December 1991.
18 For the Luxembourg draft see Europe Documents (*Agence Europe*) No. 1722/1723, 5 July 1991.
19 The Dutch had counted on the support of the Germans, but the Germans were persuaded otherwise by the French foreign minister. David Buchan, *Financial Times*, 7/8 December 1991. See also *Agence Europe*, 30 September 1991.
20 Hurd had taken the first step towards a deal on defence in a private conversation with the Italian foreign minister De Michelis in Rome on Easter Monday, 1 April. David Buchan, 'Why a temple proved stronger than a tree', *Financial Times*, 7/8 December 1991.
21 *The Guardian*, 12 December 1991.
22 *Financial Times*, 11 December 1991.
23 Ibid., 12 December 1991.

4 RATIFICATION

1 Article R.
2 See Belmont European Policy Centre, *The New Treaty on European Union* vol. 2, pp.21–6, Brussels, February 1992.
3 Many nationalist politicians in the UK argued for a referendum, how-ever.
4 EC Bulletin 6/92, 1.1.3.
5 EC Bulletin 12/92, I.15–29.
6 This eccentric Irish Protocol (no. 17) had to be interpreted by a further Declaration on 1 May 1992 so as not to impede freedom to travel or of information.
7 EC Bulletin 6/92, 1.1.6.
8 EC Bulletin 9/92, 1.1.2.
9 Embarrassingly, Brunner was (until sacked) also *chef de cabinet* of Commission Vice-President Martin Bangemann.
10 Unofficial translation.
11 Article 138(3).
12 Official Journal (OJ) C 348, 31 December 1992.
13 EC Bulletin 5/1993, 1.1.5.
14 See Law Report in *The Independent*, 3 August 1993. The judges decided that the Maastricht Treaty did not entail an abandonment or transfer of the Crown's prerogative powers but an exercise of them.
15 *The Economist*, 25 September 1993.
16 OJ C 125, 18 May 1992.
17 OJ C 21, 25 January 1993.
18 See the Commission's communication on public access, OJ C 156, 8 June 1993.
19 OJ C 125, 6 May 1993.
20 At the time of writing the interinstitutional agreement on committees of enquiry is outstanding.
21 *Growth, Competitiveness, Employment: The Challenges and Ways Forward into the*

21st Century, EC Bulletin, Supplement 6/93. See also Harry Cowie and John Pinder (eds), *A Recovery Strategy for Europe*, London, Federal Trust, 1993.
22 *Agence Europe*, 16 December 1993.

5 FISCAL AND MONETARY POLICY IN EMU

1 *Report on Economic and Monetary Union in the European Community and Collection of Papers submitted to the Committee for the Study of Economic and Monetary Union*, Brussels, EC Commission, 1989.
2 EC Commission, *One Market, One Money*, European Economy no. 44, September 1990; *Report on EMU*, 1989, op. cit.: see especially paper by Alexandre Lamfalussy, 'Macro-coordination of fiscal policies in an economic and monetary union'.
3 Andrew Blake and Peter Westway, 'Should the Bank of England be independent?', *National Institute Review* no. 143, February 1993.
4 Tommaso Padoa-Schioppa and Fabrizio Saccomanni, *Agenda for Stage Two: Preparing the Monetary Platform*, London, Centre for Economic Policy Research Occasional Paper no. 7, 1992.
5 Willem Buiter and others, *'Excessive Deficits': Sense and Nonsense in the Treaty of Maastricht*, London, Centre for Economic Policy Research, Discussion Paper no. 750, 1992.
6 G.M. Caporale, 'Fiscal solvency in Europe: budget deficits and government debt under European Monetary Union', *National Institute Review* no. 140, May 1992.
7 Sir Donald MacDougall, 'Economic and Monetary Union and the European Community Budget', *National Institute Review* no. 140, May 1992.
8 Charles Goodhart, *Fiscal Policy and Emu*, London School of Economics Financial Markets Group Special Paper no. 31, 1990.
9 *One Market, One Money*, op. cit.

6 COMMON FOREIGN AND SECURITY POLICY

1 Simon Nuttall writes in a personal capacity and his views do not necessarily reflect those of the European Commission.
2 Finn Laursen and Sophie Vanhoonacker (eds), *The Intergovernmental Conference on Political Union*, Maastricht, European Institute of Public Administration, 1992.
3 Jacques Delors, *European Integration and Security*, Alastair Buchan Memorial Lecture, in *Survival* no. XXXIII (2), 1991.
4 Articles J.4.6, J.10 and N.2.
5 Op. cit., p.107.
6 A letter by an assistant Under-Secretary of State Bartholomew, leaked in February 1991, was notable for its particularly cautious attitude to autonomous European activity.
7 Article J.1.
8 Article J.4.
9 Article J.11.1 combined with the references in Title V *passim*.
10 Article L.
11 Articles C and J.8.
12 Listed in Articles J.1.2, J.2 and J.3 respectively.
13 Article J.8.2, para 2.
14 Article J.5.4, para 2.
15 Article J.4.2.

16 Article J.4.4–5.
17 Declaration No. 30.
18 Article K.3.2(b).
19 Article K.5.
20 Article 100c.
21 Article 109.3–4.
22 Declaration No. 28 reads: 'The Conference agrees that the division of work between the Political Committee and the Committee of Permanent Representatives will be examined at a later stage, as will the practical arrangements for merging the Political Cooperation Secretariat with the General Secretariat of the Council and for cooperation between the latter and the Commission.'
23 Article J.5.1–3.
24 This incorporates the previous EPC Directorate in the Secretariat General, the Inspectorate of External Delegations, and the Directorate responsible for the management of the External Delegations, as well as three new Directorates responsible on a geographical basis for political relations with Europe, the developed world and the developing world.
25 Declaration No. 30.
26 Article J.9.
27 Article J.4.2.
28 Article J.4.6.
29 Article J.10.

7 EUROPEAN CITIZENSHIP AND COOPERATION IN JUSTICE AND HOME AFFAIRS

1 Malcolm Anderson and Monica den Boer wrote the sections on justice and home affairs co-operation; Gary Miller wrote on citizenship.
2 Legislative proposals on the easing of border controls were made as early as 1984 and directives on the right of residence were put forward in 1989. For the related policy areas see EC Commission, *Abolition of Controls on Persons at Intra-Community Borders*, Com(88)640 final, December 1988.
3 The basic Schengen Agreement of 14 June 1985 was complemented by the 'Schengen Convention' of 19 June 1990 on the gradual suppression of internal border controls, which laid down the necessary measures for the application of the original accord. Schengen is a village in Luxembourg where the Agreement was signed.
4 Convention of the Member States of the European Communities on the crossing of their external borders and the Convention of 15 June 1990 determining the state responsible for examining applications for asylum lodged in one of the Member States of the Communities.
5 See Andrew Evans, 'European Citizenship: A novel concept in EEC law', *The American Journal of Comparative Law*, vol. 32, 1984, pp.679–715, p.683.
6 *A People's Europe: Reports from the Ad Hoc Committee*, EC Bulletin, Supplement 7/1985.
7 *Tindemans Report on European Union to the European Council*, EC Bulletin, Supplement 1/1976.
8 European Parliament, *Draft Treaty Establishing the European Union*, OJ C 77, 19 March 1984.
9 European Parliament, *Declaration of Fundamental Rights and Freedoms*, Doc. A2–3/89, adopted 12 April 1989.
10 The Spanish proposals on European Citizenship of 7 September 1990 raised

the possibility of the right to vote for EC citizens ultimately being extended to national elections.

11 *Intergovernmental Conferences: Contributions by the Commission*, EC Bulletin, Supplement 2/91.

12 Belgian Government, *Aide-mémoire*, Brussels, 20 March 1990, p.5.

13 David Martin (rapporteur), *Second Interim Report Drawn up on Behalf of the Committee on Institutional Affairs on the Inter-governmental Conferences in the Context of Parliament's Strategy for European Union*, European Parliament, 25 June 1990, Doc A 3–166/90, adopted 11 July 1990.

14 Parliament had already been discussing this, see the De Gucht Report on a proposed uniform electoral procedure for the European Parliament elections, document PE 140.107/revised, 5 February 1991.

15 European Council, Conclusions of the Presidency, Madrid, June 1989; Spanish government, *Hacia una ciudadania europea*, mimeo, dated 7 September 1990.

16 European Council, *Conclusions of the Presidency*, Madrid 1989.

17 According to Yves Doutriaux, *Le traité sur l'Union européenne*, Paris, Editions Armand Colin, 1992, p.114, who took part in the negotiations, this was the express reason why the member states avoided any change that would lead to the incorporation of the ECHR into EC law. The European Convention on Human Rights states (in Art.1) that its rights shall be secured to everyone within the jurisdiction of its signatory states; and that 'any person' may bring a case concerning a violation of their rights.

18 Joint Declaration by the European Parliament, the Council and the Commission on Fundamental Rights adopted at Luxembourg, 5 April 1977, OJ C 103, 27 April 1977.

19 See *Stauder* v. *The City of Ulm*, Case 29/69 [1969] ECR, p.419 ff, p.425; and *Nold* v. *the Commission*, Case 4/73 [1974] ECR p.491ff, p.507.

20 Articles 48, 52 and 59 EEC respectively.

21 On 'work-seekers' see *Procureur du Roi* v. *Royer*, Case 48/75 [1976] ECR, p.497ff and *Centre Public de l'Aide Sociale de Courcelles* v. *Lebon*, Case 316/85 [1989] ECR; on freedom to receive services see *Luisi and Carbone* v. *Ministero del Tresoro*, Case 286/82 [1984] ECR, p.377ff and *Cowan* v. *Le Trésor Public*, Case 186/87 [1989] ECR.

22 Three directives were adopted by the Council on 28 June 1990 on a right of residence for students and pensioners and on a general right of residence. EC Commission, *Proposal for a Council Directive on voting rights for Community nationals in local elections in their Member State of residence*, COM (88) 371, presented to the Council on 24 June 1988, which itself was based on a report produced by the Commission in 1986.

23 OJ L 329, 30 December 1993.

24 See International Study Group on European Citizenship, *Draft Proposals*, Federal Trust, London, 1990.

25 Article 8d in conjunction with Article 138d and 138e.

26 Francis Jacobs, Richard Corbett and Michael Shackleton, *The European Parliament* (2nd edition), Harlow, Longman,1992, pp.264–66.

27 Monica den Boer and Neil Walker, 'European policing after 1992', *Journal of Common Market Studies*, vol. 31, no. 1, March 1993.

28 Simon Nuttall, *European Political Cooperation*, Oxford, The Clarendon Press, 1992.

29 J.J.E. Schutte, 'The European Market of 1993: Test for a regional model of supranational criminal justice or of interregional cooperation in criminal law', *Criminal Law Forum*, vol.3, no.1, Autumn 1991.

30 Neil Walker, 'Models of European integration and models of European police cooperation', in Malcolm Anderson and Monica den Boer (eds), *Police Cooperation across National Boundaries*, London, Pinter, forthcoming.

31 C.W.A. Timmermans, 'Free movement of persons and the division of powers between the Community and its Member States: Why do it the intergovernmental way?' in Henry G. Schermers *et al.* (eds), *Free Movement of Persons in Europe*, Dordrecht, Martinus Nijhoff Publishers, 1993.

32 Article 100c.

33 Article K.1 (1–6) and Article K.9 in conjunction with Article 100c(6).

34 Article K.1 (7–9).

35 J.H.H. Weiler, 'The transformation of Europe', *The Yale Law Journal*, 100, no.8, 1991.

36 Article K.1(5).

37 For example, an EC Drugs Monitoring Centre is being created for the exchange of information about drugs and drug addiction.

38 See Schutte, op.cit., and Timmermans, op.cit. and also Roel Fernhout, 'The United States of Europe have commenced. But for whom?', *Netherlands Quarterly of Human Rights*, 3, 1993.

39 Michael Spencer, *1992 and All That: Civil Liberties in the Balance*, London, Civil Liberties Trust, 1990.

40 Lode van Outrive, rapporteur, *Second Report of the Committee on Civil Liberties and Internal Affairs on the Entry into Force of the Schengen Agreements*, European Parliament Session Documents, A3–0336/92, 1992.

41 Article C.

42 Old Article 8a of the Treaty of Rome (as amended by the Single Act).

8 OLD POLICIES AND NEW COMPETENCES

1 Articles 130r, 130s and 130t.

2 Article 118B.

3 Article 2.1 of the Agreement.

4 Article 2.3 of the Agreement.

5 Article 2.4 and Article 4 of the Agreement. For the practical workings of the Agreement, see *Agence Europe*, 10/11 January 1994.

6 Article 1 of the Agreement.

7 See *Agence Europe*, 2 December 1993.

8 Article 129b.

9 Article 2.

10 Article 130r.

11 Article 189c.

12 All the figures cited here are in 1992 prices.

13 Article 129.

14 Article 100c.

9 THE PUBLIC FINANCES OF THE UNION

1 EC Commission, *Report of the Study Group on the Role of Public Finance in European Integration*, 2 vols, (MacDougall Report), Brussels, 1977.

2 For a review of the development of European public finances, see EC Commission, *Community Public Finance: The European Budget after the 1988 Reform*, Luxembourg, 1989; and Michael Shackleton, *Financing the European Community*, London, Chatham House/Pinter, 1990, pp.1–8.

3 Commission, *Community Public Finance*, op. cit., 1989, pp.57–9.

4 The following figures come from Commission, *Haushaltsvademekum*, Edition 1993.

5 Commission, *Community Public Finance*, op. cit., 1989, pp.57–9.

6 Geoffrey Denton, *Federalism and European Union after Maastricht*, 1993, p.39.

7 Shackleton, *Financing the European Community*, op. cit., 1990, pp.24–47.

8 Shackleton also points to the fact that before the Fontainebleau Summit of 1984, Britain was the second largest net payer, despite the fact that its per head income at the time was below or just equal to the EC average.

9 European Parliament, Working Group on Own Resources, *Own Resources of the Community*, 5 May 1980, Doc. PE 634/final, Brussels, 1980. EC Commission, *Report by the Commission to the Council and European Parliament on the Financing of the Community Budget*, COM(87)101 final, Brussels 1987. Indirect progressivity results from the definition of the 'tax' base of the new resource as the difference between GNP and the share of the VAT base in GNP.

10 Peter M. Schmidhuber, the competent Commissioner, has argued in favour of a 'true Community tax' (*Ist die Finanzverfassung der EG reformbedürftig?*, in EG-Kommission, Vertretung in der Bundesrepublik Deutschland, *Europäische Gespräche*, Heft 6, Bonn, 1991, p.7). As he refers to the position of the Parliament, one can assume that he implies that such a tax can be progressive. Shackleton, op. cit. (p.71), points to the fact that the Commission already in 1978 stated that the EC's system of financing should continue to develop towards 'true own resources'.

11 A recent survey of these new developments in economic theory is found in E.G. Furubotn and R. Richter (eds), *The New Institutional Economics*, Tübingen, 1991, pp.1–32.

12 For 'frustration', see J.R. Pennock, 'Federal and Unitary Government – Disharmony and Frustration', *Behavior Sciences*, vol. 4, 1969, pp.147–57; for 'preference cost', see Dieter Biehl, 'Financing the EEC Budget', in Remy Prud'homme (ed.), *Public Finance with Several Levels of Government*, Proceedings of the 46th Congress of the International Institute of Public Finance, Brussels, 1990. The terms 'resource' and 'preference cost' have been used instead of 'external' and 'decision-making cost' originally coined by Buchanan and Tullock in their seminal book *The Calculus of Consent*, Michigan, Ann Arbor, 1962.

13 It is not possible to develop fully here all the possible implications of the extended cost approach. But see Dieter Biehl, 'A federalist budgetary policy strategy for European Union', *Policy Studies*, vol. 6, part 2, 1985; and Dieter Biehl, 'The financial constitution of the European Community: Its deficiencies and a proposal for reform', in Preston King and Andrea Bosco (eds), *A Constitution for Europe*, Lothian Foundation Press, London, 1991, pp.75–91.

14 James M. Buchanan, 'An economic theory of clubs', *Economica*, vol. 32, 1965.

15 Geoffrey Denton writes that, until recently, subsidiarity was virtually unknown in Britain; *Federalism and European Union after Maastricht*, Wilton Park Paper 67, London, HMSO, 1993. But there exists a large body of literature, going back to Greek and medieval philosophers. For the EC context, see Jacques Delors, 'Le principe de subsidarité', in Jacques Delors, *Le nouveau concert européen*, Paris, 1992.

16 Dieter Biehl, 'Die EG-Finanzverfassung: Struktur, Mangel und Reform-möglichkeiten' in Rudolf Wildenmann (ed.), *Staatswerdung Europas?*, Baden-Baden, 1991, pp.368f.

17 This principle can be traced back to Albert Breton, 'A theory of government grants' in *Canadian Journal of Economics and Political Science*, vol. 31, 1965; and

to Wallace E. Oates, *Fiscal Federalism*, New York, Harcourt Brace Jovanovich, 1972 (the term 'correspondence' is used by Oates).

18 Denton stressed that 'direct powers of taxation in the hands of the Community itself would make it more accountable as to how funds are spent' (*Federalism and European Union*, op. cit.).

19 Articles 203(4) and 203(9) EC.

20 The text of the Interinstitutional Agreement of 1988 is also to be found in Shackleton, *Financing the European Community*, op. cit.

21 EC Commission, *Community Public Finance*, op. cit., referring to the 'Joint Declaration of the European Parliament, the Council and the Commission on various measures to improve the budgetary procedure' of 30 June 1982.

22 Commission, ibid, p.65.

23 Article 203(9) EC.

10 PROBLEMS OF GOVERNANCE IN THE UNION

1 Richard Falk, Samuel S. Kim and Robert C. Johansen, *The Constitutional Foundations of World Peace*, Albany, State University of New York Press, 1993. R.B.J. Walker and Saul H. Mendlovitz, *Contending Sovereignties: Rethinking Political Community*, Boulder, Lynne Reiner, 1990. R.B.J. Walker, *Inside/Outside: International Relations as Political Theory*, Cambridge, CUP, 1993.

2 Cited in Harvey C. Mansfield, *Taming the Prince: The Ambivalence of Modern Executive Power*, New York, Free Press, 1989, pp.257 and 270.

3 Ibid., p.291.

11 THE EUROPEAN COMMISSION

1 See for example, as a representative statement of this criticism, the Editorial in *Agence Europe*, 27/28 September 1993.

2 R. Keohane and J.S. Nye, *Power and Interdependence: World Politics in Transition*, Boston, Little, Brown and Co., 1987; William Wallace, 'Less than a federation, more than a regime: The Community as a political system', in Helen Wallace, William Wallace and Carole Webb (eds), *Policy Making in the European Community*, 2nd edition, Chichester, John Wiley & Sons, 1983.

3 *Agence Europe*, 27 July 1993.

4 Article 158.

5 Article 157.

6 See *Institutional Adaptations Necessary for an Enlarged Commission*, Brussels–Bonn, TEPSA, June 1992.

7 Article 161.

8 Sir Christopher Prout, European Parliament *Debates*, 14 September 1993.

9 See *Intergovernmental Conferences: Contributions by the Commission*, EC Bulletin Supplement 2/1991.

10 Speech to the Third Interinstitutional Conference, Strasbourg, 23 October 1990.

11 Speech to the Assizes of National Parliaments and the European Parliament, Rome, 28 November 1990.

12 *Commission Communication on Subsidiarity: The Principle of Subsidiarity*, SEC(92) 1992, 27 October 1992.

13 Case 120/78.

14 See *Joint Declaration on the 1993 Legislative Programme* in EC Bulletin Supplement 1/1993.

15 Figures based on internal Commission research studies.

16 The EC Commission's General Reports of 1989 and 1992 show that there were over 180 pieces of primary legislation in 1989 and fewer than 100 in 1992.
17 Jacques Delors, European Parliament *Debates*, 12 July 1990.
18 EC Bulletin Supplement 2/1991, op. cit.; European Parliament Resolution (Bourlanges Report) Doc A3–0085/91.
19 Article 145.
20 EC Bulletin Supplement 2/1991, op. cit.

12 REPRESENTING THE STATES

1 Pierre Gerbet, *La construction de l'Europe*, Paris, Imprimerie Nationale, 1983, p.162 ff.
2 W. Nicoll, 'Maastricht revisited' in A. Cafruny and G. Rosenthal (eds), *The State of the European Community*, vol. 2, Colorado, Lynne Riener Publishers, 1992, p.23 ff.
3 The EC Council in turn was and remains different in operation from the Special Council of Ministers of the European Coal and Steel Community, as per new Article 7 of that Treaty.
4 W. Nicoll and T.C. Salmon, *Understanding the European Communities*, Hemel Hempsted, Philip Allan, 1990.
5 There are three departures from the rules which require the Council to find unanimity if it wants to change a Commission proposal. The first is in its treatment of the Preliminary Draft Budget, which technically is not a Commission 'proposal'. The second is in the area of 'comitology', where the Council can change a 'draft measure' (something else which is not a proposal) by qualified majority. The third is in Article 189b(5) and (6), where after conciliation the Council can change a Commission proposal by qualified majority to reflect an agreement with the European Parliament, or to accept an amendment proposed by Parliament.
6 For the avoidance of doubt: what is said here concerns only the deliberations of the Council. There are authorities which can impose upon the member states: the Court of Justice; the Commission when it is exercising Treaty and secondary legislation powers under the competition policy, or its powers under Chapter VI of the Euratom Treaty, or those under Article 54 of the ECSC Treaty; the European Central Bank under Articles 105a and 108a of Maastricht.
7 *The Economist*, 25 September 1993.
8 See p.186 above.
9 If indeed this practice continues under co-decision. See W. Nicoll, 'Note the hour and file the minute', *Journal of Common Market Studies*, December 1993.
10 The minutes of the Council are confined to indicating the documents it had before it, the decisions it took with the texts of acts annexed, and the statements made by the Council, its members or the Commission (Rules of Procedure of the Council, 1987 version, Article 7). There is also a verbatim, which is transcribed, but can be consulted only by the Council Secretariat, the presidency of the meeting concerned and, only so far as it wishes to read what its representative is recorded as saying, a member state delegation.
11 R. Keohane and S. Hoffman (eds), *The New European Community: Decision-making and Institutional Change*, Boulder, Colorado, Westview Press, 1991, p.16.
12 European Parliament, Committee on Institutional Affairs, Doc. A3 0189/92, 21 May 1992, Strasbourg (the Hänsch Report), p.18. For a discussion of the

intricacies (and algebra) of voting and of majorities, see P. Budden and B.L. Monroe, *Decision-making in the EC Council of Ministers*, European Community Studies Association, University of Pittsburgh, PA, May 1993.

13 More accurately, the Budget Council draws a line when the opposition falls below 23 votes.

14 But a member state is obliged to accept something unwelcome if it is in breach of Community law – that is, the law which it itself helped to formulate, or which it accepted in its Treaty of Accession.

15 Article 108a.2 and 3.

16 See, for example, *Agence Europe*, 24 September 1993, and Ian Davidson in the *Financial Times*, 30 September 1993.

17 The French presidency of 1989 described itself initially as 'La Présidence des Communautés Européennes', but changed its style half way through. Serenely, in 1994, Greece is calling itself the 'Presidency of the European Union'.

18 W. Nicoll 'Qu'est-ce que la comitologie?', *Revue du Marché Commun*, December 1987.

19 'Subsidiarity' occurs ten times in the speech which Jacques Delors delivered at the College of Europe in 1989, one year after Margaret Thatcher had spoken there about creeping centralization.

20 Case 22/1970.

21 Article 109.1 and 2.

22 Article 6 of the Protocol on the statute of the European Central Bank.

23 The Commission's popular version *The Institutions of the European Community*, Brussels-Luxembourg, 1994, gets this wrong.

13   REPRESENTING THE PEOPLE

1 Schuman Declaration, 9 May 1950.

2 EC Court of Justice, *Isoglucose* Ruling, Cases 138 and 139/79.

3 For an analysis of the development of the Parliament's powers, see Francis Jacobs, Richard Corbett and Michael Shackleton, *The European Parliament* (2nd edition), Harlow, Longman, 1992.

4 For an account of the IGC on political union and of Parliament's impact on it, see R.G. Corbett, 'The Intergovernmental Conference on Political Union', *Journal of Common Market Studies*, September 1992, or, in greater detail, *The Treaty of Maastricht: From Conception to Ratification*, Harlow, Longman, 1993.

5 For a detailed list, see the annex to this chapter, pp.225–8.

6 Resolutions on the IGC in the context of Parliament's strategy for European Union; Minutes of the EP of 11 July 1990 and 22 November 1990 (based on the Martin Reports, Doc. A3–166/90 and A3–270/90).

7 See the annex.

8 See p.191 above.

9 Article 206.

10 Article 188b.

11 Article 4.

12 Article 138c.

13 Resolution on a uniform electoral procedure: a scheme for allocating the seats of Members of the European Parliament. Minutes of the European Parliament, 10 June 1992 (based on De Gucht Report, A3–186/92).

14 Resolution on the conclusions of the European Council meeting in Edinburgh. Minutes of the European Parliament, 16 December 1992.

15 *Agence Europe*, 4 November 1993.
16 In which case, the Council may act by a qualified majority.

EUROPEAN UNION AND THE RULE OF LAW

1 Kieran Bradley is responsible for Part I of this chapter and Alastair Sutton for Part II. The views expressed by Kieran Bradley are personal, and do not necessarily represent those of the European Parliament; his thanks are due to Joseph Weiler and Richard Corbett for their comments on the text, though they bear no responsibility for any errors of fact or appreciation.
2 For a brief summary of the main opposing views, see Rowland Dworkin, *A Matter of Principle*, Oxford, The Clarendon Press, 1986, pp.11–13.
3 The question of the validity of the Treaty will not be examined here; it is difficult to see which court would have jurisdiction and against what criteria its validity would be judged, other than the constitutional courts of the member states (e.g. the judgement of the *Bundesverfassungsgericht* of 12 October 1993).
4 For the sake of brevity, only the legal order of the EEC Treaty is considered here; 'EEC' denotes the Treaty provision before modification by the Treaty of Maastricht, 'EC' indicates the post-modification numbering.
5 [1991] ECR I-6079; *Draft European Economic Area Agreement I*, 14 December 1991, OJ 1992 C 110/11.
6 Case 294/83, *Les Verts* v. *European Parliament* [1986] ECR 1339, 1365.
7 See, respectively, Case C-260/89, E.R.T. [1991] ECR I-2925, and Joined Cases C-6 and 9/90, *Francovich and others* [1991] ECR I-5357.
8 Koen Lenaerts, 'Constitutionalism and the many faces of federalism', 38 *American Journal of Comparative Law*, 1990, pp.205, 220. Even national derogations for matters such as public policy (e.g. Article 36 EC) and national security (Article 223) are subject to Community supervision.
9 The assent and negative assent ('co-decision') procedures, however, enable the Parliament to thwart the wishes of a unanimous Council, while the Commission can prevent the adoption of a Council act by refusing to submit a proposal.
10 The term 'national interests' is used *faute de mieux* to indicate the interests governments pursue in the Council; see generally, Weiler, 'The transformation of Europe', 100 *Yale Law Journal*, 1991, pp.2403, 2406, fn 7.
11 The term 'negative assent' procedure is sometimes used as an alternative to 'co-decision' (which the UK government, especially, dislikes) to describe the Article 189b procedure.
12 A number of direct challenges by member states to Council measures for incompetence are currently pending.
13 Case 43/75 [1976] ECR 455; the Court's reasoning could be used to support the view that the 'Luxembourg Compromise' of 1966 was illegal.
14 Joined cases C-181/91 and C-248/91, *European Parliament* v. *Council and Commission*, not yet reported in ECR; in the latter case, Parliament had challenged the power of the Commission to implement an aid budget agreed upon by the member states.
15 Case 45/86, *Commission* v. *Council* [1987] ECR 1493.
16 The reason appears from its pleadings in the *Hormones* case, where the Council claimed that it enjoyed a discretionary power to determine the primary purpose, and hence the legal basis, of a measure; the criterion 'principal objective' would in effect be a subjective test.

17 Now both provisions enable the Council to act by a qualified majority, though only Article 100a gives Parliament a veto power.

18 Case C-300/89 *Commission* v. *Council* [1991] ECR 2867; for references, see Bradley, 'L'arrêt dioxyde de titane: Un jugement de Salomon?', 1992 *Cahiers de droits européens*, p.603.

19 Case 68/86, *United Kingdom* v. *Council* [1988] ECR 855.

20 J.-P. Jacqué and J.H.H. Weiler, 'On the road to European Union – a new judicial architecture', *Common Market Law Review*, no.27, 1990, pp.184, 200.

21 The judgement of the *Bundesverfassungsgericht* of 12 October 1993 on the constitutionality of the German law allowing ratification of the Treaty provides several examples of such concerns.

22 See EC Bulletin 12/92, 1.15–1.22.

23 Joseph Weiler has recently suggested that 'the appropriate criterion for judicial review would be reasonableness and excess of jurisdiction' (Weiler, 'Journey to an unknown destination', *Journal of Common Market Studies*, vol. 31, 1993, p.438); but as these were already available to the Court as grounds for annulment pre-Maastricht, the added value of judicial review under the second paragraph of Article 3b is not readily apparent.

24 There may exist intermediate positions between these two approaches, where, for example, procedural judicial review shades into substantive review (Martin Shapiro, 'The Giving Reasons Requirement', *The University of Chicago Legal Forum*, 1992); this is a dilemma which arises for the Court in the general context of its enforcement of the procedural requirements of the Treaty, rather than specifically in relation to subsidiarity.

25 See, respectively, the *ERTA* and *Stölting* cases, Case 22/70 [1971] ECR 263 and Case 138/78 [1979] ECR 713. For judicial deference to the judgement of a national legislator, see Case C-159/90, *SPUC* v. *Grogan* [1991] ECR I-4685, 4739.

26 Indeed, the extent of these new obligations was seen by a majority of the Irish Supreme Court as a material qualification of the sovereignty of the state in the conduct of foreign affairs (*Crotty* v. *An Taoiseach* [1987] 2 CMLR 666).

27 In his essay in the *Festschrift* for Mr Justice Walsh, James Casey has suggested that the *Crotty* judgement 'involves nothing less than a new constitutional right – to have government' (including foreign affairs) 'conducted in accordance with the mandates of the Constitution' (in James O'Reilly (ed.), *Human Rights and Constitutional Law*, Dublin, Round Hall Press, 1992, p.190); the European Union does not guarantee such a right.

28 Parliament may also enjoy some formal influence over the administrative expenditure for the CFSP (Article J.11.2), though this is unlikely to add to its leverage over substantive policy choices.

29 The Court may be given jurisdiction under conventions between the member states concerning 'matters of common interest' (Article K.3.2c), though these would constitute international agreements rather than measures of Community law.

30 See the judgement of the *Bundesverfassungsgericht* of 12 October 1993.

31 As related in the Tenth Commission report on the application of Community law, COM (93) 320 final, 28 April 1993.

32 Opinion in Case 30/88, *Greece* v. *Commission* [1989] ECR 3711, 3726.

33 Part II is written by Alastair Sutton.

34 Court of Justice Cases 26/62 and 6/64 respectively.

35 Joined Cases 6/90 and 9/90, ECR [1991] I, 5357.

36 Commission Communication, 'Making the most of the internal market: Strategic programme', COM (93) 632 final, 22 December 1993.

37 Issues which need to be addressed in this connection include the wider and more transparent dissemination of EC legal texts, training in EC law, facilitating access to courts and the full implementation of the Brussels and Rome Conventions on judicial cooperation.

38 COM (93) 576 Final of 16 November 1993.

39 See, for example, Iva Van Bael, 'Insufficient judicial control of EC Competition Law enforcement', in *International Antitrust Law and Policy*, Annual Proceedings of the Fordham Corporate Law Institute, 1992.

40 OJ L 257, 21 September 1993 on Council Regulation (EEC) No. 4064/89 of 21 December 1989 on the Control of Concentrations between Undertakings.

41 Advocate-General Rozes has said: 'The Commission has a wide discretion in deciding whether or not to commence procedures under Regulation 17 but . . . a completely discretionary power of assessment on the part of the administration is incompatible with the concept of law on which the Community legal order is based. . . . Individuals . . . have the right to expect the discretion to be exercised properly since the provision conferring that power was also adopted in their interest' in *Schmidt* v. *Commission*, Case 210/81, 1983 ECR 3045.

42 *British American Tobacco Company Ltd.* and *R J Reynolds* v. *Commission*, Joint cases 142 and 156/84 1987 ECR 4566.

43 One of the clearer statements of judicial policy in this field is in the *Grundig* case: 'The exercise of the Commission's powers necessarily implies complex evaluations on economic matters. A judicial review of these evaluations must take account of their nature by confining itself to an evaluation of the relevance of the facts and of the legal consequences which the Commission deduces therefrom. This review must in the first place be carried out in respect of the reasons given for the decisions which must first set out the facts and the considerations on which the said evaluations are based'; *Consten and Grundig* v. *Commission* 56 and 58/64 1966 ECR 299.

44 *Flat Glass* Case T-68, 77 and 78/89, ECR 1992, II, 1403; and *BASF* v. *Commission*, Joint cases T-79, 89, T-84/86, 89 etc. 1992 CMLR 357.

45 Case 354/90 ECR 1991, I, 5505.

46 Case 41/92, judgement of June 10, 1993 (not yet published in the ECR).

47 Case 221/89 ECR 1991 I – 3905 and Case 354/90 ECR 1991 I – 552, respectively.

48 'The Council, acting unanimously on the initiative of the Commission or a Member State, may decide to apply Article 100(c) of the Treaty establishing the European Community to action in areas referred to in Article K.1(1) to (6), and at the same time, determine the relevant voting conditions relating to it . . .'

15 BUILDING THE UNION: POLICY, REFORM, CONSTITUTION

1 p.142.

2 p.82.

3 See Harry Cowie and John Pinder (eds), *A Recovery Strategy for Europe*, London, Federal Trust, 1993.

4 pp.142–3.

5 p.99.

6 p.94.

7 pp.112–21.
8 p.109.
9 p.163.
10 p.230.
11 pp.250–1.
12 pp.208–14, 192–3.
13 pp.185, 192.
14 p.50.
15 p.183.
16 pp.180, 186–7.
17 Article D.
18 See Andrew Duff (ed.), *Subsidiarity Within the European Community*, London, Federal Trust, 1993.
19 pp.235–7.
20 pp.167–9.
21 p.197.
22 p.20.

INDEX

accountability: for budgetary expenditure 140; of Central Bank 76; need for greater levels of 61–2, 266

acquis communautaire law 260–1

agriculture: Common Agricultural Policy (CAP) 125, 149, 150, 152, 166, 234; equalisation in spending policies 151–2; Maastricht provisions on 7, 125; Special Committee for Agriculture 195

Albania, possibility of joining European Community 12

Anderson, M. and den Boer, M., on justice and home affairs 275

assent procedure for European Parliament 212, 213–214

'Assizes' (Conference of Parliaments of the European Community) 41, 217, 218

Association Agreements with EC 245, 261; enforcement of 261

asylum policy 115, 264, 275, 290n.

Atlantic alliance 8–9, 88, 97; *see also* Nato

Austria; application for EC membership 12, 15, 205, 261; EEA Agreement with EC 260–1; and Emu 82; neutrality 97; and transport policy 133

Bank of Credit and Commerce International (BCCI) 77

Bank for International Settlements 77

banking system: banking supervision 77; centralisation of 72–3, 75–6; Maastricht provisions for 196–7; and market intervention 78; monetary policy and central bank

independence 75–6; and single currency 21; support for Emu 42, 271

Belgium: and political union 44; ratification of Maastricht Treaty 60; regional devolution of power 14

Belmont European Policy Centre 197

Blake, A. and Westaway, P., on central bank independence 75

border controls 105–6, 290n.; External Borders Convention 105, 114, 119, 120, 121; implications of abolition of internal frontiers 245; and security 112–14

Bosnia 5, 97

Bradley, K. and Sutton, A., on European Court of Justice 276

Britain *see* United Kingdom

Brittan, Sir Leon 95

Brussels, European Council meeting at (1993) 181–2

Buchanan, J. and Tullock, G. on resource costs 145

Buiter, W., on fiscal policy 78

Bulgaria: application for EC membership 12, 15; Association Agreement with EC 245, 261

bureaucracy 162, 163

Cash, Bill 64

centralisation: and federalism 10; of financial and economic policy 72–3; fiscal stabilisation without 80–2

CFSP *see* Common Foreign and Security Policy (CFSP)

Christopherson, Henning 55

'Citizen's Europe' 244

citizenship 15, 26, 29–30, 104–22; democratic deficit between EC and